Introduction to Information Science

Introduction to Information Science

David Bawden and Lyn Robinson

facet publishing

© David Bawden and Lyn Robinson 2012

Published by Facet Publishing
7 Ridgmount Street, London WC1E 7AE
http://www.facetpublishing.co.uk

Facet Publishing is wholly owned by CILIP: the Chartered Institute
of Library and Information Professionals.

David Bawden and Lyn Robinson have asserted their right
under the Copyright, Designs and Patents Act 1988 to be
identified as authors of this work.

British Library Cataloguing in Publication Data
A catalogue record for this book is available from the British Library.

ISBN 978-1-85604-810-1

First published 2012

Text printed on FSC accredited material.

Typeset from author's files in 10/13 pt Revival 565 and Frutiger by
Flagholme Publishing Services.
Printed and made in Great Britain by CPI Group (UK),
Croydon CR0 4YY.

Contents

List of figures

Preface

Our aim in writing this book was to describe in outline, and to set into context, all the important topics within the information science discipline. Since this covers a very wide area, we have not covered any topic in elaborate detail. We have, rather, pointed out the topics and issues, described them briefly and shown how they fit together, explained the terminology, and shown where more detail can be found. The result, we hope, is a good introduction to the 'logic and language' of information science. It is intended primarily for students of information science and related topics, but should be accessible to practitioners.

We have gone into particular detail for those topics not well covered elsewhere. For topics such as information technology, information organization and information retrieval, where there are numerous good sources, we have mainly restricted ourselves to an outline with references. We have not given details of systems, metadata formats and the like, as these change often and can easily be found on the web.

While we have tried to give up-to-date information, we are well aware that books can get out of date rapidly if they attempt to give too much detail, and so we have focused on basic principles which should not go out of fashion too quickly. Our book has a slightly different emphasis from other texts in the information sciences. We have emphasized concepts and theories, as we believe that a good understanding of these is of more use in the long term than specifics of current systems, services and techniques. We have also emphasized the historical dimension, as we believe it is essential to understand where the discipline and its constituents came from, and why some things are as they are.

Our approach is rooted in the literature, with copious references, presented at the end of each chapter for ease of access. Our hope is that the text of this book will be sufficient to give a basic understanding of the whole area, and that readers will follow the references for details and examples of those aspects in which they are most interested. The summary text and boxes, and the key references, at the end of each chapter are intended to convey the basic messages in a concise way. The section 'Additional resources' mentions a diverse range of sources complementing this book.

We owe particular thanks to our international A to Ž of foreword writers – Theresa Dirndorfer Anderson, Andrew Dillon, Jonathan Furner, Birger Hjørland, Fidelia Ibekwe-SanJuan and Maja Žumer – for their insightful comments.

We are grateful to our students at several institutions for comments on drafts of this book, and on earlier lecture materials from which it emerged, to David Haynes and Andrew Robson for assistance with depiction of models, and to Helen Carley, Sarah Busby, Kathryn Beecroft and Lin Franklin at Facet Publishing for encouragement and practical assistance. Access to resources was made possible by the efficient assistance of the staffs of City University London Library, University College London Library, the City of London public library service and the British Library. We received a great deal of assistance in identification and reproduction of images from, inter alia, Tom Wilson, Boyd Rayward, Gheorghe Lazarovici, Marco Merlini, Erica Mosner (Institute of Advanced Study, Princeton), Raphaele Cornille and Stéphanie Manfroid (Mundaneum, Mons), Mari Melguizo (AT&T Laboratories), Jackie Brown (British Library), Ann Rossiter (SCONUL), Stephen Greenberg (National Library of Medicine), Jonathan Eaker (Library of Congress), Martha Walker and Susette Newbury (Cornell University Library) and Chris Southerns and David Prudames (British Museum).

David Bawden and Lyn Robinson

Forewords

Information science and 21st century information practices: creatively engaging with information

Theresa Dirndorfer Anderson
Senior Lecturer, Centre for Creative Practice and Cultural Economy, University of Technology, Sydney, Australia

This book invites us to imagine the future of information science, which the authors frame as a field of study (Chapter 1). Moving away from the pursuit of all-encompassing meanings helps us to navigate the complexity associated with various views in information science and, as the authors explain, '. . . be relaxed about the varied approaches and methods which may be applied to information problems.' Information sciences (in the plural), they go on to explain, are dispersed. As an information researcher positioned in a centre of creative practice and cultural economy (areas unlikely to be considered traditional domains of information science), I welcome this pragmatism. It is nonetheless helpful to discuss (as the authors go on to do) whether or not we can identify a 'core' of information science and to consider the 'big questions' of information science in all their multifaceted complexity.

For me that complexity places information sciences at a crossroads as we face the challenge of handling ideas and knowledge. We need to balance our traditional areas of expertise in this regard with the new skills and strategies needed to thrive in contemporary digital contexts where, more than ever before, we have opportunities to creatively engage with information in a range of digital, analog and hybridized forms bouncing in-between. The pre-eminent role information plays in lives increasingly unfolding in digital and mobile spaces provides new opportunities for information researchers and practitioners to be cultural shape-shifters, guiding our communities and clients through the dynamic, highly mediated, networked worlds that require them to engage with information in increasingly inventive ways.

At this crossroads, the big question for me takes the following form: how can we continue to provide leadership in relation to navigating, using and managing information, while at the same time insert ourselves into conversations and planning about institutional and infrastructure strategies needed to cultivate and sustain the creative literacies increasingly called for in our information worlds? It is a question that presents challenges as well as opportunities for the field of information science. I have a personal fondness for the way Howkins articulates the challenge:

> The main question of our age is how we live our lives. As we struggle with this, we face other questions. How do we handle ideas and knowledge, both our own and other people's? What relationship to ideas do we want? Where do we want to think?
>
> Howkins (2009, 1)

I believe there is great opportunity for us to become key players in the new creative information ecologies Howkins discusses. If we examine this challenge in the context of research and discovery, for instance, it is not so much the access to information but the capacity to engage with that information in creative, imaginative ways that contributes to research success.

The challenges of contemporary information practice and information spaces discussed in Chapter 10 therefore resonate strongly with me and the future promise that I believe the study of information science offers. How should we respond to the new ways of working with and using information likely to continue to emerge? What role can we play in e-research and dynamic forms of scholarly communication? Can we design information spaces that respond to the human need for reflection or contemplation some of the time, and stimulation to kick-start creativity and innovation at other times? As researchers and as practitioners, we are invited to think about the systems and spaces we want to carve out for ourselves and for the people we seek to support through our research and our professional practice.

The highly networked and increasingly complex information ecologies and workplace milieux emerging in 21st-century life call for creative as well as critical capacities for engaging with information. Trying to be creative in such landscapes, however, is fraught with challenges, not least because the fast access to information often taken for granted may be at the expense of time needed for creative thinking and reflection. Insight and inventiveness are needed to solve problems and devise workarounds. Nurturing such capacities, in my view, involves providing opportunities to experience 'imperfect' information, to engage with ambiguities and to create the spaces and times for deeper reflection. Effectively engaging with information in any given context calls for self-awareness about one's own thresholds for these ambiguities and uncertainties.

By responding to these contemporary challenges, be it as information researchers or as practitioners, we have an opportunity to take on a stewardship role within our communities. We can become cultural shapeshifters – helping to shape the services, infrastructures and policies that support those communities as they strive to be more creative and inventive in their engagements with information.

Reference

Howkins, J. (2009) *Creative ecologies: where thinking is a proper job*, St Lucia, Queensland: University of Queensland Press.

The emerging discipline of information

Andrew Dillon

Dean and Yule Regents Professor of Information Studies at the School of Information, University of Texas, Austin, USA

One wonders if there is really a need for another book introducing information science to the world. Surely we have so many already that the best any new volume can hope to offer is topicality or currency? Perhaps we need new ones because the field ceases to remain still, or the emergence of every new technology seems to require expression once more of the importance of organization, context and human use. Either answer is plausible enough but I think there is a simpler one. We don't have a best introduction yet. No single book I can pull from my shelves or locate on Amazon, our collective digital library in the second decade of the 21st century, provides the appropriate weaving of materials together to do justice to this meta-discipline we call information. Not since Machlup and Mansfield's edited (1983) tome *The Study of Information*, now sadly out of print and extortionately priced on the used market, have I felt comfortable handing a student one text and saying 'this' is the one. Consequently, my piecemeal approach to referencing the core has often translated into confusion in students' minds over what exactly they should be reading.

While the searches for compelling and unifying definitions of information and information science or studies are engaging, I am not convinced by the underlying implication, oft mooted by critics, that we cannot really be a field until we agree such definitions. What hope would there ever be for disciplinary emergence if we had to agree definitions in advance? Further, I suspect many fields could really split hairs about their own definitions and for me there is more to understanding what makes a discipline real than the wording of its self-description. At the very least we should identify the commonalities among the scholastic efforts of those who call themselves information scientists, for it is in looking at what people do rather than what they say that we often find the truth. I am very pleased that David and Lyn have presented ample evidence of doing just this in their efforts at showcasing the logic and language of information science.

The dynamic nature of the information field is perhaps the reason so many of us who work in it ended up here, and it is in an examination of current academic movements within the field that I want to offer one way of understanding our field. It is certainly trendy for university administrations to speak encouragingly of interdisciplinary efforts but the reality is that few universities or departments are prepared for the enormous efforts involved in enabling scholarship across fields. Transcending disciplinary boundaries requires an understanding and appreciation of the publication norms and distributions in each area, a sense of the pressing concerns and questions within each and an awareness of how work is funded and recognized as valuable. In an odd way, these abilities reflect the very nature of work in information studies, where examinations of scholarly and documentary practices, the analysis of research impact and overlap, and concern for describing and managing the interactions of people with information and its underlying technologies are core. It is no coincidence that in these times new schools of information are emerging across the globe and organizing collectively to better explain and market their roles to various audiences, not least their own university administrations. Perhaps it is here, rather than in pursuit of agreeable definition, that we should be looking to better understand our role and purpose as a scholarly effort.

If there are defining characteristics of iSchools, they must at least include these three elements to my mind:

1 A recognition that no existing discipline has a monopoly on appropriate theory and method for studying information, hence any genuine information school must contain an intellectually diverse faculty willing to engage collectively in shared problems;
2 An understanding and treatment of information that conceives of it as mediated by people and technology across multiple environments, rather than one based on the practices of traditional agencies of collection (libraries, archives, museums, etc.);
3 A commitment to research activities that seek answers to fundamental and pressing questions about information in all human endeavors.

It would take more than my allotted space to develop this argument fully but I am convinced these three criteria cannot be applied generally to the majority of academic units claiming authority within information studies. Some, like computer science, might make a claim on meeting one or perhaps two criteria (at a stretch) but would surely fail the test of interdisciplinary commitment.

Many traditional LIS programs might meet the interdisciplinary criterion but surely would find it more difficult to claim a genuinely research-centric approach to non-agency based information problems. All three, are in my view, only met by genuine schools of information, be they members of the emerging iSchool Caucus or not. And it is the future of such schools that will determine the trajectory of the field.

In this light, I see the future of our collective concerns with information in a bright light. I would not presume to place limits on the type of intellectual pursuits information scientists will engage in over the next two decades, though I suspect concerns with the intelligent exploitation of massive data sets, improved search, better curation of the digital record, and innovative human interfaces to information will remain central. But we are entering a phase of rapid growth in internet usage (can you still believe that the majority of the people on our planet have yet to experience this wonder?) and the forces at work trying to exercise control over it all are not all motivated by the same goals or concerns. If nothing else, there is a call to arms here for better, serious, theoretically strong scholarship on information and its role in our world. The labels and the naming arguments that characterize too much of the discourse in this domain in the last few decades are unimportant here, what matters now is that a real information science emerges that can live up to the challenges of the times. If enough of us are up for the fight, then information science might just come of age and blossom in the years ahead.

The scope of information science

Jonathan Furner
Associate Professor, Department of Information Studies, University of California, Los Angeles, USA

By a variety of measures, information science is in excellent health. The community supports several academic journals and conferences of the highest quality, the iSchools movement continues to grow, and the impact of pure and applied research is keenly felt on the design and development of products and services of many kinds, which benefit society and culture in many ways. A couple of years ago, the publication of the magisterial 3rd edition of the *Encyclopedia of library and information sciences* provided an especially compelling demonstration of the breadth, depth and vibrancy of the field, in terms not only of problems addressed but also of approaches taken.

So it's all the more inexplicable that – until now – we really haven't had much of a choice when it comes to introductory textbooks. I remember coming across Brian and Alina Vickery's *Information science in theory and practice* on the shelves where I worked as a library assistant in 1988 and thinking, 'Yes – this is the field for me.' A quarter of a century on, I'm never completely comfortable in my recommendations of similarly inspirational introductions. (Occasionally I've wondered to myself what such a text should now be like; but it's a very good thing I've never attempted to write one. I would get stuck on the first chapter, going round and round on two questions: 'But . . . is information science really a science?' and, maybe even less constructively, 'But . . . is information science really about information?') I should make it clear at this point that the authors of the present work were absolutely adamant that this foreword should not be used to provide a testimonial for their book. But I also feel the need, very strongly, to put on record that a lot of people have been waiting quite some time for just this book.

My hope and expectation is that newcomers to the field will be inspired by the book to take information science in bold and productive directions. If the field is to continue to have impact at the levels that it has had in the recent past, then clearly it must continue to generate knowledge of fairly specific kinds (e.g., of people's information needs, and of the ways those needs may be satisfied most effectively) that allows for continuous improvements in the design of information access systems. But I think there are three other prerequisites for the ongoing relevance of the field whose significance may not be quite so obvious.

First, we need to appreciate that information science has a history. This history certainly didn't begin with Google. It didn't begin with MEDLINE, and it didn't begin with the memex. It didn't even begin with the Répertoire bibliographique universel. It's a history that is replete both with stories of success and stories of failure. All are stories from which we can and should continue to learn. We can only do so if these stories continue to be retold in ways that make their relevance to contemporary concerns clear.

Secondly, we need to appreciate that information science has an ethical dimension. Decisions taken in the design of information systems and services may be judged not only on the basis of the success with which those systems and services perform their designated functions, but also in accordance with their tendency to produce consequences that are just, or equitable, or respectful of the rights of various groups of agents. Many of the most intractable problems in information science derive from some form of conflict among fundamental ethical principles, and are less technical than they are social or cultural.

Thirdly, and most generally, we need to appreciate that information science is about people. It's quite common these days to see information science or its sister fields described as having a focus on 'information, people, and technology.' This is undoubtedly a useful summary, but almost as often it's also clear that the speaker self-identifies with either a systems- or a business-focused orientation. There remains almost unlimited scope for the development of a humanistically oriented information science – and by that I don't mean one that focuses narrowly on serving the information needs of humanities scholars, but one in which the potential benefits of taking humanistic or idiographic approaches (historical, ethical, philosophical, cultural, interpretive, etc.) are fully explored.

There are many ways of defining the scope of information science, of course, and equally many ways of tracing the outlines of a productive future for the field. Ultimately, our selection of the boundaries that each of us draws around it is much less important than our choosing to devote our time and efforts to it. So long as our main goal continues to be to contribute, in ways large or small, to the general project of making the world a better place, the forecast is good. I have no doubts that, for many years to come, this wonderful book will serve as one of the very best places for people to start to make a difference.

A fascinating field and a pragmatic enterprise

Birger Hjørland
Professor of Information Science, Royal School of Library and Information Science, Copenhagen, Denmark

Information science is a fascinating field. It is basically about helping people find the books, articles, pictures, music, information, etc., they need or would like to read or experience. Information specialists help students, researchers and everybody else to find the documents they need in order to solve tasks, including writing thesis and research papers. Such documents used to be kept in physical libraries, archives and museums but are increasingly available in digital form, sometimes free, sometimes with toll access. We may term all this 'the information ecology' and information specialists are those people studying this universe in order to help people utilizing it optimally for the specific purposes that people have.

Although much information is available in digital form, the study of information is not identical with the study of computers, information technology or communication technology. Information science is rather about knowledge production in society and how this knowledge is materialized in documents, including digital documents, and how it is organized, labelled and managed, in order to serve different groups and individuals (this definition is adapted from Jack Andersen). Information science is about what Google and Wikipedia can do for you, but it is also about what Google and Wikipedia cannot do for you, what else needs to be consulted. It is about how to improve access to information by progress both in computer-based retrieval and in forms of information services provided by information professionals. Such information services include the teaching of 'information literacy' to students and helping professionals, for example medical doctors, doing evidence-based practice. Another way to describe the difference between computer science and information science is to say that for the first the interaction between humans and computers is a core topic. In the case of information science it is rather the interaction between people and the whole information ecology. This makes an important difference, although the computer is certainly a central tool in information science.

Information science has many specific branches. Some specialize in specific technologies, for example, the new wave of 'social technologies' or specific user groups (e.g. library and information services for children). Some subfields cover kinds of processes such as information seeking and retrieval or knowledge organization and information architecture. Some specialize in specific domains, for example cultural, social or scientific information. All these branches are not just studied by information professionals, but are interdisciplinary by nature. That means that also information science itself is at the same time a monodiscipline in its own right and an interdisciplinary enterprise drawing from other fields and depending on input from other fields. The unique focus of information science in relation to other disciplines is described above: the study of the information ecology in order to facilitate its utilization to many specific purposes. It follows that information science is a pragmatic enterprise: it studies knowledge and information for a purpose, in order to make progress and to improve things (well aware that 'progress' and 'improvement' may mean different things to different people).

What is important and critical for the further development of information science at the present time? I believe this has to do with on the one hand the need *to develop a general perspective* that keeps the field together and helps information scientists and information professionals to get a clear identity in relation to other fields in this multidisciplinary field; first of all, perhaps, in relation to computer scientists. On the other hand it is necessary to *develop a body of specific information science knowledge related to all major branches of knowledge.* Knowledge and information is always specific, it is always about something concrete (including, of course, concrete philosophical questions). There are obvious limits to a pure generalist or universalist approach. Therefore more domain-analytic studies are also urgently needed.

The writing of textbooks has generally low prestige in the academic world. I believe this is unjust, at least in some fields. Most information specialists only know a narrow part of the field, lacking an understanding of information science as a whole. It is important both in the educational context and in the scientific and professional context that we have a clear identity: that we can understand and argue why the different subfields exist, and all contribute to strengthen the whole field from their own corner. Strong parts and a strong whole are mutually dependent. Therefore it is important to work on the whole, by writing textbooks, by studying the history and theories of the field and in other ways. To write textbooks in highly fragmented fields is a challenge, and unfortunately many textbooks provide very narrow and one-sided views of information science.

I believe this book is the best introduction to information science available at present. It tackles both the philosophical basis and the most important branches, and it is based on solid knowledge about the contemporary literature of the field. If students have the knowledge provided by this introduction, this would be a fine basis on which to go further with specific problems.

A slippery and ubiquitous concept

Fidelia Ibekwe-SanJuan
Associate Professor,Information and Communication Studies, University of Lyon 3, France

Information science is about research and practice on how people collect, organize, store, retrieve and disseminate information and use it, both at individual and social levels. As an academic discipline, information science is often assimilated with information technology, with computer science, the internet or even the web. Few practitioners and scholars are aware of the real nature of this field which originated in the late 19th century from the foundational works done by European pioneers on documentation and bibliography management. The field has grown since its emergence in the 1960s, alongside progress done in computer science and in telecommunications. The evolution of the field is impacted by that of the web and the changes it has wrought in the ways in which information is handled, accessed and disseminated in our digital society. These rapid changes make information science an exciting field but also one that continually faces new challenges and seeks methods to address them. Hence, the field has continually had to interact with many other fields of education and research, in order to devise theories and methods suitable to tackle the ever-growing number of information-centric needs.

The present book by David Bawden and Lyn Robinson renders a historical and illuminating account of the major figures and contributions in the field. It is a comprehensive but accessible analysis of issues that the field has been dealing with. From a discussion of the epistemological positions and paradigms which form the foundations of the field, to a summary of research in more applied areas like domain analysis, information retrieval and informetrics, the reader is offered a concise and pedagogical insight into the cogent contributions in the field. Because information is a slippery and ubiquitous concept, books devoted to the specific way in which this interdisciplinary field – library and information science – deals with information-centric problems, go a long way in distinguishing the contributions this field has made to the global information society.

The future of information science

Maja Žumer

Professor of Information Science, Department of Library and Information Science and Book Studies, University of Ljubljana, Slovenia

> The future is always beginning now
>
> Mark Strand

Information is at the centre of our society. It is what we often talk about, it appears frequently in the media, it is often labelled as our most important asset. Even our time is, taking into account the importance of information, labelled the 'information age'. We feel threatened by information overload, some may even suffer from information anxiety. On the other hand we cannot survive without it; we need information every moment of our lives.

And yet information science, the science having information at its focus, is experiencing an identity crisis. This is not new. For more than half a century information scientists have had to explain, over and over again, what their discipline was, and repeat that they were neither computer scientists nor librarians, while closely cooperating with them – and others. Could the reason be the interdisciplinary nature of the field? So outsiders notice the methods and theories taken from psychology, sociology, statistics, philosophy, etc., and do not see the added value of information science, particularly the focus on the object of the research: information.

Or is it because 'information' itself is so vaguely and variously defined? Or have information scientists never had good public relations skills, so that they could communicate the message and become more visible? Part of the problem, at least in some environments, may also be attributed to the often used phrase 'library and information science' (LIS). While possibly accepted by librarians, the phrase does not do justice to information scientists, limiting them to the context of libraries only.

While all this may seem a less important issue – information science has, after all, survived and flourished – the lack of understanding of information science is the highest hurdle for the implementation of its research results in practice. As the result, we encounter websites which are completely unintuitive, information systems aimed at the general public for which one needs specific training (e.g. library catalogues), unattractive interfaces, confusing subject arrangements, and so on. Let us take library catalogues as an example. Researchers have been confirming over and over again that current catalogues are still anchored in the card catalogue paradigm, and thus not intuitive and easy to use compared to similar or competitive services such as Amazon or Google. New conceptual models of the bibliographic universe have been developed and successfully verified with the users; we therefore have an excellent foundation for the development of new bibliographic information systems. But, with the exception of a handful of prototype implementations, nothing much has changed.

Information scientists have developed a very detailed understanding of human information behaviour, and one would expect these findings to be used in the development of information systems to support more efficient and effective interaction, resulting in the right information at the right time. But that has not happened; at least not enough.

What is there for information science in the future? I have no doubt that both basic and applied information science research is needed more than ever. Coming to information science at a later period in life (via mathematics and computing), I am still fascinated with its potential and implications. So many answers are still missing and so much has not been implemented yet.

The future of information science lies in the hands of the young generation – the young researchers who come into the field with novel ideas, who are willing to think out of the box, while not losing the big picture. It is our duty as educators and advisers to support them in their growth into competent and confident researchers of the future.

As for the future, your task is not to foresee it, but to enable it.

Antoine de Saint-Exupéry

List of acronyms

AACR	Anglo-American Cataloguing Rules
ACM	Association for Computing Machinery
ADI	American Documentation Institute
ANSI	American National Standards Institute
API	Application Programming Interface
ASCII	American Standard Code for Information Interchange
ASI	Academic Standards Institute
ASIS	American Society for Information Science (now ASIST)
ASIST	American Society for Information Science and Technology
ASLIB	Association of Special Libraries and Information Bureaux (UK)
ASK	Anomalous State of Knowledge
BC	Bliss Classification
BC2	Bliss Classification (second edition)
BCE	Before Common Era (equivalent to BC)
BL	British Library
BSI	British Standards Institute
CC	Colon Classification
CI	Competitor, or Competitive, Intelligence
CILIP	Chartered Institute of Library and Information Professionals (UK)
CLEF	Cross Language Evaluation Forum (or Conference and Labs of the Evaluation Forum)
CLIR	Cross Language Information Retrieval
CPU	Central Processing Unit
CRG	Classification Research Group
CSCW	Computer Supported Collaborative Work
DBMS	Database Management System
DC	Dublin Core
DCMI	Dublin Core Metadata Inititaive
DDC	Dewey Decimal Classification
ECM	Enterprise Content Management
EDRMS	Electronic document and records management system

eGMS	electronic Government Metadata Standard (UK)
ELIS	Everyday Life Information Seeking
FID	International Federation for Information and Documentation
FOSS	Free and Open Source Software
FRAD	Functional Requirements for Authority Data
FRBR	Functional Requirements for Bibliographic Records
FRSAD	Functional Requirements for Subject Authority Data
GDI	General Definition of Information
GIS	Geographic Information Systems
GLAM	Galleries, Libraries, Archives and Museums
HCI	Human Computer Interaction
HR	Human Relations
HTML	Hypertext Markup Language
HTTP	Hypertext Transfer Protocol
IA	Information Architecture
ICP	International Cataloguing Principles
ICT	Information and Communication Technology
IGUS	Information Gathering and Utilizing System
IFLA	International Federation of Library Associations
IIB	Institut International de Bibliographie (later FID)
IIS	Institute of Information Scientists (UK – now CILIP)
IM	Information Management
IO	Information Overload OR Information Organization
IRM	Information Resource Management
ISAD(G)	International Standard for Archival Description (General)
ISBD	International Standard Bibliographic Description
ISI	Institute for Scientific Information
ISO	International Standards Organization
IT	Information Technology
JISC	Joint Information Systems Committee (UK)
KM	Knowledge Management
KO	Knowledge Organization
LCC	Library of Congress Classification
LCSH	Library of Congress Subject Headings
LIS	Library and Information Science
LISA	Library and Information Science Abstracts
LISTA	Library and Information Science and Technology Abstracts
LMS	Library Management System
LOM	Learning Object Metadata
MARC	Machine Readable Cataloguing
METS	Metadata Encoding and Transmission Standard

MODS	Metadata Object Description Schema
MTC	Mathematic Theory of Communication (Shannon/Weaver)
NISO	National Information Standards Organization (USA)
NIST	National Institute of Standards and Technology (USA)
NLM	National Library of Medicine
OA	Open Access
OAI	Open Access Initiative
OAIPMH	Open Access Initiative Protocol for Metadata Harvesting
OCLC	Online Computer Library Centre
OD	Open Data
OJS	Open Journals Systems
OPAC	Online Public Access Catalogue
OpenDOAR	Open Directory of Open Access Repositories
OSI	Open Society Institute
OSS	Open Source Software
OWL	Web Ontology Language
PDA	Personal Digital Assistant
PI	Philosophy of Information
QR	Quick Response (codes)
RDA	Resource Description and Access
RDBMS	Relational Database Management System
RDF	Resource Description Framework
RFID	Radio Frequency Identification
SE	Social Epistemology
SCONUL	Society of College, National and University Libraries (UK)
SKOS	Simple Knowledge Organization System
SLA	Special Libraries Association
SNA	Social Network Analysis
SQL	Structured Query Language
SSCI	Social Science Citation Index
STEM	Science, Technology, Engineering and Medicine
TCP/IP	Transmission Control Protocol / Internet Protocol
TEI	Text Encoding Initiative
TMI	Too Much Information
TREC	Text Retrieval Conference
UDC	Universal Decimal Classification
UDK	see UDC
UK	United Kingdom
UKMARC	obsolescent national version of MARC (UK)
UMLS	Unified Medical Language System
UNIMARC	international variant of MARC

URI	Uniform Resource Identifier
URL	Uniform Resource Locator
USMARC	obsolescent national variant of MARC (USA)
USA	United States of America
VLE	Virtual Learning Environment
VLSI	Very Large Scale Integration
VRA	Visual Resources Association (metadata standard)
VRE	Virtual Research Environment
W3C	World Wide Web Consortium
WHO	World Health Organization
WIPO	World Intellectual Property Organization
WWW	World Wide Web
XML	Extensible Markup Language

CHAPTER 1

What is information science? Disciplines and professions

Information science is, or should be, involved with the whole concept of knowledge in whatever form its manifestations may take.

Jesse Shera (1973, 286)

Apparently, there is not a uniform conception of information science. The field seems to follow different approaches and traditions: for example, objective approaches versus cognitive approaches, and the library tradition versus the documentation tradition versus the computation tradition. The concept has different meanings, which imply different knowledge domains. Different knowledge domains imply different fields. Nevertheless, all of them are represented by the same name, information science. No wonder that scholars, practitioners and students are confused.

Chaim Zins (2007, 341)

The chunky concepts which make up our field's intellectual core (e.g. knowledge, information, communication, representation) are neither owned by information science nor likely to be assembled into an entirely credible canon without the judicious addition of perspectives and approaches taken from established disciplines such as computer science, linguistics, philosophy, psychology and sociology, as well as from newer fields such as cognitive science and human-computer interaction.

Blaise Cronin (2008, 466)

Let us not restrict ourselves to grubbing around in the garden patch of a limited, little information science, restricted to the relationship between information and machine. Instead, let us expand, reach out, embrace and explore the wider world of information, to develop a vision of information science as a central synthesising discipline in understanding not simply information, but the world we live in. Because the world we live in is surely a world of information.

Tom Wilson (2010)

Introduction

The subject of this book is information science. We begin by asking what information science is, as an academic discipline and profession. Obviously, and simplistically, it is the science of information. But what does this mean?

There are three main answers to this question (Buckland, 2012). One considers information science as being concerned with computing, algorithms and information technologies, a second with information as related to entropy in information theory and information physics, a third with information science as being concerned with information recorded in documents, with meaning and knowledge, and hence as growing from the older disciplines of librarianship and documentation. We will focus on the third of these in this book, although we will mention aspects of the other two at appropriate points. We will therefore be following the kind of definition which goes back at least as early as Borko (1968), and is expressed by Saracevic (2010, 2570) as:

> Information science is the science and practice dealing with the effective collection, storage, retrieval and use of information. It is concerned with recordable information and knowledge, and the technologies and related services that facilitate their management and use.

This gives us a general idea of the nature of the subject. But there is still scope for much difference in viewpoint as to exactly what the subject comprises. In the most thorough investigation yet, Zins (2007) reported fifty different explanations and definitions of information science, based on a Delphi study of experts. They ranged from circular arguments ('information science is what information scientists do') to the polemic ('information science is a self-serving attempt to ennoble what used to be called library science') to the very broad ('information science is the totality of the process of communication and understanding, both intra- and inter-personally'). Although they all had some concept of information at their centre, it is hard to see how they fit easily into any coherent single explanation of, or paradigm for, the subject. A range of other authors have expressed similarly diverse views as to the best way, in detail, to understand the information science discipline; see Robinson (2009) for details. Hjørland (2000) gives a thorough and detailed analysis of many aspects of the library and information disciplines to the end of the 20th century.

But we will need to examine it in more detail, following the approach put forward by one of us in a journal article (Robinson, 2009).

The nature of information science

Information science is clearly both an academic discipline and an area of professional practice. We will think first about the discipline, although we should note that there have always been some doubts as to what extent it is a real discipline, still less a 'true science' (Robinson, 2009; Buckland, 2012).

One way to accommodate the wide range of views about, and diverse approaches to, the subject within a coherent framework is to regard information science as a *field of study*; using this phrase in the specific sense of Paul Hirst, the philosopher of education (Hirst, 1974). A field of study is an alternative to 'disciplines' based on a unique form of knowledge, such as mathematics or the physical sciences, and to 'practical disciplines' based on one of the forms of knowledge but oriented to solving practical problems, such as engineering or medicine. For Hirst, a field of study is focused on a topic or subject of interest, using any of the forms of knowledge – sociological, mathematical, philosophical etc. – which may be helpful in studying it. Bawden (2007a) argues that it may be appropriate to regard information science as such a field of study, focused on the topic of information. This is in order to keep the subject within sensible bounds, and also to restrict the focus to recorded information, produced and used by humans, as is also suggested by Bates (1999). Information science is then understood as:

> a multidisciplinary field of study, involving several forms of knowledge, given coherence by a focus on the central concept of human recorded information

This is reminiscent of the insistence of Machlup and Mansfield (1983) that the field should be described as the information sciences, emphasizing the plural, to show the breadth of approach needed; see Webber (2003) for more discussion of this. It is also in accord with Tom Wilson's rallying cry quoted at the beginning of this chapter (Wilson, 2010). We will follow this broad approach through this book.

We can go on, following Robinson (2009), to argue that we can give some more precision to this general idea by arguing that the focus on recorded information can be expressed specifically as a focus on the *communication chain* of recorded information: from its creation, through dissemination, indexing and retrieval, use, and archiving or disposal. This is implied in many earlier explanations of the subject, but noting it explicitly helps to clarify what are the concerns of information science. Details of the chain, and the ways in which it is being changed by new technologies, are discussed in Chapter 10.

We can then explain more precisely what an information scientist does, in terms of both research and scholarly study and of practice, through the components of *domain analysis*. We will discuss this more fully in Chapter 5. For now, we will just note that there are a number of aspects which represent both the activities of the information practitioner and the ways in which research and study are carried out. Examples are user studies, historical studies, studies of terminology, research on indexing and retrieval, and so on.

This gives us a conceptual model for information science as an academic discipline, comprising the study of the components of the communication chain through the aspects of domain analysis. This is developed further in Robinson (2009). For our purpose, it gives us the understanding of information science which we shall use throughout this book.

> Information science can best be understood as a field of study, with human recorded information as its concern, focusing on the components of the communication chain, studied through the perspective of domain analysis.

The 'field of study' idea allows us to be relaxed about the varied approaches and methods which may be applied to information problems. However, there is still a concern, discussed by many authors, about what kind of discipline it is.

What kind of discipline is information science?

One way of assessing this is to see where the subject fits within the academic structure of universities. We would, for example, always expect to find physics and chemistry in science faculties, and thereby conclude that they were scientific subjects. However, the information sciences tend be dispersed. To take the example of a selection of departments of library and information science in universities in the British Isles at the time of writing (December 2011), we find them spread across faculties as follows: informatics (5), business schools (3), social sciences and human sciences (3), arts and social sciences (2), arts (1), education (1), science (1). The same is true in other countries. This shows the varied ways in which information science is viewed.

And, indeed, the literature shows a similar variety of views. It has been called, among many other things, a meta-science, an inter-science, a postmodern science, an interface science, a superior science, a rhetorical science, a nomad science, an interdisciplinary subject which should be renamed knowledge science, and a subject which may assume the role once played by philosophy in mediating science and humanism; see Robinson (2009) for references.

There has been a growing consensus over the years that information science is a social science; see, for example, Roberts (1976) and Cronin (2008). Domain analysis, which is fundamental to our view of the subject, is based on the idea that groups of people have common information practices and interests and concerns, and is therefore primarily a social theory, and that this implies that information science is primarily a social science (Hjørland and Albrechtsen, 1995).

Or perhaps it is no sort of science at all; Arms (2005) and Buckland (1996a) suggested it might be seen as a liberal art, and Buckland (2012) argues that it is, above all else, a form of cultural engagement. The philosopher Luciano Floridi, of whom we will hear more in subsequent chapters, suggests that it is applied philosophy of information (Floridi, 2002).

Having formed an idea, though certainly not a precise definition, of what kind of discipline information science is, and what its focus of interest is, we can now ask what are its constituent parts, and whether there is an irreducible 'core' of the subject.

Constituents and core

Debates about what topics and subjects make up information science, and which of these are its essential 'core', have rumbled on in the literature for many years. They have typically taken two forms: attempts to enumerate the components of information science and attempts to produce 'maps', literal or metaphorical, showing how these parts fit together.

The curriculum for information science education has been much debated over the years; its core has been argued to comprise a variety of topics, including human-computer interaction, information literacy, information management, documentation, library management, knowledge management, information organization, information society studies, bibliometrics, information seeking, and information retrieval; see Mezick and Koenig (2008), Bawden (2007b), Lørring (2007) and Robinson and Bawden (2010). The recommendations by professional bodies, such as ASIST and CILIP, are correspondingly broad.

Mappings of information science, or the broader LIS, typically produced by the methods of informetrics to be discussed in Chapter 8, give similar results; for a review, see White (2010), and for recent examples, see Milojevic, Sugimoto, Yan and Ding (2011), Åström (2010) and Janssens, Leta, Glänzel and De Moor (2006). They typically identify informetrics, information retrieval, information seeking, information management and library/archive studies as major recognizable components.

We have to conclude that this confirms the picture of information science as a broad and diverse discipline, and that it is difficult to point to a small and unambiguous set of topics which comprise it. In this book, the chapter structure reflects our desire to be comprehensive as to the topics which are of importance to information science.

Although we have so far focused on information science itself, there are other information-related disciplines which link to information science from several different perspectives, and we now consider these.

Other information disciplines

Information science has overlaps with numerous other disciplines and professions. Indeed, because of its status as a meta-discipline, a little like philosophy or education, it can be seen to have links with all other disciplines, since all have some information and knowledge extensions, and hence information scientists may contribute to all (Bates, 1999; 2007). However, we will look here at those where there is an evident overlap in terms of common interests and concepts. The conceptual model discussed above allows us to analyse these in a rather formal way, showing how they are linked through one of the aspects of domain analysis; computing, for example, links through the indexing and retrieval component, and sociology and information society studies through the user studies approach (Robinson, 2009). Zhang and Benjamin (2007) have also offered an interesting conceptual model of information-related fields, which they collectively term the I-field. This is based on interactions of four components – information, people, technology and organizations and society – set within particular domains and contexts. However, here we will just look informally at six important overlaps: collections; technology; social; communication; management and policy; and domain specialism.

Collection overlap

Arguably the most evident overlap is with the collection disciplines and professions: librarianship, archiving and heritage, sometimes referred to as the GLAM (galleries, libraries, archives and museums) sector. Information science grew from a speciality – documentation and special librarianship – within this sector, and a composite field of 'library and information science' (LIS) is generally recognized, albeit with stresses and strains from the amalgamation of two distinct camps (Dillon, 2007), which Bates (2007) distinguishes as 'information sciences' and the 'disciplines of the cultural record'. Increasing convergence (or perhaps reconvergence, since these institutions often began as united entities) between the 'memory institutions' of this sector, in an increasingly digital environment, emphasizes this overlap; see, for example, Hughes (2012, part 1), Given and McTavish (2010) and Davis and Shaw (2011, Chapter 13). These aspects are discussed in Chapter 12.

Technology overlap

The other very obvious overlap is with the information technology disciplines: computer science and information systems. Information retrieval, digital libraries, repositories and similar areas, discussed in Chapter 7, are important overlap areas, as is the study of human-computer interaction; all of these have, at various times, been claimed as integral parts of information science.

Social overlap

The more information science is regarded as a social science, the more significant this overlap becomes. It is most clearly seen in information society and social informatics studies, discussed in Chapter 11.

Communication overlap

Technical communication, the writing of abstracts, translation, information design and so on have always been regarded as an area of interest to information science. There is also an overlap with journalism and publishing, and with the new area of digital humanities. These aspects are discussed further in Chapter 10. Through information and digital literacies, discussed in Chapter 13, there is a link to broader areas of communication and learning.

Management and policy overlap

Information management and information policy, generally regarded as within information science, naturally overlap with knowledge management, business intelligence and other 'general' management and policy-making areas, as is discussed in Chapter 12.

Domain specialism overlap

In the past, it was taken for granted that an information scientist would be some kind of a subject specialist; in legal information, medical information, scientific information, etc. This is no longer the case, but there is still an important overlap area between information science and the knowledge of a subject area. In healthcare, for example, subject expertise is still of great importance, and this has spawned the practitioner roles of 'clinical librarian', 'health informaticist' and 'informationist' (Robinson, 2010; Dalrymple, 2011; Brettle and Urquhart, 2012). To distinguish them from true subject specialists (doctors, in the previous example), it has been suggested that such people be called 'domain-generalists' (Hjørland, 2000).

These overlaps, and the 'field of study' status, imply that information science, whatever else it may be, is inherently multidisciplinary and interdisciplinary. This is often spoken of as a strength of the field, although there is a downside: Dillon (2007), for example, argues that the diversity of the field may prevent the establishment of an agreed core of methods and theories, as conventional disciplines have.

Given the number and extent of overlaps, and with other disciplines and professions concerned about 'information matters', it is reasonable to ask if there is any unique place for information science.

The uniqueness of information science

It is clear that many other professions are interested in components of the communication chain: publishers are concerned with dissemination, computer scientists with information retrieval, and so on. Even accepting that information science is a meta-discipline, surely it must have some 'academic turf' of its own? We, and others argue, that the uniqueness of information science lies in its concern for *all* aspects of the communication chain; others are interested in specific aspects, but only the information sciences see their concern as being the totality. We might also name some aspects of information organization and information behaviour, unaffected by technology or by context, which are the particular concern of the information sciences. But our main claim to a unique area is the totality of the communication chain; for more discussion, see Robinson and Bawden (2012), Robinson (2009) and Robinson and Karamuftuiglou (2010).

Another way in which the distinctive nature of disciplines is shown is by the questions which they set out to answer by research, and the problems they aim to solve in practice. There have been a number of sets of 'big questions' proposed for the information sciences. As examples, we can give two sets of three general questions for the field, proposed by two American professors, shown in the box below: the first set by Marcia Bates of the University of California, Los Angeles, and the second set by Andrew Dillon, of the University of Texas at Austin. All these questions are centred around information, all are complex and require a multifaceted approach to have any hope of success in answering them, and they combine theoretical understanding with practical value; good metaphors for the discipline as a whole.

To show the range of questions which might interest the information sciences in the broadest sense, we have have included two from the American physicist John A. Wheeler, whose ideas will be mentioned again in Chapter 4 when we discuss 'information physics'; the idea that information may be a feature of the physical universe, analogous to, or even more fundamental than, matter and energy. His 'Big Questions' related to physics and cosmology, but the two quoted here touch on information: is it the case that information is an underlying reality in the universe, and how does meaning emerge in the physical world.

We will now look briefly at the history and development of information science as a profession and discipline, at its professional bodies, and at the way in which information scientists have been, and are, educated.

History of information science

Information science first became known as a discipline during the 1950s. The terms 'information science' and 'information scientist' were first used by Jason Farradane in the mid-1950s (Shapiro, 1995). Farradane, a British scientist born in Hampstead, London, to Polish parents, was originally named Levkowitz, and

---

Some 'big questions' for the information sciences

What are the features and laws of the recorded-information universe?

How do people relate to, seek, and use information?

How can access to recorded information be made most rapid and effective?

Marcia Bates

What is the essential nature of information that might relate diverse endeavours (communicating, maintaining biological life, learning and finding) where the term is employed meaningfully?

How do we move from an information provision model (storage, retrieval, management etc.) to one where we identify and shape the manner in which information nourishes a culture, an organization or an individual?

How might we positively influence the cyberinfrastructure as the majority of the world joins us online?

Andrew Dillon

It from bit?

What makes meaning ?

John A. Wheeler

---

adopted his new name as a tribute to his scientific heroes, Michael Faraday and J. B. S. Haldane. Although his initial concept of an information scientist was a specialist in the handling of scientific and technical information, Farradane pioneered the teaching of information science as a distinct subject, and was among those who argued for a 'true science of information', along the lines of the natural sciences (Farradane, 1976; Bawden, 2008).

The emergence of the information science discipline was promoted by a number of causes. Although there have been librarians and archivists from the earliest days of writing and recorded information, formal information professions and disciplines came into existence only in the 19th century. The German librarian Martin Schrettinger used the term *bibliothekswissenschaft*, which may be reasonably translated 'library science', in 1808, to encompass the tasks of cataloguing, classification, shelf arrangement and library management.

Information science *per se* stems from the communications revolution of the 19th century, which will be discussed in the next chapter, and with the simultaneous emergence of scientific and technical disciplines (Meadows, 2004). The consequent need to deal with the large volumes of literature, and scientific and technical literature in particular, led to the emergence in the early 20th century of the *documentation* movement, pioneered by Paul Otlet, which espoused a 'scientific' approach to the storage and retrieval of recorded information.

There were other influences underlying the birth of information science, which we will briefly mention: for overviews and references on various aspects of the early history, see Robinson and Bawden (2012), Larivière, Sugimoto and Cronin (2012), Bawden (2008), Robinson (2009), Hahn and Buckland (1998), Williams (1997), Buckland (1996b), Buckland and Liu (1995), Ingwersen (1992), Meadows (1987), Rayward (1997, 1985), and Shera and Cleveland (1977).

The increased awareness of technical information as a resource for science-based industries led to the establishment of special libraries, and to the idea of 'information work' as distinct from librarianship. These, compared with traditional libraries, had a much more proactive role, a strong subject focus, and an interest in all forms of information, not just formally published documents (Ditmas, 1950). The need to deal with the 'information explosion', the very rapid expansion in publications of all kinds dealing particularly with scientific and technical information during and after the 1939–45 war, was discussed at the influential 1948 Royal Society Conference on scientific information.

The growing application of new technologies to information handling, initially mechanized documentation techniques, and then the digital computer, provided the technological background for the new science (Black, 2007). Vannevar Bush's influential Memex concept of personal information management with access to the world's information, combined with Shannon and Weaver's Mathematical Theory of Communication, and the new 'informetrics' laws, such as Bradford's law of scattering (all to be discussed in later chapters), held out the prospect of a genuinely scientific approach to information management.

The establishment of a new discipline or profession has typically been recognized, since the 19th century, by the setting up of a professional body to represent it. The first such body in the area that was to spawn information science was an international body for the co-ordination of the activities of the documentation movement. The Institut International de Bibliographie (IIB), later renamed as the International Federation for Information and Documentation (FID), was established by the two Belgian pioneers of documentation, Paul Otlet and Henri La Fontaine, in 1895. Lasting until the new millennium, it can claim to be the first recognizable information science association (Rayward, 1997).

On a smaller scale, several associations were set up for special librarians. The Special Libraries Association (SLA), founded in the USA in 1909, is still thriving as a worldwide body today; for an account of its development, see SLA (1984). In the UK, the Association of Special Libraries and Information Bureaux (ASLIB), was formed in 1924 with the aim of co-ordinating the activities of specialist information services in the UK and a role as a national intelligence service for science, commerce and industry (Muddiman, 2005). ASLIB still exists today, as an organization mainly promoting information management. National groups of special librarians were formed in many other countries. The UK was rather slow off the mark, perhaps because of the existence of two other bodies catering for a relatively small sector; the Industrial Group of the Library Association was formed only in 1971 (Mason, 1991). It still survives, though now combined into a group also catering for commercial, legal and science librarians.

The two main bodies representing information science *per se* formed later, and had shorter lives in their 'pure' form. The American Documentation Institute, created in 1937, became the American Society for Information Science in 1968. It renamed itself as the American Society for Information Science and Technology in 2000. In the UK, the Institute of Information Science (IIS) was formed in 1958, and joined with The Library Association to form the Chartered Institute of Library and Information Professionals (CILIP) in 2002. While each association had its particular reasons for the change, the fact that both felt that it was sensible for information science to enter a wider grouping – with technology or with the collection disciplines – illustrates what was said above about its multidisciplinary nature.

Specialized journals are also a feature of a mature discipline. Of the major information science journals today, the longest-established is *Journal of Documentation*, the name reflecting its origins in the field of documentation when it was founded in 1945. Both the main information science associations founded journals: *Journal of the American Society for Information Science and Technology* (formerly *Journal of the American Society for Information Science*) in 1950, and the IIS's *Journal of Information Science* (formerly *The Information Scientist*) in 1967. The last of the major specific information science journals, *Information Processing and Management*, was founded as *Information Storage and Retrieval* in 1963. Of course, information science material is published in a much wider range of journals; some of the more significant of these are listed in the additional resources at the end of the book.

Finally we consider professional education. The first formalized educational programmes for the information sciences came with the establishment of courses in librarianship at the University of Göttingen in 1886, and the University of Columbia in 1887 – the latter established by Melville Dewey – and at Leipzig and Barcelona, both in 1915, followed by the creation of London University's School of Librarianship (later attached to University College London) in 1919. Graduate studies began at the University of Chicago in 1926, and in London a few years later. The first signs of an information science education came with a course specifically for science graduates in London in 1929, though this closed for lack of interest in 1935. Modern information science education began in 1961, when Jason Farradane set up an evening course in 'collecting and communicating scientific knowledge' at Northampton College of Advanced Technology. This led to the establishment of a Masters course in information science at the Centre for

Information Science when the College became City University London in 1965 (Robinson and Bawden, 2010). Other courses in the subject were developed worldwide in the following years, typically conjoint library and information departments (Um and Feather, 2007; Mezick and Koenig, 2008).

A new development in information education is the iSchools movement. Based mainly in the USA, with some international representation, iSchools are academic departments taking a broad view of information science, as the interaction of information, people and technology: the iField of Zhang and Benjamin (2007).

One recurrent question has been to what extent education in the information sciences should be focused on theories and principles, as against training in practical techniques. We strongly advocate the former, believing that it is much more valuable for students to gain an understanding of principles and concepts on which they can build throughout their professional lives, rather than ephemeral, and sometimes trivial, points of practice, and this has been the basis of our courses at City University London (Robinson and Bawden, 2010). We are encouraged in this viewpoint by evidence from studies of graduates (see, for instance, Simmons and Corrall, 2011), and by the views of two eminent figures from the past, who both had experience as practitioners and teachers: Jesse Shera from the USA and Brian Vickery from Britain:

> Librarianship can be an intellectual discipline in its own right, and education is not a substitute for experience, but a preparation for it. Librarianship . . . must abandon the practice of putting its students through 'little fake experiences in the classroom'. We must teach pupils theory, not techniques: principles, not practice.
>
> Jesse Shera (1973, 335)

> Only in a very static profession can one be trained to slot in immediately to an available job, and our profession is far from static. It is more beneficial for the students to give them a generalized grounding in a wide variety of professional activities and concerns, so that they will have some background knowledge for no matter what job is first available. For those who seek it, our subject also has its cultural value, which can contribute to a general education.
>
> Vickery (2004, 29)

This is our justification for focusing on principles and concepts, at the expense of practical details, in this book.

Summary

Information science has changed greatly in nature since its inception. Rather than forming a focused science of information, with its own methods and theories, it has overlapped with other disciplines, making use of many and varied methods, and contributing some to other areas. Its practice has also changed. From a situation where most practitioners were subject-specialist information providers, often dealing with scientific information, we have moved to a point where they take a much wider variety of roles. We will review this diversity, and the principles and concepts which underlie it, in the rest of this book.

- It is sensible to speak of the information sciences in the plural, to emphasize the breadth, multidisciplinary nature, and interconnectedness of the field.
- It is a field of study, focused on recorded information, and requiring a variety of perspectives and methods.
- Growing out of special librarianship and documentation, it has strong links with IT and computing, and with the collection disciplines.
- Although it underlies and supports practice, it is a valid academic discipline in its own right, and educational programmes based on concepts and principles are the most valuable.

Key readings

Michael Buckland, What kind of science can information science be?, *Journal of the American Society for Information Science and Technology*, 2012, 63(1), 1–7.

Lyn Robinson, Information science: communication chain and domain analysis, *Journal of Documentation*, 2009, 65(4), 578–91.

Marcia Bates, Defining the information disciplines in encyclopedia development, *Information Research*, 2007, 12(4), paper colis29 [online] available at http://informationr.net/ir/12-4/colis29.html.

Andrew Dillon, LIS as a research domain: problems and prospects, *Information Research*, 2007, 12(4), paper colis03 [online] available at http://informationr.net/ir/12-4/colis/colis03.html.

[Four papers which present, in clear terms, differing views of the information sciences.]

References

Arms, W. Y. (2005) Information science as a liberal art, *Interlending and Document Supply*, 33(2), 81–4.

Åström, F. (2010) The visibility of information science and library science research in bibliometric mapping of the LIS field, *Library Quarterly*, 80(2), 143–159.

Bates, M. J. (1999) The invisible substrate of information science, *Journal of the American Society for Information Science*, 50(12), 1043–50.

Bates, M. J. (2007) Defining the information disciplines in encyclopedia development, *Information Research*, 12(4), paper colis29 [online] available at http://informationr.net/ir/12-4/colis29.html.

Bawden, D. (2007a) Organised complexity, meaning and understanding: an approach to a unified view of information for information science, *Aslib Proceedings*, 59(4/5), 307–27.

Bawden, D. (2007b) Information seeking and information retrieval: the core of the information curriculum, *Journal of Education for Library and Information Science*, 48(2), 125–38.

Bawden, D. (2008) Smoother pebbles and the shoulders of giants: the developing foundations of information science, *Journal of Information Science*, 34(4), 415–26.

Black, A. (2007) Mechanisation in libraries and information retrieval: punched cards and microfilm before the widespread adoption of computer technology in libraries, *Library History*, 23(4), 291–300.

Borko, H. (1968) Information science: what is it?, *Journal of the American Society for Information Science*, 19(1), 3–5.

Brettle, A. and Urquhart, C. (eds) (2012) *Changing roles and contexts for health library and information professionals*, London: Facet Publishing.

Buckland, M.K. (1996a) The 'liberal arts' of library and information science and the research university environment, in Ingwersen, P. and Pors, N.O. (eds), *Second International Conference on Conceptions of Library and Information Science: Integration in Perspective, 1996, Proceedings*, Copenhagen: Royal School of Librarianship, pp 75–84, available from http://people.ischool.berkeley.edu/~buckland/libarts.html.

Buckland, M. K. (1996b) Documentation, information science and library science in the USA, *Information Processing and Management*, 32(1), 63–76.

Buckland, M. K. (2012) What kind of science can information science be?, *Journal of the American Society for Information Science and Technology*, 63(1), 1–7.

Buckland, M. K. and Liu, Z. (1995) History of information science, *Annual Review of Information Science and Technology*, 30, 385–416.

Cronin, B. (2008) The sociological turn in information science, *Journal of Information Science*, 34(4), 465–75.

Dalrymple, P. W. (2011) Data, information, knowledge: the emerging field of health informatics, *Bulletin of the American Society for Information Science and Technology*, 37(5), 41–4.

Davis, C. H. and Shaw, D. (2011) *Introduction to information science and technology*, Medford NJ: Information Today.

Dillon, A. (2007) LIS as a research domain: problems and prospects, *Information Research*, 12(4), paper colis03 [online] available at http://informationr.net/ir/12-4/colis/colis03.html.

Ditmas, E. M. R. (1950) The literature of special librarianship. *Aslib Proceedings*, 2(4) 217–43.

Farradane, J. (1976) Towards a true information science, *The Information Scientist*,

10(3), 91–101.

Floridi, L. (2002) On defining library and information science as applied philosophy of information, *Social Epistemology*, 16(1), 37–49.

Given, L. M. and McTavish, L. (2010) What's old is new again: the reconvergence of libraries, archives and museums in the digital age, *Library Quarterly*, 80(1), 7–32.

Hahn, T. B. and Buckland, M. K. (eds) (1998) *Historical studies in information science*, Medford NJ: Information Today.

Hirst, P. (1974) *Knowledge and the curriculum*, London: Routledge and Kegan Paul.

Hjørland, B. (2000) Library and information science: practice, theory and philosophical basis, *Information Processing and Management*, 36(3), 504–31.

Hjørland, B. and Albrechtsen, H. (1995) Toward a new horizon in information science: domain-analysis, *Journal of the American Society for Information Science*, 46(6), 400–25.

Hughes, L. M. (ed.) (2012) *Evaluating and measuring the value, use and impact of digital collections*, London: Facet Publishing. Part 1: Digital transformations in libraries, museums and archives.

Ingwersen, P. (1992) Information and information science in context, *Libri*, 42(2), 99–135.

Janssens, F., Leta, J., Glänzel, W. and De Moor, B. (2006) Towards mapping library and information science, *Information Processing and Management*, 42(6), 1614–42.

Larivière, V., Sugimoto, C. R. and Cronin, B. (2012) A bibliometric chronicling of library and information science's first hundred years, *Journal of the American Society for Information Science and Technology*, 63(5), 997–1016.

Lørring, L. (2007) Didactical models behind the construction of an LIS curriculum, *Journal of Education for Library and Information Science*, 48(2), 82–93.

Mason, D. (ed) (1991) *Information for industry: twenty one years of the Library Association Industrial Group*, London: Library Association Publishing.

Meadows, A. J. (1987) *The origins of information science*, London: Taylor Graham.

Meadows, J. (2004) *The Victorian scientist: growth of a profession*, London: British Library.

Machlup, F. and Mansfield, U. (1983) Cultural diversity in studies of information, in Machlup, F. and Mansfield, U. (eds), *The study of information: interdisciplinary messages*, New York NY: Wiley, pp 3–59.

Mezick, E. M. and Koenig, M. E. D. (2008) Education for information science, *Annual Review of information Science and Technology*, 42, 593–624.

Milojevic, S., Sugimoto, C. R., Yan, E., and Ding, Y. (2011) The cognitive structure of library and information science: analysis of article title words, *Journal of the American Society for Information Science and Technology*, 62(10), 1933–53.

Muddiman, D. (2005) A new history of ASLIB (1924–1950), *Journal of Documentation*, 61(3), 402–28.

Rayward, W. B. (1985) Library and information science: an historical perspective,

Journal of Library History, 20(2), 120–36.

Rayward, W. B. (1997) The origins of information science and the International Institute of Bibliography/International Federation for Information and Documentation, *Journal of the American Society for Information Science*, 48(4), 289–300.

Roberts, N. (1976) Social considerations towards a definition of information science, *Journal of Documentation*, 32(4), 249–57.

Robinson, L. (2009) Information science: communication chain and domain analysis, *Journal of Documentation*, 65(4), 578–91.

Robinson, L. (2010) *Understanding healthcare information*, London: Facet Publishing.

Robinson, L. and Bawden, D. (2010) Information (and library) science at City University London: fifty years of educational development, *Journal of Information Science*, 36(5), 618–30.

Robinson, L. and Bawden, D. (2012) Brian Vickery and the foundations of information science, in Gilchrist, A. and Vernau, J. (eds), *Facets of knowledge organization*, Bingley: Emerald, 281–300.

Robinson, L. and Karamuftuoglu, M. (2010) The nature of information science: changing models, *Information Research*, 15(4), paper colis717, available from http://informationr.net/ir/15-4/colis717.html.

Saracevic, T. (2010) Information science, *Encyclopedia of Library and Information Sciences* (3rd edn), Abingdon: Taylor & Francis, 1:1, 2570–85.

Shapiro, F. R. (1995) Coinage of the term *Information Science*, *Journal of the American Society for Information Science*, 46(5), 384–5.

Shera, J. (1973) *Knowing books and men: knowing computers too*, Littleton CO: Libraries Unlimited.

Shera, J. H. and Cleveland, D. B. (1977) History and foundations of information science, *Annual Review of Information Science and Technology*, 12, 249–75.

Simmons, M. and Corrall, S. (2011) The changing educational needs of subject librarians: a survey of UK practitioner opinions and course content, *Education for Information*, 28(1), 21–44.

SLA (1984) Special Libraries Association: 75 years of service, New York NY: Special Libraries Association, available at http://www.sla.org/pdfs/history/75years_publication.pdf.

Um, A. Y. and Feather, J. (2007) Education for information professionals in the UK, *International Information and Library Review*, 39(3/4), 260–8.

Vickery, B. (2004) *A long search for information*, Occasional Papers No. 213, Graduate School of Library and Information Science, University of Illinois at Urbana-Champaign, available from http://www.ideals.illinois.edu/handle/2142/3808.

Webber, S. (2003) Information science in 2004: a critique, *Journal of Information Science*, 29(4), 311–30.

White, H. D. (2010) Bibliometric overview of information science, *Encyclopedia of*

Library and Information Science, Abingdon: Taylor & Francis, 1:1, 534–45.

Williams, R. V. (1997) The documentation and special library movements in the United States, 1910–1960, *Journal of the American Society for Information Science*, 48(9), 775–781.

Wilson, T. D. (2010) Information and information science: an address on the occasion of receiving the award of Doctor Honoris Causa, at the University of Murcia, September 2010, *Information Research*, 15(4), paper 439 [online] available at http://InformationR.net/ir/15-4/paper439.html.

Zhang, P. and Benjamin, R. I. (2007) Understanding information related fields: a conceptual framework, *Journal of the American Society for Information Science and Technology*, 58(13), 1934–47.

Zins, C. (2007) Conceptions of information science, *Journal of the American Society for Information Science and Technology*, 58(3), 335–50.

CHAPTER 2

History of information: the story of documents

The written word – the persistent word – was a prerequisite for conscious thought as we understand it

James Gleick (2011, 37)

Technology trends and their social impacts can be described in broad terms, but such summaries are extreme simplifications, imagined aggregations of the myriad details of any number of individuals, their actions and the consequences. And each detail involves a personal history far to rich and detailed to be fully comprehended. It is only by attempting to reconstruct the details of specific developments, and of actual persons in their complex and ever-changing contexts, that one can begin to comprehend what was going on.

Michael Buckland (2006, 3)

I like the dreams of the future better than the history of the past.

Thomas Jefferson

Introduction

In this chapter we will give some historical context for the rest of the book, by looking at the development of recorded information, and the documents which carry it, throughout time. We will do this only very briefly and informally; there are many detailed treatments of the history of information provision and dissemination, and we will not try to replicate these in any way. We will give a historical perspective on specific topics in several of the chapters which follow; the history of information science itself has already been mentioned in the first chapter.

It is sometimes suggested that, since information science is a relatively young discipline, there is no need to think about the history of anything which came before, say, 1950. We disagree. Some appreciation of the history of information and documents, as well as being of interest in its own right, can help give a perspective on current problems and solutions. Although contexts and technologies may change, many information issues remain constant over time, and a historical perspective can be of practical, as well as academic, value. It is not possible to understand current information provision, and plan for its improvement, without appreciating how it has come to take the form which it has, and what commonalities and analogies there may be with past information environments. And we are not, in fact, faced with the choice posed by the opening quotation from Thomas Jefferson: reflecting on the information past can help us envisage the information future. For thoughtful analyses of the importance of a historical perspective for the information sciences, see Aspray (2011), Pawley (2005), Rayward (1996), Warner (1999), Spink and Currier (2006) and Weller (2007).

Historical studies come in many forms and flavours, with different perspectives, interests and methods; for an overview, see Donnelly and Norton (2011) and Tosh (2010). For the information sciences, historical accounts have fallen into a number of categories:

- history of libraries, archives and information services
- history of information policies and infrastructures
- history of publishing, books and reading
- history of information technologies (and not just digital ones)
- history of the information disciplines and professions
- origins of the information society
- studies of the cultural and social contexts of information communication and use.

See Black (2006) for a thorough review of all these forms of historical enquiry. As examples of classic 'library history' and 'book history', see the three-volume Cambridge *History of Libraries in Britain and Ireland* (Cambridge University Press, 2006) and the five-volume Ashgate *History of the Book in the West* (Ashgate, 1210). As good examples of histories of particular libraries, see Harris (1998) and Conaway (2000), and of a form of collection Singer (2010). For a detailed account of the history of information resources and services in one domain, healthcare, see Robinson (2010, Chapter 2). For good examples of studies of the development of information technologies, see Bourne and Hahn (2003), Rayward and Bowden (2004) and Buckland (2006).

The last of these points has developed into a new sub-discipline, 'information history'. This is a rather newer, and still a minority, approach, compared with the more traditional 'history of libraries'; see Weller (2007, 2008). It is the study of all aspects of information in societies of the past; how it was understood, used, organized, managed, collected, disseminated, etc. It is therefore a branch of history focused on an intangible central object of study; analogous to histories of such things as humour or fear. Very often however, it will necessarily be studied through a focus on the physical documents which convey information, and how people have produced and used these.

A very different, and intriguing, approach to history considers the normal practice of regarding history as beginning with the first writing as too parochial. 'Big history' seeks to take a much longer view, setting the human past within the whole history of the universe, and the emergence of complexity (see, for example, Spier, 2010). Starting from the beginning of the universe, this considers first the emergence of complexity in its physical constituents, then the emergence of complex chemistry, then the biological era, and only lastly the period of cognition and communication. While way outside the normal considerations of human information history, this approach is of interest for those who consider information an intrinsic feature of the universe, as will be discussed in Chapter 4 .

Here, we will not follow any of these approaches. We look at the historical development of documents, and the systems and services set up to deal with them, in a brief and informal manner, to set the context for what follows in the rest of the book.

Information ages?

It is tempting, in trying to present a short and simple account of a complex and long-term development, to write of distinct 'information ages' based on 'information revolutions'. And there is no doubt that a series of developments in the communication of information have largely dictated the information environment which followed; language, recorded signs and symbols, writing and scripts, printing, mass communications, the digital computer, and the internet are typically taken as the defining developments. However, this is rather too simplistic a viewpoint; no form of history falls into such neat periods, and developments happen at different points in different parts of the world. In outlining the history of documents, therefore, we will follow the timeline without invoking such distinct categories. For general overviews, see Gleick (2011) for a history of communication of information, Robinson (1995, 2009) for writing and scripts, Twyman (1998) for printing, and Zeegers and Barron (2010), Manguel (1997, 2008), Feather (2005) and Finkelstein and McCleery (2005), for libraries, books and reading.

Prehistory and the ancient world

Information communication began with spoken language, but we can only speculate how information may have been transmitted through oral communication. It is only with the origins of recorded information – which, as the opening quotation from James Gleick reminds us, transforms the nature of human thought and knowledge – that we can begin a history of information, based around documents.

The earliest artefacts which we might reasonably describe as documents are cave paintings, and other forms of rock art, the oldest believed to be about 40,000 years old. The purpose of these drawings of animals and people, and seemingly abstract designs, cannot be known, though this has not stopped a lot of speculation. Whether it is reasonable to call them 'documents' is a moot point; but they show that the people of that time had the means to record signs and symbols, and thereby communicate across time, whatever their purpose may have been (Bahn, 2010).

Symbolic inscriptions believed to be the first forms of writing date back to 5000 years BCE, and appear on portable stone artefacts; messages can now be sent across space as well as time. Figure 2.1 shows an example of such; one of the Tartaria tablets from Romania, believed by some experts to be the earliest form of writing yet found, though this is still a matter of controversy.

Figure 2.1
Tartaria tablet; an example of proto-writing (Photograph by Marco Merlini, reproduced courtesy of EURO INNOVANET)

True writing – the agreed repertoire of signs or symbols that is used to reproduce clearly the thoughts and feelings that the writer wishes to express – appeared over 5000 years ago. It used to be thought that it was invented once, in Babylonia, and transmitted to the rest of the world, but expert opinion now holds that writing was invented independently at least four times: in Mesopotamia, Egypt, China and Mesoamerica. The earliest accurately dated writings, from both Egypt and Mesopotamia, are from around 3300 BCE, although some experts claim earlier examples. We will focus on the descendants of these writings, and their consequences in the western world. For aspects of information in the ancient world, see Brosius (2003), Houston (2004), and Too (2010).

Mesopotamian writings used the cuneiform script, written on clay tablets using sharpened reeds as writing implements. In Egypt, the hieroglyphic and hieratic scripts were written in ink on a variety of materials: the stereotypical papyrus, but also wood, stone and pottery. Because of the nature of the materials used, and the durability of clay tablets, we know much more of collections in Mesopotamia than their equivalents in Egypt. Figure 2.2 shows an example of such a tablet, showing a human head, a triangular symbol for bread, and number symbols; probably an administrative record of food rations.

Figure 2.2 *Cuneiform tablet (reproduced courtesy of British Museum)*

The earliest collections were attached to palaces and temples; there is little evidence of organization or intent, and it is not clear if any distinction was made at that time between library and archives. At a later stage, there is evidence of different kinds of collections, encompassing religious material, government records, business and trade records, family documents such as genealogical tables, property and inheritance matters, and astrological predictions, scientific and medical texts, literary works and correspondence of all kinds. Three examples can be given from Mesopotamia, showing the size and sophistication of document collections in the ancient world.

The library/archive at the palace of Ebla, in modern Syria, active between 2600 and 2300 BCE, comprised tablets stored on wooden shelves, with different types of materials held in separate rooms. Two 'archive rooms' held over 17,000 tablets of commercial, legal and administrative records. Another room held collections of dictionaries, proverbs, epic narratives, myths, hymns, incantations and rituals. Others contained material on botany, zoology, mineralogy and mathematics. There was even what might be regarded as an early form of reference collection. Many tablets were devoted to lists of persons and items, often in order of precedence and importance: gods, kings, professions, animals, stones, etc. The ordering of items in the rooms was maintained by rudimentary written classification tables.

The temple at Sippar, in modern Iraq, active over a very long period, had a library of tablets stored in brick pigeonholes (see Figure 2.3). Over 50,000 items

Figure 2.3
Sippar tablet library (reproduced courtesy of the British Museum)

have been found, divided into records of the temple's activities, including business records and literary texts.

Finally, from the later part of this period, the palace of Assurbanipal at Nineveh, again in modern Iraq, built around 650 BCE, had a large, well organized and catalogued collection, with around 10,000 distinguishable works on 30,000 tablets, arranged by subject in different rooms. They were stored in earthenware jars on wooden shelves, related items kept together in a basket, with a front tablet describing the set; each tablet had an identification tag, noting its location 'jar-shelf-room'. An early form of catalogue, also written on clay tablets, was provided near the door of each room, giving for each work present its title, opening words, number of tablets comprising the work, and its location symbol.

Less is known about libraries and archives in ancient Egypt, although it is clear from surviving writings that they existed. Their materials – papyrus and later parchment – have for the most part not survived, and the physical structures have yet to be found. The only convincing example is from the Temple of Edfu, in Upper Egypt, where there is evidence of a small number of scrolls being kept in a recess, a list of titles of the scrolls being carved on the wall nearby; there is, however, doubt as to whether this can be considered as a true library.

So it is clear that in the ancient world we can see already some of the elements of an information infrastructure; physical spaces, with different types of material arranged by location; descriptions of work, and parts of works; shelf lists, locator tags, and early forms of catalogue; subject arrangement; lists and early classifications; reference works; and multiple copies of texts, with master copies of important works held centrally.

The classical and medieval worlds

The alphabet, invented in Phoenicia around 1200 BCE, used a small number of symbols to replace the much larger symbol sets of cuneiform and hieroglyphic writing, and could be used to write different languages, greatly increasing the flexibility of representation. The Phoenician alphabet influenced the Aramaic/Hebrew and Greek alphabets, leading to the first substantial bodies of alphabetic writings. Libraries and record centres became widespread throughout the classical world of Greece and Rome, and included the first recognizable public and private libraries. Tables of contents and bibliographies, in a recognizable modern form, were developed. Initially texts were written on

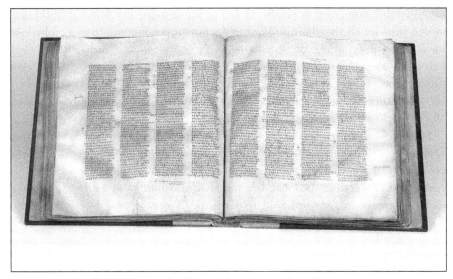

Figure 2.4 *Codex Siniaticus (© The British Library Board)*

papyrus rolls, stored on shelves, or in pigeon-holes or chests; tags or smaller scrolls were attached to identify title and author. Scrolls were later supplanted by the *codex*, the forerunner of the modern book, stemming from wooden writing tablets tied together. The *Codex Siniaticus*, a manuscript of the Christian Bible written in the 4th century, shown in Figure 2.4, is a well known example.

The best known library of this period is, of course, the Great Library of Alexandria in Egypt, founded by Alexander the Great in the 4th century BCE, and developed by the Ptolomaic kings over the following centuries (El-Abbadi and Fathallah, 2008). A centre for scholarship, it was believed at its height to contain over 400,000 Greek papyrus manuscripts: essentially all of human knowledge at that time. Its famous *Pinakes* catalogue, written over many scrolls, was divided according to the classification of its creator, Callimachus. This had sections for philosophy, law, history, medicine, natural history and miscellanea, with literature divided into rhetoric, lyric, comedy, tragedy and epic works. Including a general guide to the literature of the day, it is regarded as the first recognizably modern form of bibliographic tool.

These developments of the classical period continued throughout medieval times. Parchment, able to be written on on both sides and better able to accept illuminations, became the norm, with the sheets folded and sewn together in codex form.

This was the period of the illuminated manuscript, now the treasures of many national libraries. Other forms of information representation – maps, musical notations, and mathematical symbolism – were developed, the last using the so-called Arabic numerals, originally an Indian innovation. The Islamic world was at that time much ahead of the West in document production, having embarked on a major programme of translating Greek, Persian and Indian texts, and extending them by original scholarship (Al-Khalili, 2010; Lyons, 2009). This process was pioneered by the 'House of Wisdom' (Bayt al-Hikma) established in 9th-century Baghdad by the Abbasid caliph Al-Ma'mun, who wished to collect all the world's books under one roof.

For much of this period in the West, writing, and to a large degree reading, was focused in religious institutions, monasteries and cathedrals, with collections of almost exclusively parchment codices. But by the end of the 12th century secular scribes were banding together into guilds and workshops, works in local languages – as opposed to Latin or Greek – were becoming more common, and treatises on mathematics, logic, philosophy and astronomy began to appear, often translated from Arabic. It is not unreasonable to suggest that, two hundred years before the introduction of printing, a publishing industry had been established.

This was promoted by the rise of secular universities throughout Western Europe, stimulating a need for multiple authoritative copies of texts. This was coupled with a demand for popular and professional books, including medical texts, educational books, novels and cookery books. The production of manuscripts attained a professional status, with scribal fraternities and apprenticeship schemes. Paper had reached Europe in the 12th century, a Chinese innovation passed on via the Arabic world. However, it was initially used only for formal documents, and not for books. The first paper mill in England was established at the end of the 15th century, to meet the demands of printers.

Toward the end of the period, several European monarchies – for example, those of England, France, Austria and Hungary – established royal collections, which provided the foundations of later national libraries; see Tanner (2008) for an account of the Hungarian example. University libraries appeared, some of which survive to the present day, at Oxford, Cambridge, Paris, Padua and elsewhere.

Catalogues of this period were accession lists of authors and titles, and served to support an active programme of document loans between monasteries. The first union catalogues were created; in 14th-century Paris, for example, the Sorbonne university library had a union catalogue of several Parisian libraries. Secular classification was typically based on the classical seven liberal arts – the *trivium* of grammar, rhetoric and dialectic (or logic) and the *quadrivium* of arithmetic, geometry, music and astronomy. This form of classification was first devised in the 6th century by Flavius Magnus Aurelius Cassiodorus, a philosopher and theologian, living in the last days of the Roman world. Religious classifications met the needs of their institutions; typically by the ecclesiastical calendar and the names of saints, so that material appropriate for reading on each day could easily be located.

The age of print

Printing with moveable characters had been established in China, where characters of baked clay were used initially, for several centuries before it was introduced into Europe in the middle of the 15th century. Credit is usually given to Johannes Gutenberg, who established a press in Mainz in 1455, his colleague Peter Schoeffer having discovered a viable method of casting the letters using an alloy of tin and lead. The first printing press was set up in England in 1476, by William Caxton; the first product was *The Dictes or Sayings of the Philosophers*. For a history of printing, see Twyman (1998).

Printing houses spread throughout Europe throughout the next century, combining the talents of compositors, engravers and type-casters, to give a recognizably modern printing industry, able to produce both text and images, though by a rather clumsy process with images reproduced separately, initially on wood-block carvings, and later on metal plates. Printing had two general effects. The availability of multiple identical copies of works, calling for bibliographic tools – catalogues, bibliographies, tables of contents, and indexes – in which there was a single description for a printed work, rather than for each unique handwritten manuscript. And printing led to the original 'information explosion', with many more copies of more titles, of an increasingly diverse nature (Eisenstein, 1993; Bawden and Robinson, 2000).

The first bibliographies in a modern sense appeared at this stage; notably Conrad Gesner's *Bibliotheca Universalis* of 1545, which pioneered ideas of selection, arrangement and indexing. Gesner, who has been described as the first would-be universal bibliographer and the last to have had any chance of succeeding, managed to include 15,000 titles in Hebrew, Greek and Latin, estimated at 20–25% of the total available at the time. Classification schemes were developed by many scholars, among the best known being those of Francis Bacon and Gottfried von Leibnitz.

The first scientific journals were established in 1665, the Paris-based *Journal des Savants*, first published on 5 January, just claiming precedence over the *Philosophical Transactions of the Royal Society* of London, which first published on 6 March.

In the 17th century advances in printing technology led to both a more rapid production process and the ability – through lithography – to allow text and images to be printed at the same time. This led to the increased numbers and readership of newspapers, magazines and scientific and professional journals. This was also the period of the appearance of major reference tools – such as Chambers *Cyclopedia* (1728), Diderot's *Encyclopédie* (1761), Samuel Johnson's *Dictionary*

(1755), and the *Encyclopedia Britannica* (1768) – as well as national and subject bibliographies, and further ideas of classification and bibliographic principles. National libraries and 'memory institutions' began to appear: the British Museum and its associated library in 1753 and the Bibliothèque Nationale in 1789.

The 19th century

The 19th century saw the advent of mass communications, due to the adoption of the products of the industrial revolution for the purposes of information dissemination, and laid the foundations of the modern information environment. The first steam-powered presses, introduced early in the century, increased the rate of printing considerably, but this soon went up by orders or magnitude (see box). Steamships and steam trains provided rapid and reliable transport for this new volume of printed material. An interesting example of the way in which steam-powered printing and transport affected the creation and dissemination of information is given in Fyfe's (2010) account of the Edinburgh-based publishers W & R Chambers. For an interesting account of how the technical developments of this period built on the intellectual insights of the Enlightenment, see Headrick (2000), and for overviews of other general issues of the period, as they affected society and individuals respectively, see Weller and Bawden (2005, 2006).

A much greater range of books and serial publications was produced, both popular and academic: in particular, many more specialized scientific and professional journals, monographs and textbooks, to meet the needs of the

---

Machine age printing

'The old wooden hand press had been able to make 250 impressions an hour . . . the Stanhope iron press, imported from the USA, allowed an impression to be made with one pull instead of two, cutting the time and effort in half, but this was still hand printing, something that Caxton . . . would just about have recognized. In 1810 the *Annual Register* was printed on an early version of the steam-powered press, which could produce a dizzying 400 impressions an hour. Then the Koenig and Bauer press arrived from Saxony. This could print up to 1,800 impressions an hour [and was adopted to print the *Times*]. By 1828 the *Times* was using Applegarth and Cooper presses, designed by their own chief printer. These machines could produce 4,000 sheets an hour . . . The How rotary press, invented in the USA in 1846, was first installed in Britain by *Lloyd's Weekly* in 1855, followed in 1857 by the *Times*, which soon had it printing 20,000 sheets an hour.'

From J Flanders, *Consuming passions: leisure and pleasure in Victorian England*, London: HarperPress, 2006

rapidly professionalizing and specializing scientific and technical activities (Meadows, 2004). Communication in general improved, with the introduction of the telegraph in the 1830s, national postal services in the 1840s and the telephone in the 1870s. Photography was introduced in the 1840s, and three decades later photographs were commonly being reproduced in printed documents. Charles Babbages' analogue computers of the 1830s, although their concept proved to be beyond what the technology of the time could deliver, gave intimations of things to come.

A range of library and information services was created during the 19th century: national libraries, such as the Library of Congress (1800); specialized national information institutions, such as the French Académie Nationale de Médicine and the US National Library of Medicine (1836); memory institutions such as the UK Public Records Office (1838) and National Gallery (1824); many academic and professional societies, typically with their own library and/or archive; modern university libraries; the first abstracting and indexing services – *Chemisches Zentralblatt* (1830) for chemistry and *Index Medicus* (1879) for medicine; and public library services, both subscription (fee-paying) and free. For studies of the last, from a UK perspective, see Sturges (2003) and Glasgow (2003).

The intellectual tools for dealing with information also made major advances. Anthony Panizzi's 91 rules (expanded from the original 73) for the British Museum library catalogue of 1841 were a major development (Carpenter, 2002), paralleled by the principles developed by Charles Jewett for the library of the Smithsonian Institute in the USA. Dewey's decimal classification first appeared in 1876, and the first modern subject headings lists appeared towards the end of the century.

Such familiar information-handling tools as filing cabinets, standard-sized envelopes, pencils with erasers, paper-clips and typewriters were also developed during this period, and the card index and catalogue became the major tool for information management (Krajewski, 2011). In many ways, despite technical advances, the information environment remained largely Victorian until the end of the 20th century.

The 20th century

The 20th century saw the introduction of new forms of analogue document; photography, cinematography, sound recording, microforms, and – later – audio and video tape. Mechanization was introduced to documentation, in the form of punched cards, edge-notched cards, optical co-incidence cards and microforms, which allowed complex searches using Boolean logic, based on detailed indexing; an example of edge-notched card equipment is shown in Figure 2.5.

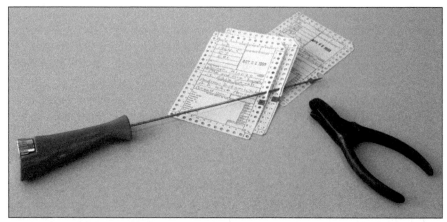

Figure 2.5 *Edge-notched card retrieval (Courtesy of the Cornell University Library)*

The advent of the digital computer at the mid-point of the 20th century led to convergence of formats; text, images, sounds, and video all became digital. New intellectual tools, such as faceted classifications and thesauri, were introduced, in an attempt to deal with the increasing volumes of materials in all formats; see Chapter 6. Many discipline-specific information services were introduced; see Powell (2000) for the development of one important example, *Chemical Abstracts*. Information and knowledge management became established disciplines, and the concept of an 'information society', to be discussed in Chapter 11, was conceived. For overviews of developments in this period, see Rayward (2008), Black and Brunt (1999) and Black, Muddiman and Plant (2007).

At the end of the century, the introduction of the internet and world wide web, and the advent of social media, brought about new forms of document and of communication, leading to repeatedly voiced suggestions that this is a change in the information environment as dramatic as, and potentially even more far-reaching than, that due to printing, or even writing. These 20th-century developments are covered in the relevant chapters.

Figure 2.6
Paul Otlet (© Mundaneum, centre d'archives, Mons, Belgique)

The centuries-old desire for universal bibliographic control was pursued by the

Figure 2.7 *The Mundaneum (© Mundaneum, centre d'archives, Mons, Belgique)*

new 'documentation movement', pioneered by the Belgian scholars Paul Otlet and Henri La Fontaine. Making use of new intellectual and physical tools for information organization, Otlet – particularly through his Mundaneum documentation centre and his influential book *Traité de documentation* (1934) – foreshadowed the origins of information science, as noted in the previous chapter; see Rayward (1994) for an overview of Otlet's significance. Otlet is shown as a young man in Figure 2.6, and a part of the Mundaneum with its manager Louis Masure in the centre, in Figure 2.7. (We are grateful to Boyd Rayward for the identification of Masure.) Ultimately the idea of a single bibliographic control centre proved impractical, and the objective is now pursued through international standards and programmes, national bibliographies, and bibliographic description standards, as we will discuss in Chapter 6.

Summary

This overview of the history of information has necessarily been brief, and somewhat simplistic. Economic, social, technical and academic developments have gone alongside the growth of knowledge, and the technologies and systems which have tried to control the resulting increases in information, records and documents. These developments have never been as orderly as they may seem, as each influences, and is influenced by, the others. We can, nonetheless, learn lessons from the information past, and use them to understand the information present, and to imagine the information future.

> • Understanding the history of information and documents is not only intrinsically interesting, but is helpful in understanding the present, and in seeing analogies with past problems and issues.
> • There are several different approaches and perspectives in the study of the history of information and documents.
> • The developments which have, in turn, changed the information environment drastically have been language, writing, printing, mass communications, and networked digital information.
> • We live in what is still, to a large extent, a Victorian information environment.

Key readings

William Aspray, The history of information science and other traditional information domains: models for future research, *Libraries and the Cultural Record*, 2011, 46(2), 230–48.

Margaret Zeegers and Deidre Barron, *Gatekeepers of knowledge: a consideration of the library, the book and the scholar in the Western world*, Oxford: Chandos, 2010. [Two authoritative and readable texts, focusing on the history of information science and of librarianship respectively.]

References

Al-Khalili, J. (2010) Pathfinders: the golden age of Arabic science, London: Allen Lane.

Aspray, W. (2011) The history of information science and other traditional information domains: models for future research, *Libraries and the Cultural Record*, 46(2), 230–48.

Bahn, P. (2010) *Prehistoric rock art: polemics and progress*, Cambridge: Cambridge University Press.

Bawden, D. and Robinson, L. (2000) A distant mirror?; the Internet and the printing press, *Aslib Proceedings*, 52(2), 51–7.

Black, A. (2006) Information history, *Annual Review of Information Science and Technology*, 40, 441–73.

Black, A. and Brunt, R. (1999) Information management in business, libraries and British military intelligence: towards a history of information management, *Journal of Documentation*, 55(4), 361–74.

Black, A., Muddiman, D. and Plant, H. (2007) *The early information society: information management in Britain before the computer*, Aldershot: Ashgate.

Bourne, C. P. and Hahn, T. B. (2003) *A history of online information services*, Cambridge MA: MIT Press.

Brosius, M. (ed.) (2003) *Ancient archives and archival traditions: concepts of record-keeping in the ancient world*, Oxford: Oxford University Press.

Buckland, M.K. (2006) *Emanuel Goldberg and his knowledge machine*, Westport CT: Libraries Unlimited.

Carpenter, M. (2002) The original 73 rules of the British Museum: a preliminary analysis, *Cataloguing and Classification Quarterly*, 35(1/2), 23–36.

Conaway, J. (2000) *America's Library: the story of the Library of Congress 1800–2000*, New Haven CT: Yale University Press.

Donnelly, M. and Norton, C. (2011) *Doing history*, London: Routledge.

Eisenstein, E. (1993) *The printing revolution in early modern Europe*, Cambridge, Cambridge University Press.

El-Abbadi, M. and Fathallah, O. M. (eds) (2008) *What happened to the ancient library of Alexandria?*, Leiden: Brill.

Feather, J. (2005) *A history of British publishing* (2nd edn), London: Routledge.

Finkelstein, D. and McCleery, S. (2005) *Introduction to book history*, London: Routledge.

Fyfe, A. (2010) Steam and the landscape of knowledge: W&R Chambers in the 1830s–1850s, in Ogborn, M. and Withers, C. J. W. (eds), *Geographies of the book*, Farnham: Ashgate, 51–78.

Glasgow, E. (2003) Two public libraries in Victorian Liverpool, *Library History*, 19(2), 129–41.

Gleick, J. (2011) *The information: a history, a theory, a flood*, London: Fourth Estate.

Harris, P. R. (1998) *A history of the British Museum Library 1753–1973*, London: British Library.

Headrick, D. (2000) *When information came of age: technologies of knowledge in the age of reason and revolution, 1700–1850*, Oxford: Oxford University Press.

Houston, S. D. (ed.) (2004) *The first writing: script invention as history and process*, Cambridge: Cambridge University Press.

Krajewski, M. (2011) *Paper machines: about cards and catalogs, 1548–1929*, Cambridge MA: MIT Press.

Lyons, J. (2009) *The House of Wisdom: how the Arabs transformed Western civilization*, London: Bloomsbury.

Manguel, A. (1997) *A history of reading*, London: Flamingo.

Manguel, A. (2008) *The library at night*, London: Yale University Press.

Meadows, J. (2004) *The Victorian scientist: growth of a profession*, London: British Library.

Pawley, C. (2005) History in the library and information science curriculum: outline of a debate, *Libraries and Culture*, 40(3), 223–8.

Powell, E. C. (2000) A history of Chemical Abstracts Service, 1907–1998, *Science and Technology Libraries*, 18(4), 93–110.

Rayward, W. B. (1994) Visions of Xanadu: Paul Otlet (1868-1944) and hypertext, *Journal of the American Society for Information Science*, 45(4), 235–50.

Rayward, W. B. (1996) The history and historiography of information science: some reflections, *Information Processing and Management*, 32(1) 3–17.

Rayward, W. B (ed.) (2008) *European modernism and the information society*, Aldershot: Ashgate.

Rayward, W. B. and Bowden, M. E. (eds) (2004) *The history and heritage of scientific and technological information systems*, Medford NJ: Information Today Inc.

Robinson, A. (1995) *The story of writing*, London: Thames and Hudson.

Robinson, A. (2009) *Writing and script: a very short introduction*, Oxford: Oxford University Press.

Robinson, L. (2010) *Understanding healthcare information*, London: Facet Publishing.

Singer, C. A. (2010) Ready reference collections: a history, *Reference and User Services Quarterly*, 49(3), 253–64.

Spier, F. (2010) *Big history and the future of humanity*, Chichester: Wiley-Blackwell.

Spink, A. and Currier, J. (2006) Towards an evolutionary perspective for human information behaviour: an exploratory study, *Journal of Documentation*, 62(2), 171–93.

Sturges, P. (2003) Great city libraries of Britain: their history from a European perspective, *Library History*, 19(2), 93–111.

Tanner, M. (2008) *The Raven King: Matthias Corvinus and the fate of his lost library*, London: Yale University Press.

Too, Y. L. (2010) *The idea of the library in the ancient world*, Oxford: Oxford University Press.

Tosh, J. (2010) *The pursuit of history* (5th edn), Harlow: Longman.

Twyman, M. (1998) *British Library Guide to Printing History*, London: British Library.

Warner, J. (1999) An information view of history, *Journal of the American Society for Information Science*, 50(12), 1125–6.

Weller, T. (2007) Information history: its importance, relevance and future, *Aslib Proceedings*, 59(4/5), 437–48.

Weller, T. (2008) *Information history – an introduction*, Oxford: Chandos.

Weller, T. and Bawden, D. (2005) The social and technological origins of the information society: an analysis of the crisis of control in England, 1830–1890, *Journal of Documentation*, 61(6), 777–802.

Weller, T. and Bawden, D. (2006) Individual perceptions: a new chapter on Victorian information history, *Library History*, 22(2), 137–56.

Zeegers, M. and Barron, D. (2010) *Gatekeepers of knowledge: a consideration of the library, the book and the scholar in the Western world*, Oxford: Chandos.

CHAPTER 3

Philosophies and paradigms of information science

Librarians know very well how to do what they do, but they never concern them-selves with why they do it. They understand the *Können* but the *Wissen* has escaped them. Their discipline is a vast accumulation of technical details rather than a body of organized abstract principles that can be applied in concrete situations – a body of knowledge known and understood by all members of the guild and one that librari-ans have themselves created.

Jesse Shera (1973, 262)

There is nothing so practical as a good theory

Kurt Lewin, German-American psychologist

Introduction

In this chapter we will consider some of the overarching approaches to the study of information, and of information science. Specific theories – of information-related behaviour, and of Shannon's mathematical theory of communication, for example – will be covered in their appropriate chapters. Here, we will look at the general ways in which we can understand the discipline and practice of information science; these may be termed philosophies, paradigms or meta-theories, or may be said to be the asking of 'meta-questions', or the examination of the presuppositions on which the field is based; for more discussion and examples of these terms, see Vickery (1997), Hjørland (1998) and Bates (2005).

Consideration of these theoretical foundations are as important for practice as for academic study. As the quote from Jesse Shera, above, reminds us, the information disciplines have for too long been concerned with the detail of practical activities – technical and organizational – without a proper understanding of what is being done, and why. As Hjørland (1998, 606) puts it, philosophies and meta-theories

have a fundamental impact on theories about users, their cognition and information seeking behaviour, on subject analysis, and on classification. They have also fundamental impact on information retrieval, on the understanding of 'information', on the view of documents and their role in communication, on information selection, on theories about the functions of information systems and on the role of information professionals.

Shera was writing specifically of library science, but concerns about the lack of a coherent body of disciplinary theory as the basis for study and practice have also been made for the other information sciences. Hjørland (1998) comments that it is difficult to give even one good example of an explicit theory in information; what we have are theories taken from other fields, and some 'unconscious attitudes' guiding research and practice. An analysis of over 1000 information science articles by Pettigrew and McKechnie (2001) confirmed this view; explicit theories were mentioned in only one third of the articles, a majority being theories brought in from other disciplines. Where theories from within information science itself were present, these were typically from a wide range of rather specific theories, such as models of information seeking, rather than broader theoretical perspectives. This is further confirmed by the identification of 72 theories of information behaviour, most originating from outside the information sciences, by Fisher, Edelez and McKechnie (2005). Although there has been an increased emphasis on theory within the information sciences over recent years, the field still remains without a convincing theoretical foundation of its own. The British astronomer-turned-information scientist Jack Meadows, reviewing the arguments for theory in a vocational subject, wrote over twenty years ago that 'even if the Holy Grail of a generalized theory of information science is possible, we still have some way to go before we can attain the vision' (Meadows, 1990, 63); we have to conclude that the situation is still the same.

To see why this may be, and what is used in its place, we will give an overview, necessarily brief and at the level of an outline, of some of the main philosophies and paradigms adopted by the information sciences. We include a particularly extensive set of literature references, so that the interested reader can follow up aspects of interest to them in more detail than we can provide here.

Philosophy and the information sciences

At the risk of over-simplifying, we can say crudely that philosophical thought addresses three kinds of question:

- meta-physics and ontology – what is it to 'be', and what kinds of things can exist
- epistemology – what is it to 'know', what can we know, and how can we be sure of our knowedge
- ethics – how can actions be 'right', and how should we act.

All three of these aspects have clear relevance to information science, and the information disciplines. Metaphysics (the study of what can exist) and ontology (the study of fundamental categories and kinds of things) addresses the existence and nature of entities such as information, documents, relevance, aboutness, and many more. Epistemology questions what is meant by knowledge, with very practical consequences for knowledge management. Ethics questions what is right use of information, and touches on issues such as censorship and privacy.

For a more thorough and nuanced discussion of the nature of philosophy, and its relation to the information sciences, see the review article by Jonathan Furner (2010). He reminds us that we may take a philosophical approach to the information sciences in two ways: analysing the nature of the disciplines from a philosophical viewpoint, and analysing the nature of entities which are important for the subject.

We will look at some of the metaphysical and epistemological issues in Chapter 4, which deals with basic concepts of information science, and ethics in Chapter 11, where social issues are considered. In this chapter we will consider the general influence of philosophy on the information sciences, and the ways in which philosophy and philosophers have been applied, and at some general philosophical positions and their consequences.

Many philosophers over the centuries have written on topics of importance to information science: knowledge, meaning, categories, classification, concepts, naming and labelling, and so on. But relatively few have directly addressed the topics from a perspective which is directly useful for the information sciences; Luciano Floridi, Fred Dretske and Karl Popper are among them. Equally few have been the examples of scholars within the information sciences making genuine philosophical contributions, as distinct from calling on philosophies and philosophers in support of their views; these include Jesse Shera, Marcia Bates, Birger Hjørland and Michael Buckland. The contributions of both these groups will be discussed below and in Chapter 4.

In this chapter, we will first briefly outline some of the main philosophical positions which may be taken within our discipline, and some of the associated paradigms for its study. A brief analysis of the way in which philosophers and philosophies have been used in support of research and scholarship in information science is then given, followed by a discussion of three particularly important examples.

Philosophical positions

The categorization of philosophical viewpoints according to positions, perspectives or schools of thought is subtle and complex, and we will make no attempt to do it justice here. But it is worthwhile noting, in a very broad-brush sense, that there are some fundamentally different positions in the philosophy of the information sciences. To a large extent, they reflect the very old division between the philosophical positions of *realism*, which holds that an objective reality exists, independent of the mind which contemplates it, and *idealism*, in which reality is regarded as subjective, and constructed by human minds. Numerous variants of these positions, and others, have been proposed, of which we will consider three, which have been particularly significant applied to philosophical analysis in the information sciences: realism, constructivism and critical theory.

This is not, of course, the only typology of philosophical and metatheoretical positions in information science. Hjørland (1998, 2005), for example, compares empiricism, rationalism, positivism and historicism as epistemological approaches, showing how they affect the practical processes of classification, indexing, collection development, and the assessment of relevance. Bates (2005) discusses and compares 13 metatheoretical positions: historical, constructivist, constructionist, philosophical-analytical, critical theory, ethnographic, socio-cognitive, cognitive, bibliometric, physical, engineering, user-centred, and evolutionary. We will discuss some of Bates' positions later, under the heading of 'paradigms'; for the moment, our three-way typology will give a flavour of the differences between such approaches.

Realism

There are a number of different forms of the realist position, but we will understand it, in the straightforward way expressed by Deutsch (2011, 11), as 'the commonsense, and true, doctrine that the physical world really exists, and is accessible to rational enquiry'. This position has been a popular one in information science, particular among many of the founders of the field who came from a scientific or technical background. Hjørland (2004) gives a strong defence of this position as a foundation for the information sciences.

A strongly realist stance will lead to a preference for quantitative and 'laboratory-style' research and evaluation methods. Realist perspectives also underlie concepts of domain analysis, to be discussed in Chapter 5.

Readers with a strong interest in these topics may note that variants of the realist position have been presented with relevance to the information sciences, including *pragmatic realism* (Hjørland, 2004), *critical realism* (Dobson, 2002; Wikgren, 2005), *realist phenomenology* (Budd, Hill and Shannon, 2010; Budd, 2012) and *structural realism* (Floridi, 2011).

Constructivism

We use this term to cover a number of related positions, all sharing the common view that reality is constructed by individuals, and that, rather than a single objective reality, we must consider numerous subjective realities, created by individuals and social groups. The relationships between constructivism, constructionism and several other related concepts are complex, and the terms not used consistently: Talja, Tuominen and Savolainen (2005) give a clear account.

This kind of position underlies several 'user-centred' theories of information-related behaviour, such as Dervin's 'Sense-Making' and Kuhlthau's 'information search process', which will be discussed in Chapter 9. It also leads to a preference for a qualitative and holistic style of research and evaluation; see, for example, Budd (2001).

Critical theory

Critical theory is a term initially associated with the philosophers of the Frankfurt School, most notably Adorno and Habermas, but usually more broadly interpreted, so that 'in both the broad and the narrow senses . . . a critical theory provides the descriptive and normative bases for social inquiry aimed at decreasing domination and increasing freedom in all their forms' (Bohman, 2010). We use the term here in the broad sense, to include structuralist, post-structuralist and post-modernist theory, which shares similar aims and nature, and is associated with many continental European philosophers, such as Bourdieu, Derrida, Foucault, Barthes, Lacan, Deleuze and Guattari.

The impact of this kind of theory on the information sciences has been relatively limited and piecemeal: see Day (2005), Radford and Radford (2005), and Cronin and Meho (2009) for reviews and analysis, and the papers in the collection edited by Leckie, Given and Buschman (2010) for examples. Cronin and Meho, referring to 'French theory' because of the number of philosophers of this stance from that country, identify 16 such philosophers cited in four main library and information journals: Latour, Foucault and Bourdieu top the list. They point out that, despite vigorous criticisms (see, for example, Sokal and Bricmont, 1997), these approaches have been increasingly adopted in a variety of subject areas, perhaps more in the humanities and social science than in the sciences, and may be expected to make more impact on the information sciences in the future.

The methods and applications of this approach are varied, but have generally been applied in the information sciences to challenge prevailing theories and practices, in areas including information organization, bibliometrics, library and information service provision, and methods for research and evaluation.

These general philosophical positions are very often implicit and unacknowledged in research and practice within information science. More visible are the general ways in which the subject is conducted ('paradigms') and changes in this ('turns'), and we will now look at some of the more important of these.

Paradigms and turns

The idea of a *paradigm*, a term made popular by the philosopher of science Thomas Kuhn, is that of a collection of beliefs about the subject matter of a field, and a set of agreements about how the subject should be studied. Numerous paradigms for the information sciences have been named, including the system paradigm, the user paradigm, the behavioural paradigm, the information paradigm, the object paradigm, the bibliometric paradigm, the cognitive paradigm, the communication paradigm, the physical paradigm, and the socio-cognitive paradigm. Some of these overlap, and others have not been influential; Hjørland (1995, 2002), Ellis (1992, 1996), Ingwersen and Järvelin (2005) and Cronin (2008) discuss and compare some of them, and critique the whole idea of paradigms in the information sciences.

A *turn*, in this context, implies a fairly rapid change of direction within a field of study, affecting which topics are thought to be relevant and important, and also affecting views of the best ways of studying them; or, as Jan Nolin (2007) more formally calls it, 'some sort of cognitive interruption with a research tradition'. A turn can be seen, in a broad-brush view, as equivalent to the adoption of a new paradigm. As with paradigms, numerous 'turns' have been claimed for the information sciences: Nolin and Åström (2010) identify the cognitive turn, the informational turn, the user-centred turn, the epistemological turn, and the pragmatic turn. They note that these often have wider scope than just the information sciences; the cognitive turn, for example, originated in psychology. Cronin (2008) mentions also the user turn and the sociological turn, both in information studies, and the linguistic turn, of wider scope, but impacting on our disciplines.

It is important to realize that, in any discipline and most certainly in information science, the emergence of a new paradigm does not mean the cessation of work based in older paradigms; the process is more one of addition, and perhaps gradual replacement. For example, we will see below that the oldest significant paradigm in information science is the systems paradigm, which implies a particular style of research. Although newer paradigms began to be embraced from the 1970s, one can still see research being carried out very much according to the systems paradigm, where this is suited to the research aims. As Davis and Shaw (2011, 231) say, it may be better to consider such paradigms as mutually dependent, rather than mutually exclusive; after all, without users in a social context there is no purpose for an information system, and without some system there can be no users.

To simplify this rather complicated picture, we will look at the three major information science paradigms: the systems, cognitive and socio-cognitive paradigms.

The systems paradigm

The systems paradigm is often called the physical paradigm, and sometimes referred to as the archetypal paradigm (Ellis, 1996), and sometimes – for reasons which will become clear – the Cranfield paradigm. It is associated with a 'scientific' or 'experimental' approach to the evaluation of information systems and services, and dates from the 1960s.

Its basic assumption, following a strongly realist position, is that information systems may be analysed in isolation from the real messy world of users, information needs, and so on; and moreover that the parts of systems can also be analysed independently. It is usually associated with the evaluation of computerized systems, particularly for information retrieval, but can be applied to a wider variety of systems and services. Typically, research under this paradigm compares such things as retrieval algorithms and indexing languages, using test collections of documents with test queries.

In a looser sense, this paradigm can be identified over a longer time period, in the context of the creation, rather than the evaluation of retrieval tools. Writing of Paul Otlet's pioneering documentation initiatives, discussed in Chapter 2, Rayward (1994) criticizes a rather naïve assumption that objective true facts can readily be gleaned from document collections, and notes that Otlet displayed little interest in the nature or needs of users of his systems.

Although experimental tests of retrieval systems had been carried out earlier, the studies which really launched this style of research were the Cranfield experiments. These were carried out at the library of what was then the Cranfield College of Aeronautics in England in stages between 1957 and 1966, although they had been preceded by smaller-scale tests of indexing at the same institution as far back as 1953; accounts of the research and its significance are given by Ellis (1996) and by papers in the volume edited by Sparck Jones (1981). The driving force behind the work was Cyril Cleverdon, the college librarian, who had a strong belief in the use of scientific methods to improve library and information provision.

The Cranfield tests were carried out in paper-based systems, and compared classification and indexing tools used in the libraries of that time; very different from what would be thought of as retrieval research today. Nonetheless, they exemplify the system paradigm very well: repeated analyses of retrieval performance when small parts of the system – for instance the indexing language – are varied, with quantitative measures of the results. The information system is, in essence, treated like a physical system, and the tests are carried in the same style as in a scientific laboratory. The Cranfield studies were the first time in which information organization and retrieval tools had been analysed and tested empirically, rather than being discussed in a theoretical and philosophical way. 'Their main findings', says Ellis (1996, 177), 'represent the nearest to concrete scientific achievements the field has ever had'.

They have certainly been, and remain, very influential in determining the ways in which information systems are developed and evaluated; one important example is the on-going annual TREC (Text Retrieval Conference) series of comparative retrieval system evaluations, conducted very much in the spirit of this paradigm (Voorhees and Harman, 2005; Harman and Voorhees, 2006). More broadly, David Ellis wrote in 1992 (57) that the paradigm had been applied to 'the evaluation of best match searching algorithms, relevance feedback systems, full text retrieval, chemical structure searching [etc.]. For its adherents it is a paradigm which has far from lost its fascination or its ability to suggest new research problems'. The same is certainly true 20 years later. This approach has also provided concepts, such as the measures of recall and precision to be mentioned in Chapter 7, which are now part of the basic vocabulary of the information sciences.

Although the details are of historic interest only, the papers in the volume edited by Sparck Jones (1981) give a good overview of the kind of research carried out within this paradigm at the height of its influence.

Although this 'experimental' style of research is obviously of most value for system development, it has also been applied to evaluate and compare different forms of operational information services, where strictly quantitative measures are realistic. For example, one study of the effectiveness of document delivery services involved the replacement of journal subscriptions by fast document supply, and a quantitative comparison of time and cost factors (Evans, Bevan and Harrington, 1996).

Successful though this style of research was, and remains, for some purposes, its limitations were soon recognized. In isolating elements of systems for evaluation, this approach removes entirely from explicit consideration the human users of information and information systems. This limitation led to the introduction of an approach which specifically deals with the individual: the cognitive paradigm.

The cognitive paradigm

Drawing on the so-called 'cognitive turn' in psychology and similar subjects, within the information sciences this approach focuses on the cognition of information users: what they know and what they think, and how this affects how they seek and use information. It also led to the idea that a machine could have cognition, and in turn to the enthusiasm for the development of so-called 'expert systems', software systems claimed to be able to think in the way an expert person does; this approach was very popular during the 1980s (see, for example, Brooks, 1987), but enthusiasm has waned, as the difficulties involved have become clearer.

This approach began to influence information science from the 1970s onwards: see, for example, Belkin (1990), Ellis (1992, 1996) and Ingwersen (1992, 1996);

for later reflective reviews, see Ford (2004) and Ingwersen and Järvelin (2005). Among the main proponents were Bertie Brookes and Nick Belkin. Brookes, a professor at University College London, was – as we shall see later in this chapter – much influenced by Karl Popper's philosophical views, and in particular his view that the internal 'world' of the human mind can interact with a world of objective information, recorded in documents. He argued that this could form the basis for a philosophy of information science, with human cognition at the forefront, and derived what he called the 'fundamental equation of information science', discussed below, on this basis (Brookes, 1980). Belkin, who was a graduate student with Brookes, has been for many years a professor at Rutgers University in the USA, best known for his studies of interactive information retrieval systems.

A number of theories and models were advanced, based on cognitive aspects of information use, and particularly aimed at information retrieval applications; for an overview and analysis see Ingwersen (1999). The best known example is the idea of an Anomalous State of Knowledge (ASK), advanced by Nick Belkin (Belkin, Oddy and Brooks, 1982). This assumes that a user recognizes some anomaly or inadequacy in their knowledge of some issue – perhaps they simply do not know something, or they have contradictory information on some point, or they have come to doubt their knowledge – which they then translate into an information need, and then into queries to some kind of information system. The answers go some way to resolving the anomaly in their knowledge, but may generate more information needs.

This kind of analysis led to ideas for retrieval systems built on different principles to those generally available, typically with a much greater degree of interaction. This interaction is needed to map between the cognitive states of the participants, machines as well as users; Belkin (1984) identified 17 different relevant mental models, held by the authors who created the knowledge base, the knowledge representation system, the users, and intermediaries (people who might use the system on behalf of users, e.g. information specialists). Necessarily, this focuses on the individual person, and neglects the effects of any social interactions in information; nor does it allow for similarities in information use by particular groups, e.g. by occupation or by educational status, although these are known to be very significant. Attempts have been made to extend the strictly individualistic cognitive paradigm to include social factors, a well known example being the set of models presented by Ingwersen and Järvelin (2005).

To an extent, the cognitive paradigm has been supplanted by more socially oriented approaches, although work is still carried out on information implications of individual cognition; for example in cognitive aspects of geographic information use (Raper, 2007) or in the application of Brookes' equation (Todd, 1999a; Bawden, 2011). And, as Budd (2011) reminds us, the field of cognitive science is itself advancing, offering new concepts and perspectives of potential value to information science. The cognitive viewpoint has also had a great influence on ideas of 'information behaviour' (Savolainen, 2007), as will be discussed in Chapter 9.

Nonetheless, the next step, starting in the mid-1990s was a more explicit inclusion of social factors into theories of information behaviour, seeking and use. Of course, as Cronin (2008) reminds us 'the social' has influenced the information sciences long before that date – see, for example, Shera (1971) – but its importance was increasingly recognized leading to our next major paradigm of information science: the socio-cognitive approach.

The socio-cognitive paradigm

The socio-cognitive paradigm, also referred to as the domain-analytic paradigm, is closely associated with the Danish scholar Birger Hjørland (1995; 2002). It forms the basis for the important concept, both theoretical and practical, of domain analysis, which will be the subject of Chapter 5. We will therefore now look quite briefly at the nature of the paradigm *per se*. As its name implies, it considers an interaction between the social and the individual worlds.

Introducing this approach, Hjørland (1995) makes the point that it is social at its basis; it locates information science among the social sciences, rather than among the 'mentalistic' or psychological subjects, as might be implied by the cognitive paradigm. It certainly does not ignore the individual, and does not imply that there is a uniform 'group think' in information terms; rather it sees 'an interplay between domain structures and individual knowledge, an interaction between the individual and the social level' (Hjørland, 1995, 409).

But the socio-cognitive view is primarily about shared knowledge, not individual mental models. It is at root an epistemological theory, inspired by the theory and sociology of knowledge; its social groups, or 'domains' – typically those involved with an academic subject or a profession – are defined by their knowledge bases. These are 'discourse communities', linked by the kinds of knowledge they communicate, and the ways this communication happens. It is also, in philosophical terms, a realist approach: 'trying to find the basis for information science in factors that are external to the individualistic-subjective perceptions of the users as opposed to . . . the behavioural and cognitive paradigms' (Hjørland, 1995, 400).

Nor is it a truly novel theory; Hjørland argues that many previous approaches within information science shared its assumptions – it has had a 'quasi-existence' – but that they are made explicit for the first time in the statement of this paradigm. As he points out, 'most people, including librarians and information scientists, intuitively perceive that domain-specific knowledge plays a major role in the information retrieval process' (Hjørland, 1995, 417).

Like other paradigms and turns mentioned above, it does not originate solely in information science, but reflects developments in areas such as psychology, linguistics and education, where 'it is not the isolated abstract individual as much as it is the discourse community and its individuals, which constitutes the focus of current research' (Hjørland, 1995, 409).

The socio-cognitive paradigm is by no means the only approach stemming from the 'social turn' in information science: another example is the application of practice theory (Talja, 2010; Lloyd, 2010), although Savolainen (2007) notes that the idea of information practice has much in common with domain analysis. It is, however, a particularly interesting and influential approach. Its practical outcome, the methods of domain analysis, will be considered in detail in Chapter 5.

It is clear that no single paradigm dominates research and practice in information science. Some commentators have seen this as demonstrating a weakness in the subject; most regard it as a healthy situation for a relatively new, and distinctly multidisciplinary, area, as was suggested in Chapter 1.

Having considered broad paradigms and philosophies, we will now look in more detail at some of the philosophers and philosophies that have influenced the information sciences.

Philosophers and information science

As was mentioned earlier, some of the issues and topics of interest to information science have been the subject of philosophical enquiry for very many years. The nature of knowledge, and what we can know, is obviously one such; this will be discussed below, in the section on Karl Popper, and again in Chapter 4. Other long-standing philosophical topics of this sort are the nature of *concepts*, analysed from the time of Plato and Aristotle, via Wittgenstein, to present-day philosophy, and of evident central relevance to information science. (Stock, 2010; Hjørland, 2009), and similarly *categories*, a basic intellectual tool derived from Aristotle and Kant of importance for subject analysis and indexing (Barite, 2000). Indeed, all of intellectual subject analysis and classification rests on philosophical foundations: see, as recent examples, Mai (2010) on bias and trust, Furner (2009) on identity, Gnoli and Poli (2004) on levels of reality, and Olson (2001) on sameness and difference. The principles of information ethics also have a philosophical basis, as will be discussed in Chapter 11.

However, most of the literature of the information sciences reveals a less coherent picture. A scan through the more academic journals of the field will yield a good number of articles, paying serious tribute, or quick lip-service, to some philosopher or school of philosophy. This, and the sheer number of philosophers name-checked, gives the impression of a somewhat dilettante approach; what Brian Vickery (1997, 458) described as 'examining the ideas of a . . . philosopher, extracting principles and offering them as presuppositions upon which information science may be based', or as Luciano Floridi (2002, 47) laments '[information] researchers have been lured by a variety of friendly but pre-established philosophies instead of fighting for their own place in the philosophical field'.

Perhaps, however, this use of philosophy and philosophers should not be criticized too much, if at all. As with the proliferation of paradigms, it is an indicator of an evolving and wide-ranging field of study, seeking for useful insights where it may find them. As an indicator, the box below shows a number of philosophers, and some ways in which their ideas have been related to the information sciences, with references. This is very far from a complete list, nor is it a list of 'best' or endorsed examples; simply a quick insight into the range of philosophers cited in the information science literature.

Philosophers and information science: some examples	
C. S. Pierce	**knowledge organization**
Thellefsen, T. L. and Thellefsen, M. M. (2004) Pragmatic semiotics and knowledge organization, *Knowledge Organization*, 31(3), 177–87.	
Hegel and the Scottish Common Sense philosophers	**classification**
Olson, H. A. (2004) The ubiquitous hierarchy: an army to overcome the threat of a mob, *Library Trends*, 52(3), 604–16.	
Heidegger	**concept of a 'work'**
Day, R. E. (2008) Works and representation, *Journal of the American Society for Information Science and Technology*, 59(10), 1644–52.	
Wittgenstein	**language in information systems and retrieval**
Blair, D. C. (2006) *Wittgenstein, language and information: back to the rough ground*, Dordrecht: Springer.	
Bourdieu	**nature of the library and information science discipline**
Weller, T. and Haider, J. (2007) Where do we go from here? An opinion on the future of LIS as an academic discipline in the UK, *Aslib Proceedings*, 59(4/5), 475–82.	
Foucault	**concept of information poverty**
Haider, J. and Bawden, D. (2007) Conceptions of 'information poverty' in LIS: a discourse analysis, *Journal of Documentation*, 63(4), 534–57.	
Deleuze and Guattari	**information organization**
Robinson, L. and Maguire, M. (2010) The rhizome and the tree: changing metaphors for information organisation, *Journal of Documentation*, 66(4), 604–13.	

continued on next page

Philosophers and information science: some examples (*continued*)	
Foucault and Derrida	**archive theory**
Manoff, M. (2004) Theories of the archive from across the disciplines, portal: *Libraries and the Academy*, 4(1), 9–25.	
Foucault and Habermas	**knowledge organization**
Andersen, J. and Skouvig, L. (2006) Knowledge organisation: a sociohistorical analysis and critique, *Library Quarterly*, 76(3), 300–22.	
Husserl and Heidegger	**information seeking**
Budd, J. M. (2005) Phenomenology and information studies, *Journal of Documentation*, 61(1), 44–59.	
Parmenides, Plato and Aristotle	**classification**
Olson, H. A. (1999) Exclusivity, teleology and hierarchy: our Aristotelean legacy, *Knowledge Organization*, 26(2), 65–73.	
Arendt	**archives and records management**
Caswell, M. (2010) Hannah Arendt's world: bureaucracy, documentation and banal evil, *Archivaria*, no. 70 (Fall 2010), 1–25.	

We will now look at three particularly important examples of the overlap between philosophy and the information sciences: Karl Popper and objective epistemology; Jesse Shera and social epistemology; and Luciano Floridi and the philosophy of information.

Karl Popper and objective epistemology

Sir Karl Popper, though Austrian by birth, spent most of his adult life in Britain, being for many years professor of philosophy at the London School of Economics. He is known first as a philosopher of science, particularly noted for his ideas about the nature of science being defined by the falsifiability of its concepts, and secondly as a political philosopher, and particularly for his espousal of the idea of 'open society'. His scientific and political views were driven by a constant thread running through his work; that our knowledge always is imperfect, though it can be improved by rational criticism. For overviews of Popper's life and work, see Popper (1992) and Notturno (2000; 2002).

This led him to the part of his work of most relevance to the information sciences: his ideas of 'evolutionary epistemology' and 'objective knowledge'. He held that knowledge advances and grows in a way analogous to biological evolution, with theories being removed and replaced by better ones, through falsification by observation, experiment and critical argument: we send our theories out to die in our place, he dramatically put it. And he sought to get away from traditional philosophical views of knowledge as a justified, true belief held by an individual person, seeking to replace it by an objective body of knowledge; 'knowledge without a knowing subject'. To support this, he proposed a system of three 'worlds': World 1, of physical items; World 2, the subjective mental content of individual knowledge; and World 3, of communicable, objective knowledge. We will look at Popper's ideas of knowledge in more detail in the next chapter.

Popper's ideas were taken up particularly enthusiastically by Bertie Brookes, introduced earlier as a founder of the cognitive paradigm in information science. He hailed Popper's ideas as the most appropriate philosophical foundation for the information sciences (Brookes, 1980). The task of the information sciences was to understand World 3 of objective knowledge, as instantiated in World 1 objects – documents of all kinds – and its interactions with the cognition of the user, Popper's World 2. On this basis, Brookes derived what he termed the 'fundamental equation of information science, as shown in the box below.

Popper's ideas can be used to make sense of practical issues of information handling: see, for example, an analysis of healthcare information in these terms (Bawden, 2002). Brookes' espousal of them, and in particular of the World 3 concept, were immediately criticized (for example, by Neill (1982) and by Rudd (1983)), on essentially the same grounds as wider philosophical criticism: that they are an unnecessary 'mystification', introducing spurious and unnecessary complexity. But perhaps, as Nutturno (2000, 139 and 145) says, 'most contemporary philosophers regard World 3 as an unfortunate product of Popper's old age: as incoherent, irrelevant and perhaps, if the truth be told, a bit ridiculous . . . [but] . . . most philosophers who reject Popper's theory of World 3 simply do not understand it'; see Chapter 3 of Notturno (2002) for a concise and comprehensible philosophical defence of the idea. And it has been found useful for analysis of information science contexts; see, for example, Bawden (2002) and Abbott (2004). It therefore should be considered as one of the fundamental bases of the information sciences.

Popper's political views, and especially his concept of open society, have also had an influence on information science, as will be discussed in the chapter dealing with the information society, while his ideas on problem solving have been applied in analysis of how people find and use information; see, for example, Ford (2004).

Jesse Shera and social epistemology

With social epistemology, we have the only case of developments and conceptions in the information sciences making an impact on philosophy itself. In the entry for 'Social Epistemology' in the *Stanford Encyclopedia of Philosophy*, Goldman (2010) writes that

> perhaps the first use of the phrase 'social epistemology' appears in the writings of a library scientist, Jesse Shera, who in turn credits his associate Margaret Egan . . .

Shera was particularly interested in the affinity between social epistemology and librarianship. He did not, however, construct a conception of social epistemology with very definite philosophical or social-scientific contours.

Brookes' fundamental equation of information science

Bertie Brookes concluded a line of research which he had followed for several years, by publishing in 1980 what he described as 'the fundamental equation of information science'. This equation, which he had put forward in various forms, was there presented as:

$$K (S) + \Delta I = K (S + \Delta S)$$

A knowledge structure, $K (S)$ is changed into an altered knowledge structure $K (S + \Delta S)$ by an input of information, ΔI. ΔS is an indicator of the effect of the modification. The same information may have different effects on different knowledge structures. It is a description of the information communication process as it affects one individual's knowledge, and hence is regarded as a foundation of the cognitive paradigm in information science. Cole (1994) used it as a 'baseline' for a consideration of a subjectivist construction of information, while Ingwersen (1992) derived extended versions of the equation.

Brookes himself, and numerous authors subsequently, have pointed out that this is not an equation in the usual mathematical sense; Todd (1999b), Cornelius (2002a) and Budd (2011), in reviewing the value and applicability of the equation, give accounts of these viewpoints. The equation as presented gives us no way of quantifying the amount of information of knowledge in $K (S)$, nor any way of deriving the difference – qualitative or quantitative – between it and $K (S + \Delta S)$, although Cole (1997) has shown one way in which this might be done. Brookes acknowledged that it was pseudo-mathematical and over-simple, and that its terms and symbols were undefined. Neill (1982, 36) suggested that just the undefined '+' sign 'contained an entire discipline'.

Despite this lack of 'equation-ness' about Brookes' equation, it has been often quoted as a qualitative summary of a central issue within the information sciences; it was cited over 100 times in the 30 years after its publication. As Cornelius (2002a, 407) says, 'It may have been unoperational in information systems, but it has remained operational as a general consideration, even if not in experimental design, within information retrieval theory and within information science's theorizing of information'. It has also been applied to a very limited degree in practice: qualitatively, as a framework for the study of general public information utilization for health information (Todd, 1999a), and for developing a typology of information seeking (Bawden, 2011), and quantitatively in a study of archaeological research (Cole, 1997). However, 'for the most part . . . the equation remains as a rather reproachful reminder of how far we are from fulfilling Brookes' research programme' (Bawden, 2008, 419)

Goldman goes on to point out that, although the phrase may be Shera's, many philosophers before and after Shera have addressed the issue of the social nature of knowledge.

John Budd (2008, 107), writing from the perspective of a library science academic, suggests that 'after Shera coined the phrase, philosophers discovered social epistemology', drawing attention to those who did the developing, particularly Alvin Goldman. Zandonade (2004) discusses in more detail the influence of Shera on philosophy, citing Steve Fuller as among his successors. And of the influence of Shera's ideas, there can be no doubt; Furner (2002) assesses his work as one of the more successful attempts to define a theoretical foundation for the information sciences. It is also reasonable to regard it as an intellectual infrastructure for the idea of an information society, as discussed in Chapter 11.

Jesse Shera, dean of the library school at Case Western Reserve University for many years, was the leading American library and information academic of his generation. As we have already seen in this chapter, he was a strong advocate for the need for a theoretical basis for our disciplines, and social epistemology, for him, was the answer. He gave much credit for the development of social epistemology to his colleague Margaret Egan, whose early death has led to her contribution being rather overlooked; an article by Jonathan Furner (2004) redresses this.

The theory was first introduced in a joint paper (Egan and Shera, 1952), and developed by Shera in numerous publications, culminating in a monograph summarizing it all (Shera, 1970). For recent retrospective reviews see Zandonade (2004) and Fallis (2006), and for a philosophical analysis, which concludes that there is a strong relation between Shera's concepts and the cognitive paradigm discussed above, despite the very different terminologies used, see Furner (2002). Shera saw social epistemology as the solution to librarianship's search for an intellectual foundation, and also as the bridge between theory and practice. He regarded it as the totality of the processes by which a society collectively achieved a state of knowing. 'The focus of this new discipline', he wrote (Shera, 1968, 9), 'should be upon the production, flow, integration and consumption of all forms of communicated thought throughout the entire social fabric'. There is some resonance here with the idea of the study of the communication chain, proposed as the basis for information science in Chapter 1. However, while the emphasis there was on domain analysis and the study of documents, Shera focused firmly on sociological analysis. And he saw a very close relationship between social epistemology and librarianship; Shera always regarded himself as first and foremost a librarian, despite his involvement in documentation and information science. To do a proper job, and to move on beyond specific skills, the librarian must possess:

a true mastery over the means of access to recorded knowledge . . . not only a thorough understanding of the nature of that knowledge, but also an appreciation of the role of knowledge in that part of society in which he operates

Shera (1968, 9)

The direct legacy of the ideas of Shera and Egan has been limited; as Budd (2008) puts it, despite his many publications over the years, Shera never really arrived at a coherent theory that could be practically applied in the information disciplines. And there has been little interest from others in developing social epistemology into a true foundation for research or practice in the information disciplines. Zandonade (2004) lists numerous reasons for this. For a specific philosophically based criticism of social epistemology as a basis for the information sciences, see Floridi (2002).

However, the general principles remain of interest: Gorman (2000), for example, believes that Shera's ideas contribute to the ethos and values of librarianship, and suggests that the components of social epistemology would form a good basis for a curriculum for the education of library science students, while Budd (2002) argues that, while it might not be *the* conceptual framework for the information disciplines it does offer *a* useful framework. And Budd (2008) and Zandonade (2004) draw attention to philosophical developments starting from social epistemology which may be of relevance to our disciplines in the longer term.

Luciano Floridi and the philosophy of information

Luciano Floridi is an Italian-born professor of philosophy, holding positions at the Universities of Hertfordshire and Oxford in England. He has published widely on the philosophy of information, computing and information technology, and we shall meet him again in the chapters dealing with basic concepts and with information ethics. Here we will briefly consider his ambitious scheme referred to as the Philosophy of Information, sometimes abbreviated as PI. His ideas are set out in an academic monograph (Floridi, 2011), and in a short and accessible introduction (Floridi, 2010).

Floridi has said that, to put it at its simplest, the philosophy of information is 'philosophy of our time, for our time'; the philosophy, one might say, of an information society. A little more fully, he says that it addresses all aspects of the concepts and nature of information, including the ways that it is used and studied. He writes that the essential message of his 2011 book is

. . . quite simple. Semantic information is well formed, meaningful and truthful data. Knowledge is relevant semantic information properly accounted for: humans are the only known semantic engines and conscious inforgs (informational organisms) in the universe who can develop a growing knowledge of reality; and reality is the totality of information (note the crucial absence of 'semantic').

This is not at all a philosophical justification for, or analysis of, what we might regard as the sciences of information; rather information is being placed as a crucial concept for philosophy itself. Virtually any philosophical issue may be rephrased, according to Floridi, in informational terms.

Floridi acknowledges that information is an elusive concept; that answering the question of what it is constitutes the hardest and most central problem of its philosophy. He suggests that information may be understood from three perspectives: as reality (patterns in the physical world); about reality (semantic and meaningful); and for reality (genetic information, algorithms and recipes). He presents seven approaches to defining information – information theoretic, algorithmic, etc.), discusses them in detail, and settles for the semantic approach, mentioned above, which 'defines information in terms of data space: information is well formed, meaningful and truthful data'. We will look at these in more detail in the next chapter, when we consider the concept of information.

Part of Floridi's scheme is the idea of the *inforg*, a conscious informational organism such as a human being. This idea is somewhat similar to the concept of the IGUS (Information Gathering and Utilizing System) proposed by the American physicists Murray Gell-Mann and Jim Hartle; for a popular account, see Gell-Mann (1994). Readers will be pleased to know that Floridi is able to show that we, as inforgs, are neither zombies, nor artificial agents.

Perhaps the most ambitious aspect of this philosophy of information is that which addresses the issue of the nature of reality itself. Floridi argues for an 'informational ontology', with information as the fundamental stuff of the physical universe. However, he takes issue with those physicists who see the universe as a kind of digital computer, arguing instead for 'information structural realism'. The arguments are detailed and technical, but they amount to the proposal of a real and objective physical world, whose constituent structures can be known, and understood in terms of information.

Floridi's ideas have caused a good deal of interest, and indeed controversy, in the information sciences, not least for his suggestion that library and information science may be defined as 'applied philosophy of information' (Floridi, 2002; 2004). PI provides the theoretical foundations for LIS, the latter being interested not in information *per se*, as is PI, but in the narrower sense of information recorded in documents. Floridi (2002, 46) can then define the information sciences in this way:

Library and Information Science as Applied Philosophy of Information is the discipline concerned with documents, their life cycles and the procedures, techniques and devices by which these are implemented, managed and regulated. LIS applies the fundamental principles and general techniques of PI to solve definite, practical problems and deal with specific, concrete phenomena. In turn, it conducts empirical research for practical service-oriented purposes . . . thus contributing to the development of basic research in PI.

This seems a reasonable proposal, and Floridi's emphasis on information recorded in documents and on their lifecycle is very much in accord with ideas of information science proposed throughout this book. Nonetheless, Floridi's proposal has been criticized by some commentators from the information sciences; typically on grounds such as that it takes too restrictive a definition of information, that it does not allow fully for the social contexts of information and knowledge, and that its view of the practice of the information disciplines is too limited. For an example of such a critique, see Cornelius (2002b).

Despite these criticisms, it seems that Floridi's PI seems to offer the best option currently available as a basis for a fundamental philosophy of the information sciences. There is now a need, as Furner (2010) points out, for its value to be determined by research into the detailed applications of PI to information science problems.

Summary

The fact, made clear we hope in this chapter, that there is no single philosophy, paradigm or theory to act as a foundation for the information science need not be a cause for pessimism. This is a relatively new, and highly multidisciplinary field, and it is natural that there should be several contenders, reflecting different issues and perspectives.

This view should not be mistaken for complacency. We believe that the search for a satisfactory foundation for the discipline is a vital task which will bring benefits to practice as much as to academia. For the moment, however, we are

- There is no single generally accepted philosophical or theoretical foundation for the information sciences; rather a variety of alternatives have been suggested.
- The sequence of 'turns' or paradigm changes, system to user/cognitive to social, has left a variety of alternative theoretical and methodological alternatives.
- Floridi's PI gives the promise of a viable foundational basis
- Further development in foundational theory and philosophy of the information sciences is important both for the academic subjects and the practical disciplines.

left with a variety of paradigms and theories, part competing and part complementing each other. It seems that, at present, Floridi's philosophy of information offers the best promise for development into a generally acceptable foundation, but much work is needed to test this.

Key readings

Jonathan Furner, Philosophy and Information Studies, *Annual Review of Information Science and Technology*, 2010, 44, 161–200.

[A clearly written literature review of the whole topic.]

Luciano Floridi, *Information – a very short introduction*, Oxford: Oxford University Press, 2010.

[An accessible introduction to the topic.]

The *Epistemological Lifeboat* site gives short and reliable accounts of philosophical concepts of relevance to information science: http://www.iva.dk/jni/lifeboat.

Philosophy resources

Anyone intending to study philosophical aspects in depth will need to use the literature of philosophy, as well as that of information science. Furner (2010) gives a useful list of relevant sources.

A popular and accessible book, which gives a clear introduction to philosophical issues for beginners, is Brian Magee's *The story of philosophy*, London: Dorling Kindersley, 2010.

A list of readings, with introductions and commentaries, from the major works of many of the philosophers of particular relevance to information science is given in the volume edited by Gerad Delanty and Piet Strydom, *Philosophies of the social sciences: the classic and contemporary readings*, Maidenhead: Open University Press, 2003.

A standard reference is the *Stanford Encyclopedia of Philosophy*, available at http://plato.stanford.edu.

References

Abbott, R. (2004) Subjectivity as a concern for information science: a Popperian perspective. *Journal of Information Science*, 30(2), 95–106.

Barite, M. G. (2000) The notion of category: its implications in subject analysis and in the construction and evaluation of indexing languages, *Knowledge Organization*, 27(1/2), 4–10.

Bates, M. J. (2005) An introduction to metatheories, theories and models, in Fisher, K. E., Erdelez, S. and McKechnie, L. (eds), *Theories of information behaviour*, Medford NJ: Information Today, 1–24.

Bawden, D. (2002) The three worlds of health information, *Journal of Information Science*, 28(1), 51–62.

Bawden, D. (2008) Smoother pebbles and the shoulders of giants: the developing foundations of information science, *Journal of Information Science*, 34(4), 415–26.

Bawden, D. (2011) Brookes equation: the basis for a qualitative characterization of information behaviours, *Journal of Information Science*, 37(1), 101–8.

Belkin, N. J. (1984) Cognitive models and information transfer, *Social Science Information Studies*, 4(2/3), 111–29.

Belkin, N. J. (1990) The cognitive viewpoint in information science, *Journal of Information Science*, 16(1), 11–15.

Belkin, N. J., Oddy, R. N. and Brooks, H. M. (1982) ASK for information retrieval: Part 1. Background and theory, *Journal of Documentation*, 38(2), 61–71.

Bohman, J., Critical theory, in Zalta, E. N. (ed.), *The Stanford Encyclopedia of Philosophy* (Spring 2010 edition), [online] available at http://plato.stanford.edu/archives/spr2010/entries/critical-theory.

Brookes, B. C. (1980) The foundations of information science. Part 1: philosophical aspects, *Journal of Information Science*, 2(3/4), 125–33.

Brooks, H. M. (1987) Expert systems and intelligent information retrieval, *Information Processing and Management*, 23(4), 367–82.

Budd, J. M. (2001) *Knowledge and knowing in LIS: a philosophical framework*, Lanham MD: Scarecrow Press.

Budd, J. M. (2002) Jesse Shera, social epistemology and praxis, *Social Epistemology*, 16(1), 93–8.

Budd, J. M. (2008) *Self-examination: the present and future of librarianship*, Westport CT: Libraries Unlimited.

Budd, J. M. (2011) Revisiting the importance of cognition in information science, *Journal of Information Science*, 37(4), 360–8.

Budd, J. M. (2012) Phenomenological critical realism: a practical method for LIS, *Journal of Education for Library and Information Science*, 53(1), 69–80.

Budd, J. M., Hill, H. and Shannon, B. (2010) Inquiring into the real: a realist phenomenological approach, *Library Quarterly*, 80(3), 267–84.

Cole, C. (1994) Operationalizing the notion of information as a subjective construct, *Journal of the American Society for Information Science*, 45(7), 465–76.

Cole, C. (1997) Calculating the information content of an information process for a domain expert using Shannon's mathematical theory of communication: a preliminary analysis, *Information Processing and Management*, 33(6), 715–26.

Cornelius, I. (2002a) Theorizing information for information science, *Annual Review of Information Science and Technology*, 36, 393–425.

Cornelius, I. (2002b) Information and its philosophy, *Library Trends*, 52(3), 377–86.

Cronin, B. (2008) The sociological turn in information science, *Journal of Information Science*, 34(4), 465–76.

Cronin, B. and Meho, L. I. (2009) Receiving the French: a bibliometric snapshot of the impact of 'French theory' on information studies, *Journal of Information Science*, 35(4), 398–413.

Day, R. E. (2005) Post-structuralism and information studies, *Annual Review of Information Science and Technology*, 39, 575–609.

Davis, C. H. and Shaw, D. (eds) (2011) *Introduction to information science and technology*, Medford NJ: Information Today.

Deutsch, D. (2011) *The beginning of infinity: explanations that transform the world*, London: Allen Lane.

Dobson, P. J. (2002) Critical realism and information systems research: why bother with philosophy?, *Information Research*, 7(2), paper no. 124, available at http://InformationR.net/ir/7-2/paper124.html.

Egan, M. E. and Shera, J. H. (1952) Foundations of a theory of bibliography, *Library Quarterly*, 22(2), 125–37.

Ellis, D. (1992) The physical and cognitive paradigms in information retrieval research, *Journal of Documentation*, 48(1), 45–64.

Ellis, D. (1996) *Progress and problems in information retrieval* (2nd edn), London: Library Association Publishing.

Evans, J., Bevan, S. J. and Harrington, J. (1996) BIODOC: access versus holdings in a university library, *Interlending and Document Supply*, 24(4), 5–11.

Fallis, D. (2006) Social epistemology and information science, *Annual Review of Information Science and Technology*, 40, 475–519.

Fisher, K. E., Erdelez, S. and McKechnie, L. (eds) (2005) *Theories of information behaviour*, Medford NJ: Information Today.

Floridi, L. (2002) On defining library and information science as applied philosophy of information, *Social Epistemology*, 16(1), 37–49.

Floridi, L. (2004) LIS as applied philosophy of information: a reappraisal, *Library Trends*, 52(3), 658–65.

Floridi, L. (2010) *Information – a very short introduction*, Oxford: Oxford University Press.

Floridi, L. (2011) *The Philosophy of Information*, Oxford: Oxford University Press.

Ford, N. (2004) Modeling cognitive processes in information seeking: from Popper to Pask, *Journal of the American Society for Information Science and Technology*, 55(9), 769–82.

Furner, J. (2002) Shera's social epistemology recast as psychological bibliology, *Social Epistemology*, 16(1), 5–22.

Furner, J. (2004) A brilliant mind: Margaret Egan and social epistemology, *Library Trends*, 52(4), 792–809.

Furner, J. (2009) Interrogating 'identity': a philosophical approach to an enduring issue in knowledge organization, *Knowledge Organization*, 36(1), 3–16.

Furner, J. (2010) Philosophy and Information Studies, *Annual Review of Information Science and Technology*, 44, 161–200.

Gell-Mann, M. (1994) *The quark and the jaguar: adventure in the simple and the complex*, London: Little Brown.

Gnoli, C. and Poli, R. (2004) Levels of reality and levels of representation, *Knowledge Organization*, 31(3), 151–60.

Goldman, A. (2010) Social epistemology, in Zalta, E. N. (ed.), *The Stanford Encyclopedia of Philosophy (Summer 2010 edition)*, [online], available at http://plato.stanford.edu/archives/sum2010/entries/epistemology-social.

Gorman, M. (2000) Our enduring values: librarianship in the 21st century, Chicago: American Library Association.

Harman, D. K. and Voorhees, E. M. (2006) TREC: an overview, *Annual Review of Information Science and Technology*, 45, 113–55.

Hjørland, B. (1995) Toward a new horizon in information science: domain-analysis, *Journal of the American Society for Information Science*, 46(6), 400–25.

Hjørland, B. (1998) Theory and metatheory of information science: a new interpretation, *Journal of Documentation*, 54(5), 606–21.

Hjørland, B. (2002) Epistemology and the socio-cognitive perspective in information science, *Journal of the American Society for Information Science and Technology*, 53(4), 257–70.

Hjørland, B. (2004) Arguments for philosophical realism in library and information science, *Library Trends*, 52(3), 488–506.

Hjørland, B. (2005) Empiricism, rationalism and positivism in library and information science, *Journal of Documentation*, 60(1), 130–155.

Hjørland, B. (2009) Concept theory, *Journal of the American Society for Information Science and Technology*, 60(8), 1519–1728.

Ingwersen, P. (1992) *Information retrieval interaction*, London: Taylor Graham.

Ingwersen, P. (1996) Cognitive perspectives of information retrieval interaction: elements of a cognitive IR theory, *Journal of Documentation*, 52(1), 3–50.

Ingwersen, P. (1999) Cognitive information retrieval, *Annual Review of Information Science and Technology*, 34, 3–52.

Ingwersen, P. and Järvelin, K. (2005) *The turn: integration of information seeking and retrieval in context*, Dordrecht: Springer.

Leckie, G. J., Given, L. M. and Buschman, J. D. (eds) (2010) *Critical theory for library and information science*, Santa Barbara CA: Libraries Unlimited.

Lloyd, A. (2010) Framing information literacy as information practice: site ontology and practice theory, *Journal of Documentation*, 66(2), 245–58.

Mai, J.-E. (2010) Classification in a social world: bias and trust, *Journal of Documentation*, 66(5), 627–42.

Meadows, J. (1990) Theory in information science, *Journal of Information Science*, 16(1), 59–63.

Neill, S. D. (1982) Brookes, Popper and objective knowledge, *Journal of Information Science*, 4(1), 33–39.

Nolin, J. (2007) What's in a turn?, *Information Research*, 12(4), paper colis11, available at http://InformationR.net/ir/12-4/colis/colis11.html.

Nolin, J. and Åström, F. (2010) Turning weakness into strength: strategies for future LIS, *Journal of Documentation*, 66(1), 7–27.

Notturno, M. A. (2000) *Science and the open society: the future of Karl Popper's philosophy*, Budapest: Central European University Press.

Notturno, M. A. (2002) *On Popper*, London: Wadsworth.

Olson, H. A. (2001) Sameness and difference: a cultural foundation of classification, *Library Resources and Technical Services*, 45(3), 115–22.

Pettigrew, K. E. and McKechnie, L. (2001) The use of theory in information science research, *Journal of the American Society for Information Science and Technology*, 52(1), 62–74.

Popper, K. (1992) *Unended quest: an intellectual autobiography (revised edition)*, London: Routledge.

Radford, G. P. and Radford, M. L. (2005) Structuralism, post-structuralism and the library: de Saussure and Foucault, *Journal of Documentation*, 61(1), 60–78.

Raper, J. (2007) Geographic relevance, *Journal of Documentation*, 63(6), 836–52.

Rayward, W. B. (1994) Visions of Xanadu: Paul Otlet (1868–1944) and hypertext, *Journal of the American Society for Information Science*, 45(4), 235–50.

Rudd, D. (1983) Do we really need World III? Information science with or without Popper, *Journal of Information Science*, 7(2/3), 99–105.

Savolainen, R. (2007) Information behaviour and information practice: reviewing the 'umbrella concepts' of information-seeking studies, *Library Quarterly*, 77(2), 109–32.

Shera, J. H. (1968) An epistemological foundation for library science, in Montgomery, E. B. (ed.), *The foundations of access to knowledge*, Syracuse NY: Syracuse University Press, 7–25.

Shera, J. H. (1970) *Sociological foundations of librarianship*, Bombay: Asian Publishing House.

Shera, J. H. (1971) The sociological relationships of information science, *Journal of the American Society for Information Science*, 22(2), 76–80.

Shera, J. H. (1973) *Knowing books and men: knowing computers too*, Littleton CO: Libraries Unlimited.

Sokal, A. and Bricmont, J. (1997) *Fashionable nonsense: postmodern intellectuals' abuse of science*, New York NY: Picador.

Sparck Jones, K. (ed.) (1981) *Information retrieval experiment*, London: Butterworth.

Stock, W. G. (2010) Concepts and semantic relations in information science, *Journal of the American Society for Information Science and Technology*, 61(10), 1951–69.

Talja, S. (2010) Jean Lave's practice theory, in Leckie, G. J., Given, L. M. and Buschman, J. D. (eds), *Critical theory for library and information science*, Santa Barbara CA: Libraries Unlimited, 205–20.

Talja, S., Tuominen, K. and Savolainen, R. (2005) 'isms' in information science:

constructivism, collectivism and constructionism, *Journal of Documentation*, 61(1), 79–101.

Todd, R. J. (1999a) Utilization of heroin information by adolescent girls in Australia: a cognitive analysis, *Journal of the American Society for Information Science*, 50(1), 10–23.

Todd, R. J. (1999b) Back to our beginnings: information utilization, Bertram Brookes and the fundamental equation of information science, *Information Processing and Management*, 35(6), 851–70.

Vickery, B. (1997) Metatheory and information science, *Journal of Documentation*, 53(5), 457–76.

Voorhees E. M. and Harman, D. K. (2005) *TREC: experiment and evaluation in information retrieval*, Cambridge MA: MIT Press.

Wikgren, M. (2005) Critical realism as a philosophy and social theory in information science?, *Journal of Documentation*, 61(1), 11–22.

Zandonade, T. (2004) Social epistemology from Jesse Shera to Steve Fuller, *Library Trends*, 52(4), 810–32.

CHAPTER 4

Basic concepts of information science

Where is the life we have lost in living?
Where is the wisdom we have lost in knowledge?
Where is the knowledge we have lost in information?

T. S. Eliot, *Choruses from 'The Rock'*

It is hardly to be expected that a single concept of information would satisfactorily account for the numerous possible applications of this general field.

Claude Shannon

Information is information, not matter or energy.   Norbert Wiener

Introduction

In this chapter, we will consider some of the basic concepts of the information sciences: information and knowledge, documents and collections, relevance and 'aboutness', and information use and users.

It may seem strange to find that there is still debate about the nature of these very fundamental ideas: as strange, perhaps, as finding a doctor who had no idea what a 'disease' or a 'treatment' was, or an engineer who had no idea what was meant by 'materials' or 'design'. That is not to say that there need be a perfect understanding of these concepts; doctors treated diseases, sometimes quite effectively, long before they had any realistic idea of what caused them. But most professions expect to have some understanding of the basic concepts with which they deal.

'Information', 'knowledge', 'document', and so on, are tricky concepts, which can have many different meanings, and can be understood in many different ways. These are not just academic matters; they can have a real effect on professional practice. What someone understands by 'knowledge', for example, and its relation to 'information', will determine how they go about the practical business of 'knowledge management'. And what a librarian or information specialist understands by a 'document' will determine what sort of things they keep on their shelves or in their computer files.

We begin by looking at perhaps the most fundamental of concepts: information itself, and knowledge.

Information and knowledge

Shannon and Wiener and I
Have found it confusing to try
To measure sagacity
And channel capacity
By $\Sigma\ p_i \log p_i$

Anonymous, *Behavioural Science*, 1962, 7 (July issue), 395

Information, argued John Feather and Paul Sturges in the 1997 Routledge *International Encyclopaedia of Information and Library Science*, is probably the most used, and the least precisely understood, term in the library and information world.

The best way to understand the concept of 'information' has been debated for many years; the more so as the ideas of the 'information age' and 'information society' have gained currency. The 'commonsense' meaning of the word relates to knowledge, news or intelligence, given and received, so that someone becomes 'informed'. But the word has had many different meanings over the years; its entry in the full Oxford English Dictionary of 2010, which shows its usage over time, runs to nearly 10,000 words.

Even within an information science context, the term has been understood with different connotations, as we shall see later.

To show the variety of ideas available, information has been explained, among many other things, as being as shown in the box below. This subset of the many definitions and explanations available shows their diversity, from simple to complex. Some relate information to concepts such as 'data' or 'knowledge', which then themselves require explanation. Some set the idea of information firmly in the context of communication between people; others see it as a more general concept, to do with structure, pattern, and organization. In this chapter, we can do no more than mention some of the more influential and interesting ideas put forward, allowing the reader to follow these up, and to find others, via the references.

Despite much effort, there is still no consensus as to what information 'really is', still less any 'theory of information', usefully applicable in all contexts; we will look at two theories for which this claim may be made later. The problem is made worse by the fact that the word is used rather differently in many different subject areas; for an early, and very influential, overview of this diversity, see Machlup and Mansfield (1983). As Capurro and Hjørland (2003, 356 and 396) say:

. . . almost every scientific discipline uses the concept of information within its own context and with regard to specific phenomena . . . There are many concepts of information, and they are embedded in more or less explicit theoretical structures.

Varied conceptions of information: 'information is . . . '

fragmented knowledge (Bertie Brookes)

knowledge packaged for a user (CILIP Body of Professional Knowledge)

meaningful data (Luciano Floridi)

an assemblage of data in a comprehensible form capable of communication and use (John Feather and Paul Sturges)

patterns of self-organized complexity, providing meaning-in-context and promoting understanding (David Bawden)

communicated signs (Claude Shannon)

a change of structure (Nick Belkin and Steve Robertson)

a stimulus originating in one system that affects the interpretation by another system of either the second system's relationship to the first or of the relationship the two systems share with a given environment (Andrew Madden)

a difference which makes a difference (Gregory Bateson)

some pattern of organization of matter and energy given meaning by a living being (Marcia Bates)

an abstract concept, which manifests itself by organizing systems (Tom Stonier)

We will now look briefly at the use of the information concept in different contexts; specifically in the physical and biological sciences, as opposed to its more familiar usage in the social and information sciences. We can only consider this in outline, referring the reader to more detailed accounts below.

Information: physical, biological, social

The idea of information as a feature of the physical world arose through studies of the thermodynamic property known as *entropy*, through the work of physicists such as Ludwig Boltzmann and Leo Szilard. Entropy, usually understood as a measure of the disorder of a physical system, is also associated with the extent of our knowledge of it; put crudely, if a system is disordered, we have little knowledge of where its components are, or what they are doing. A formal mathematical link may be made between entropy and information, when information is defined in the way required by Shannon's theory, discussed below. Analysis of the relation between information and physical entropy led Rolf Landauer to propose his well known aphorism 'information is physical'.

Information must always be instantiated in some physical system; for the kinds of information of interest to the information sciences, this would be a human brain or some kind of document.

The idea of information as a physical entity has received increasing attention in recent decades. Information has been proposed as a fundamental aspect of the physical universe, on a par with – or even more fundamental than – matter and energy. One of the originators of this approach was the American physicist John Wheeler, who coined the phrase 'it from bit' to express the idea that physical reality is, in some way, generated from information; his views are surveyed, critiqued and extended in papers in Barrow, Davies and Harper (2004). Currently active proponents are Lee Smolin, who has suggested that the idea of space itself may be replaceable by a 'web of information', and David Deutsch, who proposes that information flow – essentially what changes occur in what order – determines the nature of everything that is. 'The physical world is a multiverse', writes Deutsch (2011, 304), 'and its structure is determined by how information flows in it. In many regions of the multiverse, information flows in quasi-autonomous streams called histories, one of which we call our universe'.

Similarly, in biology, the discovery of the genetic code and associated developments in molecular biology have led to the idea that information is a fundamental biological property, and that the transmission of information may be as fundamental – or more fundamental – a property of living things as metabolism, reproduction, and other signifiers of life.

Fascinating though these ideas are, we cannot pursue them further here; interested readers should begin with the overviews given by Gleick (2011), Floridi (2010), Davies and Gregersen (2010), Vedral (2010) and von Baeyer (2004).

The question then naturally arises as to whether these scientific ideas of information have any relevance for the information sciences, as we understand them in this book; or whether it just happens that the English word 'information' is used to mean quite different things in different contexts.

Very different views have been taken. Some authors have devised quite elaborate schemes to link physical, biological and human information. The British academic Tom Stonier, in a series of three books, advanced a model of information as an abstract force promoting organization in systems of all kinds: physical, biological, mental and social, and including recorded information (Stonier, 1990; 1992; 1997).

Marcia Bates, a well known American information science scholar now Professor Emerita at the University of California Los Angeles, has advanced a similar all-encompassing model, which she terms 'evolutionary' (Bates, 2005; 2006). It relies on a number of inter-related 'information-like' entities:

- Information 1 – the pattern of organization of matter and energy
- Information 2 – some pattern of organization of matter and energy given meaning by a living being
- Data 1 – that portion of the entire information environment available to a sensing organism that is taken in, or processed, by that organism
- Data 2 – information selected or generated by human beings for social purposes
- Knowledge – information given meaning and integrated with other contents of understanding.

This model, while all-encompassing and one of the more ambitious attempts at integrating information in all its contexts, remains at a conceptual and qualitative level, and introduces a potentially confusing multiplicity of forms of information and similar entities.

Others have denied that it is at all useful to try to make such a direct link. Cole (1994) and Hjørland (2007), for example, argue against any equating of the idea of information as an objective and measurable 'thing' to the kind of information of interest in library and information science; this information, they argue, is subjective in nature, having meaning to a person in a particular context.

Still others have proposed that it is an open, though interesting, question. One of the authors of this book has suggested that we may see information in human, biological and physical realms as being related through emergent properties in complex systems; one does not look for direct equivalences, but for more subtle linkages (Bawden, 2007a; 2007b).

It seems clear that the question as to whether there can be any generally applicable theory of information in all contexts is an important one. However, as Jonathan Furner (2010, 174) puts it 'the outlook for those who would hold out for a 'one size fits all' transdisciplinary definition of information is not promising'. The best known potential contender so far is Shannon's information theory, to which we now turn.

A mathematical theory of information, with a little semiotics

The closest approach to a universal formal account of information is Shannon's 'information theory', originated by Claude Shannon, and properly referred to as Shannon-Weaver-Hartley theory, in recognition of those who added to it and gave it its current form. This gives a rigorous mathematical basis for calculating the amount of information that can be transmitted through a medium or channel, and is an important tool for communication engineers. It has been widely applied to introduce the concept of information into the physical and biological sciences. But – despite much effort – this theory has made little impact on the theory or practice of librarianship or information science. As the limerick which opens this section reminds us, it is not easy to use a single equation to calculate the value both of telecommunications capacity and of human knowledge.

The first quantitative measures of information came from the US Bell Laboratories, which supported the work of the three pioneers – Harry Nyquist, Ralph Hartley and Claude Shannon – and in whose in-house journal the first writings in what would come to be termed 'information theory' were published. These focused, naturally enough, on the set of engineering issues around the transmission of messages across various kinds of physical communication network. Gleick (2011) gives a good account of their work.

The initial steps were taken by Nyquist, who in 1924 showed how to estimate the amount of information which could be transmitted in a channel of given bandwidth; the focus of his paper was on the telegraph. He did not, however, use the term 'information', writing instead of the 'transmission of intelligence'. These ideas were developed by Hartley in 1928, who established a quantitative measure of information, so as to compare the transmission capacities of different systems. He titled his paper 'Transmission of information', and used the word throughout. Nyquist and Hartley thereby arguably originated one of the modern uses of the term.

Hartley emphasized that this measure was 'based on physical as contrasted with psychological considerations'. The meaning of the messages was not to be considered; information was regarded as being communicated successfully when the receiver could distinguish between sets of symbols sent by the originator.

His measure of information, understood in this way, was the logarithm of the number of possible symbol sequences. For a single selection, the associated information, H, is the logarithm of the number of symbols, s.

$$H = \log s$$

This in turn was generalized by Claude Shannon (Figure 4.1) into a fuller theory of communication, in an article of 1948, which was later republished in book form (Shannon and Weaver, 1949). It is interesting to note that the original modest claim of the article to be describing *A* mathematical theory of communication had been trans-

Figure 4.1
Claude Shannon (reproduced courtesy of the Library of Congress)

muted by the time the book was published to *The* mathematical theory. It was never claimed to be a theory of information, and it is perhaps unfortunate that it has been widely known as such; it is better to stick with Shannon's title of mathematical theory of communication (MTC). Its basic characteristics are set out in the box here.

Warren Weaver, a distinguished mathematician, scientific administrator and proponent of the public understanding of science, contributed an essay entitled *Recent contributions to the mathematical theory of communication* to the book. Roughly paralleling and expounding Shannon's more lengthy technical article, Weaver's contribution – philosophical, non-mathematical, wide-ranging, and considerably easier to read – has arguably had greater influence in spreading the ideas of information theory than any of its originators.

Shannon's Mathematical Theory of Communication

Shannon's article confines itself to a mathematical and technical derivation of what was still being referred to as communication, rather than information, theory. Shannon, noting that he is following Nyquist and Hartley in developing general theory of communication, defined the fundamental problem of communication as the accurate reproduction at one point of a message selected from another point. Meaning is ignored: 'these semantic aspects of communication are irrelevant to the engineering problem' (Shannon and Weaver, 1949, 3). What matters is that the actual message in each case is one which is selected from the set of possible messages, and the system must cope with any selection. If the number of possible messages is finite, then the information associated with any message is a function of the number of possible messages.

Shannon derives his well known formula for H, the measure of information

$$H = - K \sum p_i \log p_i$$

where p_i is the probability of each symbol, and K is a constant defining the units. The minus sign is included to make the quantity of information, H, positive; necessarily a probability will always be less than 1, and the log of such a number is always negative.

Shannon pointed out that formulae of the general form $H = - \sum p_i \log p_i$ appear very often in information theory, as measures of information, choice and uncertainty; the three concepts seem almost synonymous for his purposes. Shannon then gave the name 'entropy' to his quantity H, since the form of its equation was that of entropy as defined in thermodynamics.

Weaver took a much broader scope in his essay, generalizing Shannon's purely engineering concept of information. But he had to note that 'the concept of information developed in this theory at first seems disappointing and bizarre – disappointing because it has nothing to do with meaning, and bizarre because it deals not with a single message but rather with the statistical character of a whole ensemble of messages, bizarre also because in these statistical terms the two words *information* and *uncertainty* find themselves to be partners' (Shannon and Weaver, 1949, 116). Weaver, however, argued that these are merely temporary reactions, and that a 'real theory of meaning' might follow.

Shannon's was not the only attempt to derive a mathematical theory of information, based on ideas of probability and uncertainty. The British statistician R. A. Fisher derived such a measure, as did the American mathematician Norbert Wiener, the originator of cybernetics. The latter's mathematical formalism was the same as Shannon's but, confusingly, he treated information as the negative of physical entropy, associating it with structure and order, whereas Shannon equated information with entropy. Shannon's information is, in effect, the opposite of Wiener's, which has caused confusion ever since for those who seek to understand the meaning of the mathematics. A similar idea to Wiener's conception of information as negative entropy had been proposed by the German physicist Erwin Schrödinger, one of the pioneers of quantum mechanics, who had suggested that living organisms feed upon negative entropy. The idea of information as the opposite of entropy was popularized, with the snappy title of 'negentropy', by Leon Brillouin (1956), who first advocated the wide use of information theory in science. It has since been applied widely, some might say too widely, in subjects including economics, psychology and theology. For overviews of these intriguing ideas, see Floridi (2010) and Gleick (2011).

Shannon's theory gives the only convincing quantitative measure of information yet derived, and a great deal of work has been done to try to apply it in a variety of disciplines. Numerous attempts have been made to extend it to deal with meaningful semantic information, and to develop mathematical models for information flow, by authors such as Bar-Hillel, Dretske, Devlin and Barwise; for overviews, see Floridi (2011a) and Cornelius (2002), and for interesting examples see Karamuftuoglu (2009) and Cole (1997). However, these have had very limited impact on the theory and practice of information science.

The reason for this can be understood from a consideration of information from a semiotic viewpoint (see, for example, Liebenau and Backhouse, 1990). This shows us that any communication of information can be understood at four 'levels':

- empiric: the physical transmission
- syntactic: the language or coding used
- semantic: the meaning of the message
- pragmatic: the significance of the message to a recipient in a particular context.

'Information theories', following Shannon's MTC, deal almost exclusively with the syntactic level; while libraries and information services – though they must consider these levels – are generally more concerned with meaning and significance of information. Hence the failing of these theories, so far, to inform the principles and practice of librarianship and information science.

We will now turn to how information, as it is generally regarded within the sciences which focus on human recorded information, is understood.

Information for information science

Even when we consider only information within the library and information disciplines, there are a variety of views as to how information is to be understood; see Bawden (2001) for a short overview, Ma (2012), Cornelius (2002) and Capurro and Hjørland (2003) for detailed reviews, and Belkin and Robertson (1976) and Belkin (1978) for older, but still interesting, perspectives.

In an influential paper from 1991, Michael Buckland distinguished three uses of the term 'information':

- Information-as-thing, where the information is associated with a document
- Information-as-process, where the information is that which changes a person's knowledge state
- Information-as-knowledge, where the information is equated with the knowledge which it imparts.

Information-as-thing regards information as physical and objective; or at least being 'contained within' physical documents, and essentially equivalent to them. The other two meanings treat information as abstract and intangible. Buckland gives arguments in favour of the information-as-thing approach, as being very directly relevant to information science, in as much as it deals primarily with information in the form of documents; as we shall see later in this chapter, Buckland is associated with the 'documentation' approach to the subject.

Information-as-process underlies theories of information behaviour with focus on the experience of individuals, such as those of Dervin and Kuhlthau, which we shall consider in a Chapter 9.

Information-as-knowledge invokes the ideas that information and knowledge are closely related; as does the formulation of Bates, noted above. The exact relation, however, is not an obvious one.

The ideas, though useful, do not constitute a precise or formal description of information. We have seen that the information theoretic approach has severe limitations for our purposes. The only current candidate is the General Definition of Information (GDI), proposed by Luciano Floridi as part of his Philosophy of Information, discussed in Chapter 3 (Floridi, 2011b; 2010). As we noted there, Floridi analyses the ways in which information may be understood, and opts to regard it from the semantic viewpoint, as 'well formed, meaningful and truthful data'. Put formally, the GDI states that:

GDI)   σ is an instance of information, understood as semantic content, if and only if:
    GDI.1) σ consists of *n data*, for n ≥≥ 1;
    GDI.2) the data are *well formed*;
    GDI.3) the well formed data are *meaningful*.

Data is understood here as simply a lack of uniformity; a noticeable difference or distinction in something. To count as information, a collection of data must be well formed (put together correctly according to relevant syntax), meaningful (complying with relevant semantics), and truthful; the latter requires a detailed analysis of the nature of true information, as distinct from mis-information, pseudo-information and false information. A 'map' of the full set of types of information in this theory is shown in Figure 4.2; note the positioning of information in Shannon's sense away from issues of truth, meaning and knowing.

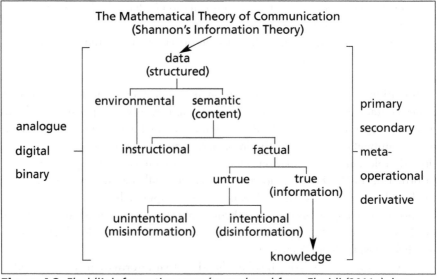

Figure 4.2 *Floridi's information map (reproduced from Floridi (2011a), by permission of Oxford University Press)*

Floridi sees information as related to knowledge, since knowledge and information are part of the same 'conceptual family'. Information is 'converted' to knowledge by being interrelated, which may be expressed through network theory. Informally:

what [knowledge] enjoys and [information] lacks ... is the web of mutual relations that allow one part of it to account for another. Shatter that, and you are left with a pile of truths or a random list of bits of information that cannot help to make sense of the reality that they seek to address.

Floridi (2011b, 288)

Furthermore, information which is meaningful must also be relevant in order to qualify as knowledge, and this aspect may also be formally modelled, as also the distinction between 'knowing', 'believing' and 'being informed'.

Floridi's GDI and its consequences give us what is currently the only formal and detailed analysis of the information concept of potential direct value for information science.

Finally, we will conclude this section by considering conceptions of knowledge of relevance for information science, several of which have already been mentioned by virtue of their link to the information concept.

Knowledge for information science

There are two main models – models, that is, in a very simple, conceptual and almost pictorial sense – used to describe the relation between information and knowledge in the information sciences. Though both are useful, they are incompatible. They differ in how the idea of knowledge is understood, and – since this is really a matter of how we use a label – it cannot be said that one could be right and the other wrong.

One model, stemming from Popper's epistemology, mentioned in the last chapter, uses 'knowledge' to denote World 2, the subjective knowledge within an individual person's mind. 'Information' is used to denote communicable knowledge, exchanged between people or recorded; this is Popper's World 3 of objective knowledge, necessarily encoded in a World 1 document, or physical communication. Information, in this model, is the form in which knowledge is communicated; 'knowledge in transit'.

The second model regards information and knowledge as the same kind of entity. Knowledge is seen as a form of 'refined' information, set into some form of larger structure, and both information and knowledge may be internal, in someone's mind, or external, encapsulated in some kind of document. This is usually presented as a linear progression, or a pyramid, from 'data', through 'information' to 'knowledge', perhaps with 'wisdom' or 'action' at the far end of the spectrum or the apex of the pyramid, as shown in Figure 4.3 on the next page; see, for example, Ackoff (1989), Rowley (2006; 2011) and Frické (2009). Some variations include 'capta' – data in which we are interested – between data and information (Checkland and Holwell, 1998). We have seen that both Bates and Floridi advocate views of information which allow for such a relation with data

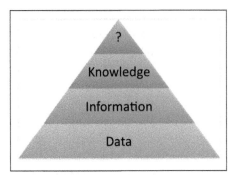

Figure 4.3 *The D-I-K-? hierarchy*

and with knowledge. Zins (2007) presents many definitions of data, information and knowledge, and their interrelation, given by participants in a Delphi study on the nature of information science.

If the incompatibility of these models causes concern, they can be integrated, but at the cost of having to distinguish two forms of knowledge: communicable, objective knowledge instantiated in documents, and personal, subjective knowledge in people's heads.

Knowledge has been studied by philosophers for many centuries, as the subject of epistemology. The usual view in that context is that it is to be understood as 'justified, true belief'; that is to say, for something to count as knowledge it must be believed by someone, for rational reasons, and it must be true.

This viewpoint poses problems for the information sciences (Buckland, 2012). When we think of knowledge, it is usually as the contents of collections of documents, rather than something which a particular person believes. The British Library, for example, has as its mission to 'advance the world's knowledge'; we doubt if they are concerned to discover who believes the contents of each item in their collections. Justification is also somewhat different in our content. Most philosophical argument justifies belief through sense perceptions; someone believes something because they saw something, heard something, etc. However, justification in a library and information context is likely to be based on information gained from some kind of document. This fits into epistemology in the form of 'testimony'; a kind of evidence in which philosophers are becoming increasingly interested, and which overlaps with the ideas of social epistemology discussed in Chapter 3; see, for example, Audi (1997), Goldman (2009) and Adler (2010). Finally, there is a particular problem with the 'truth' criterion. Particularly with scientific and technical material, we can be sure that most of our current knowledge base is 'untrue', in the sense that it will be superseded in time, by better theories, more accurate observations, improved technologies, etc. It seems counter-intuitive to suggest, on this basis, that we have 'no knowledge'.

Some recent developments from philosophy have gone some way to provide new perspectives on knowledge, more appropriate for the information sciences. One has been mentioned already in previous chapters; this is the idea of Karl Popper of knowledge 'without a knowing subject', and consequently of a World 3 of objective knowledge which includes errors and inconsistencies. Popper's 'objective epistemology' (1979) views the totality of things – including information and its communication – as explicable by a system of three 'Worlds'. World 1 is the physical world, of people, books, computers, buildings, etc. World 2 is the internal, subjective mental state of an individual, including their personal knowledge. World 3 is the world of communicable, objective knowledge – or information – with which libraries and information centres deal. So, we may see the communication of information as involving all three of these 'worlds': a person may read a book (World 1), understanding the information it contains (World 3), and assimilating it into their own personal knowledge (World 2).

Other developments include:

- Luciano Floridi's (2010; 2011b) conception of knowledge in the Philosophy of Information, which, while generally respecting established philosophical ideas, adapts them to deal with the 'information context'.
- David Deutsch's (2011) concept of 'explanatory knowledge', which comprises our best rational explanations for the way the world is; such knowledge is inevitably fallible and imperfect, and our task is to improve it, not to justify it.
- Jonathan Kvanvig's (2003) idea of knowledge as 'understanding', allowing for contradictions and inconsistencies.
- Michael Polanyi's (1962) ideas of 'personal knowledge' (somewhat similar to Popper's World 2), which have acted as a basis for some conceptions of the practice of knowledge management; see, for example, Tsoukas (2005) and Day (2005).

It seems likely that some of these ideas will prove valuable in providing a precise understanding of knowledge in a form useful for our disciplines.

Finally, we should note that, although most consideration of knowledge for the information sciences has focused on the Western rational and scientific tradition, there has also been some interest in preserving the indigenous knowledge of peoples in the developing world and making it accessible, as we will discuss in Chapter 12. These forms of knowledge may differ radically from Western norms, being based in experiences, stories and even dreams, and typically having very different forms of classification of material and means of dissemination (Stevens, 2008; Maina, 2012).

We now turn to the next pair of fundamental concepts: documents and collections, dealing first with documents.

Documents

'The debate about whether "information" or "document" is the primary object of study in information science', writes Karamuftuoglu (2009), 'is a complex and multifarious one'. Throughout the debates about what information really is, there has been a strong trend which argues that this is not an important issue, since librarians and information scientists do not handle information at all, they handle documents. Certainly, these documents carry information, but they are not the same thing. And, as we have seen in earlier chapters, the documentation movement of the first half of the 20th century was one of the predecessors of information science.

The usual dictionary definition of 'document' is a paper, or other object, conveying some information, evidence or proof. The word comes from the Latin *docere*, to teach or to inform, with '-ment' implying the means.

It might therefore be thought that the meaning of 'document' is straightforward, and that the only issues that can arise relate to the differences between printed and electronic documents. This is far from the case. It can be argued that, if a 'document' is some physical thing which records thoughts or ideas – information – then we should include paintings, sculpture, and perhaps even any artefact, as documents. But then, what about geological specimens in museums, carefully labelled and collocated with similar minerals; might we not go to look at them to find out about the mineral, as an alternative to reading about it in a book – which is clearly a document. An antelope in the wild may be just an antelope; but in a zoo, placed where it can be studied, in surroundings indicative of its natural habitat, does it not convey information? And is an information-bearing 'thing' not a document? If a photograph of the lunar surface is a document, why not the real thing seen through a telescope? And so on.

The debates about what can count as a document have been very much associated with the work of Michael Buckland, whose views on 'information-as-thing' we noted earlier in this chapter. A British-born information scientist, who has spent much of his career as a distinguished professor in the United States, Buckland has espoused the centrality of the document idea for information science, looking backward to its origins in the documentation movement and forward to the newer ideas of document theory. A concise review of the whole topic and its history is given by Lund and Skare (2010).

Buckland brought the issues to attention in his influential 1997 article on 'What is a document?'. His views stem from his advocacy of 'information-as-thing', as against 'information-as-knowledge' or 'information-as-process' (Buckland, 1991), discussed earlier in this chapter, and hence the idea that a document is a physical entity. Reviewing and critiquing the views of 20th-century European documentalists, including Paul Otlet, Suzanne Briet and Donker Duyvis, he showed how they extended the idea of a document beyond printed texts, and indeed beyond items created with the intention of communicating information. The emphasis moved from communication to evidence: a document was some physical item which gave evidence, and was in that way informational.

However, there had to be something else: to count as a document, the item had to be placed in relation to other evidence-bearing items, by being put in a collection, indexed, cross-referenced, etc. This is exemplified in the box here, using the examples of Briet quoted by Buckland.

Object	Document
star in the sky	No
photo of star	Yes
stone in river	No
stone in museum	Yes
animal in wild	No
animal in zoo	Yes

There are practical consequences of accepting this wider view of document: whole sub-disciplines such as museum documentation only make sense if it is accepted. The practice of botanical gardens, such as Kew Gardens in London, of arranging library books, dried herbarium specimens and living plants according to the same classification scheme is another example. The emphasis is on whether some item functions as a document, rather than what its physical form or nature may be.

Buckland's presentation has been reviewed and updated by several authors, including Buckland himself (1998), Frohmann (2009) and Kallinikos, Aaltonen and Marton (2010), particularly with respect to the specific issues of digital documents. These cannot be defined by form, medium or location in the way that physical documents can, being less 'solid' and permanent; hence the pragmatic 'documentation' approach, defining a document by function, is particularly appropriate. Analyses have been given of the document nature of religious icons (Walsh, 2012), museum objects (Latham, 2012), and even landforms (Grenersen, 2012). An intriguing new form of document is the *DNA barcode*, a small segment of genetic code, unique to a particular organism. They may be used to aid identification of all forms of living things, for example, identifying invasive organisms or illegal imports at national borders, or verifying validity of herbal remedies. They even hold out the prospect of a hand-held device, akin to *Star Trek*'s tricorder, which can process a sample to extract the sequence, and compare it with a remote database (Savolainen et al., 2005; Chase, 2008).

Even if we restrict ourselves to regarding documents as being some physical entity deliberately created for the purpose of conveying information, we still find some difficulties. In particular, we may have a problem deciding when two documents are 'the same'. If I have a copy of a textbook, and you have a copy of the same edition of the same book, then these are clearly different objects. But in a library catalogue they will be treated as two examples of the same document. What if the book is translated, word for word, as precisely as possible, into another language: is it the same document, or different? At what point do an author's ideas, on their way to becoming a published book, become a 'document'?

These are quite difficult issues philosophically, and pose real practical problems for resource description, in particular for library cataloguing codes. They led to the development of the Functional Requirements for Bibliographic Records (FRBR) model (Carlyle, 2006), discussed in the context of information organization in Chapter 6. FRBR distinguishes four levels:

- work: 'a distinct intellectual or artistic creation', e.g. Shakespeare's *Hamlet*
- expression: 'the intellectual or artistic realization of a work', e.g. the English text of *Hamlet*
- manifestation: 'the physical embodiment of an expression of a work', e.g. a specific edition of *Hamlet*
- item: 'a single exemplar of a manifestation', e.g. this copy of this edition of *Hamlet* in my hand.

However, there has been scope for disagreement on how these four levels should be understood (see, for example, Zhang and Salaba, 2009). Are adaptations or abridgements of an original to be considered as different expressions of the work, or as new works? When do small changes in a text, perhaps just the correction of errors when a book is reprinted, make a new expression, rather than just variations of the original expression? Do we need the idea of a 'superwork', to include commentaries, criticisms, different formats – e.g. a film based on a book? And so on. It seems that much of this ambiguity stems from the basic question of what is a document and, similarly, what is a 'work' (see, for example, Smiraglia, 2001).

Collections

Collections, in the sense of interest to the information sciences, and documents go naturally together. As we have seen, one of the things which makes a document a document is that is in an organized collection of related documents; and it is difficult to envisage a collection of information without documents.

> Collection: a number of objects collected or gathered together, viewed as a whole; a group of things collected and arranged.
>
> *Oxford English Dictionary*

The concept of a collection – an organized set of information-bearing items chosen for a particular purpose in a particular context or environment, and usually unique to that situation – is fundamental to the information sciences. Clayton and Gorman (2001, xii) describe a library collection as 'an assemblage of physical information sources combined with virtual access to selected and organized information sources'. The library is the archetypical form of information collection: as Corrall (2012, 3) puts it ' . . . the whole notion of a library is fundamentally associated with the idea of a collection, to the extent that the words "library" and "collection" are almost synonymous.' However, the same principles apply to collections in records centres, archives, museums, galleries, and all forms of information centre. For overviews, see Fieldhouse and Marshall (2012), Cullingford (2011) and Hughes (2012). Issues of collection management will be discussed in Chapter 12.

A useful distinction, though not an absolute one, is between two forms of collection:

- collections of ideas, embodied in documents
- collections of objects, which may provoke ideas in the viewer.

The former is typified by the library, the latter by the gallery.

It is the selection and organization of the collection, with items having some rationally assessed similarity, which distinguishes the typical information collection from the 'cabinet of curiosities' style of seemingly anarchic or random objects, intended to provoke surprise, awe or humour. (For thoughts on the relevance of the cabinet of curiosities to library and information science, see Divelko and Gottlieb, 2003 and Frohmann, 2009.)

With different forms of documents, and other items, and with other purposes, it forms the basis for the activities of information centres, libraries, records centres, and archives, museums (of all kinds, including natural history) and galleries (although the last might not consider the information-bearing nature of the items to be the most important). The disciplines which underlie these professional activities are often referred to as the 'collection sciences'.

The 'collection' in each of these cases may refer to the totality of their information resources, or to a sub-set: for example, a special collection within a library devoted to some topic, or the records of a particular organization within an archive centre.

The move towards a digital information environment has implications for the nature of the collection itself, as well as the practicalities of managing it.

Few collections are truly digital – examples of such would be the digital libraries created rapidly to deal with natural disasters – and these fully digital collections may be assembled very rapidly, in a way which physical collections cannot be. Conversely, very few collections now avoid any digital dimension. Managing 'hybrid' or 'complex' collections presents particular problems of maintaining consistency of approach, and presenting the collection in a unified way.

The move to digital collections generally means a move from 'ownership' and 'location' to 'access', as has been recognized for many years. The collection takes on a dynamic and impermanent nature, with varied and unpredictable lifecycles, and to some degree no longer under local control.

Any digital resource, perceived as a single entity by its users, may in fact be a composite or aggregate of distributed sources: a collection, composed of such entities is even more an aggregate. Given that the resources of which it is composed will often link to other resources, it becomes very difficult to place a 'boundary' around the collection, clearly distinguishing what is inside it. Furthermore, a single digital resource may be simultaneously in several digital collections, which could not happen in the pre-digital world.

This means that such a collection can no longer be thought of as a set of physical items in a particular location, or even a collection of digital items on a particular computer, but rather a means of selecting items from the universe of knowledge. The collection may be defined as 'a set of criteria for selecting resources from the broader information space', with collection membership defined 'through criteria rather than containment' (Lagoze and Fielding, 1998).

We will now consider the final set of fundamental concepts, those which arise largely from studies of information retrieval and seeking: relevance, aboutness and information use.

Relevance and aboutness

In an early paper, Wilson (1978) identified five 'fundamental concepts of information retrieval': information; aboutness; relevance; information need; and information use. More have been introduced over the years, to the point where Jansen and Rieh (2010) were able to present 17 'theoretical constructs of information searching and information retrieval'.

We have already considered the nature of information. The other concepts here fall into two groups: those concerned with the *aboutness* of a document, and its *relevance* in relation to a search or query; and those concerned with information needs and use. The concept of *relevance* has received particular attention; see for example Nolin (2009), Saracevic (1975; 2007), Borlund (2003) and Mizzaro (1997). As Jansen and Rieh (2010, 1525) say

> It is difficult to find a concept that has generated more discussion in or had more impact on the fields of information searching and information retrieval than has relevance. Relevance plays a most significant, fundamental and central role in all aspects of information retrieval and information searching, including theory, implementation and evaluation.

Tefko Saracevic, a Croatian-born professor of information science with a long career in the USA, is well known for his studies of relevance over three decades: he goes so far as to suggest that it is 'a, if not even *the*, key notion in information science in general and information retrieval in particular' (Saracevic, 2007, 915). This strong claim is based on the idea that much research and practice in information science is based on the simple idea that information systems provide answers to queries, and that each of these answers is relevant or not relevant to the question asked; in turn this is linked to the *aboutness* of the information retrieved. This concept, stating what a document is about – its subject matter – might appear straightforward, but has in fact been the topic of much debate; see Hjørland (2001) for an overview.

But it is the nature of relevance that has received most discussion over many years. 'Intuitively', says Saracevic (1975, 324) 'we understand quite well what relevance is. It is a primitive "y' know" concept . . . for which we hardly need a definition'. But when the idea is studied more closely for theory or research, it is not at all simple. There has even been controversy about such a basic issue as whether relevance is objective – a document is relevant to the query or it is not – or whether it is subjective – it is relevant if a particular user on a particular occasion thinks it is; see Hjørland (2004) and Abbott (2004).

However, it is in the evaluation of information retrieval systems that relevance becomes a complex and slippery concept, particularly when real users with real information needs are involved. Documents may be judged as relevant but not interesting, as irrelevant but useful, as relevant but not as relevant as other documents, as relevant if presented first in a results list but not relevant if presented last, and so on. The necessity to ignore such issues in laboratory-style investigations is one of the limitations of the systems paradigm, as discussed in Chapter 3.

To take an example used by one of the authors of this book many years ago (Bawden, 1990), suppose that the query is for information on 'treatment of migraine'. When the relevance of the results is considered, the first question is whether the documents are indeed about this topic; whether, in effect, the retrieval system including is indexing is working well. The second question is whether the user considers them relevant.

The first question is easily answered, by reading the documents. The second is more subtle. One document may be an account of recent advances in migraine treatment; the second may be review of the pharmacological action of a drug, or the biography of a famous doctor, with the treatment of migraine mentioned in passing. Although both are formally relevant – the system is working correctly in retrieving them – it is likely that most users would judge the first to be relevant and the second not; although if the aim were to compile a complete bibliography they might both be considered relevant. Further, users will often bring in other factors in deciding whether items are relevant, in the sense of being useful answers to their queries. The first document, although clearly the right topic, may be, for example, rather old, or written in a language which the user cannot read, or even written by an author with whom they have professional disagreements; and for any of these, or many other reasons, will be judged not relevant.

Furthermore, a user's opinion of the relevance of any particular document may change as the results are examined. The 'recent advances' document may be judged relevant if it is the first to be examined; but if several similar documents have already been seen, so that no new information is added, this decision may change. More generally, as a search progresses and it becomes clear what information is available on a topic, the user's view of what is relevant may change considerably. Taylor, Zhang and Amadio (2009) discuss this phenomenon, and give an example of the way in which relevance judgements changed as a group of students searched for information on a business topic. They found a variety of criteria other than simple aboutness being used, particularly the clarity of writing in the documents, and the students' ability to understand the information. For similar findings, see Taylor (2012).

The nature of relevance in particular contexts is also problematic: Raper (2007), for example, discusses geographic relevance, where the output from geographic information systems (GIS) must be judged in terms of place, space and time, as well as other attributes.

To deal with these complexities, a variety of frameworks for understanding different degrees and levels of relevance has been devised, and concepts such as pertinence, utility, usefulness and topicality have been advanced as alternatives to simple relevance; see, for example, Nolin (2009), Saracevic (2007), Borlund (2003), Mizzaro (1997), Bawden (1990) and Buckland (1983) for reviews and examples. These go a long way from the simple yes/no idea of relevance, originally devised for retrieval experiments: it has been suggested, for example, that relevance is best modelled by the mathematics of fractals (Ottaviani, 1994). There is still no completely satisfactory way of dealing with the relevance concept, either in theory or for practical system evaluation.

Information use and users

Turning to issues of information use and users, by contrast with the attention to the idea of relevance, the nature of *information use* has been very little studied, and there have been few attempts to give conceptual clarity to this very basic idea. In two of the few studies of this kind, Savolainen (2009) compares approaches to understanding information use, and Fleming-May (2011) analyses the related idea of *library use*. Other studies have looked at information use in terms of its context within the users' life and work, and at information practices and information for performing tasks; these will be discussed in the chapter on information behaviour.

These analyses have shown that the concept of information use is a complex and multifaceted one, and one which is changing in newer digital environments, particularly with the growth of social media. In particular, the rather restricted view of a 'user' as a passive recipient and consumer of certain limited types of information, typically held by information practitioners of the past, has been supplanted by the recognition that a much wider range of activities needs to be included; this view is typified by the suggestion that 'information users' would be better regarded as 'information players' (Nicholas and Dobrowolski, 2000).

Summary

All of the concepts discussed in this chapter are contested, and views of them have changed considerably over time.

Information and knowledge, and the relationship between them, are indeed slippery concepts. The significance of any link between the ideas of information in the physical, biological and social worlds remains unclear, while even within the information sciences there are alternative ways of regarding the concepts. Shannon's MTC has proved unsuitable as the basis for a formal treatment of information in our discipline; perhaps Floridi's GDI will be more successful. New approaches to knowledge may be more helpful for our purposes than traditional viewpoints.

Documents and collections are clearly entities of fundamental importance to the information sciences; but theory is weak here, and there are elements of ambiguity in how we understand these concepts, even before we consider the changes brought about by the transition to a largely digital information environment. Even ideas such as relevance and information user, whose meaning might be thought to be intuitively obvious, have complexities when analysed fully.

Further study of these fundamental entities and concepts can be of benefit to both research and practice.

- The fundamental concepts of the information sciences include information, knowledge, documents, collections, relevance and aboutness, and information use and users.
- All of these are contested concepts, whose nature and significance are still debated.
- Shannon's MTC has proved too limited as a theoretical basis for the information sciences; Floridi's GDI, and some of the newer concepts of knowledge, show promise in this respect.
- Further study of the fundamental concepts of the information sciences is important both for the academic subjects and the practical disciplines.

Key readings

Luciano Floridi, *Information – a very short introduction*, Oxford: Oxford University Press, 2010.
[A short and readable account of Floridi's approach, with concise reviews of other aspects.]

James Gleick, *The information: a history, a theory, a flood*, London: Fourth Estate, 2011.
[A readable account of many aspects of the information concept, centred around the development of Shannon's theory.]

Michael Buckland, What is a 'document'?, *Journal of the American Society for Information Science*, 1997, 48(9), 804–9.
[A classic review of the issue.]

Tefko Saracevic, Relevance: a review of the literature and a framework for thinking on the notion in information science. Part II: nature and manifestations of relevance, *Journal of the American Society for Information Science and Technology*, 2007, 58(13), 1915–33.
[A recent review of the issues.]

References

Abbott, R. (2004) Subjectivity as a concern for information science: a Popperian perspective, *Journal of Information Science*, 30(2), 95–106.

Ackoff, R. L. (1989), From data to wisdom, *Journal of Applied Systems Analysis*, 16(1), 3–9.

Adler, J. (2010) Epistemological problems of testimony, in Zalta, E. N. (ed.), *Stanford Encyclopedia of Philosophy* (Winter 2010 edition) [online] available at http://plato.stanford.edu/archives/win2010/entries/testimony-episprob.

Audi, R. (1997) The place of testimony in the fabric of knowledge and justification, *American Philosophical Quarterly*, 34(4), 405–22.

Barrow, J. D., Davies, P. C. W. and Harper, C. L. (2004) *Science and ultimate reality*, Cambridge: Cambridge University Press.

Bates, M. J. (2005) Information and knowledge: an evolutionary framework for information, *Information Research*, 10(4), paper 239 [online] available at http://informationr.net/ir/10-4/paper239.html.

Bates, M. J. (2006) Fundamental forms of information, *Journal of the American Society for Information Science and Technology*, 57(8), 1033–45.

Bawden, D. (1990) *User-oriented evaluation of information systems and services*, Aldershot: Gower.

Bawden, D. (2001) The shifting terminologies of information, *Aslib Proceedings*, 53(3) 93–8

Bawden, D. (2007a) Information as self-organised complexity: a unifying viewpoint, *Information Research*, 12(4), paper colis31, available at http://informationr.net/ir/12-4/colis/colis31.html.

Bawden, D. (2007b) Organised complexity, meaning and understanding: an approach to a unified view of information for information science, *Aslib Proceedings*, 59(4/5), 307–27.

Belkin, N. J. (1978) Information concepts for information science, *Journal of Documentation*, 34(1), 55–85.

Belkin, N. J. and Robertson, S. E. (1976) Information science and the phenomenon of information, *Journal of the American Society for Information Science*, 27(4), 197–204.

Borlund, P. (2003) The concept of relevance in IT, *Journal of the American Society for Information Science and Technology*, 54(10), 913–25.

Brillouin, L. (1956) *Science and information theory*, New York NY: Academic Press.

Buckland, M. K. (1983) Relatedness, relevance and responsiveness in retrieval systems, *Information Processing and Management*, 19(4), 237–41.

Buckland, M. K. (1991) Information as thing, *Journal of the American Society for Information Science*, 42(5), 351–60.

Buckland, M. K. (1997) What is a 'document'?, *Journal of the American Society for Information Science*, 48(9), 804–9.

Buckland, M. K. (1998) What is a 'digital document'?, *Document Numérique*, 2(2), 221-230, available from http://people.ischool.berkeley.edu/~buckland/digdoc.html [An amended version of Buckland's 1997 paper, with more emphasis on digital documents.]

Buckland, M. K. (2012) What kind of science can information science be?, *Journal of the American Society for Information Science and Technology*, 63(1), 1–7.

Capurro, R. and Hjørland, B. (2003) The concept of information, *Annual Review of Information Science and Technology*, 37, 343-411.

Carlyle, A. (2006) Understanding FRBR as a conceptual model: FRBR and the bibliographic universe, *Library Resources and Technical Services*, 50(4), 264–73.

Chase, M. W. (2008) Barcoding life, in *McGraw Hill Yearbook of Science and Technology 2008*, New York NY: McGraw Hill, 35–7.

Checkland, P. and Holwell, S. (1998) *Information, systems and information systems – making sense of the field*, Chichester: Wiley.

Clayton, P. and Gorman, G. E. (2001) *Managing information resources in libraries: collection management in theory and practice*, London: Library Association Publishing.

Cole, C. (1994) Operationalizing the notion of information as a subjective construct, *Journal of the American Society for Information Science*, 45(7), 465–76.

Cole, C. (1997) Calculating the information content of an information process for a domain expert using Shannon's mathematical theory of communication: a preliminary analysis, *Information Processing and Management*, 33(6), 715–26.

Cornelius, I. (2002) Theorising information for information science, *Annual Review of Information Science and Technology*, 36, 393–425.

Corrall, S. (2012) The concept of collection development in the digital world, in Fieldhouse, M. and Marshall, A. (eds), *Collection development in the digital age*, London: Facet Publishing, 3–25.

Cullingford, A. (2011) *The special collection handbook*, London: Facet Publishing.

Davies, P. and Gregersen, N. H. (2010) *Information and the nature of reality: from physics to metaphysics*, Cambridge: Cambridge University Press.

Day, R. E. (2005) Clearing up 'implicit knowledge': implications for knowledge management, information science, psychology, and social epistemology, *Journal of the American Society for Information Science and Technology*, 56(6), 630–5.

Deutsch, D. (2011) *The beginning of infinity: explanations that transform the world*, London: Allen Lane.

Divelko, J. and Gottlieb, K. (2003) Resurrecting a neglected idea: the reintroduction of library museum hybrids, *Library Quarterly*, 73(2), 160–198.

Fieldhouse, M. and Marshall, A. (eds) (2012) *Collection development in the digital age*, London: Facet Publishing.

Fleming-May, R. A. (2011) What is library use? Facets of concept and a typology of its application in the literature of library and information science, *Library Quarterly*, 81(3), 297–320.

Floridi, L. (2010) *Information – a very short introduction*, Oxford: Oxford University Press.

Floridi, L. (2011a) Semantic conceptions of information, in Zalta, E.N. (ed.), *Stanford Encyclopedia of Philosophy (Spring 2011 edition)* [online] available at http://plato.stanford.edu/archives/spr2011/entries/information-semantic.

Floridi, L. (2011b) *The philosophy of information*, Oxford: Oxford University Press.

Frické, M. (2009) The knowledge pyramid: a critique of the DIKW hierarchy, *Journal of Information Science*, 35(2), 131–42.

Frohmann, B. (2009) Revisiting 'what is a document?', *Journal of Documentation*, 65(2), 291–303.

Furner, J. (2010) Philosophy and information studies, *Annual Review of Information Science and Technology*, 44, 161–200.

Genersen, G. (2012) What is a document institution? A case study from the South Sámi community, *Journal of Documentation*, 68(1), 127–33.

Gleick, J. (2011) *The information: a history, a theory, a flood*, London: Fourth Estate.

Goldman, A. I. (2009) Social epistemology: theory and applications, in O'Hear, A. (ed.), *Epistemology: Royal Institute of Philosophy Supplement 64*, Cambridge: Cambridge University Press, 1–18.

Hjørland, B. (2001) Towards a theory of aboutness, subject, topicality, theme, domain, field content . . . and relevance, *Journal of the American Society for Information Science and Technology*, 52(9), 774–8.

Hjørland, B. (2004) Arguments for philosophical realism in library and information science, *Library Trends*, 52(3), 488–506.

Hjørland, B. (2007) Information: objective or subjective/situational? *Journal of the American Society for Information Science and Technology*, 58(10), 1448–56.

Hughes, L. M. (ed.) (2012) *Evaluating and measuring the value, use and impact of digital collections*, London: Facet Publishing.

Jansen, B. J. and Rieh, S. Y. (2010) The seventeen theoretical constructs of information searching and information retrieval, *Journal of the American Society for Information Science and Technology*, 61(8), 1517–34 .

Kallinikos, J., Aaltonen, A. and Marton, A. (2010) A theory of digital objects, *First Monday*, 15(6), available from http://firstmonday.org/htbin/cgiwrap/bin/ojs/index.php/fm/article/view/3033/2564.

Karamuftuoglu, M. (2009) Situating logic and information in information science, *Journal of the American Society for Information Science*, 60(1), 2019–31.

Kvanvig, J. L. (2003) *The value of knowledge and the pursuit of understanding*, Cambridge: Cambridge University Press.

Lagoze, C. and Fielding, D. (1998) Defining collections in distributed digital libraries, *D-Lib Magazine*, (November 1998) [online] available from http://www.dlib.org/dlib/november98/lagoze/11lagoze.html.

Latham, K. F. (2012) Museum object as document: using Buckland's information concepts to understand museum experiences, *Journal of Documentation*, 68(1), 45–71.

Liebenau, J. and Backhouse, J. (1990) *Understanding information*, London: Macmillan.

Lund, N. W. and Skare, R. (2010) Document theory, *Encyclopedia of Library and Information Sciences* (3rd edn), 1:1, London: Taylor & Francis, 1632–9.

Ma, L. (2012) Meanings of information: the assumptions and research consequences of three foundational LIS theories, *Journal of the American Society for Information Science and Technology*, 63(4), 716–23.

Machlup, F. and Mansfield, U. (1983) *The study of information; interdisciplinary messages*, New York NY: Wiley.

Maina, C. K. (2012) Traditional knowledge management and preservation: intersections with library and information science, *International Information and Library Review*, 44(1), 13–27.

Mizzaro, S. (1997) Relevance: the whole history, *Journal of the American Society for Information Science*, 48(9), 810–32.

Nicholas, D. and Dobrowolski, T. (2000) Re-branding and re-discovering the digital information user, *Libri*, 50(3), 157–162.

Nolin, J. (2009) 'Relevance' as a boundary concept: reconsidering early information retrieval, *Journal of Documentation*, 65(5), 745–67.

Ottaviani, J. S. (1994) The fractal nature of relevance: a hypothesis, *Journal of the American Society for Information Science*, 45(4), 263–72.

Polanyi, M. (1962) *Personal knowledge*, Chicago IL: University of Chicago Press.

Popper, K. R. (1979) *Objective knowledge: an evolutionary approach (revised edition)*, Oxford: Clarendon Press

Raper, J. (2007) Geographic relevance, *Journal of Documentation*, 63(6), 836–52.

Rowley, J. (2006) Where is the wisdom that we have lost in knowledge?, *Journal of Documentation*, 62(2), 251–70 .

Rowley, J. (2011) The wisdom hierarchy: representations of the DIKW hierarchy, *Journal of Information Science*, 33(2), 163–80.

Saracevic, T. (1975) Relevance: a review of and a framework for the thinking on the notion in information science, *Journal of the American Society for Information Science*, 26(6), 321–43.

Saracevic, T. (2007) Relevance: a review of the literature and a framework for thinking on the notion in information science. Part II: nature and manifestations of relevance, *Journal of the American Society for Information Science and Technology*, 58(13), 1915–33.

Savolainen, R. (2009) Information use and information processing: comparison of conceptualizations, *Journal of Documentation*, 65(2), 187–207.

Savolainen, V., Cowyn, R. S., Vogler, A.P., Roderick, G. K. and Lane, R. (2005) Towards writing the encyclopaedia of life: an introduction to DNA barcoding, *Philosophical Transactions of the Royal Society: Biology*, 360(1462), 1805–11.

Shannon, C. E. and Weaver, W. (1949) *The mathematical theory of communication*, Urbana IL: University of Illinois Press.

Smiraglia, R. P. (2001) *The nature of a 'work': implications for the organization of knowledge*, Lanham MD: Scarecrow Press.

Stevens, A. (2008) A different way of knowing: tools and strategies for managing indigenous knowledge, *Libri*, 58(1), 25–33.

Stonier, T. (1990) *Information and the internal structure of the universe*, Berlin: Springer-Verlag.

Stonier, T. (1992) *Beyond information: the natural history of intelligence*, Berlin: Springer-Verlag.

Stonier, T. (1997) *Information and meaning: an evolutionary perspective*, Berlin: Springer-Verlag.

Taylor, A. (2012) User relevance choice and the information search process, *Information Processing and Management*, 48(1), 136–53.

Taylor, A., Zhang, X. and Amadio, W. J. (2009) Examination of relevance criteria choices and the information search process, *Journal of Documentation*, 65(5), 719–44.

Tsoukas, H. (2005) *Complex Knowledge: studies in organizational epistemology*, Oxford: Oxford University Press.

Vedral, V. (2010) *Decoding reality: the universe as quantum information*, Oxford; Oxford University Press.

Von Baeyer, C. (2004) *Information: the new language of science*, Harvard MA: Harvard University Press.

Walsh, J. A. (2012) 'Images of God and friends of God': the holy icon as document, *Journal of the American Society for Information Science and Technology*, 63(1), 185–94.

Wilson, P. (1978) Some fundamental concepts of information retrieval, *Drexel Library Quarterly*, 14(2), 10–24.

Zhang, Y. and Salaba, A. (2009) *Implementing FRBR in libraries: key issues and future directions*, New York NY: Neal-Schuman.

Zins, C. (2007) Conceptual approaches for defining data, information and knowledge, *Journal of the American Society for Information Science and Technology*, 58(4), 479–93.

CHAPTER 5

Domain analysis

If information science is to be taken seriously as a field of study, it is important that basic theories are formulated and examined in the field. Domain analysis is one serious attempt to consider the basic problems in IS. Anybody working in the field should care about the arguments that have been or might be raised for or against this view.

Birger Hjørland (2010, 1653–4)

Introduction

Domain analysis is a 'metatheoretical framework for library and information science . . . the basic claim in [domain analysis] is that "domains" of knowledge are the proper object of study for LIS' (Hjørland, 2010, 1648). It is also a very practical framework for understanding information on particular topics, and for particular groups, and underlies the work of the subject specialist information practitioner. It provides a valuable link between research and practice in the information sciences.

The idea was conceived by, and remains closely associated with, Birger Hjørland, Professor of Information Science at the Royal School of Librarianship and Information Science, Copenhagen. Hjørland – whose work on the philosophy and concepts of information science we have already encountered in earlier chapters – has for many years been one of the foremost authorities on the foundations of information science and of knowledge organization.

We will use Hjørland's meaning of domain analysis here; but note that the phrase has sometimes been used in the library and information literature with a more restrictive meaning, usually relating either to bibliometric analysis or to classification.

Domain analysis as a theory for information science

As we saw in Chapter 3, the idea of domain analysis was initially introduced in association with the socio-cognitive paradigm, for information science, as an alternative to the cognitive and behavioural paradigms (Hjørland and Albrechtsen, 1995). These latter approaches focused on the individual, and their personal knowledge, behaviours, preferences, information needs, opinions of relevance, etc. By contrast, wrote Hjørland and Albrechtsen,

> The domain analytic paradigm in information science (IS) states that the best way to understand information in IS is to study the knowledge domains as thought or discourse communities ... Knowledge organization, structure, co-operation patterns, language and communication forms, information systems, and relevance criteria are reflections of the objects of the work of these communities and of their role in society.

They acknowledge that this is not an entirely new idea, and that previous approaches have shared its assumptions: as Tennis (2003) puts it 'domain analysis is done in many ways and by many people in information science'. It had not, however, previously been stated fully or explicitly. Talja (2005) gives early examples of this kind of approach.

As understood by these authors, domain analysis is a realist approach in philosophical terms; it seeks a basis for information science in factors external to the individual, which are objective rather than subjective, and which may be located in the expertise and practices of subject specialists. If we wish to design an information system for Scandinavian geography, Hjørland and Albrechtsen say, the obvious approach is to design it according to how Scandinavia actually is, not according to the way some particular users think it is; we would probably want to use geographers as the relevant domain experts to advise us. However, it is not necessary to adhere to this philosophical viewpoint to make pragmatic use of domain analysis; see, for example, Feinberg (2007) for a more subjective approach.

They also argue that domain analysis, being based on groupings of people with common interests and concerns, is primarily a social theory, and that this implies that information science is primarily a social science. (As we noted in Chapter 1, we interpret this as meaning a field of study, with a focus on information in a social context.) More specifically, this is a *socio-cognitive* approach, since it considers the communication of knowledge within groups of people:

> Domain analysis consequently does not conceive users in general, but sees them as belonging to different cultures, to different social structures, and to different domains of knowledge. Information producers, intermediaries, and users are more or less connected in communities that share common languages, genres and other typified communication practices.
>
> Hjørland (2010, 1652); for a fuller discussion, see Hjørland (2002a)

This theoretical background to domain analysis has influenced views of the nature of information science, and its practice: as Sundin (2003) puts it 'domain analysis has, during the last decade, developed as an important theoretical approach within library and information science'. And, in particular, as we saw in Chapter 1, we can understand information science as the application of the methods of domain analysis to the information communication chain (Robinson, 2009).

Domain analysis also has considerable practical value for the information scientist, and for information specialists generally, as we will see later.

What is a domain?

In straightforward pragmatic terms, an information domain is the set of information systems, resources, services and processes associated with a group of users with common concerns and a common viewpoint, and sharing a common terminology. This will typically be: an academic subject area, e.g. theoretical physics or philosophy; a professional or trade, e.g. accountancy or clock-making; or an 'everyday' hobby or concern, e.g. cookery or job-seeking.

There are some overlaps and complications. Medicine, law and engineering, for example, are all professions and also academic subjects. History may be the concern of the professional historian, the student of history (at any level, from junior school to university), and the layperson (either as a recreational interest, or for some specific purpose, e.g. researching family history). Domains may be defined generally or specifically, with this in mind.

More formally, Hjørland (2010, 1650) suggests that a domain may be 'a scientific discipline or a scholarly field. It may also be a discourse community connected to a political party, a religion, a trade or a hobby'. Domains, he suggests, are defined and explained by three dimensions: ontological, epistemological and sociological. The ontological dimension defines the domain by its main object of interest: botany by plants, history by the past, theology by the Divine, etc. This is the most usual way of defining a domain. The epistemological dimension relates to the kind of knowledge in the domain, or perhaps different kinds of knowledge associated with different paradigms or ways of understanding. The sociological dimension relates to the kind of people and groups involved in the domain.

These three dimensions interact in a rather complex way, and it is necessary to produce something more concrete in order to apply domain analysis to a specific case. Hjørland (2002b, 2010) suggests that 11 'aspects' or 'approaches' to the study of domains can be derived from the three dimensions, as discussed in the next section.

Other commentators have extended these ideas. Tennis (2003) argues that use of Hjørland's 11 approaches does not delineate exactly what a domain is, in any particular case. He adds two 'axes', to help definition of domains:

1 'Areas of modulation' set parameters on the names and extension of the domain, specifying what is included and not included, and what the domain

may sensibly be called (e.g. is Transpersonal Psychology different from psychology *per se*, or is it a part of mainstream psychology?).

2 'Degrees of specialization' set the 'intension' of a domain, i.e. the focus of its specialization (Hinduism, for example, is a qualified domain of religion, with lesser extension (scope) and greater intension (specialized focus), and also indicates intersection, when domains overlap (e.g. medical ethics).

See Hjørland and Hartel (2003), and Feinberg (2007), for further discussion of how a domain is described, or constructed.

Sundin (2003) extends the domain analytical approach by using tools from the theory of professions, looking at professional interests, power relations, and occupational identities, in an examination of the professional domain of nursing. Morado Nascimento and Marteleto (2008), in similar vein, take ideas from Bourdieu's sociology of culture to better understand the nature of domains, and the rationale for information practices within particular domains.

One might also add to the specified 11 aspects: including, for example, issues of the evaluation and analysis of information, and standards and quality and reliability issues, which differ considerably between domains.

These debates imply that domain analysis must be treated as a general approach, rather than a precise algorithm: as Hartel (2003) puts it, investigations are conducted 'in the general domain analytical spirit'.

Aspects of domain analysis

Hjørland (2002b) introduced 11 'aspects' of domain analysis; essentially things which feature in study and practice of information with specific domains. They are expressed in slightly different words in various publications, but are summarized in the box here.

Aspects of domain analysis

1 Resource guides and subject gateways
2 Special classifications and thesauri
3 Indexing and retrieval special features
4 User studies
5 Bibliometric studies
6 Historical studies
7 Document and genre studies
8 Epistemological and critical studies
9 Terminologies, languages for special purposes, discourse analysis
10 Structures and institutions in communication of information
11 Cognition, knowledge representation and artificial intelligence.

It is worth noting that these approaches straddle the boundary between what is generally regarded as 'research' (e.g. user studies or bibliometrics) and what is usually regarded as 'professional practice' (e.g. producing literature guides, and knowledge organization tools). This is an attractive feature of the approach, as it emphasizes the desirable links between research and practice in the information sciences.

It is worth taking each of these aspects in turn, and examining its nature with some examples. It should be noted that this is not a definitive list, and other aspects could be added, though it has been satisfactory for most analyses carried out in practice.

Resource guides

The preparation and use of resource guides stems from the long-standing involvement of information specialists in subject bibliography and guides to the literature, albeit that it is now most commonly expressed in the form of resource guides and subject gateways in digital formats. Such guides may be generally applicable and publicly available, or may be for in-house use, relating to sources available within a particular institution. There is a strong relation between this aspect of domain analysis and the promotion of digital literacy for specific subjects, discussed in Chapter 13. An examination of existing literature guides is an essential part of preparation for information work in the area. Analysis of the context and structure of such guides, particularly their development over time, is a valuable contribution to understanding the nature of the information domain.

Information organization tools

Similarly, the creation and use of classifications, taxonomies, thesauri and other tools for information organization, which will be discussed in Chapter 6, has been the concern of information specialists for many decades. 'Creation' is most likely to be concerned with small, specialized and possibly in-house tools – taxonomies and thesauri for the most part. However, some information scientists will become involved with the updating and maintenance of subject-specific sections of major tools, such as the Dewey, UDC, Bliss and Library of Congress classification schemes, and the Library of Congress subject headings. As with literature guides, a familiarity with relevant tools is essential for any subject specialist information practitioner, while analysis of the nature and development of these tools sheds much light on information in particular domains.

Indexing and retrieval

The same is true of specialized indexing and retrieval systems, whose development and use is the concern of information specialists in those subject areas. Specialist retrieval systems, discussed further in Chapter 7, are most common in science, technology and medicine (STEM) subject areas, but are also found elsewhere. Examples are:

- chemical information systems, allowing for retrieval of substances, reactions and properties
- molecular biology systems, allowing matching of nucleotide and protein sequences
- medicines information systems, which allow identification of medicines by their actions, their appearance, and their names, the latter allowing of language variants and phonetic matching
- geographic information systems, with spatial and temporal metadata and displays
- fine arts, with image databases allowing retrieval by subject, genre and copyright and use status.

Sophisticated and specialist indexing is also often associated with STEM subjects, though is found elsewhere. Examples are:

- medicine and pharmaceuticals, with an array of indexing languages
- fine arts, which have developed exhaustive indexing languages, which also serve as informative glossaries
- archaeology and history, for which many 'local' vocabularies have been developed.

User studies

These have been a feature of the library and information landscape for several decades and are discussed in Chapter 9. Many have focused on professional or academic groups ('information needs of doctors', 'information behaviour of lawyers', 'information use by students of business and finance', etc.), and hence are relevant to the idea of information use within specific domains (Case, 2012). However, as Hjørland (2002b) points out, their value in domain analysis is limited in many cases by the lack of any theoretical basis, or investigation of any domain specific aspects; there is limited value in asking the same questions of senior business managers as of new students of geology. Studies of users and use within a particular domain may be very valuable, if the study focuses on the specific resources, tasks and knowledge of relevance to that domain.

Within a subject area, of course, there may be several very different user groups, and hence potentially different domains. Users of mathematics literature, for example, a subject with a particularly great 'reach', include: professional mathematicians; professionals in closely associated areas, for example statistics and operations research; those working in the many areas which use mathematics, hence the plethora of 'mathematics for . . . ' books; those teaching and learning mathematics, at any level from junior school to graduate school; and those interested in recreational mathematics. While these may most sensibly be counted as different domains, they are all in some sense 'users of mathematics information'.

It is of obvious importance for information scientists working in a subject area to be familiar with what is known of the information practices, behaviours and needs of those involved with that area. It may be feasible for them to carry out small and local user studies, ideally building on previous similar studies, to avoid results only of local interest.

Bibliometrics

Bibliometric studies of the literature of a subject area are similar to user studies, in that information practitioners will be more likely to make use of their results, rather than carry out such studies for themselves; although local small-scale bibliometric studies may be valuable if they can be combined or compared with other results. Bibliometric data will be valuable to any subject-specialist practitioner, in scoping the size and nature of the information base of a subject, and in assisting in collection development, as discussed in Chapter 8.

Historical perspectives

Historical studies within domain analysis comprise two distinct, though related, aspects: the study of the historical development of the subject area itself, and of its concepts, theories and practices; and the historical development of its information resources, systems and services. It is not possible to understand the second without an appreciation of the first. This forms a part of the more general study of information history, discussed in Chapter 2.

Historical aspects, as we saw in that earlier chapter, are sometimes regarded as of little relevance to practice. For domain analysis, we can make the same case for history as was made generally: that we cannot properly understand current information provision, and plan for its improvement, without understanding how it has come to be as it is.

Document and genre studies

Studies of documents and genres are of evident relevance to information practitioners in specific domains, since each domain has a typifying mix of types of document and content which defines it, very often uniquely. The changes in the types of document available as the information environment becomes largely digital, as noted in Chapter 4, makes it even more important for these factors to be studied and understood.

Some subjects have forms of documents and content very closely associated with them, e.g. chemistry (chemical structures and reactions), history (archival and primary sources), music (sheet music and recorded sound), fine arts (images and artefacts), geography (maps and atlases), astronomy (star charts), mathematics (mathematical notations), architecture (plans, drawings and models), etc. Others are typified by a very wide range of documents and content; healthcare for example, has a particularly large and diverse range of resources (Robinson, 2010).

Epistemological and critical studies

These focus on the nature and structure of knowledge in specialist subject areas. It is evident that the kind of knowledge being expressed, and the way it is communicated, differs greatly between, say, mathematics, the visual arts, and horticulture. This affects the kind of information resources which are provided, and the way in which information and knowledge are accessed. For example, Robinson (2010) notes the importance of three kinds of knowledge in the healthcare domain: *propositional knowledge*, publicly available, objective, and often of a scientific or technical nature; *practical craft knowledge*, tacit and gained by professional experience, and often associated with 'clinical intuition' and 'professional judgement'; and *personal knowledge*, subjective and gained by reflection on experience. For a fuller discussion, see Higgs, Richardson and Dahlgren (2004).

As Hjørland (2002b) emphasizes, some subject areas may have several paradigms, or schools of thought. It is important that information providers are aware of these, as otherwise information provision may be partial or confusing.

Terminology, language, discourse

The importance of terminology and special languages, and discourse analysis, will differ greatly between areas, although almost all domains, even 'everyday' or hobbyist topics, have some specific terms, or words used with a particular meaning. The way in which these terms are used, and more generally the way discourse is carried on, is also characteristic of subject areas, and needs to be appreciated by those involved with information provision.

The issue is most evident in the terminology of STEM subjects in particular, with vocabularies such as chemical nomenclature, giving unambiguous names for chemical substances, botanical and zoological nomenclatures for naming living things, and the terminologies of the medical sciences, being the most obvious. These special languages form a barrier to any information access from the outside, and one concern of the information practitioner may be to provide access in layperson's language, particularly for healthcare (Robinson, 2010).

These areas also often generate artificial languages, largely or wholly divorced from natural language: mathematical notation, chemical structure notation, and (in a different kind of domain altogether), musical and dance notations, are examples. We might also include meta-languages, such as the Unified Medical Language System (UMLS), used for purely formal information processing and vocabulary linking rather than person-to-person communication here.

However, the issue is by no means confined to these subjects: a scan of any academic bookstore will show a variety of dictionaries and glossaries for subjects such as philosophy, law, history, economics and the fine arts.

Information practitioners in subject domains have an obvious need for familiarity with any specific terminologies used, and may be able to contribute by creating and updating glossaries and similar tools. They may also be involved with another aspect of language; the translation of terminology between natural languages, for subject-specific language dictionaries or multilingual glossaries.

Structures, institutions and organizations

An understanding of how these are involved in the communication of information within a particular domain is of evident importance to information practitioners. This involves participants at all stages of the communication chain from producers, through all forms of disseminators, to users: research institutes and universities; learned societies, commercial and institutional publishers, libraries, archives, etc. These factors may differ from domain to domain in perhaps unexpected ways: to give just one example, the role of learned societies in journal publishing and database production is much more significant in mathematics than in similar subjects.

Cognition, knowledge representation and artificial intelligence (AI)

This final aspect is perhaps the least likely to have direct relevance for the information practitioner. This is particularly so since the 1980s enthusiasm for 'expert systems' able to encapsulate the knowledge in a specific domain and hence of great interest to subject specialist information scientists, has produced very little of practical value. Nonetheless, research continues on many aspects of knowledge representation, and it is important for subject specialists to be aware of developments in their areas. Perhaps the most relevant current aspects are ontologies and meta-languages such as UMLS mentioned above.

We can therefore see that of the 11 aspects, some – for example, resource guides and information organization tools – are largely regarded as practically useful activities rather than research topics, while for others – for example, knowledge representation, bibliometrics and user studies – the opposite is the case. In fact, however, all have a two-fold value, as being both tools for the practitioner and also topics for study and research. In this way, domain analysis forms a bridge between theory and practice for information science.

Practical value of domain analysis

Hjørland explains the aspects of domain analysis as being the special competencies of the information scientist; they encompass the skills and knowledge needed to provide effective information systems and services in particular subject areas, and for particular groups of users.

They therefore form the basis for subject specialist information work, as will be discussed fully later in this chapter.

One may also, in a sense, reverse this idea, and note that aspects of domain analysis may be of value in studying a subject area in information terms. If we wish to know what an academic subject, professional discipline, etc., is like 'informationally', we will want to know, for example: what kind of information and knowledge does the area encompass?; what kind and format of information resources are available, and who produces them?; what kind of special terminologies, classifications, indexes, and retrieval systems are available?; what guides to the literature, subject gateways, etc., are available?; how much is published on the topic, in what languages, and so on?; how old is the subject, and how important is older material? – and so on. All the questions are covered by the aspects of information domains.

Domain analysis will therefore be of practical importance in three ways, and to three different groups. Experienced practitioners in an area will apply its aspects: creating and using resource guides, creating and using knowledge organization tools, etc. New practitioners, or those new to a subject area, can use the aspects to gain competence: finding out what special retrieval tools are available, assessing what is known of users and their needs, etc. And researchers can use the aspects of domain analysis as a framework for examining a domain in information terms; since if one knows about all the aspects as they relate to an area, one can realistically claim to understand it. Domain analysis therefore provides a clear and direct link between research and practice in information science.

It should be noted that even the most enthusiastic proponents of domain analysis do not believe that information science research and practice should split into domain-specific subjects: there are general information science principles applicable to all domains (Hjørland, 2010).

We will now look at some specific examples of the use of domain analysis to understand information in a specific subject area.

Examples of domain analysis

The most extensive published example of domain analysis is that of Robinson (2010), who analyses the healthcare domain – which has a particularly rich and diverse set of resources and users – using all of the 11 aspects. The analysis is structured into six main sections: domain overview, including epistemological and structure or institution aspects; history; producers and users; information organization, including classifications, terminologies and knowledge representation; sources and retrieval systems, including resource guides, analysis of document types and bibliometric analysis; and information and knowledge management. This is an indication of the way in which the 11-aspect framework can be used as guide, rather than a prescriptive formalism.

Other studies which have applied some of the aspects of domain analysis to specific subjects include Hartel (2003; 2010) on cookery, Karamuftuoglu (2006) on information art, Morado Nascimento and Marteleto (2008) on architecture, Orom (2003) on fine art, and Sundin (2003) on nursing. Talja (2005) reviews earlier examples of this general approach, before the specific domain analysis formulation was described.

Domain analysis and the subject specialist

Information practitioners have taken subject specialist roles for many years. Examples include: subject specialist librarians in university or special libraries; subject specialist cataloguers in national or research libraries; information officers in biomedical research institutes or pharmaceutical companies; information researchers in business and financial institutions; and so on.

A subject specialist information practitioner is not a subject specialist *per se*: a medical information specialist is not a doctor, nor a legal information specialist a lawyer (unless they have qualified in those professions previously; it is not uncommon, particularly in commerce and industry, for such positions to be filled by subject practitioners who have switched to an information role). As Hjørland (2010, 1649) puts it: 'To be an information specialist with a given speciality is not to be a subject specialist in the ordinary sense, but rather to be an expert in information resources in that field'.

What is needed is someone with an understanding of, at least, the basic concepts of the subject – its 'logic and language' – plus specialist and deep knowledge of its information attributes, which are well expressed in the domain analysis approaches. There has always been a debate as to whether it is better to first gain subject knowledge, through degree level study and perhaps practical experience, and then to add on an understanding of, and skills in, the information aspects; or to begin with a grounding in information science, and add on the subject knowledge. But the two must both be acquired at some stage. It is essential to combine some subject knowledge, plus knowledge of subject-specific sources, users needs, etc.: the sort of aspects noted above. (Rodwell (2001) refers to this as 'subject expertise'; Hjørland (2000) as the capabilities of the 'domain generalist'. The subject background is needed to make possible the detailed insight into needs and sources, to enable the interpretation and evaluation of information, and to make the information professional credible to their users.

What does such a subject specialist do that other information professionals cannot (or prefer not to)? A variety of answers are given (see, for example, Rodwell, 2001; Hardy and Corrall, 2007; Garitano and Carlson, 2009; Jackson, 2010), most commonly:

- create user guides
- create terminologies and taxonomies
- carry out 'difficult' searches and reference queries
- evaluate and interpret information
- provide current awareness
- suggest useful new sources and collection development
- act as instructor, trainer, consultant and advisor.

The resonance with the aspects of domain analysis, discussed above, is clear.

This often leads to an overlap with the activities of the users, and with the organization as a whole: in an academic library, for example, this takes the form of an involvement with teaching. The downside, if the subject specialist role is over-emphasized, can be a concern about loss of professional identity and skills.

There has been some diminution in the perceived importance of subject specialism for the information practitioner since 1990, largely due to the view that the most important task for most information practitioners was to provide access to digital resources. The limitations of this view are now being realized; Hjørland (2010) gives a powerful argument for the need for subject knowledge by most, if not all, information practitioners. This will best be achieved by bringing domain analysis to the forefront as a main focus for research and practice in information science.

Summary

We have seen that the idea of domain analysis is a central concept for information science, linking several other important aspects: resources and retrieval systems, terminologies and classifications, user behaviour, the quantitative aspects of a literature as assessed by bibliometrics, the nature of knowledge in a subject area, the way information sources and services have developed over time, the institutions and organizations that produce and disseminate information, etc.

By focusing on particular subject areas and user groups, it provides both a theoretical framework and a set of specific activities and competencies, for researchers and practitioners in the information sciences. This gives a unique approach to both the study of, and the practical instantiation of, the information communication chain; and thereby provides a unique stance for information science, distinct from adjacent disciplines such as computer science and information systems and publishing.

- Domain analysis is a framework for studying information communication within subject areas and user groups, and for the provision of information services to such groups.
- It is a socio-cognitive approach, based on examining the nature of knowledge within social groups, and implications for information provision.
- It provides a basis for the work of the subject specialist information practitioner.
- It provides a bridge between research and practice in the information sciences.

Key readings

Birger Hjørland, Domain analysis in information science, in *Encyclopedia of Library and Information Science* (3rd edn), 1:1, 1648–54, Abingdon: Taylor & Francis, 2010. [A concise overview of the ideas and applications.]

Birger Hjørland, Domain analysis in information science. Eleven approaches – traditional as well as innovative, *Journal of Documentation*, 2002, 58(4), 422–64. [Explanations and examples of the eleven original aspects of domain analysis.]

References

Case, D. O. (2012) *Looking for information: a survey of research on information seeking* (3rd edn), Bingley: Emerald.

Feinberg, M. (2007) Hidden bias to responsible bias: an approach to information systems based on Haraway's situated knowledge, *Information Research*, 12(4), paper colis07, available from http://InformationR.net/ir/12-4/colis/colis07.html.

Garitano, J. R. and Carlson, J. R. (2009) A subject librarian's guide to collaborating on e-science projects, *Issues in Science and Technology Librarianship*, no. 57, available from http://www.istl.org.

Hardy, G. and Corrall, S. (2007) Revisiting the subject librarian: a study of English, law and chemistry, *Journal of Librarianship and Information Science*, 39(2), 79–91.

Hartel, J. (2003) The serious leisure frontier in library and information science: hobby domains, *Knowledge Organisation*, 30(3/4), 228–38.

Hartel, J. (2010) Managing documents at home for serious leisure: a case study of the hobby of gourmet cooking, *Journal of Documentation*, 66(6), 847–76.

Higgs, J., Richardson, B. and Dahlgren, M. A. (eds) (2004) *Developing practice knowledge for health professionals*, London: Butterworth-Heinemann.

Hjørland, B. (2000) Library and information science: practice, theory and philosophical basis, *Information Processing and Management*, 36(3), 504–31.

Hjørland, B. (2002a) Epistemology and the socio-cognitive perspective in information science, *Journal of the American Society for Information Science and Technology*,

53(4), 257–70.

Hjørland, B. (2002b) Domain analysis in information science. Eleven approaches – traditional as well as innovative, *Journal of Documentation*, 58(4), 422–64.

Hjørland, B. (2010) Domain analysis in information science, in *Encyclopedia of Library and Information Science* (3rd edn), 1:1, 1648–54, Abingdon: Taylor and Francis.

Hjørland, B. and Albrechtsen, H. (1995) Toward a new horizon in information science: domain-analysis, *Journal of the American Society for Information Science*, 46(6), 400–25.

Hjørland, B. and Hartel, J. (2003) Afterword: ontological, epistemological and sociological dimensions of domains, *Knowledge Organisation*, 25(4), 162–201.

Jackson, M. (2010) *Subject specialists in the 21st century library*. Oxford: Chandos.

Karamuftuoglu, M. (2006) Information arts and information science: time to unite?, *Journal of the American Society for Information Science and Technology*, 57(13), 1780–93.

Morado Nascimento, D. and Marteleto, R. M. (2008) Social field, domains of knowledge and informational practice, *Journal of Documentation*, 64(3), 397–412.

Orom, A. (2003) Knowledge organization in the domain of art studies – history, transition and conceptual changes, *Knowledge Organization*, 30(3/4), 128–43.

Robinson, L. (2009) Information science: communication chain and domain analysis, *Journal of Documentation*, 65(4), 578–91.

Robinson, L. (2010) *Understanding healthcare information*, London: Facet Publishing.

Rodwell, J. (2001) Dinosaur or dynamo? The future for the subject specialist reference librarian, *New Library World*, 101(1), 48–52.

Sundin, O. (2003) Towards an understanding of symbolic aspects of professional information: an analysis of the nursing domain, *Knowledge Organisation*, 30(3/4), 170–81.

Talja, S. (2005) The domain analytic approach to scholars' information practices, in Fisher, K. E., Erdelez, S. and Mckechnie, L. (eds), *Theories of information behavior*, Medford NJ: Information Today, 123–7.

Tennis J. T. (2003) Two axes of domains for domain analysis, *Knowledge Organisation*, 30(3/4), 191–5.

CHAPTER 6

Information organization

The first step in wisdom is to know the things themselves: this notion consists in having a true idea of the objects: objects are distinguished and known by classifying them methodically and giving them appropriate names. Therefore, classification and name-giving will be the foundation of our science.

Carl Linnaeus

Cataloguers would lose much of their status if it were shown that most cataloguing is a trivial job easily done by clerical staff.

Maurice Line

Introduction

The organization of information, and information resources, is one of the fundamental aspects of the information sciences. In essence, this amounts to classifying and name-giving: as essential in our sciences as Linnaeus proclaimed it to be in his, though for rather different reasons. It is an extensive and complex subject in its own right, but fortunately it has a particularly wide range of textbooks and articles. We will outline the main topics and issues within the subject, pointing to where more detailed treatments can be found. One of the main aspects of the subject is the way in which relatively old tools and techniques are being adapted to the modern information environment. Therefore, although up-to-date materials are important, older texts may also be very useful. The fundamentals of the subject, particular some of the theory of classification and indexing, go back many years, and – as we saw in Chapter 2 – some of the main tools used today have their origins in the 19th century. They were developed as part of the attempt to provide bibliographic control of printed materials; to record, identify and make accessible all the intellectual output of humanity, as expressed in recorded knowledge. They, and newer equivalents, are now being used to provide access to the rapidly expanding stock of digital material.

We will look first at some of the fundamental issues of information organization, before examining the main tools: terminology, metadata, resource description, systematic and alphabetic subject description and abstracting. Texts covering several of these aspects in detail include Chowdhury and Chowdhury (2007), Taylor (2004), Chan (2007) and Svenonious (2000). For a more detailed examination of all aspects of information organization in one subject domain – healthcare – see Robinson (2010, Chapter 4).

This subject is referred to as either 'information organization' or 'knowledge organization'. Usually these terms are treated as synonymous. But they remind us that the purpose may be either understanding the structure of knowledge itself, or the pragmatic purpose of arranging documents; initially physical documents on shelves, latterly digital documents in a virtual space. The questions raised have been asked since the earliest days of philosophy: is there a single 'natural' classification of everything in the world?; on what basis do we assign things to categories?; how do our mental concepts relate to physical things?; how distinct can two things be, and still be given the same name?; and so on. There is a great deal of theory underlying all organizations of information and knowledge; whether classification schemes for documents or scientific taxonomies – of plants, animals, rocks, stars, and many more.

For an overview of the theoretical bases for documentary information organization, see Svenonious (2000), Tennis (2008) and Hjørland (2003, 2008a), and for theoretical underpinnings of various aspects, see Hjørland (2008b, 2009, 2011), Hjørland and Pedersen (2005), Hjørland and Shaw (2010), and Weinberg (2009).

Controlled vocabulary and facet analysis

These are two fundamental concepts, both of which appear in several aspects of information organization.

A controlled vocabulary is, at its simplest, just a list of terms which are to be used for indexing and retrieval; examples are keyword lists, subject headings, classifications, taxonomies, thesauri, authority lists, and others. They 'control' the variability and redundancy of natural language. The opposite is an uncontrolled vocabulary: full-text, freely chosen keywords and tags, etc. The argument about whether controlled or uncontrolled vocabularies are 'best' has rumbled on for many years, quite pointlessly. The obvious answer is that a combination of both is desirable: controlled vocabulary for consistency, and to use term relations; uncontrolled for precision, and for new terms.

Facet analysis involves dividing the concepts within a subject domain into consistent sections. For example, the subject of 'historic buildings' might have the facets PURPOSE (house, church, school . . .), STYLE (Gothic, classical, Arts and Crafts . . .), CONSTRUCTION (stone, brick, timber . . .), AGE (Victorian, medieval . . .), etc. This style of analysis finds use in the construction of classifications and thesauri, the design of interfaces, the construction of complex search logics, and more (La Barre, 2010; Broughton, 2006a).

We can now begin to look at the tools for information organization, beginning with the most familiar: terminology lists.

Terminologies

A *terminology* or *term list* is generally taken to mean the words and phrases used in the communication of information in a particular subject or field; interpreted broadly, it includes words and phrases in common usage. Terminology resources encompass a number of overlapping categories: general dictionaries, scholarly, introductory or abridged, and illustrated; multilingual dictionaries; dictionaries and glossaries for specific subjects; special-purpose dictionaries, of rhyming words, quotations, crossword clues; and thesauri, in the sense of Roget's word finder, rather than the retrieval thesauri discussed below. We might also include dictionaries of the proper names of persons ('biographical dictionaries') or places (geographical dictionaries or gazetteers). Once the epitome of the quality-assured printed volume, these kinds of tools are now increasingly digital in format, and beginning to be produced by crowd-sourcing, particularly for popular use.

There is some overlap between subject terminology tools, such as glossaries, and the subject heading lists, thesauri and taxonomies discussed below. Both kinds may be used to provide terms for indexing, and equally both may be used to help understand the 'logic and language' of a subject. There is also overlap between the 'people and places' lists and the authority files used in cataloguing and resource description. They are primarily intended to fulfil the requirements noted by Buckland (2008) for the 'general reference' function: to provide, or confirm, facts (in this case, to explain the meaning or significance of a word or phrase), and to provide context for such explanation. For the origins and development of sources of this kind, see Hitchens (2005), Hüllen (2004), Mersky (2004) and Mugglestone (2005); and for current issues, see Tackabery (2005), Mugglestone (2011), Cassell and Hiremath (2011, Chapters 7, 10 and 11), and Ayre, Smith and Cleeve (2006).

Beyond subject specific dictionaries and glossaries there are also, particularly in STEM subjects, a variety of special languages and notations. Some notations, such as those of mathematics, music and dance, are languages in their own right. Others are detailed and specific terminologies, such as: nomenclatures for chemical structures and reactions (Leigh, 2011); nomenclatures and taxonomies for living things (Bowker, 2005; Heidorn, 2011), and specialized terminologies for medicines and healthcare (Robinson, 2010, Chapter 4).

The varied terminologies noted above can all provide terms for indexing, but their main purpose is communication, rather than information retrieval. Now we turn to vocabularies and standards specifically designed for indexing and retrieval, beginning with metadata, which provides 'standard containers' for descriptions of documents.

Metadata

Literally 'data about data', metadata is best understood as short, structured and standardized descriptions of information resources. The term first gained wide use in the 1990s, but the idea had been instantiated in library cataloguing rules in the mid-19th century. For an accessible introduction to metadata principles see Haynes (2004); for more detail of specific formats and schemas see Zeng and Qin (2008), Miller (2011) and Hider (2012).

Metadata records are surrogates for the original items, used in its place. The main purposes for metadata are as means to identify, retrieve, use and manage information resources. This includes: retrieval, finding required items by searching or browsing; display, deciding whether an item is likely to be useful; legal issues, noting the rights status of items; and records management, noting who has responsibility for the document, and when they should be reviewed, archived, etc. It is also desirable that metadata can be shared and exchanged; hence the requirement for standardization.

Metadata has usually been thought of as having two components: *descriptive metadata* and *subject metadata*. These were traditionally instantiated in different physical forms: for example, the distinct 'author/title catalogue' and 'subject catalogue', in libraries using drawers of catalogue cards, but both are now usually subsumed within one metadata format. Descriptive metadata describes the item itself – its title, author, date of publication or creation, physical form, etc. Subject metadata describes the content – what the item is 'about'. Subjects may be described using controlled terms – classification codes, subject headings and so on – or uncontrolled terminology – for example, terms from titles and abstracts. In terms of Popper's '3 Worlds', we can think of descriptive metadata as defining World 1 information objects, while subject metadata defines their World 3 content. Descriptive metadata answers questions such as 'what is this called?', 'who wrote it?', 'how old is it?', 'how big is it?', 'what kind of thing is it?', 'where is it?' Subject metadata answers the question 'what is it about?' The details of descriptive metadata will vary according to the physical nature of the item: e.g. 'how big is it?' will be answered in terms of pages and centimetres for a book, and megabytes for a digital resource. Subject metadata is invariant to physical form, since it describes the intrinsic content, and the same tools are therefore used regardless of form; e.g. the Dewey Decimal Classification, best known for shelf arrangement of books in libraries, is also used in internet directories.

As noted above, metadata records should be relatively short, and must be structured and standardized. By structured is meant, in effect, that a metadata record comprises fields, elements or attributes representing a distinct type of information, e.g. a title, a keyword, or an author name. In this way, we can distinguish records referring things written by Benjamin Disraeli from things written about him.

By standardized is meant that the same information is presented in the same way. Disraeli's name always appears as 'DISRAELI, BENJAMIN', or as 'BENJAMIN DISRAELI', or as 'DISRAELI B'. None is right or wrong, but there should be consistency.

As an aside, we might remember that Disraeli became Lord Beaconsfield in later life, and wrote some books under that name. It is good if our metadata collection has a link between the two. But to make such a link, two kinds of knowledge are needed: the general knowledge that it is possible for one person to have two names; and the specific knowledge that Disraeli/Beaconsfield is such a person. Human experts are good at amassing and using these kinds of knowledge, computers less so. Although automatic metadata creation is highly desirable, particularly to cope with the great quantities of digital information now available, intellectual metadata creation by expert people is still regarded as the best option to get the best quality; even though, as the opening quote from Maurice Line reminds us, even some within the information professions have doubted the mystique which has arisen about some aspects.

Some examples of currently important metadata standards which govern the content and elements of records are briefly noted below, to give an idea of their variety; for more details, see Zeng and Qin (2008) and Miller (2011).

- Machine Readable Cataloguing (MARC) is an exchange format for metadata records created according to the AACR2 and RDA cataloguing codes. In the past, there have been numerous national variants, e.g. USMARC and UKMARC, and international versions, particularly UNIMARC. MARC21 is now emerging as a new de facto international standard. Numbered fields and sub-fields are used to hold the record content.
- Dublin Core (DC) and derivatives – the best known web metadata format, DC was designed as the simplest possible useful metadata format, initially comprising just 15 elements – such as 'title', 'creator', 'subject' and 'format' – with minimal instructions for entering content. It has been expanded since, and numerous variants have been produced. One such is the UK government's e-GMS standard, which expands DC to 23 fields, including some appropriate for government material, such as 'mandate' and 'preservation'.
- Learning Object Metadata (LOM), designed to hold metadata for educational resources at all levels of granularity, from a diagram to a video clip to a textbook, and having a complex set of fields, including educationally specific elements such as 'typical age range' and 'interactivity type'.
- Text Encoding Initiative (TEI), a standard for the representation of texts in

digital form, particularly valuable for digital humanities. A series of tutorials and examples for TEI, 'TEI by example', is available at the time of writing at http://tbe.kantl.be/TBE.
- Metadata Encoding and Transmission Standard (METS), developed by the Library of Congress for archiving digital items; a modular and flexible standard. Metadata Object Description Schema (MODS) is an extension to METS to represent library cataloguing records.
- International Standard for Archival Description (General) (ISAD(G)), a metadata standard providing general guidance for description of archival records.
- Visual Resources Association (VRA) Core, a standard for description of works of visual cultures and images which document them.

These kinds of metadata standards and formats, which permit the creation of records describing information resources, are supported by a variety of languages and standards which allow their encoding and implementation in web environments; this is often seen as a move towards the *semantic web*, to be discussed in the next chapter. An important example is XML, in which several of the standards above, including LOM, METS, MODS and DC variants, are encoded. They are typically expressed as an XML *schema* with a *namespace* denoting the location of components and definitions.

The Resource Description Framework (RDF) is a general metadata model, based on the description of resources as a series of subject-relation-object expressions termed *triples*, very similar to the entity-relation database models discussed in the next chapter. It is regarded as the standard knowledge representation language for the Web. Topic maps are a rather similar kind of formal knowledge representation.

RDF and XML are used to build more specific metadata models, such as the Web Ontology Language (OWL), designed to represent ontologies, and the Simple Knowledge Organization System (SKOS), a model for representing controlled vocabularies such as classification schemes, taxonomies, subject heading lists and thesauri.

For an overview, see Antoniou and van Harmelen (2008), and as examples, see XML used to encode MARC records (Dimic, Milsavljevic and Surla, 2010), and an ontology represented in RDF to create a dataset of the sales of artworks (Allinson, 2012).

We will now look at how the first form of metadata content is provided: the description of an information item.

Resource description and cataloguing
This is the provision of descriptive metadata; presenting the physical form of a

document. The term *cataloguing* still generally refers to library material; *resource description* is more general, and increasingly used. For detailed background on cataloguing, see Bowman (2003) and Welsh and Batley (2012).

Charles Ammi Cutter, the American librarian who was one of the 19th-century originators of modern ideas of resource description, argued that a catalogue should fulfil the following functions (phrased in more modern idiom):

- to allow a user to *find* a resource, for which they know one or more of author, title or subject
- to *show* what resources are available written by particular authors or on specified subjects
- to *help* the user choose the best resource for their needs, by *edition* (date, publisher, etc.) and by *character* (style, level, etc.).

These are still very relevant aims. A commonly quoted set of aims for catalogues of printed libraries was:

- *location* – identifying where particular resources are to be found
- *collocation* – bringing associated works (e.g. by the same author, or on the same subject, or in a series of books or reports) together
- *information* – providing directly some needed information (e.g. a full bibliographic reference, the full name of an author, the exact name of a corporate author).

These are also still relevant, even in a digital environment, if we think of resources being brought together dynamically on screen, rather than physically on a shelf.

These sets of general aims have been expanded into lists of more specific 'principles', which can guide the creation of explicit cataloguing codes, and other protocols for resource description. They also serve the desire for universal bibliographic control, by proving a consistent description for all published documents. See Bowman (2006) for an account of early developments. Most modern library cataloguing codes stem from the influential 'Paris Principles', approved by an international conference on cataloguing principles in 1961. The latest set of such principles is IFLA's 'Statement of International Cataloguing Principles' (ICP), which is inclusive of more types of resource than earlier principles (Tillett and Cristán, 2009); for a commentary on this, see Guerrini (2009).

Cataloguing codes, used in libraries for many decades, include very detailed rules for the precise description of such things as authors' names and editions of a work, and for specification of such things as the names of illustrators and translators, influenced by the need for precise identification of specific printed documents, particularly books, in large collections. The best known of these codes is AACR (Anglo-American Cataloguing Rules). The printed form of the 1998 revision of the second edition of these rules (AACR2) includes 26 chapters over 676 pages: an indication of the necessary complexity of such rules.

AACR is based upon a more general standard, the ISBD (International Standard Bibliographic Description), dating from the early 1970s, which dictates at a more general level what can be said in describing a bibliographic item. This requires the following elements to be specified: title and statement of responsibility ['author']; edition; material, or type of publication ['physical form']; publication, distribution, etc. ['publisher']; physical description [size, etc.]; series; note; standard number and terms of availability. AACR specifies, in considerable detail for consistency, how these are to be expressed.

The limitations of cataloguing codes such as AACR led to the development of the Functional Requirements for Bibliographic Records (FRBR) model, which is beginning to make an impact on cataloguing systems and practices (IFLA, 1998; Zhang and Salaba, 2009). It is based on an entity-relation model, of the kind discussed in the databases section of the next chapter, which shows the relations between different kinds of documents, and their attributes, and the people and organizations which create and disseminate them; an example is shown in Figure 6.1.

As was mentioned in Chapter 4, FRBR distinguishes four levels – work, expression, manifestation, and item – but these are not entirely satisfactorily

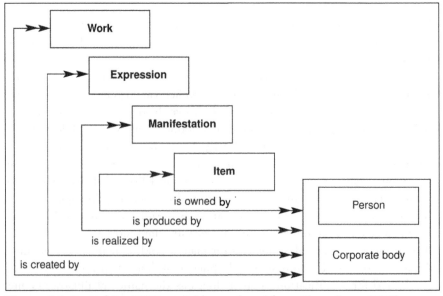

Figure 6.1 *Part of the FRBR model (reproduced from Chowdhury, 2010)*

defined. Nonetheless, there is some evidence that this is a 'natural' way of looking at bibliographic entities (Pisanski and Žumer, 2010), as well as resting on a formal model.

Typically, library cataloguing has allowed searching at the 'manifestation' level, and display of results at the 'item' level. The FRBR model should allow for more flexible search and display, to allow for greater precision – e.g. 'retrieve records for this edition of this book, where there is a copy available for loan in a library to which I have access' – and also with more generality – e.g. everything on Shakespeare's *The Tempest*: the play itself, in its various editions, novels based on it, translations, commentaries, audiobook versions, and film versions, including related films, such as *Forbidden Planet* and *Prospero's Books*.

However, there has been disagreement on how these four levels should be understood, stemming from the basic questions of what is a document (discussed in earlier chapters) and what is a 'work' (Smiraglia, 2001).

FRBR, and the associated Functional Requirements for Authority Data (FRAD), which provides standard forms for the names or people, organizations, works, etc. (Patton, 2009), and Functional Requirements for Subject Authority Data (FRSAD) for subject description (Salaba, Zeng and Žumer, 2011), form the 'conceptual foundation' for the cataloguing standard which is intended to replace AACR2: Resource Description and Access (RDA). It is intended to be used beyond the library world, in the wider collection environment; in museums and archives, for example. For overviews, see Oliver (2010) and Anhalt and Stewart (2012).

Unlike AACR, RDA has been designed around a formal data model, and it avoids the complexity of separate rules for describing different kinds of material. However, it has been designed for compatibility with AACR, so that existing catalogue records need not be modified. It has been criticized from its inception as too much influenced by AACR, and hence stuck in the past; see, for example, Coyle and Hillman (2007). Its implementation was delayed, and it is still uncertain to what extent major libraries and information services will support it in its current form (Anhalt and Stewart, 2012).

We will now look at the tools used for describing subjects; the 'aboutness' of a document. Following the usual convention, we will divide them into *systematic* and *alphabetic* tools; classifications and taxonomies, and subject headings and thesauri, respectively. However, we should note that there is some overlap between the two; classification schemes often have alphabetic indexes, so that the place/s of specific subjects in the scheme can be quickly found, while alphabetic vocabularies which show broader and narrower terms can be drawn out as a taxonomy. We should also note the importance of tools which can map or translate between different vocabularies, linking the way a concept is treated in each. These are sometimes termed *crosswalks*, if they convert between two specific vocabularies or metadata format. There are also *metavocabularies*, which link several vocabularies or terminologies; an example is the Unified Medical Language System (UMLS), which links healthcare vocabularies (Robinson, 2010).

But first, we need to briefly look at a rather imprecisely used term; ontology.

Ontologies

There is no single, generally accepted meaning of 'ontology' within the information sciences. The term, coming from the Greek *ontos*, 'that which exists', has been used, and still is used within philosophy to mean the study of what kinds of things can exist, and how they can be described. It is sometimes used to describe, informally, a general set of things of concern; the ontology of an area in this sense would be the major concepts within it.

The term has been adopted within computer science to mean a formal description of a domain of knowledge, in terms of the entities within it, and their relationships. Understood in this way, many controlled vocabularies – classification schemes, taxonomies and thesauri in particular – would be regarded as ontologies, albeit rather simple ones, and they are often described as such, particularly in the context of the semantic web. The term is sometimes reserved for vocabularies with a rich set of relationships, more than the synonym/hierarchy/associative relations common to retrieval vocabularies. For example, biomedical ontologies use relations such as 'is contained in', 'adjacent to', 'preceded by', 'transformation of', and 'has participant' (Smith et al., 2005).

Systematic vocabularies: classification and taxonomy

Classifications, categorizations and taxonomies are all forms of knowledge organizations which aim to show the relationships between concepts – generally hierarchical relationships – by bringing together terms representing similar meanings. They are therefore referred to as 'systematic' vocabularies: constructed according to a 'system'. For detailed overviews of classification, both theory and practice, see Broughton (2005), Hunter (2009) and Bowker and Star (2000); a very clear brief account of principles, including applications in a web environment, is given by Slavic (2011).

The theory of classification can get very complex (see, for example, Langridge, 1992; Beghtol, 2010; Bowker, 2005; Bowker and Star, 2000; Hjørland and Pedersen, 2005; and Hjørland, 2008b), but some pragmatic points can be stated simply:

- Classification shows the relations between concepts; particularly, though not exclusively, hierarchical concepts.
- Classification is a process of categorizing concepts into mutually exclusive sets, by rational principles of division.
- Particular items can rarely be classified absolutely, but rather on the basis of overall similarity.

To be sensible and usable, a classification must:

- apply to similar things
- give sets similar in nature and size
- apply consistent criteria for division
- apply one criterion at a time.

These principles are always obeyed in formally designed classifications, but may be broken down into simpler taxonomies and categorizations.

All classifications have some form of *notation*; a numeric or alphanumeric code which reflects the structure of the classification, and shows the relationship between its component parts. For example, in the Dewey Decimal Classification the number 425 is used for 'grammar of standard English'. The decimal notation structure shows that this is part of class 420 'English and Old English', itself part of class 400, 'Language'. Classificatory notation has the advantage of being language-independent; a book on a particular topic will have the same notation in any library in the world which uses that classification.

There is some interrelation between systematic and alphabetic vocabularies. An alphabetic indexing vocabulary which shows broader and narrower terms in detail can be displayed as a hierarchical classification, while the 'top terms' of a thesaurus or set of subject headings can be used as a set of broad categories or a taxonomy.

Classification is a similar process to indexing; however, it is usual for just one classification notation to be assigned. This is not strictly necessary, unless the intention of classification is to provide a single place for the physical location of an item. For computerized material, as many classification codes as appropriate can be applied.

The simplest form of systematic vocabulary is a *categorization*, a simple form of classification, with limited structure and detail. 'Broad' categorizations are so called because they include wide subject concepts within each category. These are useful for browsing and for physical arrangement.

They are used in several settings: in libraries, particularly public or school libraries where a simple structure with a high degree of browsability is required, or where fiction is a large component of stock; in bookshops (both in the high street and online); and as an additional search tool in some computerized databases, particularly in the humanities and social sciences. They are also present in many web directories and portals.

These are a simple form of classification, with little or no hierarchical structure, rarely going down more than one level, and often breaking the rules about single principle of division. For example, a bookshop may well have a general category for COOKERY, sub-divided into such things as VEGETARIAN COOKERY, CHINESE COOKERY, MICROWAVE COOKERY, etc. It is unlikely that it would divide to further levels, CHINESE VEGETARIAN COOKERY, etc., and it is unlikely that the shop owner would be worried by the inconsistent division by ingredients, region, cooking instruments etc. Such systems work because they are generally small-scale – browsers in a bookshop can see much of the stock and categories at one glance – and are geared closely to the needs of the users and the nature of the material. The same argument justifies their use for simple navigating access to a collection of digital material.

More complex is a *taxonomy*: a classification devised for a particular environment or set of information. They usually reflect the local conditions closely, and are adapted to the local 'culture'. They are usually modified and extended more frequently than other information organization tools. See Lambe (2007) for an overview of this kind of taxonomy. The term is, of course, also still used in an older sense: a scientific classification of some aspect of the natural world. Taxonomies are usually intellectually constructed, but may be automatically generated. They are a popular tool for organizing digital information resources, always supporting browsing, and sometimes searching as well.

Taxonomies may well 'break the rules' of classification, for example by allowing the same concept to appear at different levels, if this is helpful to the user's browsing. They may be a high-level description of subject matter – for example a 'corporate taxonomy' is a way of expressing the interests of an organization, so as to, for example, organize material on an intranet. This kind of taxonomy may link into a thesaurus for more detailed terminology. Alternatively, taxonomies may include many specific examples – names of places, people or departments, for example, as well as general concept headings – and may have more similarity with a thesaurus than a library classification. They may also include much descriptive information about the concepts and items, and be a kind of information-giving tool. Taxonomies are typically used to give access to diverse forms of materials – databases, documents, e-mails, people – and hence to support knowledge management programmes.

More complex and all-encompassing are the oldest established vocabularies of this kind: *enumerative* classifications, devised for physical arrangement of library materials, and more recently used also for subject retrieval of digital information. Enumerative classifications aim to list completely – to enumerate – all aspects of knowledge within their scope; they are invariably hierarchically arranged, dividing and subdividing knowledge; the Dewey classification, for example, is divided into ten main classes, each class into ten divisions, and each division into ten sections, with further sub-division as needed; its structure at the divisions level (with headings simplified for clarity) is shown in Figure 6.2, typifying this kind of enumerative classification.

They are well suited for arranging large volumes of material, especially when a physical arrangement, with a place for each item, is required, and hence are

Second Summary
The Hundred Divisions

000   **Computer science, knowledge & systems**
010   Bibliographies
020   Library & information sciences
030   Encyclopedias & books of facts
040   [Unassigned]
050   Magazines, journals & serials
060   Associations, organizations & museums
070   News media, journalism & publishing
080   Quotations
090   Manuscripts & rare books

100   **Philosophy**
110   Metaphysics
120   Epistemology
130   Parapsychology & occultism
140   Philosophical schools of thought
150   Psychology
160   Logic
170   Ethics
180   Ancient, medieval & eastern philosophy
190   Modern western philosophy

200   **Religion**
210   Philosophy & theory of religion
220   The Bible
230   Christianity & Christian theology
240   Christian practice & observance
250   Christian pastoral practice & religious orders
260   Christian organization, social work & worship
270   History of Christianity
280   Christian denominations
290   Other religions

300   **Social sciences, sociology & anthropology**
310   Statistics
320   Political science
330   Economics
340   Law
350   Public administration & military science
360   Social problems & social services
370   Education
380   Commerce, etiquette & folklore
390   Customs, etiquette & folklore

400   **Language**
410   Linguistics
420   English & Old English languages
430   German & related languages
440   French & related languages
450   Italian, Romanian & related languages
460   Spanish & Portuguese languages
470   Latin & Italic languages
480   Classical & modern Greek languages
490   Other languages

500   **Science**
510   Mathematics
520   Astronomy
530   Physics
540   Chemistry
550   Earth sciences & geology
560   Fossils & prehistoric life
570   Life sciences; biology
580   Plants (Botany)
590   Animals (Zoology)

600   **Technology**
610   Medicine & health
620   Engineering
630   Agriculture
640   Home & family management
650   Management & public relations
660   Chemical engineering
670   Manufacturing
680   Manufacture for specific uses
690   Building & construction

700   **Arts**
710   Landscaping & area planning
720   Architecture
730   Sculpture, ceramics & metalwork
740   Drawing & decorative arts
750   Painting
760   Graphic arts
770   Photography & computer art
780   Music
790   Sports, games & entertainment

800   **Literature, rhetoric & criticism**
810   American literature in English
820   English & Old English literatures
830   German & related literatures
840   French & related literatures
850   Italian, Romanian & related literatures
860   Spanish & Portuguese literatures
870   Latin & Italic literatures
880   Classical & modern Greek literatures
890   Other literatures

900   **History**
910   Geography & travel
920   Biography & genealogy
930   History of ancient world (to ca. 499)
940   History of Europe
950   History of Asia
960   History of Africa
970   History of North America
980   History of South America
990   History of other areas

Consult schedules for complete and exact headings

Figure 6.2 *Top-level structure of the Dewey classification (reproduced from Bowman, 2005)*

widely used for library classification. They have limitations in dealing with very detailed subject description, and with items involving several concepts; the extent to which they cover all of knowledge has also been critiqued (Zins and Santos, 2011). They are also unsuitable for rapidly changing subject fields, since they cannot be revised frequently. Topics such as 'Internet' and 'AIDS/HIV', which rapidly generated large volumes of literature, caused problems for enumerative classifications, which initially had no place for them. Because they are widely used internationally, their revision is generally in the hands of international committees, which produce revisions of particular sections and subsections at infrequent intervals.

Nonetheless, enumerative classifications are still the main tools for subject description used in library catalogue records, and are used for organizing internet resources in some web portals.

The best-known and most widely used examples are: the Dewey Decimal Classification (DDC), devised by the American librarian Melville Dewey and first published in 1876; the Universal Decimal Classification (UDC), first created in 1905 by the documentalists Paul Otlet and Henri La Fontaine, who have been mentioned in previous chapters, as an extension of Dewey's scheme; and the Library of Congress Classification (LCC), devised by that library, and begun in 1901. They have all undergone continual revision; Dewey, for example, is now in its 22nd edition. Even so, they show their origins: for example, Dewey's main structure shown above reflects both the 19th-century Western world, and the 'liberal arts' setting in which it was created. Although all widely used enumerative classifications have been updated in detail, major restructuring is unpopular because of the upheaval which would be caused to large libraries which use them for physical arrangement of material. For detailed treatment of the Dewey classification, see Bowman (2005), Chan (2007, Chapter 13) and Satija (2007).

Dewey, and particularly UDC, which was designed to deal better with detailed analysis of technical material than Dewey, have acquired a 'synthetic' or 'number building' facility in recent editions. Rather than list (enumerate) notations for every possible concept, notations can be built up. This capacity was present from the start, with tables of subdivisions, for types of materials, time periods and geographical areas, which could be linked to class numbers. This can be taken further by combining subjects. To give a simple example, to classify a book on 'agricultural research in Japan' in Dewey, we would first decide that the main concept was 'agriculture' to be qualified by the concepts of 'research' and 'Japan', the latter two taken from tables of general concepts, applicable in many cases. So, since agriculture has the notation 630, research is 072, and Japan is 052, we can construct the class number:

630.72052   agricultural research in Japan

UDC goes further than this, in that whole sections of the classification are 'synthetic', allowing class numbers to be built up as needed. In this way, the enumerative classifications are adopting some of the nature of faceted classifications, discussed later. For accounts of the UDC and its recent development, see McIlwaine (1997) and Slavic, Cordeiro and Riesthuis (2008).

The 'purest' example of a large enumerative classification is the Library of Congress Classification (LCC), which has limited synthetic capabilities. Despite this, and the fact that it is designed by and for one specific national library, it is increasingly popular in academic libraries worldwide, while the National Library of Medicine classification, effectively a sub-set of LCC, is widely used in healthcare libraries; in the UK, a local variant, the Wessex classification, is generally used. LCC provides very detailed, sometimes idiosyncratic, subject listings, based upon enumeration within 19 major classes, e.g. H for social sciences and R for medicine, giving entries such as:

HQ9261   reform and reclamation of adult prisoners
R601-602   food and food supply in relation to public health

For a detailed account of LCC, see Chan (2007, Chapter 14).

Finally, *analytico-synthetic* classifications, commonly termed faceted classifications, are designed to classify complex material, at a high level of subject specification. Terminology is grouped into related concepts by facet analysis (hence analytic), from which the classification for any item can be constructed (hence synthetic); these classifications can then cope with new concepts, in a way in which enumerative schemes cannot (although, as noted above, the enumerative schemes are gaining synthetic capabilities).

Faceted classifications were devised by the Indian librarian S. R. Ranganathan in the 1930s. Ranganathan's Colon Classification (named for the punctuation mark which characterizes its notation), the first universal classification of this type, has been little used outside the Indian subcontinent; for an overview of this scheme, see Satija and Singh (2010). Ranganathan's ideas led to the creation of many faceted classification schemes in specific subject areas, particularly in science, technology and social sciences. This type of scheme was very popular during the 1950s and 60s for classifying specialized or technical material, particularly in systems using techniques of mechanized documentation and, later, early applications of computers.

They rapidly lost popularity, however, because of their perceived complexity and difficulty of use – their notations are certainly unfriendly to the casual user, they are not well suited for physical arrangement of material, and they are relatively little used today. The only major scheme of this sort, apart from the Colon Classification, still under development is the second edition of the Bliss

Classification (BC2); the first edition was an enumerative scheme, and was entirely revised. This is regarded as an influential and theoretically sound scheme, but again has little practical use (Broughton, 2010).

We now move to the second major type of controlled vocabulary; alphabetic.

Alphabetic vocabularies: subject headings and thesauri

There are several kinds of alphabetic controlled vocabularies in which the terms – words or phrases – are arranged in alphabetical order. There are no well defined distinctions between them; in general, the distinction lies in how much information is provided about each term, including term definitions and inter-relations.

Keyword lists are the simplest form of alphabetic controlled vocabulary. Often they consist of nothing more than a list of 'approved terms'; sometimes they include synonyms. They are a simple and cheap form of terminology to develop and use, but are very limited in their usefulness, and applicable only to small files and unsophisticated users.

Subject headings are lists of terms – often quite lengthy to represent complex concepts – which are used for indexing for retrieval, and sometimes browsing. They will generally include synonyms, and sometimes hierarchical and 'SEE ALSO' relations. Complex subject heading lists can be very similar to thesauri. On the other hand, the simpler forms are little more than lists of keywords. They are most commonly used in situations where only one heading, or only a few, are added to each record, e.g. library databases and bibliographies.

The Library of Congress Subject Headings (LCSH) is the most widely known and widely used terminology of this sort; it provides subject indexing in many library databases, and increasingly in digital environments. A very large vocabulary, first published in 1914, it has over 270,000 terms, covering all subject areas. Examples of terms are:

Halloween cookery
Snails as carriers of disease
Overweight women in art
Electronic reserve collections in libraries
Virus diseases in children
Church work with the baby boom generation
Space flight on postage stamps.

These examples illustrate the way in which these headings link together several concepts. For a detailed overview of LCSH, see Broughton (2012), and for explanations of its applicability in digital resources see Walsh (2011) and Yi and Chan (2010).

Thesauri are of particular importance, as they are a sophisticated form of terminology, which can be very powerful in giving effective access to digital information; they are also the only retrieval terminology defined by national and international standards, though not all vocabularies called thesauri observe their prescriptions. For detailed coverage of thesauri, see Broughton (2006b) and – sound on the principles though dated in detail – Aitchison, Gilchrist and Bawden (2000).

Thesauri are listings of terms with inter-term relations shown. There are various relations which may be used, but the standard set (that is, literally, the set defined by the relevant international standards: ISO 2788 for monolingual thesauri) is:

SY   synonym
BT   broader term
NT   narrower term
RT   related term

Another useful relation is 'Top Term' or 'Heading Parent', identifying the hierarchy in which the term occurs.

One of the set of synonyms will be a 'preferred term', giving an unsymmetrical USE/USE FOR relation. All the other relations are generally symmetric. The standard also requires *scope notes*, notes giving definitions or explanations of terms, and/or prescribing their use in indexing. An example of a term in thesaurus form is shown in Figure 6.3 on the next page.

Thesauri have generally been used for both indexing and searching, but they may also be used in the form of an 'indexing thesaurus' (to provide extra terms to aid free-text searching) or a 'search thesaurus' (to suggest extra terms for a searcher to use in querying a full-text database).

The process of constructing a thesaurus involves an initial analysis of the subject area, in the same way that would be used to construct a faceted classification; indeed a thesaurus and a classification can be two 'faces' of the same scheme. More usually, the classification structure is used simply as a framework to derive the terms with their interrelationships that will form the thesaurus.

Having reviewed methods for describing resources and their subject content, we conclude this chapter by looking at two long-established ways of organizing and controlling information; the writing of abstracts and summaries of lengthy items, and the indexing of documents and collections.

Abstracting

An abstract is 'a brief but accurate representation of the contents of a document'

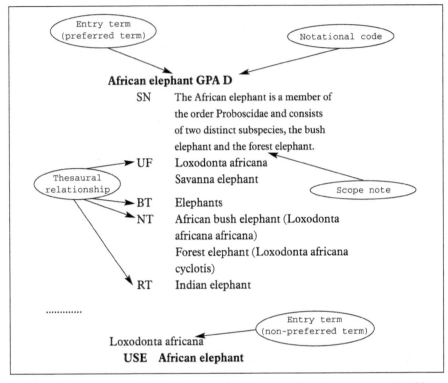

Figure 6.3 *Example of thesaurus term (reproduced from Broughton, 2006b)*

(Lancaster, 2003) or, more formally according to the relevant ISO standard 'an abbreviated, accurate representation of the contents of a document, without added interpretation or criticism and without distinction as to who wrote the abstract'.

Abstracting has a long history; summaries of articles have been used as means of keeping up with the scientific, medical and professional literature in particular for many years. Borko and Bernier (1975) suggest that its origins can be traced back to classical times, with the first recognizable abstracting journals, and sections for abstracts in general journals, dating from the 17th century, their use expanding greatly in the 19th century, together with the creation of subject-specialist abstracting and indexing services such as Index Medicus and Chemical Abstracts. For overviews, apart from the book by Borko and Bernier, see Chowdhury (2010, Chapter 8) and Koltay (2010); Alonso and Fernandez (2010) give a conceptual model for studying abstracts and abstracting.

Abstracts may vary in a number of respects, and so may be categorized differently. A fundamental difference is whether they are *informative*, intended to give sufficient information to be a replacement for the original, or *indicative*, giving just enough information for a reader to decide whether the item is of interest. They also vary:

- by length, from the verbose and 'literary' to the terse and 'telegraphic'
- by the extent of criticism and interpretation of the original
- by the extent to which they are 'targeted' or 'slanted' to a particular interest, or type of user, as against attempting to be balanced and objective.

The writing of abstracts is governed by international standard: ISO 214 (1976) 'Abstracts for publications and documentation'. Publishers and database producers also have *de facto* standards; see, for example, Montesi and Owen (2007). There is a general tendency for abstracts to become more 'structured', with a consistent set of elements which are present. There still remains debate about the most effective ways to make abstracts useful; see, for example, Hartley and Betts (2008, 2009), Zhang and Liu (2011) and Ripple et al. (2011). This is of particular importance as more reliance is placed on abstracts because of information overload (Nicholas, Huntington and Jamali, 2007). This is potentially troubling, as studies have shown that typically 20% of abstracts contain significant inaccuracies – usually presenting the subject matter of the main document in an unreasonably positive light.

Automatic abstracting has been a goal for many years, since the first research on the topic, carried out by H. P. Luhn in the late 1950s. Much effort has been expended since then on the design of systems, using a variety of approaches to automatic abstracting and summarizing: see Chowdhury (2010) for an overview. Nonetheless, most practical abstracting within information systems and services is still largely an intellectual task.

Indexing and tagging

An index is usually understood as a systematic arrangement of entries designed to enable users to locate information in a document, or in a collection of documents. The process of producing such an index is 'indexing', and those who do it are 'indexers'; it is governed by international standards ISO 5963 (1985) 'Examining documents, determining their subjects and selecting index terms' and ISO 999 (1996) 'Guidelines for the content, organization and presentation of indexes'. The classic text on the indexing process is Lancaster (2003); for a review of the theoretical and historical background, see Weinberg (2009).

It is usually taken to mean the assignment of a number of terms from an alphabetic vocabulary, by contrast with classifying, where a systematic vocabulary is used. If no controlled vocabulary is used, the process is called 'free term indexing'. While this is likely to capture very precise and up-to-date terminology, the use of isolated keywords means that no semantic relations between terms can be made visible. Free keywording has attracted interest recently, as 'folksonomy' or 'social tagging', whereby internet materials, such as web pages, photographs, videos and catalogue records for books, are freely indexed by users (Ding et al., 2009; Mai, 2011; Park, 2011; Voorbij, 2012). The long-term usefulness of this, and how it might be combined with, or complement, traditional intellectual indexing, is unclear. One response from information practitioners has been to look for ways to combine tagging with controlled vocabulary structures; see, for example, Šauperl (2010) for the UDC, and Yi and Chan (2009) for LCSH .

There are many types of index: 'back of the book' indexes; indexes of the content of a journal issue or volume; cumulative indexes to journals, newspaper and magazines; database indexes; and indexes to pages on internet or intranet sites. An index may be to a *collection of items*, e.g. indexing a database, an intranet, or an Internet directory, or to a *single item*, e.g. indexing the contexts of a book, or a report, or a volume of a journal. In the case of collections, the index directs users to a particular item within the collection. In the single item case, the index 'points to' a page or a section within the item.

The basic principles in the production of any index – the 'indexing process' – are largely the same, regardless of the type of index. Indexing is a process of firstly deciding what the item being indexed is about ('content analysis') and then deciding how best to represent this 'aboutness' ('term selection'). The indexer must identify abstract concepts, and then match these with appropriate terms. This may be contrasted with the simple automatic indexing of full-text, in which terms are selected from the document on the basis of concordance (all words are chosen), statistical analysis (terms which occur relatively frequently are chosen) or positional analysis (terms in the title, abstract, first paragraph, etc. are chosen) This latter approach can be done perfectly well by machine, since it deals simply with text strings, with no identification of underlying concepts. It is this concept analysis which makes indexing an intellectual process. The justification for continuing to use human, intellectual indexing, rather than the much cheaper automatic indexing, is that human analysis gives an index which is more useful and usable. Though not particularly consistent: many studies have shown that the best degree of consistency which can be obtained between human indexers does not exceed 50%.

Intellectual indexing is claimed to have a number of significant advantages over full-text searching, or production of concordances by computer – which amounts to the same thing – in addition to concept analysis. The human indexer can deal readily with:

homographs – words which are spelt the same, but have different meanings;

synonyms – different words with the same meaning;

inferences – where the main subject word is implied, but never used;

and with the difference between significant and trivial 'passing' mentions of a word.

Automatic indexing systems, although becoming much more capable, have problems with all these aspects. A variety of software systems is available, to produce indexes automatically or to aid the human indexer, such as Cindex, Macrex and Sky Index (Coates, 2009).

Intellectual indexing of a particular document can be regarded as a three-stage process:

- understanding of the content: the indexer decides what the document is 'about'
- analysis of the content: the indexer decides which concepts are to be indexed, and to what depth
- translation of concepts into indexing terms: the indexer chooses the most appropriate terms from the alphabetic vocabulary being used (e.g. a thesaurus or list of subject headings).

The two generally accepted principles of indexing are:

- include all concepts thought to be of interest to users of the index
- index at the most specific level that the indexing vocabulary allows.

These are rather general ideas; the indexer has to interpret them. The two main criteria for indexing are:

- exhaustivity: the extent to which all possible concepts are included
- depth: the degree of specificity with which concepts are described.

Indexing which is both exhaustive and deep is usually regarded as the 'gold standard', but the other three possibilities (deep but not exhaustive, etc.) may be appropriate in different circumstances.

Summary

Tools for information organization have changed slowly; some of these used today, more than a century after they were first introduced, would seem familiar to Melville Dewey and Anthony Panizzi. The dramatic changes in the technical means by which documents are created and disseminated has not been matched by the intellectual means by which they are managed. Whether automated methods will be devised to do the same job as current tools, and whether folksonomies and the like will prove effective in the long term, remains to be seen.

- Information organization remains at the heart of information science, its importance enhanced in new information environments
- New forms of descriptive metadata have emerged to deal with new forms of document, while subject description has been little altered.
- The right balance between expert human input, automated processes, and social tagging has yet to be established
- Long-established theories and concepts remain important, despite technical advances

---

Key readings

Elaine Svenonius, *The intellectual foundation of information organization*, Cambridge MA: MIT Press, 2000.

[A thorough treatment of basic issues.]

Grigoris Antoniou and Frank van Harmelen (2008) *A semantic web primer* (2nd edn), Cambridge MA: MIT Press.

[Accessible analysis of the new forms of information organization.]

References

Aitchison, J., Gilchrist, A. and Bawden, D. (2000) *Thesaurus construction and use: a practical manual* (4th edition), London: Aslib.

Allinson, J. (2012) OpenART: open metadata for art research at the Tate, *Bulletin of the American Society for Information Science and Technology*, 38(3), 43–8.

Alonso, M. I. and Fernandez, L. M. (2010) Perspectives of studies on document abstracting: towards an integrated view of models and theoretical approaches, *Journal of Documentation*, 66(4), 563–84.

Anhalt, J. and Stewart, R. A. (2012) RDA simplified, *Cataloging and Classification Quarterly*, 50(1), 33–42.

Antoniou, G. and van Harmelen, F. (2008) *A semantic web primer* (2nd edn), Cambridge MA: MIT Press.

Ayre, C., Smith, I. A. and Cleeve, M. (2006) Electronic library glossaries: jargonbusting essentials or wasted resource?, *Electronic Library*, 24(2), 126–34.

Beghtol, C. (2010) Classification theory, *Encyclopedia of Library and Information Sciences* (3rd edn), Abingdon: Taylor & Francis, 1045–60.

Borko, H. and Bernier, C. L. (1975) *Abstracting concepts and methods*, New York NY: Academic Press.

Bowker, G. C. (2005) *Memory practices in the sciences*, Cambridge MA: MIT Press.

Bowker, G. C. and Star, S. L. (2000) *Sorting things out: classification and its consequences*, Cambridge MA: MIT Press.

Bowman, J. (2003) *Essential cataloguing*, London: Facet Publishing.

Bowman, J. (2005) *Essential Dewey*, London: Facet Publishing.

Bowman, J. H. (2006) The development of description in cataloguing prior to ISBD, *Aslib Proceedings*, 58(1/2), 34–48.

Broughton, V. (2005) *Essential classification*, London: Facet Publishing.

Broughton, V. (2006a) The need for a faceted classification as the basis of all methods of information retrieval, *Aslib Proceedings*, 58(1), 49–72.

Broughton, V. (2006b) *Essential thesaurus construction*, London: Facet Publishing.

Broughton, V. (2010) *Bliss Bibliographic Classification Second Edition, Encyclopedia of Library and Information Sciences*, Abingdon: Taylor & Francis, 1:1, 650–9.

Broughton, V. (2012) *Essential Library of Congress Subject Headings*, London: Facet Publishing.

Buckland, M.K. (2008) Reference library service in the digital environment, *Library and Information Science Research*, 30(2), 81–5.

Cassell, K. A. and Hiremath, U. (2011) *Reference services in the 21st century* (2nd edn revised), London: Facet Publishing.

Chan, L. M. (2007) *Cataloguing and classification: an introduction* (3rd edn), Lanham MD: Scarecrow Press.

Chowdhury, G. G. (2010) *Introduction to modern information retrieval* (3rd edn), London: Facet Publishing.

Chowdhury, G. G. and Chowdhury, S. (2007) *Organizing information: from the shelf to the web*, London: Facet Publishing.

Coates, S. (2009) Software solutions, *Indexer*, 27(4), 168–72.

Coyle, K. and Hillman, D. (2007) Resource Description and Access (RDA). Cataloguing Rules for the 20th Century [sic], *D-LIB Magazine*, 13(1/2), Jan/Feb 2007, available from: http://www.dlib.org/dlib/january07/coyle/01coyle.html.

Dimic, B., Milsavljevic, B. and Surla, D. (2010) XML schema for UNIMARC and MARC21, *Electronic Library*, 28(2), 245–262.

Ding, Y., Jacob, E. K., Zhang, Z., Foo, S., Yan, E., George, N. L. and Guo, L. (2009) Perspectives on social tagging, *Journal of the American Society for Information Science and Technology*, 60(12), 2388–2401.

Guerrini, M. (2009) In praise of the unfinished: the IFLA Statement of International Cataloguing Principles 2009, *Cataloguing and Classification Quarterly*, 47(8), 722–40.

Hartley, J. and Betts, L. (2008) Revising and polishing a structured abstract: is it worth the time and effort? *Journal of the American Society for Information Science and Technology*, 59(12), 1870–7.

Hartley, J. and Betts, L. (2009) Common weaknesses in traditional abstracts in the social sciences, *Journal of the American Society for Information Science and Technology*, 60(10), 2010–18.

Haynes, D. (2004) *Metadata for information management and retrieval*, London: Facet Publishing.

Heidorn, P. B. (2011) Biodiversity informatics, *Bulletin of the American Society for Information Science and Technology*, 37(6), 38–44.

Hider, P. (2012) *Information resource description: creating and managing metadata*, London: Facet Publishing.

Hitchens, H. (2005) *Dr Johnson's Dictionary – the extraordinary story of the book that defined the world*, London: John Murray.

Hjørland, B. (2003) Fundamentals of knowledge organization, *Knowledge Organization*, 30(2), 87–111 .

Hjørland, B. (2008a) What is knowledge organization (KO)?, *Knowledge Organization*, 35(2/3), 86–101.

Hjørland, B. (2008b) Core classification theory: a reply to Szostak, *Journal of Documentation*, 64(3), 333–42.

Hjørland, B. (2009) Concept theory, *Journal of the American Society for Information Science and Technology*, 60(8), 1519–36.

Hjørland, B. (2011) The importance of theories of knowledge: indexing and information retrieval as an example, *Journal of the American Society for Information Science and Technology*, 62(1), 72–7.

Hjørland, B. and Pedersen, K. N. (2005) A substantive theory of classification for information retrieval, *Journal of Documentation*, 61(5), 582–97.

Hjørland, B. and Shaw, R. (2010) Concepts: classes and colligation, *Bulletin of the American Society for Information Science and Technology*, 36(3), 2–4, available from http://www.asis.org/Bulletin/Feb10/Bulletin_FebMar10_Final.pdf.

Hüllen, W. (2004) *A history of Roget's Thesaurus: origins, development and design*, Oxford: Oxford University Press.

Hunter, E. J. (2009) *Classification made simple* (3rd edn), Aldershot: Ashgate.

IFLA (1998) Functional Requirements for Bibliographic Records, produced by the IFLA, Study Group on the Functional Requirements for Bibliographic Records, Munich: K. G. Saur: available from http://www.ifla.org/VII/s13/frbr/frbr.pdf.

Koltay, T. (2010) *Abstracts and abstracting: a genre and skills for the 21st century*, Oxford: Chandos.

La Barre, K. (2010) Facet analysis, *Annual Review of Information Science and Technology*, 44, 243–86.

Lambe, P. (2007) *Organizing knowledge: taxonomies, knowledge and organisational effectiveness*, Oxford: Chandos.

Lancaster, F. W. (2003) *Indexing and abstracting in theory and practice* (3rd edn), London: Facet Publishing .

Langridge, D. W. (1992) *Classification: its kinds, systems, elements, and applications*, London: Bowker-Saur.

Leigh, G. J. (2011) *Principles of Chemical Nomenclature 2011: a guide to IUPAC recommendations*, London: Royal Society of Chemistry.

Mai, J-E. (2011) Folksonomies and the new order: authority in the digital disorder, *Knowledge Organization*, 38(2), 114–22.

McIlwaine, I. C. (1997) The Universal Decimal Classification: some factors concerning its origins, development and influence, *Journal of the American Society for Information Science*, 48(4), 331–9.

Mersky, R. M. (2004) The evolution and impact of legal dictionaries, *Legal Reference Services Quarterly*, 23(1), 19–35.

Miller, S. J. (2011) *Metadata for digital collections: a how-to-do-it manual*, London: Facet Publishing.

Montesi, M. and Owen, J. M. (2007) Revision of author abstracts: how it is carried out by LISA editors, *Aslib Proceedings*, 5991, 26–45.

Mugglestone, L. (2005) *Lost for words: the hidden history of the Oxford English Dictionary*, New Haven CT: Yale University Press.

Mugglestone, L. (2011) *Dictionaries: a very short introduction*, Oxford: Oxford University Press.

Nicholas, D., Huntington, P. and Jamali, H. R. (2007) The use, users, and role of abstracts in the digital scholarly environment. *Journal of Academic Librarianship*, 33(4), 446–53.

Oliver, C. (2010) *Introducing RDA: a guide to the basics*, London: Facet Publishing.

Park, H. (2011) A conceptual framework to study folksonomic interaction, *Knowledge organization*, 38(6), 515–29.

Patton, G. E. (ed.) (2009) *Functional requirements for authority data: a conceptual model*, Munich: K. G. Saur.

Pisanski, J. and Žumer, M. (2010) Mental models of the bibliographic universe. Part 1: mental models of descriptions, *Journal of Documentation*, 66(5), 643–67.

Ripple, A. M., Mork, J. G., Knecht, L. S. and Humphries, B. L. (2011) A retrospective cohort study of structured abstracts in MEDLINE, 1992–2006, *Journal of the Medical Library Association*, 99(2), 160–2.

Robinson, L. (2010) *Understanding healthcare information*, London: Facet Publishing.

Salaba, A., Zeng, M. L. and Žumer, M. (eds) (2011) *Functional requirements for subject authority data (FRSAD): a conceptual model*, Munich: de Gruyter.

Satija, M. P. (2007) *The theory and practice of the Dewey Decimal Classification system*, Oxford: Chandos.

Satija, M.P. and Singh, J. (2010) Colon Classification (CC), *Encyclopedia of Library and Information Sciences* (3rd edn), Abingdon: Taylor & Francis, 1:1, 1158–68.

Šauperl, A. (2010) UDC and folksonomies, *Knowledge Organization*, 37(4), 307–17.

Slavic, A. (2011) Classification revisited: a web of knowledge, in Foster, A. and Rafferty, P. (eds), *Innovations in information retrieval*, London: Facet Publishing, pp 23–48.

Slavic, A., Cordeiro, M. I. and Riesthuis, G. (2008) Maintenance of the Universal

Decimal Classification: overview of the past and preparation for the future, *International Cataloguing and Bibliographical Control*, 37(2), 23–9.

Smiraglia, R. P. (2001) *The nature of a work: implications for the organization of knowledge*, Lanham MD: Scarecrow Press.

Smith, B., Ceusters, W., Klagges, B., Köhler, J., Kumar, A., Lomax, J., Mungall, C., Neuhaus, F., Rector, A. L. and Rosse, C. (2005) Relations in biomedical ontologies, *Genone Biology*, 6(5):r46 [online] available at http://genomebiology.com/content/pdf/gb-2005-6-5-r46.pdf.

Svenonious, E. (2000) *The intellectual foundation of information organization*, Cambridge MA: MIT Press.

Tackabery, M. K. (2005) Defining glossaries, *Technical Communication*, 52(4), 427–33.

Taylor, A. G. (2004) *The organization of information* (2nd edn), Santa Barbara CA: Libraries Unlimited.

Tennis, J. T. (2008) Epistemology, theory and methodology in knowledge organization: towards a classification, metatheory and research framework, *Knowledge Organization*, 35(2/3), 102–12.

Tillett, B. B. and Cristán, A. L (2009) *IFLA cataloguing principles: the statement of international cataloguing principles (ICP) and its glossary in 20 languages*, Munich: K. G. Saur. Also available online at http://www.ifla.org/publications/statement-of-international-cataloguing-principles.

Voorbij, H. (2012) The value of LibraryThing tags for academic libraries, *Online Information Review*, 36(2) [online EarlyCite file.].

Walsh, J. (2011) The use of Library of Congress Subject Headings in digital collections, *Library Review*, 60(4), 328–43.

Weinberg, B. H. (2009) Indexing: history and theory, *Encyclopedia of Library and Information Sciences* (3rd edn), Abingdon: Taylor & Francis, 1:1, 2277–90.

Welsh, A. and Batley, S. (2012) *Practical cataloguing: AACR, RDA and MARC21*, London: Facet Publishing.

Yi, K. and Chan, M. L. (2009) Linking folksonomy to Library of Congress subject headings: an exploratory study, *Journal of Documentation*, 65(6), 872–900.

Yi, K. and Chan, L. M. (2010) Revisiting the syntactical and structural analysis of Library of Congress Subject Headings for the digital environment, *Journal of the American Society for Information Science and Technology*, 61(4), 677–87.

Zeng, M. L. and Qin, J. (2008) *Metadata*, London: Facet Publishing.

Zhang, C.and Liu, X. (2011) Review of James Hartley's research on structured abstracts, *Journal of Information Science*, 37(6), 570–6.

Zhang, Y. and Salaba, A. (2009) *Implementing FRBR in libraries: key issues and future directions*, New York NY: Neal-Schuman.

Zins, C. and Santos, P. (2011) Mapping the knowledge covered by library classification schemes, *Journal of the American Society for Information Science and Technology*, 62(5), 877–901.

CHAPTER 7

Information technologies: creation, dissemination and retrieval

The change from atoms to bits is irrevocable and unstoppable ... Computing is not about computers any more. It is about living.

Nicholas Negroponte (1995, 4 and 6)

As more information is represented digitally, human-computer interaction (HCI) broadly defined, becomes more central to information science.

Jonathan Grudin (2011, 369)

Introduction

In this chapter, we will give an overview of the information technologies which underlie the information sciences, and some of the more important application areas. This is obviously a very wide area, and whole books are written about many of the topics within it. We shall attempt no more than to mention and briefly discuss each of the topics within this area and give references to where more details can be found. Our aim is simply to give an overall picture of what technologies are important to the information scientist and how they relate to one another. Many readers will be familiar with much of this material and we ask them to consider this a refresher course.

We will look initially at the nature of technology generally, and information technology in particular, setting the scene for what follows. We will then examine the nature of digital computers and their software systems, the networks which connect them, some of the new physical forms they are taking, and some ideas of the future of computing. We will cover the ways in which people interact with computers, and the ways in which IT systems are envisaged and designed. Finally we consider some of the important applications – particularly information retrieval and digital libraries – showing how they can be understood as following and facilitating the communication chain.

What are information technologies?

'Technology', from the Greek *techné*, meaning art, skill or craft, is usually taken to mean the understanding of how to use tools, in the broadest sense of the word.

The term *information technology* was first used in the 1950s, to describe the application of mechanized documentation and the new digital computers, but it came to be widely used in the 1980s to describe the much wider spread use of computers, particularly the first personal computers, and of the computer networks which pre-dated the internet. Early in that decade, Peter Zorkoczy (1982, 3), in one of the earliest books devoted to the subject, commented that the phrase was 'a relatively recent and perhaps not particularly well chosen addition to the English language'. Pointing to the various ways in which the term was understood, he declined to give an exact definition; we will follow his example.

The concept of information technology is usually associated with computers and networks. But, in a wider sense stemming from the original meaning of the word, the technologies of information include all the tools and machines which have been used to assist the creation and dissemination of information throughout history, as discussed in Chapter 2; from ink and paper, through printing, to mechanized documentation technologies and the photocopier. Ben Shneiderman (2003) gives a thoughtful mediation on the nature of information technology, and its empowering effects, while Nicholas Negroponte (1995) provides an early, and very prescient, account of the impacts of IT; Markus Krajewski (2011) examines the idea of card index files as a 'universal paper machine', the forerunner of the computer.

While not ignoring the past and present significance of these, we will focus here on digital technologies. In doing so, we take the view expressed by Paul Gilster, whom we will meet again in Chapter 13, to the effect that all information today is digital, has been digital, or may be digital. And, pragmatically, digital technologies are more complex and rapidly changing than others.

This last point is summed up well by Moore's Law, which states that the number of components which can be placed inexpensively into the integrated circuits which are the basis of all modern digital devices roughly doubles every two years. This means that processing speed, storage capacity, and other metrics of computer power also increase at the same rate.

Impressive though this is, advances in information technology are not due to this alone. Largely as a result of these advances, digital devices have become more interconnected with each other, more integrated into other sorts of equipment and product, much smaller, and more pervasive, affecting all aspects of life and work which have any information component. With this background, we will now look in outline at the digital technologies which have affected all aspects of the communication chain over the past decades.

Digital technologies

We will describe these aspects only in outline; see Ince (2011) and White and Downs (2007) for more detailed but still accessible accounts, and for a readable account of the historical development of the digital computer see Hally (2005).

Any digital device represents data in the form of *binary digits* or *bits*. Patterns of bits may represent data or instructions. A collection of eight bits is known as a *byte*. Quantities of data are represented as multiples of bytes, for example:

kilobyte	one thousand	(10^3) bytes
megabyte	one million	(10^6) bytes
gigabyte	one billion	(10^9) bytes

There is an older convention, based on binary notation which was rather different. A kilobyte would be defined as 10^2 bytes, i.e. 1024 bytes, rather then 1000. A gigabyte, under this understanding, is actually 1,073,741,824 bytes. These variants have now been renamed kibibytes, mebibytes and gibibytes by the standards authorities, but the ambiguity persists.

Any character or symbol may be represented in binary notation, but this requires an agreed coding. The most widely used code since the beginning of the computer age has been the American National Standards Institute's ASCII (American Standard Code for Information Interchange) code, but it is limited to the Latin alphabet, Arabic numerals and a few other symbols. It is being supplanted by Unicode, which can handle a wider variety of symbols and scripts. It can do this by having a long coding string, up to 32 bits, while ASCII is restricted to 7 bits; the more bits in the code, the more different symbols can be coded. Codes provide arbitrary representations of characters; for example, the ASCII code for the letter L is 1001100.

The basic architecture of the digital computer has not changed since it was set out by John von Neumann, shown in Figure 7.1 on the next page with an early working computer, in 1945. A Hungarian-born mathematician and physicist, von Neumann spent most of his life in the USA, working on a variety of topics, including nuclear physics, quantum mechanics, game theory, information theory and – not least – the fundamentals of computing. His design, which gave the first formal description of a single-memory stored-program computer, is shown, in a modernized form, in Figure 7.2 (on page 135). This is generally referred to as the von Neumann architecture, although he clearly drew from his collaborations with other US computer pioneers, such as Presper Eckert and John Mauchly.

This architecture is general-purpose, in the sense that it can run a variety of programs. This distinguishes it from special-purpose digital computers which carry out only one task; there, are several such computers, for example, in the

Figure 7.1 *John von Neumann with the computer of the Institute of Advanced Study (Alan Richards photographer. From The Shelby White and Leon Levy Archives Center, Institute for Advanced Study, Princeton, NJ, USA)*

appliances in most kitchens in the developed world and several in any modern car. A von Neumann machine loads and runs programs as necessary, to accomplish very different tasks. Ince (2011, 6–7) expresses this in words, to give a working definition of a computer:

> A computer contains one or more processors which operate on data. The processor(s) are connected to data storage. The intentions of a human operator are conveyed to the computer via a number of input devices. The result of any computation carried out by the processor(s) will be shown on a number of display devices.

The heart of the computer, the *processor*, often referred to as the *central processing unit (CPU)*, carries out a set of very basic arithmetic and logical operations with instructions and data pulled in from the *memory*, also referred to as *main* or *working* memory. This sequence is referred to as the *fetch-execute cycle*. Two components of the processor are sometimes distinguished: an *arithmetic and logic*

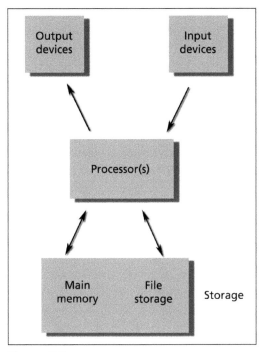

Figure 7.2
Von Neumann architecture (Reproduced from Ince, 2011, by permission of Oxford University Press)

unit, which carries out the operations, and a *control unit*, which governs the operations of the cycle.

While programs and data are being used, they are kept in the memory. While they are not being used, they are stored long-term in the *file storage*. Items in memory are accessible much more rapidly than items in file storage. Memory is much more expensive, so computers have much more file storage than memory; the computers on which this book was written have 1 and 2 gigabytes of memory and 75 and 250 gigabytes of file storage respectively. Although these are much larger than the memory and file storage on computers of past years, the principle remains the same. For example, the IBM XT personal computer, introduced in 1983, had 256 kilobytes of memory and 10 megabytes of file storage.

Data comes into the computer through its *input devices* and is sent into the outside world through the *output devices*. The components are linked together through circuits usually denoted as a *bus*, sometimes referred to more specifically as a *data bus* or an *address bus*.

All of these components have undergone considerable change since the first computers were designed. Processor design has gone through three main technological stages. The so-called 'first generation' of computers used valves as processor components, and the 'second generation' used transistors. Computers of the 'third generation', including all present-day computers, use circuits on 'silicon chips', using methods of very-large-scale integration (VLSI), which allows millions of components to be placed on a single computer chip; see Ince (2011) for a readable introduction to this technology. The tangible result of this has been a great increase in processing speed, typically measured as the number of instructions per second; the computer on which these words are being typed has a processor speed of 2 Gigahertz, meaning two billion instructions per second.

The storage elements of the computer's memory comprise regular arrays of silicon-based units, each holding a bit of data, and created using the same VLSI methods as processors. Earlier generations of computers used so-called 'core storage', with data held on tiny magnetized elements arranged in a three-dimensional lattice; again each element held one bit of data.

File storage, holding data and programs that are not needed immediately, has always used magnetic media, which can hold large volumes of data cheaply, provided quick access is not required. Earlier generations of computers used a variety of tapes, drums and disks; current computers use so-called *hard disks*, rapidly spinning magnetizable disks, with moveable arms with *read/write heads*, to read data from or write data to any area of the disk. Regardless of the technology, each area holds one bit of information, according to its magnetic state.

Input devices fall into three categories: those which take input interactively from the user; those which accept data from other digital sources; and those which convert paper data into digital form. The first category comprises the venerable QWERTY keyboard, originally developed for typewriters in the 1870s, together with more recently developed devices: the mouse and other pointing devices, and the touch-screen. The second category comprises the silicon-memory data stick, replacing the various forms of portable magnetic 'floppy disks' used previously, and the ports and circuits by which the computer communicates with networked resources. The third category is that of the scanner, digitizing print and images from paper sources.

Output devices are similarly categorized in the same three ways. There are the display screens, which allow user interaction through visual and sound output; those which output digital data – data sticks and network circuits and ports; and those which print paper output; typically now laser or inkjet printers for personal and office use, and commercial digital printers. These latter have revolutionized the production of printed documents, as we shall discuss further in Chapter 10, for two main reasons. They make the unit cost of the printing of one document the same as that of many, allowing, most notably, print-on-demand books; for the impact of such devices in a library setting, see Arlitsch (2011). And they allow text and images to be handled in an integrated way, since both are represented as binary data patterns, and the basic printing unit for each is the pixel, the smallest point which can be displayed on a screen or printed on a page. This contrasts with early forms of printing, in which they had to be treated in a different way; older books usually have images on separate pages from print. Computerized phototypesetting began to be employed in the 1960s, with full digital printing in the 1980s; see Cope and Phillips (2006) and Twyman (1998) for more details, and Chapter 10 for more on the consequences.

Having outlined the nature of the isolated digital computer, we will now consider the networks which connect them together.

Networks

No computer today lives an isolated life. All are connected via some form of network to others, to enable communication, and information access and sharing. Since the 1990s the internet and the world wide web have become ubiquitous, such that it has become difficult to think of information technologies without these at centre stage. We will look in outline at some network concepts and examples, then moving on consider two recent developments: the grid and the cloud. For more details, presented in an accessible way, see Ince (2011), Davis and Shaw (2011, Chapter 6), Derfler and Freed (2004), and Gralla (2006).

The growth of networked computing has been driven by three factors: communications technology, software and standards. In terms of technology, older forms of network, based on co-axial cables originating in the 1880s and used for telegraph and telephone systems, have been succeeded by fibre-optic cables, and various forms of wireless transmission. These allow much faster transmission speeds and greater information carrying capacity; such systems are described loosely as *broadband*. Software systems have improved the efficiency and reliability of transmission greatly: an important example is *packet switching*, by which messages may be split up and their constituents sent by the fastest available route, being recombined before delivery.

Standards are fundamentally important, so that different forms of network, and different kinds of computers connected to them, can communicate effectively. The internet, originating in the 1960s in networks built for defence research in the USA, is a worldwide network of networks, integrated by common standards: the internet control protocols, commonly known as TCP/IP (Transmission Control Protocol/Internet Protocol). It has been estimated that in 2011 over two billion people, one third of the world's population, were users of the internet.

The world wide web, often spoken of as if it were synonymous with the internet, is in fact a major internet application. A system for allowing access to interlinked hypertext documents stored on networked computers, it originated in the work of Sir Tim Berners-Lee at the CERN, the European nuclear research establishment. Berners-Lee introduced the idea in 1989 in an internal memorandum with the modest title 'Information management: a proposal'. At the time of writing (December 2011), the original document was available at http://www.w3.org/History/1989/proposal.html. For Berners-Lee's own account of the origins and early nature of the web, see Berners-Lee (1999).

The web is based on so-called client-server architecture: a web browser, the client, on the user's computer accesses the website on the remote server computer, through the internet, and downloads the required web page. This relies on a number of standards. For example, web pages must be created using a mark-up language, typically HTML, sometimes referred to as the *lingua franca* of the internet, and be identified by a Uniform Resource Identifier, commonly referred to as a Uniform Resource Locator or URL; a Hypertext Transfer Protocol (HTTP) enables communication between client and server. Use of the web parallels that of the internet itself, with over two billion users estimated in 2011.

The internet and web, despite their great reach and influence, are by no means the only significant computer networks. Many private, local and regional networks exist, although increasingly they are using the standards of the internet and web, for compatibility.

Beyond the current network arrangement, we can see the development of new ways of connecting computers together.

Grid computing is a term used to describe a number of computers linked together by internet connections, and sometimes by high-speed network connections, so that they can work together, giving, in combination, the power of a much larger single machine; see Ince (2011) for a more detailed account, and Town and Harrison (2010) for an information retrieval example.

The *cloud* is a concept which takes networking to its ultimate extent. Rather than software and files of information being stored on individual computers, they are stored remotely, 'in the cloud' – in practice in large 'server farms' – and accessed via networks when they are needed. This is facilitated by 'cloud services', such as Apple's iCloud and Googledocs+, which control the servers and network access. Moulaison and Corrado (2011) give a good description of this technology, with case studies of particular relevance to information practitioners. We will return to the cloud as a possible future for information provision in the final chapter.

By comparison with earlier forms of computer, today's are very much more reliant on, and empowered by, network connectivity. But they are different in another way; their shapes and sizes.

Mobile and pervasive

The very first computers occupied a building. Subsequent generations occupied a large room, a small room and a desktop. The trend has continued, to give ever smaller and more mobile computing devices, exemplified by today's laptops, notebooks, tablet computers and smartphones. For examples relevant to library and information services, and issues associated with their use, see Ally and Needham (2012) and Wisniewski (2011).

The trend continues, with computing power appearing in, and being applied to, objects which would never have previously been associated with computers; a trend known as *pervasive* computing. We will give just two examples.

1 Radio Frequency Identification (RFID) tags are very small electronic

devices, which may be attached to any kind of object, and which emit radio signals; these can be read by a receiver to locate and identify the object. One obvious example is insertion in library books, where they can aid location, circulation etc. (Walsh, 2011; Palmer, 2009; Zimerman, 2011).

2 QR (Quick Response) codes are *matrix barcodes*, black and white patterns in a square format. Originally they were designed for tracking items in manufacturing or retail settings, but they have gained much wider use since many smartphones gained apps for scanning them and using the encoded information, typically displaying text or opening a webpage. They are used in museums, galleries, libraries and information centres to provide information about collection items, to provide additional information about resources and services, to offer guides, maps, audio tours and self-service hints and tips, and for marketing and promotion; for detailed and varied examples, see Ekart (2011), Walsh (2011), Whitchurch (2011) and Hoy (2011).

So far, we have thought mainly about the physical devices of information technology: the *hardware*. To make a computer do any useful tasks requires instructions, in the form of programs: the *software*.

Software

Computer users will, for the most part, interact with two forms of software: *operating systems* and *applications*.

The operating system, specific to a particular type of computer and installed on each machine, controls the hardware, and runs applications. Examples are versions of Microsoft's Windows, Apple's OS X, and Linux.

Applications software typically comes in the form of packages, for a specific purpose. Applications may either be installed on individual computers, as for example word processors, spreadsheets and web browsers typically are, or may be accessed on the web; this is usual for search engines, library management systems, social media, and the like. As we have seen, there is an increasing trend for virtually all software to be accessible from the cloud, rather then installed on individual machines.

Applications software, from the users' perspectives, typically requires the computer to carry out tasks defined at a fairly high level: search the bibliographic database for authors with this name; calculate the mean of this column of figures; insert this image into the blog post; and so on. These must be translated into a series of very specific low-level commands to be carried out by the processor. This is achieved by software features operating 'behind' the interface of the application, usually unknown to the user.

All software must be written in some kind of programming language, though this will usually be invisible to the user, who will have no reason to know what language any particular application is written in. At the risk of over-simplification, we can say there are four kinds of software language:

1 *Low-level* programming languages, also referred to as *assembly* languages or *machine code*, encode instructions at the very detailed level of processor operations; these languages are therefore necessary specific to a particular type of computer. This kind of programming is complex and difficult, but results in very efficient operation; it is reserved for situations where reliably fast processing is essential.

2 *High-level* programming languages express instructions in terms closer to user intentions, and are converted by other software systems, generally termed *compilers*, into processor instructions; programs are therefore much easier to write and to understand, and the languages can be used on different types of computer. There have been many such languages, some general purpose and some aimed a particular kind of application. The first examples were developed in the 1950s, and two of the earliest are still in use: Fortran, still a language of choice for scientific and engineering applications, and COBOL, still used in many 'legacy' systems for business applications. Currently popular are Java, C++, and C# (pronounced C sharp).

3 *Scripting* languages are a particularly significant form of high-level language, designed to support interaction, particularly with web resources; for example, to update a web page in response to a user's input, rather than reloading the page each time, or to create a *mashup*, an integration of data from several web sources. Examples are Javascript, PHP and Perl.

4 *Mark-up* languages are somewhat different in nature, as they are designed to annotate text, to denote either structural elements ('this is an author name'), presentation ('print this in italic') or both. The first such languages were designed for formatting documents for printing; an example is LaTeX. More recent examples control the format and structure of web resources; examples are HTML and XML.

An innovation in the way software is provided has come from the *open source* movement. Commercial software is usually provided as a 'black box'; the user has no access to the program code, and therefore cannot modify the system at all, nor even know exactly how it works. With open source software, the user is given the full source code – the original programs – which they are free to modify. This makes it easy to customize software to meet local needs and preferences. It also allows users to collaborate in extending and improving the systems, correcting errors, etc.; this is held by open source enthusiasts to be the best way of getting good-quality software. There is an analogy with the open access and open data initiatives, discussed in Chapter 10. Most such software is free, leading it to be known as FOSS (Free and Open Source Software). Well known examples of open source systems are the Linux operating system and the Moodle virtual learning environment; library and information examples are the Greenstone and Koha library management systems, the DSpace repository system, the Alfresco document and records management system, and GIS packages such as QGIS and GRASS. For an overview of open source systems generally, see Deek and HcHugh (2008), for an overview of library and information applications, see Hale and Hughes (2012) and Poulter (2010), and for examples of the use of specific systems, see Donnelly (2010), Biswas and Paul (2010) and Keast (2011).

Another way of getting access to the workings of software systems, though this time without having access to the source code, is via an Application Programming Interface (API). This is a facility provided by many websites, allowing external users to make use of the site's facilities in specified ways. Ince (2011) gives examples, such as a website dealing with French food and recipes which uses the Amazon API to display French recipe books and allow their purchase from Amazon without leaving the food site. A widely used API is that of Google Maps, which can be used to create location guides on one's own website. APIs can also be used to create mashups by taking data from various sources without the need for programming.

Interacting with computers

The ways in which people interact with computers, generally described under the headings of *human-computer interaction* (HCI) or of *usability*, is an area of great and increasing importance to the information sciences, as our opening quotation from Jonathan Grudin exemplifies; indeed it has sometimes been held to be the most significant area of overlap between information technology and information science. It is particularly concerned with the design and evaluation of interfaces, and has contributed greatly to some of the newer design methods mentioned below. Its methods range from surveys and interviews to the use of sophisticated instruments to track eye and hand movements as an interface is used. For overviews of these areas, see Chowdhury and Chowdhury (2011), Rogers, Sharp and Preece (2011), Grudin (2011), Dix et al. (2004), and Shneiderman et al. (2009).

A related area is that of *information visualization*. Whereas HCI responds to the opportunities for different forms of interaction offered by present-day computers, visualization responds to the challenge of the great amounts of digital data which can be obtained. This involves the use of software to help in the comprehension of large volumes of data, often by creating visual or diagrammatic representations, and by extracting and displaying crucial facts and figures from the mass. For an overview and numerous examples, see Steele and Iliinsky (2010), and for briefer exemplification, see Davis and Shaw (2011, Chapter 8). There is a link between visualization and the broader area of *data analytics* or *data mining* – extracting interesting information from large data compilations – which will be mentioned in Chapter 12.

Information systems, analysis, architecture and design

The way in which IT systems are modelled and designed has changed greatly over the past decades. This is relevant to information science practitioners for two reasons: because it influences the kind of information systems which are available; and because some of the newer methods allow much more involvement from those who are not technical experts, including many information practitioners. For an overview of recent trends and issues see Galliers and Corrie (2011).

There is dichotomy in the general methods by which IT systems are envisaged and designed, between approaches which we may categorize, at the risk of over-simplification, as 'hard' and 'soft'. Hard approaches, including most systems analysis and design and software engineering, take a positivist viewpoint; the aspects of the world being considered are real and unambiguous, and amenable to formal data modelling, metrics, fixed objectives, and structured processes of analysis. Softer approaches, including soft systems methodologies, take a more interpretivist viewpoint: there are different perspectives of the aspects of the world being studied, and all should be taken into account, through a toolbox of methods including subjective conceptual models and an emphasis on understanding the problems qualitatively.

A classic overview and comparison of methods, with particular emphasis on soft systems approaches, is given by Checkland and Holwell (1998). Peter Checkland, a British management scientist, is the originator of the soft systems approach, and still explains it more clearly than later authors: for a recent and readable account of this approach, see Checkland and Poulter (2006). There are many texts dealing with the 'harder' approaches; helpful examples are Kendall and Kendall (2010) and Britton and Doake (2005).

New trends in system design, influenced by HCI concepts and methods, and by soft systems approaches, are variously termed 'user-centred', 'participatory', 'persuasive' and 'interactive'; see, for example, Rogers, Sharp and Preece (2011), Hasle (2011) and Shneiderman et al. (2009).They emphasize an incremental, interactive approach, changing the system to suit the needs of the user, rather than forcing the user to adapt to the 'best' system. Information practitioners are often well positioned to be involved in this sort of design process.

A similar aspect of use of IT in which information practitioners are often involved is that of *information architecture* (IA). The term has a number of shades of meaning, but it is usually understood as the quest for the best way of organizing and structuring complex information spaces, typically websites, so that their users can find their way around easily, and feel that the information environment is supportive of their needs. It draws from the insights of HCI, of user-centred design, and from the 'traditional' ideas of information design on the printed page. It also relies on the ideas of categorization, taxonomy, and faceted classification, discussed in Chapter 6 to organize the layout of information. The term was coined in the 1970s by Saul Wurman, originally a 'real' architect, who came to believe that the principles behind the design of buildings and physical spaces could be applicable to information spaces; he is, perhaps, better known for his concept of 'information anxiety'. Information architecture came into its own from the late 1990s, with the expansion of the web, and the need to bring order and structure to web-based information. Dillon (2002) gives an interesting brief account of issues in the development of the subject, and Haller (2011) gives a summary of its current status. The fullest introduction, emphasizing the application of IA to large websites, is Morville and Rosenfield (2006); Morville and Calender (2010) gives copious examples for search and navigation interfaces. See Davies (2011) for an account of the use of IA to counter information overload, and Burford (2011) for a study of the practice of IA in several large organizations. For the basic principles of information design in any context, and on which IA draws, see Orna (2005), and for an interesting historical perspective, see the analysis of Paul Otlet's ideas for interfaces to information by van den Heuvel and Rayward (2011). Although IA has no agreed general theory, some pragmatic principles have emerged: Brown's (2010) 'eight principles of information architecture', shown in slightly modified form in the box on the next page, are a good example.

Having dealt with a number of general issues, we can now turn to look at some specific applications.

Applications

We will briefly review some applications of information technologies of particular importance to the information sciences. We will do this by considering their impact on aspects of the communication chain – creation, dissemination, sharing, organization and retrieval, and preservation of information – bearing in mind that the impact will include digital documents that may be printed, and paper documents that may be digitized.

Creation

The most familiar form of technology for information creation comes in the well known form of office software: word processors, spreadsheets and presentation

Principles of information architecture (adapted from Brown, 2010)

Objects: treat content as a living thing, with a lifecycle, behaviours and attributes; recognize different types of content and treat them differently.

Choices: offer meaningful choices to users, keeping the range of choices available focused on a particular task. A greater number of options can make it more difficult for people to reach a decision: people think they like having many options, but they don't (the 'paradox of choice').

Disclosure: show only enough information to help people understand what kinds of information they will find if they dig deeper. Comes from the general design principle of 'progressive disclosure': people cannot use information they are not yet interested in, or do not understand.

Exemplars: describe the contents of categories by showing examples; it's the simplest and most effective form of explanation.

Front and side doors: assume a majority of users will come to any page or piece of information other than through the home page and prescribed navigation routes; typically they come via search engine. All pages should tell the visitor where they are, and what else is available; the home page should focus on orienting new users.

Multiple classification: offer several different classifications for browsing content; allow for the users' different mental models, even for quite restricted sets of information.

Focused navigation: don't mix apples and oranges in a navigation scheme; provide access by different mechanism, for example, topic, timeliness, services; use facet analysis principles.

Growth: assume the content you have today is a small fraction of what you will have in the future; allow for growth by, for example, having a few main categories and making it easy to create sub-categories.

software. To this, we might add software packages for editing images, video and audio files created by digital devices. These are used in the creation of most 'born digital' documents of a traditional kind.

There is then a very considerable body of information in the form of, largely ephemeral, digital communications: e-mails, micro-blogging messages, social media updates, and so on.

In a less familiar context, much digital data is gathered automatically by a wide variety of monitoring instruments: from CCTV cameras to satellite imaging, and from medical diagnostic data to retailers' sales data. These create the large data sets which are the raw material for the e-research to be discussed in Chapter 10.

Dissemination

IT has affected the dissemination aspect of the communication chain in a number of ways. Publishing has been affected in two main ways. Conventional printed documents are produced by digital printing, with the advantages noted above. And much publishing is now wholly digital, in the form of web-based publicly available materials, and in-house material published on intranets; both of these relying on what used to be termed *desktop publishing* facilities, essentially web design and content management software.

Newer forms of dissemination, most obviously blogs, rely on combining easy-to-use web page creation software, together with communication links. Mashups, referred to above, which link and integrate information from disparate sources by use of APIs and scripting languages, are a similar new form of dissemination; for an overview of mashups with library and information examples, see Engard (2009).

Another form of dissemination promoted by IT systems is digitization of physical items: books, newspapers and other texts, and also images, museum objects, etc. This makes large collections of older material, as well as individual rare and valuable items, much more widely available than their physical instantiation would permit. This process involves hardware (scanners) and software (image manipulation and content management); see Zhang and Gourley (2008) and Terras (2010) for overviews.

Finally, we should mention *machine translation*, as a means of disseminating material in languages unfamiliar to potential users, much more widely than would be possible with human translators. After many years of unfulfilled promise, this has now reached a stage where a useful, if not perfect, translation between many language pairs is available free, or at low cost, in part due to availability of systems such as Babelfish and Google Translate. For a detailed overview of machine translation see Wilks (2009), and for examples of library and information applications see Spellman (2011) and Smith (2006).

Sharing

The technologies which support information sharing come, for the most part, in two broad categories: one, relatively long-established and relatively formal, we can categorize as *groupware*; the other, its opposite in both respects, as *social media*.

Groupware, also referred to as *collaborative software* and as *computer-supported collaborative work* (CSCW) has its origins in experimental systems developed in the 1960s, but only achieved wide adoption in the 1990s. Its core is usually taken to be systems which allow collaborative work on documents by participants remote from each other, supported by a variety of tools for communication and conferencing and virtual meetings. In commercial environments, this is most often instantiated in packages such as Lotus Notes and Microsoft Sharepoint, but a wide variety of smaller systems of all kinds are used for collaborative working.

Social media originated with the world wide web in the 1990s, on which it depends, and became seemingly ubiquitous in the new millennium. Intended primarily for informal social interactions, through messaging and exchange of media such as photographs and videos, it has begun to be adopted for business and professional activities; for early analyses of its transformative effects, see Warr (2008) and Qualman (2009). It is exemplified by Facebook, primarily a social tool, though increasingly used for marketing and promotion, and by LinkedIn, a professional networking tool.

Spanning the boundaries of these two categories are *wikis* and *media sharing* sites. Wikis are web-based systems that allow their content to be extended and modified by their users, often with little or no central control. They are now used in many contexts: the best known is the Wikipedia public encyclopedia, but the approach is used for information sharing in many diverse contexts.

Media sharing sites on the web allow users to maintain collections of their own material while simultaneously making it available for others to access. Well known examples are Flickr for photographs and LibraryThing for books.

Finally, and at a more sophisticated level of sharing, we might mention *expert systems*, an aspect of artificial intelligence. These are software systems which aim to incorporate the knowledge of a community of expert people in a very limited area, and which then manipulate this knowledge through rules and other processes in order to act as an expert person would; making diagnoses, recommending a course of action, etc. Under development since the 1970s, and steadily increasing their use for very specific tasks, they have not really fulfilled their once much-hyped potential as yet. Human knowledge, especially of the commonsense variety, has proved surprisingly resistant to being computerized.

Organization and retrieval

These are the IT applications which have usually been thought of as at the heart of information science. Nonetheless, we will treat them, as with other applications, in outline only, as there are many excellent detailed texts available. They have a close relationship with the tools and concepts of information organization discussed in the last chapter, and with issues of information management discussed in Chapter 12; here we will focus on the technical issues. This is not to ignore the fact that studies of information retrieval, in particular, have generated interesting theoretical issues; see the discussions of paradigms in Chapter 3, an account of 17 theoretical constructs of information retrieval (Jansen and Rieh, 2010), and debates on the relevance of theories of knowledge to information retrieval, indexing and browsing (Hjørland, 2011a, 2011b).

We will discuss these applications under six headings, accepting that there is overlap between them: reference handling systems, databases, information retrieval systems, digital libraries and repositories, document management systems and the semantic web.

Reference handling software is the simplest form of these systems. It allows for collections of bibliographic or website references to be created and maintained, with limited indexing, and to be output in different citation formats. Examples are RefWorks and Endnote; Zotero, Mendeley and citeulike are web-based media sharing equivalents. See Kern and Hensley (2011) for a review of their features.

Databases is a rather over-used and general term for any collection of digital information. Here we will use it in a more restricted way, to mean systems which handle structured data, typically in the form of numbers and short pieces of text: the *database management system* (DBMS) or, in an even more restricted sense, the *relational database management system* (RDBMS).

The phrase 'relational database' strictly refers to a system designed with rigorous formal rules; but the term has been misused over the years by software companies who have applied it to systems which do not meet the full criteria. The key to RDBMSs is *normalization*. This is a process of grouping data elements into clearly defined structures without redundancy, according to a data model, removing repeating data elements so that each piece of data is stored only once, and making the model depend on the relations between the data elements, rather than any particular application of the data. The data is then represented as two-dimensional tables, where each table represents a kind of thing, each row one instance of that thing, and each column one attribute of that instance of the thing. So for example, we could have a table of BOOKS, with one column for AUTHOR, one column for TITLE, and one column for DATE OF PUBLICATION. Each row represents one book, e.g.

AUTHOR	TITLE	DATE PUBLISHED
Charles Dickens	A Christmas Carol	1843
Arthur Conan Doyle	A Study in Scarlet	1887

In a library setting we might make more tables, to deal with individual copies of the books and their location, borrower names and addresses, and so on. The important point is to remove multiple storing of the same information, and to have a logical structure so that only the same sort of information appears in the same tables; we would not, for example, want to have details of borrowers in the BOOKS table, as they would have to be repeated for each book they borrowed.

Database design can get complicated, as it has a good deal of associated theory, largely developed by the British computer scientists Edgar Codd and Chris Date, while they were working for IBM in the USA in the 1960s and 70s; however, the basic ideas are quite simple. The process of modelling for databases of this kind is termed *entity-relationship* (ER) modelling, and is the basis of the RDA metadata scheme discussed in Chapter 6, on information organization. Databases of this kind use a structured query language to search the tables; the best known is SQL (Structured Query Language) used in many database systems.

There are many books and articles dealing with DBMS, at a variety of levels of rigour and detail. Connolly and Begg (2010) is thorough and relatively accessible; for detailed treatments by one of the pioneers of the topic, see Date (2003; 2011). Davis and Shaw (2011, Chapter 7) give brief and clear examples.

Information retrieval (IR) systems are usually understood to be those which handle less structured data than the facts and figures dealt with by DBMS. There may be some structure present: for example, the field structure of a typical bibliographic database, with fields for author name, title of article, source name, publication details, subject indexing etc. Or their may be little or no structure to the records in the system, as with web search engines such as Google, or the 'enterprise search' systems, such as Autonomy, which aim to deal with large volumes of diverse materials, including reports, emails, and so on.

IR systems are usually analysed in terms of system components; however, it seems that each writer has their own preferred set of components. A recent, and relatively complex, example is shown in Figure 7.3.

We will discuss IR systems in a rather simple way, considering just four main components or sub-systems: input; indexing; search; and interface. Fuller coverage is given by Chowdhury (2010) and Chu (2010) from a library and information viewpoint, and by Baeza-Yates and Ribeiro-Neto (2010) in more technical detail. Other perspectives are given in the multi-authored books edited

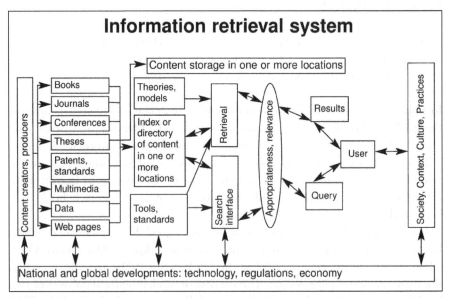

Figure 7.3 *Components of an information retrieval system (reproduced from Chowdhury, 2010)*

by Melucci and Baeza-Yates (2011), Ruthven and Kelly (2011), Foster and Rafferty (2011) and Göker and Davies (2009).

The input sub-system, depending on the purpose of the overall system, may have to include materials of a widely different kind, as in the diagram in Figure 7.3, or may handle a more restricted range. What is entered may be a whole document, for a full-text retrieval system, or a document surrogate, a shorter summary record such as a bibliographic reference. Virtually all IR systems use an 'inverted file' structure; a file of index terms, created by the indexing sub-system, with pointers from each term to the documents to which it applies, themselves held in another file in sequential order. This allows rapid look-up of relevant documents, without having to scan the whole file.

The index file is created by the *indexing* component. Indexing may be 'full-text', with every word in the document indexed, or more selective; if the latter it may be automatic, with terms chosen statistically according to their frequency of occurrence, or it may be done by an indexer. A controlled vocabulary may or may not be used, as well as, or in addition to, the terms in the original document and/or added free terms. The process of indexing was discussed in the chapter on information organization.

The heart of an IR system is its *search* component, which does the work of retrieval. Search is carried out in different ways, reflected in the 'theories/models' component in the diagram in Figure 7.3; in essence it describes the nature of algorithms used in the search process. For details, see the recommended texts and the chapters by Rasmussen (2011) and Hiemstra (2009). We will mention three main classes of models:

1 *Boolean*: this works by manipulating sets of documents indexed with particular terms, using the Boolean operators AND, OR, NOT. It is clear and straightforward: a search for '(CATS OR DOGS) NOT HORSES' produces all those documents indexed with the term CATS or the term DOGS provided they are not indexed with the term HORSES. A drawbacks is the binary all-or-nothing metric. There is no way to say that one document is all about cats, while another barely mentions them in passing; documents are indexed CATS or not. Also, users often find it difficult to express their information need in the exact way required by a Boolean search.
2 *Vector*: this approach calculates the similarity between the query and each document according to the terms in common. It is more subtle than Boolean, as it allows for different degrees of matching, rather than just yes/no, and it allows results to be ranked in order of similarity to the query.
3 *Probabilistic*: this approach includes a number of methods which attempt to calculate the probability that a document will be relevant to a query, on the basis of statistical analysis of the occurrence of terms in the query and

in the set of documents. Some of the methods use 'relevance feedback', allowing the user to assess retrieved documents as relevant or not, amending probabilities according to these judgements, and searching again; this process continues until the user is satisfied with the result.

Sometimes the Boolean model is described as 'exact' retrieval, while the other two models are denoted as 'best match'; the latter will always return some result as the closest to the query, whereas the former will return exactly what was specified, which may be nothing.

Other retrieval algorithms use fuzzy set theory and Bayesian logic (Baeza-Yates and Ribeiro-Neto, 2010); there have even been studies on analogies between the formalisms of retrieval and quantum mechanics, with potential application in the quantum computers mentioned below (van Rijsbegen, 2004; Melucci and van Rijsbergen, 2011). Some retrieval systems use information other than apparent relevance to rank the output; an obvious alternative is to present newer material first. The Google search engine's PageRank algorithm orders items according to how many other web pages link to them, a surrogate measure of the interest value of the site; and one which has spawned a small industry of 'search engine optimization' to promote sites in these rankings.

Many writings on searching assume that the user has a well defined query to put to the system, but in fact many searches involve an element of *browsing*. There are numerous purposes for browsing, including:

- finding information in a context where browsing is the only feasible method
- finding information on topics which are not clearly defined, or which are hard to specify exactly; i.e. where the information need is broad and poorly specified
- getting an overview or sample of the information in a collection
- finding items which are similar to, or dissimilar from, those which one has identified
- finding one's bearing in a subject of which one knows little
- selecting the 'right' information from a large collection of 'relevant' material
- looking for inspiration, new ideas, or just something interesting; i.e. allowing for serendipity.

Browsing has been included as a component of a number of models of information-seeking behaviour, as we will discuss in Chapter 9, although usually without clear definition. It is variously categorized as *directed, semi-directed* and *undirected,* as *systematic, exploratory* and *casual,* or as *purposive, semi-purposive* and *capricious,* and has also been described by terms such as *undirected viewing, active scanning* and *passive attention.* Some IR systems make specific provision for this kind of 'informal search', but most do not cater for it well (Bawden, 2011).

The *interface* component allows the user to put their query to the system, and to receive the results. Interfaces have changed greatly over the years, although the operations which they evoke behind the scenes have not. There have been, and still are, a variety of interface styles; see the recommended texts, Morville and Callender (2010) and Wilson (2011) for details and examples. We will mention three important general styles, which have developed to match the typical computer interfaces of the time.

The first was the *command line* interface, stemming from the 1960s and developed for the first generation of online bibliographic search systems. At least one of these, for the Dialog host system, remained in use almost unchanged over nearly 50 years. These require the user to know a limited set of commands: typically, to search for documents indexed with a term, browse the index, combine sets with Boolean operators, and display results. They also allow for searching for phrases, truncated terms beginning or ending in a certain way, terms within a specified proximity of one another, terms in particular fields of the record, and so on. For instance, in the classic Dialog system, the command:

S digital(w)library/ti AND (online OR retrieval OR search*) AND au=jones ?

will retrieve documents with the phrase 'digital libraries' in the title, and any of the terms 'online', 'retrieval' or anything beginning 'search', for example search, searches, searching, and so on, anywhere in the subject parts of the record, and an author with the name Jones.

This kind of interface gives the user complete control over a Boolean search, and allows very precise specification of detailed searches. However, it not easy to use, and the user must take some time learning the system commands. Although these types of interfaces are still available, their functions have largely been absorbed within other styles of interface.

At the opposite extreme is the simplicity of the 'search box', pioneered by Google; a single box, into which the user types whatever they wish. This may be a Boolean statement, if the system works in this way, but will more usually be just a few terms or phrases; most searches on Google are single words. This simplicity is so attractive to most users, particularly if combined with a search function which gives ranked output, that many IR systems have adopted it, accepting that it loses the control and precision possible with the command line.

An intermediate stage, often provided as an 'advanced search' function, attempts to combine the simplicity of the search box with the power of the command line, by providing a matrix of rows and columns for the user to fill in, assisted by prompts and drop-down menus, giving a limited choice of Boolean operators and field specification. The example below, Figure 7.4, from our university's OPAC, shows a search for 'digital library' as a phrase in the title, the truncated term 'retriev' in subject terms, and an author name Jones.

All these forms of interface, and variants of them, are to be found in IR systems; system designers seek to strike a balance between simplicity and precision of search specification; most users prefer simplicity most of the time.

So far, we have discussed IR systems in terms of text retrieval, by contrast with the facts and figures

Advanced Search

Enter your keywords:
Please fill in the form, select limits, and click Search (or return to Quick Search).

Title:	"digital library"	And
Subject:	retriev*	And
Author:	jones	And
Any Field:	

Search

Figure 7.4 *Advanced search function*

searching of DBMS. Although this is certainly the most widely encountered form of IT system, there are several other forms for different types of material, for example:

- citation searching, finding which documents cite a starting point document, to find newer material on that subject (Jacsó, 2004)
- image searching, using algorithms to search for features of still and moving images, rather than relying on text indexing (Enser, 2008a; Enser, 2008b; Town and Harrison, 2010)
- sound searching, to find items with names that sound similar; for example to identify medicines when all that is known is the spoken name (Robinson, 2010)
- music retrieval, with algorithms searching for features of pieces of music, rather than relying on index terms (Downie, 2003; Inskip, 2011)
- cross-language information retrieval (CLIR) (Kishida, 2005)
- chemical structure and substructure searching, retrieving records for chemical substances and reactions (Willett, 2008).

There have been many studies of the ways in which people use retrieval systems; a detailed aspect of the information behaviour which we will discuss in Chapter 9. Initially focused on system aspects, these have recently turned to examining individual preferences and styles; as examples, see Ford, Miller and Moss (2005), Chen, Magoulas, and Dimakopoulos (2005) and Vilar and Žumer (2008). Heinström (2010) has used such studies to define searching 'styles', such as the conscientious searcher, the worried searcher, and the laid-back searcher.

Studies of the use of IR systems have identified a small number of search strategies and tactics, general approaches to retrieval, used frequently; these can be put to best effect with those interfaces which give full control over Boolean searching in structured records with subject indexing. They were first described by Marcia Bates (1979), whom we met in Chapter 4; for recent comparisons, see Papaioannou et al. (2010) and Xie (2010), and for similar tactics with internet search engines see Smith (2012). A recent development has been the trend to 'social discovery' or 'social search', with search becoming a collaborative activity through means such as social bookmarking and tagging (Shneiderman, 2011; McDonnell and Shiri, 2011).

Some examples of identifiable strategies are shown in the box below: in a practical setting they will mainly be used informally and in combination, but it may be helpful to adopt them if no useful material, or too much, is being found.

Examples of search strategies for information retrieval

Berrypicking: carry out the search using a small number of search terms; choose the most interesting two or three items; read these, and then search again modifying the search terms as necessary; repeat until enough items have been found (the topic of the search may have changed in the process).

Building blocks: divide the search into distinct topics, represent each topic by a set of synonyms linked by OR and then link all the topics with AND. Begin with the topic likely to have the smallest number of documents in the collection, and stop when the number of retrieved documents is small enough to scan.

Pearl growing: start with a known relevant document, the 'seed', and look it up in the collection. Examine the index terms, and use these as starting points for a search. Examine the retrieved documents, choose relevant one, and repeat the process. Continue until no new relevant documents are found.

Successive fractions: do an initial search, using just one term, or a few terms linked with AND. Examine some of the documents found, and find terms occurring only in those which are relevant or those which are not relevant. Repeat the search, adding 'relevant' terms with AND and 'not relevant' terms with NOT. Continue until the retrieved set has been reduced to a small enough number to be scanned.

Quicksearch: divide the search into distinct topics, represent each with one index term, and search linking the terms with AND. Any relevant documents found can then be used as the 'seed' for pearl growing.

The evaluation of IR systems has been a major preoccupation of information science over many years, and has spawned its own traditions, methods and metrics; see, for example, Robertson (2008). The most widely used metrics for information retrieval are recall and precision, measuring respectively the success of a system in finding all the relevant material that there is to be found, and in returning only relevant material. They are formally defined as follows:

For a search which retrieves N documents, of which Nr are judged relevant, and there are M relevant documents in the collection:

Recall = Nr / M
Precision = Nr / N

See Robertson (1969) for a classic paper introducing this kind of metrics and Egghe (2008) and Järvelin (2011) for more recent analyses. See Chapter 14 for methods of evaluating IR systems, and Chapter 4 for a discussed of the complex question of relevance, on which all these metrics depend.

Digital libraries and repositories

Strictly speaking, a digital library would be a library whose collections and services were wholly digital, having no physical location, and being staffed by virtual librarians; perhaps Second Life avatars. No libraries have yet achieved this state, and few libraries have only digital material. By common usage, a digital library is a library offering a significant proportion of digital material and services, along with physical components; these have also been termed electronic, hybrid and virtual libraries. For explanations and analyses of the complex nature of digital libraries, and the way in which these have developed over time, see Rowlands and Bawden (1999), Bawden and Rowlands (1999), Arms (2000), Seadle and Greifeneder (2007). Candela et al. (2007) give a detailed set of definitions and models for these systems and their components.

All digital libraries provide the usual range of library services, which will be outlined in Chapter 12, but with particular differences to the way the collection is defined and maintained. The diagram in Figure 7.5 indicates the major components of a digital library, in particular showing how such a library 'extends' its collections into web resources and in the collections of other digital libraries. The diagram shows the most common arrangement, by which each form of material has its own search interface/s; there may, for example, be different interfaces for groups of databases and collections of e-journals, as well as for special collections and materials, including printed materials. The alternative, a single interface for all forms of material, is desirable, but difficult to arrange, if it is to avoid an overly simple 'lowest common denominator' approach.

Digital libraries grew from initial development in library automation (see Tedd (2007) for the early history of this in the UK), given impetus by the development of the web, and increasing availability of digital forms of traditional resources, particularly e-journals. Overviews and examples are given by Arms (2000), Chowdhury and Chowdhury (2002), Andrews and Law (2004), Lesk (2005), Bearman (2007) and Chowdhury et al. (2008). There are particular concerns about *interoperability*, the ability to search across different collections and

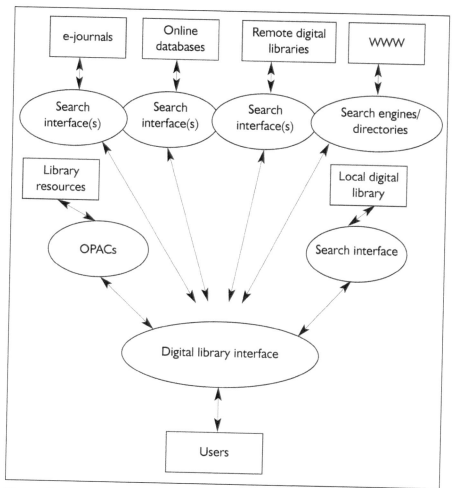

Figure 7.5 *Components of a digital library (reproduced from Chowdhury and Chowdhury, 2002)*

different libraries, requiring common standards and metadata, and *link resolver* facilities, to enable a user to switch between, for example, a record which they have found in an abstracting service and the equivalent full-text article in an e-journal collection.

Closely associated with digital libraries are *library management systems*, which can be used with both digital and printed resources to automate all library management and service functions, and which are generally structured around an online catalogue (OPAC). Current examples include: open source systems such as Koha and Greenstone: proprietary systems such as Talis, Ex Libris (Aleph and Voyager) and SirsiDynix: and the media-sharing web-based LibraryThing, designed for personal book collections but now being increasingly used in 'proper' libraries.

Repositories, which we will discuss in Chapter 10 in the context of open access, are systems for maintaining collections of documents created within an organization and making them publicly available. They are similar in concept to digital libraries, their uniqueness lying in the form of material, which means that collection building is a rather simple process, and that indexing and classification can be relatively simple. They typically use software systems specifically designed for repositories, such as DSpace and EPrints.

Electronic document and records management systems (EDRMS) handle the information flows within records centres and archives; as we will see in Chapter 12, a main feature of this environment is a clear document lifecycle, which these systems are designed to manage. Examples are HP TRIM, ECM Documentum, and the cloud-based Alfresco.

Finally, although it is not a system as such, but rather an aspiration, we should mention the *semantic web*. This refers to the idea that information on the web may be structured and encoded in such as way that its content and meaning are made explicit, so that they can be 'understood' by search engines and other software agents. The idea was first popularized by Tim Berners-Lee, the originator of the web itself, at the start of the new century (see, for example, Berners-Lee, Hendler and Lassila, 2001). It is still very much a work in progress, relying on the developments in metadata, ontologies, taxonomies, tagging, etc., discussed in Chapter 6. The concept of *linked data*, formal means by which related items can be associated by structured metadata, is also fundamental. For progress reports on its development, and relevance to information provision, see Antoniou and van Harmelen (2008), Burke (2009), Dunsire and Willer (2011) and Miller (2011, Chapter 11).

Preservation

The final stage of the communication chain, archival preservation, is both helped and hindered by information technologies. On the one hand, having digital copies of printed materials is a good safeguard against loss through fire, flood, theft, etc. On the other hand, the preservation of digital materials is in itself a major problem, and one so new that the best methods are not yet fully understood. For one thing, whereas paper documents are well known to survive for hundreds of years if properly cared for, no digital storage format has been in existence for more than 50 years, so that long-term survival cannot be demonstrated. There is also the problem of the obsolescence of formats. As storage mechanisms pass from use – who now remembers the Betamax video tape or the 8-inch floppy disk? – the data on them must be migrated to newer formats. Or the old equipment must be archived along with its data. Not for nothing do some archivists argue that the best way to ensure the survival of digital data is to print it on paper and put it in a drawer. For an overview of these issues, see Harvey (2010; 2012).

Summary

Future prospects for information technology largely stem from the seemingly inexorable increases in processing power and storage capacity; as we shall see in Chapter 15, some commentators believe that this will lead, probably around the middle of the 21st century, to a 'singularity'; a point at which the power of computers becomes so great that humans will no longer be able to understand what they are doing. Even setting these aside, possible advances include: quantum computers, based on the 'qubit', a storage element able to be in several states at once, and offering greatly enhanced processing capabilities; biological computers, using strands of DNA as the processing elements; neural computers, designed to emulate the patterns of neurons within the human brain; and various flavours of artificial intelligence, so that the behaviour of the computer, in a particular context, would be indistinguishable from that of a person.

For the moment, we can conclude that, whether or not any of these ideas comes to fruition, information technology will continue to develop and continue to affect and change the communication chain of recorded information. Information science and information technologies are intimately linked, each continually influencing the other. Researchers and practitioners in the information sciences can be designers, as well as users, of technology systems, particularly in HCI and information architecture, as well as in the obviously relevant applications in the organization and retrieval of information.

- Computers are still designed according to the concepts put forward by von Neumann in the 1940s, though their power and speed continue to increase exponentially.
- Networking and pervasive computing have greatly altered, and continue to alter the IT environment.
- All aspects of the communication chain of recorded information are affected by developments in IT.
- Information practitioners have traditionally focused on IT applications such as information retrieval and digital libraries, but are well placed to contribute to other aspects of IT development.

Key readings

Darrel Ince, *The computer: a very short introduction*, Oxford: Oxford University Press, 2011.

   [A clear and concise introduction to digital computers and networks.]

Gobinda Chowdhury, *Introduction to modern information retrieval* (3rd edn), London:

Facet Publishing, 2010.

[Gives a wide coverage of many of the topics of this chapter.]

Peter Morville and Louis Rosenfeld, *Information architecture for the world wide web: designing large-scale web sites*, Sebastopol CA: O'Reilly Media, 2006.

[Good introduction to all aspects of information architecture.]

Peter Morville and Jeffery Callender, *Search patterns*, Sebastopol CA: O'Reilly Media, 2010.

[Copious examples of search interfaces and features.]

References

Ally, M. and Needham, G. (eds) (2012) *M-libraries 3: Transforming libraries with mobile technology*, London: Facet Publishing.

Andrews, J. and Law, D. (eds) (2004) *Digital libraries: policy, planning and practice*, Aldershot: Ashgate.

Antoniou, G. and van Harmelen, F. (2008) *A semantic web primer* (2nd edn), Cambridge MA: MIT Press.

Arlitsch, K. (2011) The Espresso Book Machine: a change agent for libraries, *Library Hi Tech*, 29(1), 62–72.

Arms, W. Y. (2000) *Digital libraries*, Cambridge MA: MIT Press.

Baeza-Yates, R. and Ribeiro-Neto, B. (2010) *Modern information retrieval: the concepts and technology behind search* (2nd edn), Harlow: Addison-Wesley.

Bates, M. J. (1979) Information search tactics, *Journal of the American Society for Information Science*, 30(4), 205–14.

Bawden, D. (2011) Encountering on the road to Serendip? Browsing in new information environments, in Foster, A. and Rafferty, P. (eds), *Innovations in information retrieval*, London: Facet Publishing, 1–22.

Bawden, D. and Rowlands, I. (1999) Digital Libraries: assumptions and concepts, *Libri*, 49(4), 181–91.

Bearman, D. (2007) Digital libraries, *Annual Review of Information Science and Technology*, 41, 223–72.

Berners-Lee, T. (1999) *Weaving the web: the past present and future of the world wide web by its inventor*, London: Orion.

Berners-Lee, T., Hendler, J. and Lassila, O. (2001) The semantic web, *Scientific American*, May 2001 issue, 34–43.

Biswas, G., and Paul, D. (2010) An evaluative study on the open source digital library softwares for institutional repository: special reference to Dspace and Greenstone digital library, *International Journal of Library and Information Science*, 2(1), 1–10.

Britton, C. and Doake, J. (2005) *Software system development: a gentle introduction* (4th edn), Columbus OH: McGraw Hill.

Brown, D. (2010) Eight principles of information architecture, *Bulletin of the American Society for Information Science and Technology*, 36(6), 30–4.

Burford, S. (2011) Complexity and the practice of web information architecture, *Journal of the American Society for Information Science and Technology*, 62(10), 2024–37.

Burke, M. (2009) The semantic web and the digital library, *Aslib Proceedings*, 61(3), 316–22.

Candela, L. , Castelli, D., Pagano, P., Thanos, C., Ioannidis, G., Koutrika, G., Ross, S., Schek, H., and Schuldt, H. (2007) Setting the foundations of digital libraries: the DELOS manifesto, *D-Lib Magazine*, 13(3/4), [online] available at: http://www.dlib.org/dlib/march07/castelli/03castelli.html.

Checkland, P. and Holwell, S. (1998) *Information, systems and information systems: making sense of the field*, Chichester: Wiley.

Checkland, P. and Poulter, J. (2006) *Learning for action: a short definitive account of soft systems methodology and its use, for practitioners, teachers and students*, Chichester: Wiley.

Chen, S. Y., Magoulas, G. D. and Dimakopoulos, D. (2005) A flexible interface design for Web directories to accommodate different cognitive styles, *Journal of the American Society for Information Science and Technology*, 56(1), 70–83.

Chowdhury, G. G. (2010) *Introduction to modern information retrieval* (3rd edn), London: Facet Publishing.

Chowdhury, G. G., Burton, P. F., McMenemy, D. and Poulter, A. (2008) *Librarianship: an introduction*, London: Facet Publishing.

Chowdhury, G. G. and Chowdhury, S. (2002) *Introduction to digital libraries*, London: Facet Publishing.

Chowdhury, G. G. and Chowdhury, S. (2011) *Information users and usability in the digital age*, London: Facet Publishing.

Chu, H. (2010) *Information representation and retrieval in the digital age* (2nd edn), Medford NJ: Information Today.

Connolly, T. M. and Begg, C. E. (2010) *Database systems: a practical approach to design, implementation and management* (5th edn), Boston MA: Addison-Wesley.

Cope, B and Phillips, A. (eds) (2006) *The future of the book in the digital age*, Oxford: Chandos.

Date, C. J. (2003) *An introduction to database systems* (8th edn), Boston MA: Addison-Wesley.

Date, C. J. (2011) *SQL and relational theory* (2nd edn), Sebastapol CA: O'Reilly.

Davies, N. (2011) Information overload, reloaded, *Bulletin of the American Society for Information Science and Technology*, 37(5), 45–9.

Davis, C. H. and Shaw, D. (eds) (2011) *Introduction to information science and technology*, Medford NJ: Information Today.

Deek, F. P. and McHugh, J. A. (2008) *Open source: technology and policy*, New York NY: Cambridge University Press.

Derfler, F. J. and Freed, L. (2004) *How networks work* (7th edn), Indianapolis IN: Que.

Dillon, A. (2002) Information architecture in 'JASIST'; just where did we come from, *Journal of the American Society for Information Science and Technology*, 53(10), 821–3.

Dix, A., Finlay, J., Abowd, G. A. and Beale, R. (2004) *Human-computer interaction* (3rd edn), Harlow: Pearson.

Donnelly, F. P. (2010) Evaluating open source GIS for libraries, *Library Hi Tech*, 28(1), 131–51.

Downie, J. S. (2003) Music information retrieval, *Annual Review of Information Science and Technology*, 37, 295–340.

Dunsire, G. and Willer, M. (2011) Standard library metadata models and structures for the Semantic Web, *Library Hi Tech News*, 28(3), 1–12.

Egghe, L. (2008) The measures precision, recall, fallout and miss as a function of the number of retrieved documents and their mutual interrelations, *Information Processing and Management*, 44(2), 856–76.

Ekart, D. F. (2011) Tech tips for every librarian: Codify your collection, *Computers in Libraries*, 31(3), 38–9.

Engard, N. C. (ed.) (2009) *Library mashups: exploring new ways to deliver library data*, London: Facet Publishing.

Enser, P. (2008a) The evolution of visual information retrieval, *Journal of Information Science*, 34(4), 531–46.

Enser, P. (2008b) Visual information retrieval, *Annual Review of Information Science and Technology*, 42, 3–42.

Ford, N., Miller, D. and Moss, N. (2005) Web search strategies and human individual differences: a combined analysis, *Journal of the American Society for Information Science and Technology*, 56(7), 757–64.

Foster, A. and Rafferty, P. (eds) (2011) *Innovations in information retrieval*, London: Facet Publishing.

Galliers, R. D. and Corrie, W. L. (ed.) (2011) *The Oxford Handbook of Management Information Systems*, Oxford: Oxford University Press.

Göker, A. and Davies, D. (eds) (2009) *Information retrieval: searching in the 21st century*, Chichester: Wiley.

Gralla, P. (2006) *How the Internet works* (8th edn), Indianapolis IN: Que.

Grudin, J. (2011) Human-computer interaction, *Annual Review of Information Science and Technology*, 45, 369–430.

Hale, M. and Hughes, M. (2012) *Open source systems in libraries*, London: Facet Publishing.

Haller, T. (2011) Is information architecture dead?, *Bulletin of the American Society for Information Science and Technology*, 38(1), 42–3.

Hally, M. (2005) *Electronic brains: stories from the dawn of the computer age*, London: Granta.

Harvey, R. (2010) *Digital curation: a how-to-do-it manual*, London: Facet Publishing.

Harvey, R. (2012) *Preserving digital materials* (2nd edn), Berlin: de Gruyter.

Hasle, P. (2011) Persuasive design: a different approach to information systems (and information), *Library Hi-Tech*, 29(4), 569–72.

Heinström, J. (2010) *From fear to flow: personality and information interaction*, Oxford: Chandos.

Hiemstra, D. (2009) Information retrieval models, in Göker, A. and Davies, D. (eds), *Information retrieval: searching in the 21st century*, Chichester: Wiley, 1–19.

Hjørland, B. (2011a) The importance of theories of knowledge: indexing and information retrieval as an example, *Journal of the American Society for Information Science and Technology*, 62(1), 72–7.

Hjørland, B. (2011b) The importance of theories of knowledge: browsing as an example, *Journal of the American Society for Information Science and Technology*, 62(3), 594–603.

Hoy, M. B. (2011) An introduction to QR codes: linking libraries and mobile patrons, *Medical Reference Services Quarterly*, 30(3), 295–300.

Ince, D. (2011) *The computer: a very short introduction*, Oxford: Oxford University Press.

Inskip, C. (2011) Music information retrieval research, in Foster, A. and Rafferty, P. (eds), *Innovations in information retrieval*, London: Facet Publishing, 69–84.

Jacsó, P. (2004) Citation searching, *Online Information Review*, 28(6), 454–60.

Jansen, B. J. and Rieh, S. Y. (2010) The seventeen theoretical constructs of information searching and information retrieval, *Journal of the American Society for Information Science and Technology*, 61(8), 1517–34.

Järvelin, K. (2011) Evaluation, in Ruthven, I. and Kelly, D. (eds) (2011) *Interactive information seeking, behaviour and retrieval*, London: Facet Publishing, 113–38.

Keast, D. (2011) A survey of Koha in Australian special libraries: open source brings new opportunities to the outback, *OCLC Systems & Services: International Digital Library Perspectives*, 27(1), 23–39.

Kendall, K. E. and Kendall, J .E. (2010) *Systems analysis and design* (8th edn), Boston: Pearson.

Kern, M. K. and Hensley, M. K. (2011) Citation management software: features and futures, *Reference and User Services Quarterly*, 50(3), 204–8.

Kishida, K. (2005) Technical issues of cross-language information retrieval: a review, *Information Processing and Management*, 41(3), 433–55.

Krajewski, M. (2011) *Paper machines: about cards and catalogs, 1548–1929*, Cambridge MA: MIT Press.

Lesk, M. (2005) *Understanding digital libraries* (2nd edn), Waltham MA: Morgan Kaufmann.

McDonnell, M. and Shiri, A. (2011) Social search: a taxonomy of, and a user-centred approach to, social web search, *Program*, 45(1), 6–28.

Melucci, M. and Baeza-Yates, R. (eds) (2011) *Advanced topics in information retrieval*, Berlin: Springer.

Melucci, M. and van Rijsbergen, K. (2011) Quantum mechanics and information retrieval, in Melucci, M. and Baeza-Yates, R. (eds), *Advanced topics in information retrieval*, Berlin: Springer, 125–55.

Miller, S. J. (2011) *Metadata for digital collections: a how-to-do-it manual*, London: Facet Publishing.

Morville, P. and Callender, J. (2010) *Search patterns*, Sebastopol CA: O'Reilly Media.

Morville, P. and Rosenfeld, L. (2006) *Information architecture for the world wide web: designing large-scale web sites*, Sebastopol CA: O'Reilly Media.

Moulaison, H. L. and Corrado, E. (eds) (2011) *Getting started with cloud computing*, London: Facet Publishing.

Negroponte, N. (1995) *Being digital*, London: Hodder and Stoughton.

Orna, E. (2005) *Making knowledge visible*, Aldershot: Gower.

Palmer, M. (2009) *Making the most of RFID in libraries*, London: Facet Publishing.

Papaioannou, D., Sutton, A., Carroll, C., Booth, A. and Wong, R. (2010) Literature searching for social science systematic reviews: consideration of a range of search techniques, *Health Libraries and Information Journal*, 27(2), 114–22.

Poulter, A. (2010) Open source in libraries: An introduction and overview, *Library Review*, 59(9), 655–61.

Qualman, E. (2009) *Socialnomics*, Hoboken NJ: Wiley.

Rasmussen, E. (2011) Access models, in Ruthven, I. and Kelly, D. (eds) (2011) *Interactive information seeking, behaviour and retrieval*, London: Facet Publishing, 95–111.

Robertson, S. E. (1969) The parametric description of retrieval tests, *Journal of Documentation*, 25(1), 1–27.

Robertson, S. E. (2008) On the history of evaluation in IR, *Journal of Information Science*, 34(4), 439–56.

Robinson, L. (2010) *Understanding healthcare information*, London: Facet Publishing.

Rogers, Y., Sharp, H. and Preece, J. (2011) *Interaction design: beyond human-computer interaction* (3rd edn), Chichester: Wiley.

Rowlands, I. and Bawden, D. (1999) Digital Libraries: a conceptual framework, *Libri*, 49(4), 192–202.

Ruthven, I. and Kelly, D. (eds) (2011) *Interactive information seeking, behaviour and retrieval*, London: Facet Publishing.

Seadle, M. and Greifeneder, E. (2007) Defining a digital library, *Library Hi-Tech*, 25(2), 169–73.

Shneiderman, B. (2003) *Leonardo's laptop: human needs and the new computing technologies*, Cambridge MA: MIT Press.

Shneiderman, B. (2011) Social discovery in an information abundant world: designing to create capacity and seek solutions, *Information Services and Use*, 31(1), 3–13.

Shneiderman, B., Plaisant, C., Cohen, M. and Jacobs, S. (2009) *Designing the user interface: strategies for effective human-computer interaction* (5th edn), Boston MA: Addison-Wesley.

Smith, A. G. (2012) Internet search tactics, *Online Information Review*, 36(1), 7–20.

Smith, D. A. (2006) Debabelizing libraries: Machine translation by and for digital collections, *D-Lib Magazine*, 12(3) [online] available at http://www.dlib.org/dlib/march06/smith/03smith.html.

Spellman, R. (2011) Developing best practices for machine translation using Google Translate and OCR terminal, *Journal of Interlibrary Loan, Document Delivery and Electronic Reserve*, 21(3), 141–47.

Steele, J. and Iliinsky, N. (2010) *Beautiful visualization*, Sebastapol CA: O'Reilly Media.

Tedd, L. A. (2007) Library management systems in the UK: 1960s–1980s, *Library History*, 23(4), 301–16.

Terras, M. M. (2010) The rise of digitization: an overview, in Rikowski, R. (ed.), *Digitisation perspectives*, Rotterdam: Sense Publishers.

Town, C. and Harrison, K. (2010) Large-scale grid computing for content-based image retrieval, *Aslib Proceedings*, 62(4–5), 438–46.

Twyman, M. (1998) *British Library guide to printing history*, London: British Library.

van den Heuvel, C. and Rayward, W. B. (2011) Facing interfaces: Paul Otlet's visualizations of data integration, *Journal of the American Society for Information Science and Technology*, 62(12), 2313–26.

van Rijsbergen, C. J. (2004) *The geometry of information retrieval*, Cambridge: Cambridge University Press.

Vilar, P. and Žumer, M. (2008) Perceptions and importance of user friendliness of IR systems according to users' individual characteristics and academic disciplines, *Journal of the American Society for Information Science*, 59(12), 1995–2007.

Walsh, A. (2011) Blurring the boundaries between our physical and electronic libraries: location-aware technologies, QR codes and RFID tags, *Electronic Library*, 29(4), 429–37.

Warr, W. A. (2008) Social software: fun and games or business tools?, *Journal of Information Science*, 34(4), 591–604.

Whitchurch, M. J. (2011) QR codes and library engagement, *Bulletin of American Society for Information Science and Technology*, 38(1), 14–17.

White, R. and Downs, T. E. (2007) *How computers work* (9th edn), Indianapolis IN: Que.

Wilks, Y. (2009) *Machine translation: its scope and limits*, Dordrecht: Springer.

Willett, P. (2008) From chemical documentation to chemoinformatics: 50 years of chemical information science, *Journal of Information Science*, 34(4), 477–99.

Wilson, M. (2011) Interfaces for information retrieval, in Ruthven, I. and Kelly, D. (eds), *Interactive information seeking, behaviour and retrieval*, London: Facet Publishing, 139–70.

Wisniewski, J. (2011) Mobile usability, *Bulletin of the American Society for Information Science and Technology*, 38(1), 30–2.

Xie, I. (2010) Information searching and search models, *Encyclopedia of Library and Information Sciences* (3rd edn), London: Taylor & Francis, 1:1, 2592–2604.

Zhang, A. B. and Gourley, B. (2008) *Creating digital collections: a practical guide*, Oxford: Chandos.

Zimerman, M. (2011) Radio frequency identification (RFID): Time to take another look, OCLC *Systems and Services: International Digital Library Perspectives*, 27(2), 146–54.

Zorkoczy, P. (1982) *Information technology: an introduction*, London: Pitman.

CHAPTER 8

Informetrics

To measure is to know.

If you can not measure it, you can not improve it.

William Thomson, Lord Kelvin

The only man I know who behaves sensibly is my tailor: he takes my measurements anew each time he sees me. The rest go on with their old measurements and expect me to fit them.

George Bernard Shaw

With an uninformed reading, and taking information to be a basic constituent of the universe, informetrics seems a very broad subject. A more informed reading might narrow informetrics to the study of all quantifiable aspects of information science. The reality is . . . more modest still.

Concepción Wilson (1999, 107)

Introduction

This chapter is about measurement; specifically measurement of the quantitative aspects of the creation, communication and use of information. As the quotations above remind us, measurement is vital, but only if the right things are measured and the measurements are meaningful and up to date.

In this chapter, we will first examine the nature of informetrics and some of its components – bibliometrics, webometrics, etc. – before looking at how the subject has developed since its origins in the 1920s. We will consider the very basic question of how much information there is before looking, in a largely qualitative way, at the main 'informetric laws'; Lotka, Bradford and Zipf, and their offspring. Finally, we will look at how informetrics techniques may be applied in information research and practice, giving just an overview with examples.

Informetrics is the study of the quantitative aspects of information resources and of the communication of information. The term was introduced in 1979 by

Otto Nacke, a German documentalist and medical information specialist, and popularized by the British information scientist Bertie Brookes, mentioned in Chapter 3.

Informetrics is usually taken to include several more specific subjects. *Bibliometrics*, the study of quantitative aspects of published documentation; *webometrics* (also termed *webliometrics* or *cybermetrics*), the study of quantitative aspects of web resources, and *scientometrics*, the quantitative study of the growth and change of academic disciplines. Bar-Ilan (2010), De Bellis (2009), Björneborn and Ingwersen (2004), Hood and Wilson (2001), Wilson (1999) and Tague-Sutcliffe (1992) all give detailed accounts of the origins, meanings and interrelations of all these terms, and others which have been used for this subject.

We will also include here within the scope of informetrics three other topics: the fundamental question of how much information there is; the quantitative analysis of information networks; and the controversial application of these methods to the evaluation of research impact and productivity. Some authors have proposed still wider scope: Tague-Sutcliffe (1992), for example, argued for inclusion of topics such as: the quantitative assessment of information itself, by Shannon formula and similar measures; quantitative measures of retrieval system effectiveness, such as recall and precision; and measures of use of resources, such as library performance metrics. We find it more helpful to treat these topics in their appropriate chapters, focusing here on analysis of quantitative aspects of documents and collections.

Informetrics has both a strong theoretical base and a number of highly practical applications. As we saw in Chapters 1 and 5, it has often been regarded as one of a small number of constituents of the information science discipline, and is also one of the aspects of domain analysis. An understanding of the principles and practice of aspects of informetrics is therefore important for all information specialists.

Historical development of informetrics

We will give only a brief outline of the development of the subject here; for a more detailed account, see De Bellis (2009), Hertzel (1987, reprinted 2010), White and McCain (1989) and Wilson (1999).

The earliest study which might count as informetrics is that carried out by Francis Cole, a zoology professor at the University of Reading, England, and Nellie Eales, the curator of the zoology museum and rare book collection established by Cole. (The Cole Museum still exists at Reading University: http://www.reading.ac.uk/colemuseum.)

They studied the growth of the discipline of comparative anatomy between 1550 and 1860, using what they termed 'statistical analysis' of the literature, to analyse, for instance, contributions from different countries (Cole and Eales, 1917). They presented graphically an analysis of 6436 documents, showing changes in the subjects of anatomical study, and relating these to external influences.

A few years later, a study with wider scope was carried out by Edward Wyndham Hulme (1923), librarian at the UK Patent Office, who related the growth of scientific literature to economic development and development of civilization, using the term 'statistical bibliography'. He analysed data from annual issues of the *International Catalogue of Scientific Literature* from 1901 to 1913, counting the entries by subject – and particularly noting when subjects divided, denoting increased specialization – and by author nationality.

These studies established the nature of the topic as the counting of documents in printed collections: counts of items (books, journals, articles, etc.) and of their attributes (country, language, references, etc.). They were rapidly applied to practical problems: for example, the first use of bibliographic data for collection development, in the case of a chemistry collection in an academic library (Gross and Gross, 1927). The authors assessed how often other journals were referenced in the *Journal of the American Chemical Society*, chosen as being most representative of the activities and needs of American chemists. They noted not only the most common of the 247 journals cited, but also trends over time, so as to make cost-effective recommendations. Foreshadowing a later main bibliometric finding, they noted that valuable materials were scattered outside the discipline, recommending that journals of physics and of general science were as important as those of chemistry *per se*. Again anticipating later concerns, they pointed out that the data showed the need for materials in languages other than English – particularly German and French.

Origins of the bibliometric laws

The first general laws of what would come to be called bibliometrics, which will be discussed later in this chapter, were also developed from the 1920s onwards.

Alfred Lotka, a mathematician best known for his work in theoretical biology, was working as a statistician with the New York-based Metropolitan Life Insurance Company, when he derived the law bearing his name, concerned with the distribution of authors by their productivity (Lotka, 1926). He analysed the number of papers contributed by each first-named author mentioned in certain sections of abstracting journals in physics and chemistry. Ironically, although his law is the first of the important informetric laws, Lotka was never involved in the library and information disciplines, and the study which derived this law is a small and untypical part of his work.

Samuel Clement (usually known as just S. C.) Bradford, the librarian of the Science Museum in London, established the next development, with his 'law of scattering', showing how the periodical literature of a given subject area is distributed across journal titles (Bradford, 1934). He analysed bibliographies of geophysics and of lubrication engineering, showing the way in which the entries were spread across a range of sources, and deriving from this a practical means for librarians to choose sources for a collection. Bradford's is the only major informetric law derived by someone from the library and information sciences.

The third of the major bibliographic laws was established by George Kingsley Zipf, an American philosopher and linguist, who derived a distribution for the frequency of occurrence of words in text (Zipf, 1935). Intriguingly, Zipf wrote that an unnamed friend had pointed out this idea to him, and indeed ideas of this kind had been mentioned by several authors before Zipf systematized and promoted them (Rousseau, 2010). This formed the basis for his later 'principle of least effort' (Zipf, 1949). There has been some controversy about whether these should count as true bibliometric laws, but their influence has been great, as we shall see later. They are laws which apply to the concerns of the library and information sciences, but are of much more general applicability.

Informetric studies were given a boost by the appearance of so-called 'citation indexes'. The importance of indexes of this type is that they allow identification of which items have cited older items; this in turn leads to the identification of 'impact', when items receive many citations, and to analysis of the structure of disciplines by examining patterns of citing. Indexes to legal citations had existed for many years, but their wider value for information retrieval was realized and expounded by Eugene Garfield (1955). The main tools which made this possible, the citation indexes of Garfield's Institute for Scientific Information (ISI) – now the Thomson Reuter 'Web of Science/Web of Knowledge' services – were introduced over a period: Science Citation Index in 1961, Social Science Citation Index in 1967 and Arts and Humanities Citation Index in 1974 (Baird and Oppenheim, 1994).

By this time, the concept of bibliometrics was well established. Derek de Solla Price's 1963 book *Little Science, Big Science* used a variety of quantitative methods to document the growth of scientific and technical literature, and to relate this to the history and sociology of science. This classic work formed the basis for scientometric study of the research process through bibliometric data. The term 'bibliometrics' had itself become established, derived by Alan Pritchard (1969), as an improvement on the 'statistical bibliography' designation still in use. The term had not been used before, although Paul Otlet had used the French equivalent 'bibliométrie' in his *Traité de documentation* of 1934, mentioned in Chapter 2. There was great interest in attempting to find a common theoretical basis for the various empirical bibliometric 'laws'; see Tague-Sutliffe (1994) and Rousseau (2005; 2010) for overviews, and Fairthorne (1969) and Egghe (1985) for influential examples.

Eugene Garfield (1972) was also among the first to emphasize the potential value of citation data in the evaluation of the quality of journals, and as a tool for the evaluation of research; see Bensman (2007) for a detailed account. This was not the first time that literature analysis had been recommended, and indeed used, to assess the impact of research. George Banay (1945) was the pioneer in this respect, identifying literature references to a research programme on the treatment of mental illness at Worcester State Hospital, Massachusetts, USA. However, the availability of citation databases and analysis tools gave a boost to this concept.

At about the same time, Henry Small, a colleague of Garfield at ISI, proposed the method of co-citation analysis (Small, 1973), which examines the joint citing of two or more items by later items; the number of times this occurs shows the strength of the link between the two items. This has proved to be a very valuable method of showing connections between key documents which can be used to map the structure of subjects and disciplines. Use of computer visualization techniques alongside informetric analysis has led to visually appealing maps and other images (Börner, Chen and Boyack, 2003), exemplified by the striking *Atlas of Science* (Börner, 2010).

By the early 1970s, therefore, all the main concepts and tools of bibliometrics were in place.

The term 'scientometrics' for the quantitative analysis of the growth of science, and other academic and professional areas, had been introduced by the Russian scientist Vasily V. Nalimov, as a translation of the Russian 'naukometriya'. It became generally accepted during the 1970s, and was used as the title of the main journal of the field, launched in 1978. *Scientometrics* has published many papers with essentially bibliometric content, showing the overlap between these sub-branches of informetrics. Growth of interest in this aspect has led to wide, and sometimes controversial, use of these techniques for productivity assessment and research evaluation, applied to countries, institutions, and individuals.

The advent of the internet, and later the world wide web, quickly led to quantitative studies of resources and their inter-relations in these new environments; see Molyneux and Williams (1999) for an account of early attempts to measure the Internet. In analysing web content, it has been taken for granted that the hyperlink takes an equivalent role to that of the citation in conventional literature; the unpleasing term 'sitation' has sometimes been used. Björneborn and Ingwersen (2004) warn against pushing this analogy too far.

A wide variety of terms was devised to describe this new area of informetrics; many have fallen out of fashion, and perhaps we need not lament *web bibliometry* and *internetometrics* too much. Most commonly used now are *cybermetrics* (for quantitative studies of anything on the internet) and *webometrics* (for the more restricted area of the web), although these terms are often used interchangeably.

Cronin (2001), Björneborn and Ingwersen (2004), Thelwall, Vaughan and Björneborn (2005) and Thelwall (2008; 2010) give careful analysis of the nature, significance and terminology of the area. Availability of detailed records, 'web logs', for digital information resources allows direct analysis of their use, and to so-called 'usage bibliometrics' (Kurtz and Bollen, 2010).

We will now go on to look in more detail at the nature of the laws introduced by pioneers such as Lotka, Bradford, and Zipf. But first, we will look at what is arguably the most fundamental question of informetrics: how much information is there?

How much information is there?

Before the advent of widespread digital information, this question was generally answered in terms of counts of documents: how many books and articles had been published. More recent attempts focus on the, much larger, amount of born-digital information; an intrinsically more difficult process, with results that can only be approximate.

The first attempt in the digital era to address this question in a rigorous way was the 'How much information?' study from the School of Information Management and Systems at University of California Berkeley, USA, first carried out in 2000, and repeated in 2003 (SIMS, 2003). This estimated that about 5 exabytes of new information was stored during 2002; equal to 37,000 times the information in the Library of Congress, or 800 megabytes/30 feet (10 metres) of bookshelf content per person on the planet. However, more than three times this amount of information was communicated through electronic channels but never stored.

Later studies (Hilbert and Lopez, 2011) have suggested that the amount of information broadcast each year was approaching 2 zetabytes by 2007, and that current capacity of all information storage devices approaches 300 exabytes. Davis and Shaw (2011, Chapter 1) and Gleick (2011, Chapter 14) report other estimates of this kind. Gleick extends the question to ask how much information, in the Shannon sense, there is in the universe; apparently 10^{90} bits.

Such large numbers may seem quite divorced from the kind of information resources usually considered as relevant for the information sciences. But it is good to be aware of the scale of the 'infoverse', particularly since trends towards e-research, to be discussed in Chapter 10, will involve information specialists in the handling of much larger data sets than before.

We will now turn to look at some of the main laws of informetrics, which describe patterns and regularities in quantitative aspects of documentation, rather than dealing with information *per se*.

The main informetric laws

Someone coming afresh to this topic may well find it confusing. There are several main 'laws', with numerous variants and reformulations, some of which are given different names. There are claims that these laws can be interrelated, and reflect one underlying law or principle. They are, in any case, not rigid laws, like the laws of science, but statistical approximations, which do not hold in all circumstances. And, although all these laws may be applied in library and information contexts, some of them come from outside the field, and are of much wider applicability.

We will try to simplify matters by focusing on the three most important informetric laws, or 'families of laws' as they are sometimes termed to emphasize the different variants and formulations: Lotka, Bradford and Zipf. We will then look at the ways in which these have been interrelated and combined. Finally, we will examine a different approach to theoretical informetrics, based on network theory. The treatment will necessarily be rather simplified and qualitative, and the interested reader will need to follow the references given. Ronald Rousseau's admirably clear 2010 encyclopaedia article on 'informetric laws' is a good starting point; Wilson's 1999 *ARIST* paper reviews the issues throroughly .

Lotka

Lotka's 'Law of Scientific Productivity', as it was originally known, is an inverse square law relating the total number of documents in some collection and the number which are authored by one person. The number of people who are authors of n documents will be $1/n^2$. More formally, this is described as a power law of form C/n^a, where C is a constant and n is approximately 2. The number of authors with y documents is given by:

$$f(y) = C/y^a$$

So the number of authors producing two items will be one-quarter the number of those producing just one item; the number producing three will be one-ninth of those producing one, and so on. About 60% of authors in a collection will produce just one item. So, for every 1000 authors contributing 1 paper, there are 250 authors contributing 2 papers, 111 authors contributing 3 papers and only 60 authors contributing 4 papers, 40 authors contributing 5 papers, etc. This means that for any subject, or collection, we would expect there to be a small number of very productive people, institutions, countries, etc., and a large number of those making a small contribution. This is an example of what would later come to be called the 'long tail'.

Of course, like all the informetric laws, this is only an approximate statistical law, describing a general regularity in collections of documents; the calculations will never be exact. As we have seen, Lotka derived his result – which he described as a 'formula' or a 'distribution', rather than a law – by analysing first authorship of scientific articles, taking the data from abstracting and indexing services. It is, however, applicable to much wider contexts, whenever we have identifiable producers of documents.

Bradford

Bradford's Law of Scattering, as it is generally known, described regularities in the sources in which interesting documents are found. His original analysis examined articles (documents) in scientific journals (sources). In general, if sources relevant to a particular subject are listed in decreasing order of 'productivity' – meaning the number of relevant items included in them – then a pattern emerges. If the list of sources is divided into three parts, each containing an equal number of useful documents, then the ratio of sources in the three parts is roughly $1:n:n^2$, where n is a constant, varying between subjects and types of material. Again, this is an approximate statistical relationship, rather than anything exact.

What this means is that a small number of sources produces a large number of useful items; this is generally referred to as the 'core'. An alternative way of looking at it is that a third of useful material is scattered over a wide range of sources: another example of the 'long tail'.

Subsequent theoretical work has extended Bradford's formula to any number of groups, rather than just three. Leimkuhler (1967) produced an alternative mathematical formalism, which is sometimes referred to as Leimkuhler's Law. This may be expressed as:

$$N(r) = a \log (1 + br)$$

where $N(r)$ is the total number of items in journals of rank equal to, or lower than r; a and b are constants, depending on the nature of the collection.

Zipf

Zipf's 'Law of Word Occurrence', as it was originally known, deals with statistical regularities in what are termed 'rank/frequency' distributions. If we order the words in some text by the number of times that they occur, then the *rank* of the word – its place in the list – will be determined by its *frequency* – the number of times it occurs. Zipf's law states that, if the words are ordered in decreasing frequency, then the rank of the word multiplied by its frequency is a constant. Mathematically, for a word with an occurrence of y and a rank of r then

$$y = k/r$$

where k is a constant, depending on the context.

Benoit Mandelbrot, best known for his development of fractals, derived an alternative, and more general, formulation of Zipf's law, so that the number of times a word occurs, n, if it has rank r, is given by

$$N = C_1/(1 + C_2.r)^ß$$

where C_1, C_2 and ß are all constants depending on the context. This is generally referred to as Mandelbrot's Law.

Zipfian distributions of this kind are very general, and are found in many aspects of informetrics.

Are they all the same law?
As noted above, there was considerable interest, from the 1960s onwards, in proving that the empirical informetric laws, formulae functions and distributions (Lotka, Zipf, Bradford, Mandelbrot, Leimkuhler, etc.) had a common basis, and are essentially equivalent. Some commonality was obvious from the first. They show very similar patterns in various aspects of documents and collections, and are based on similar rankings by size or frequency of attributes. They relate in general terms to some kind of source and yield: journals-articles, authors-publications, etc. Indeed, Zipf referred to Lotka's work in first announcing his own findings. They also have obvious similarity to familiar distributions observed outside the library and information world, such as the ubiquitous Pareto principle, often referred to as the '80:20 rule', derived originally from the observation by the Italian economist Vilfedo Pareto that 80% of the wealth of Italy at the beginning of the 20th century was owned by 20% of the population. The similarity with the informetric distributions is clear.

However, considerable mathematical difficulties were encountered, and it was not for more than 50 years after the first empirical laws were derived that a satisfactory proof of their equivalence was provided. For details of this, readers with a mathematical bent are referred to Rousseau (2010) for a concise summary, and to Egghe (2005) for a detailed treatment.

There has also been interest in seeking an underlying explanation for these laws. The most commonly offered is the principle known variously as 'success-breeds-success', 'cumulative advantage', 'preferential attachment' and the 'Matthew effect'; the last from the verse in St Matthew's Gospel that states that 'For whoso-ever hath, to him shall be given, and he shall have more abundance: but whosoever hath not, from him shall be taken away even that he hath'. These all rest on the idea that the more productive a source is, in any sense, the more likely it will con-tinue to be productive; although there is always a small chance that a new source may produce the new item. An article in a journal that has been cited many times already is much more likely to be cited again than a rarely cited article; a more distinguished author will receive disproportionately more recognition for their contributions (e.g. citations) than authors who are less known; an author of many papers is much more likely to publish again than one who is less prolific; and so on.

Other explanations are more mathematical in nature: Mandelbrot argued, for example, that fractal theory was the underlying explanation for these laws. Still others point to power laws, of which the informetric laws are an example, being ubiquitous in both the physical and the social worlds. Accounts of these, and other, explanations are given by Rousseau (2010) and Newman (2005).

Network theory

A further kind of quantitative theory which fits within informetrics is network theory in its various guises. This may be adapted to study networks of different kinds, of relevance to the information sciences, from computer networks to social networks. Of obvious relevance to webometric studies, network analysis is often used in conjunction with other informetric tools. Its formal structure is very different from them, relying on the mathematics of graph theory rather than that of statistical distributions. Börner, Sanyal and Vespignani (2007) give a clear account of the underlying ideas.

Thelwall (2006) identifies four main research traditions in network analysis applied to webometrics: from statistical physics, aimed at modelling the structure and growth of the web; from computer science, aimed at facilitating information retrieval and data mining; from the information and social sciences, aimed at studying networks of people; and from the information and social sciences, aimed at studying networks of information.

For informetric applications, the most widely applied technique of this sort is social network analysis (SNA), a strategy for investigating social networks based upon the concepts of graph theory. Otte and Rousseau (2002) review its methods and informetric applicability: library and information applications include study of citation and co-citation networks, and of networks of collaborating researchers and of people seeking, accessing and sharing information.

A concept that many SNA studies are based around is the 'small world' or 'six degrees of separation' concept, which implies that large networks are structured so that all parts are connected through a small number of links . This has been applied in numerous informetrics studies; examples are a study of information-seeking behaviour in an academic library (James, 2006) and a webometric study of linkages within academic websites (Björneborn, 2006).

Although SNA is a particularly appropriate form of network analysis for informetrics, other kinds of network and graph theory may be applied; for an example of a different approach, see an analysis of the structure of the internet using network models derived from statistical physics (Pastor-Satorras and Vespignani, 2004).

Applying informetrics

As we have seen, there has been great theoretical interest in deriving and analysing informetric laws, and practical interest in producing and using tools for informetric analysis, such as citation indexes and software for carrying out citation and co-citation analysis and for visualizing the results. For many years, the only generally available tools were the ISI citation indexes and associated software. More recently other bibliographic search systems, such as Google Scholar and Elsevier's Scopus literature database system, both launched in 2004, have provided tools for bibliometric analysis (Neuhaus and Daniel, 2008). While this increased range of tools is obviously a good thing, it has to be recognized that different systems will give different results – another reason for being cautious in applying bibliometric findings. See, for example, Meho and Spurgin (2005), Meho and Rogers (2008), Li et al. (2010) and Jacso (2010).

Applications of informetrics come in two forms. There are the applications which aim at improving our understanding of documents, collections, disciplines, information behaviour, etc. This is informetrics as a tool for information research; in some cases, as an aspect of domain analysis. Then there are applications in which informetric findings are used as a direct guide to practice; in creating and improving collections, services, etc. We will consider both of these.

The literature is extensive, and has been produced over a long time period; this is a topic where older work is still of value. We will do no more than indicate a categorization of informetric applications, and give some examples. For more detailed reviews, see White and McCain (1989), Borgman and Furner (2002), Bar-Ilan (2008), De Bellis (2009) and Kurtz and Bollen (2010).

It has been evident for many years that an understanding of informetric distributions, and a willingness to use informetric data, should be of value for the management of collections in all environments, including libraries and record centres, and of information services generally; for an early example of advocacy of this kind, see Buckland and Hindle (1969) and for a recent example see Nisonger (1998). However, uptake of these methods as a routine and major tool for the management of collections, and information services in general, has been limited. Line (1994) ascribed this to the nature of service management – 'political' rather than scientific – and to the lack of consistency and reliability in the data typically available.

Changes in literature characteristics

Perhaps the most obvious application of informetrics, and the first to be realized in early bibliometric studies is the *understanding of literatures and their change over time*. Many studies have been carried out, comparing – between subject areas and over time – factors such as the amount of material published, its spread across sources, countries and languages, authorship patterns, use of citations, footnotes and acknowledgements, and many more. For an overview of principles and early development, see Tabah (1999). Examples are an analysis of the core journal literature of tropical medicine, focusing on authorship and country affiliation (Keiser and Utzinger, 2005), an analysis of the discipline of information and knowledge management based on co-citation analysis (Schlögl, 2005), and an investigation of the impact and influence of pharmacology journals based on both bibliometric indicators and usage metrics (Schlögl and Gorraiz, 2011).

Such analyses use many of the elements of bibliographic records – title, author, affiliation, subject descriptors, references, date of publication, journal (or other source) name, language, etc. – as well as records of citations to the item at a later date. Use of this last element relies on the assumption that one document cites another for rational reasons, to do with common subject matter, and an intellectual 'debt' from one to another. Studies which have examined the motivations behind citing have often found that a variety of other reasons are involved, not all of them rational or truly subject-related; citing is a complex process (Baird and Oppenheim, 1994; Cronin, 1998; Nicolaisen, 2007). People may cite others: to situate their own work in context; to give credit for related work; to correct, criticize or substantiate previous work; to identify methodologies, equipment, processes etc; to provide background reading; to give credit to pioneers; to gain credibility by association; to show membership of a 'school of thought'; to show they are well read; and for many other purposes. It is therefore unwise to place uncritical reliance on the idea that a citation reflects with a strong subject link, or an assessment of quality.

Collection management

One of the most obvious practical applications was the use of bibliometric data, particularly Bradford distributions and citation ranks, for the *development of collections*, core lists, etc. This relies on the seemingly sensible ideas that any information collection has a relatively small core, but with some material scattered over a wide range of sources, and that highly cited items are worth having. The original ideas were developed with printed literature, but are equally applicable to digital material and to the web, as exemplified by a study of the scatter of healthcare material on the web (Bhavnani and Peck, 2010). However, practical use seems to have been limited, despite the technique being specifically recommended for this purpose by, among others, Nisonger (1998) for journals, and Enger (2009) for books.

Nicolaisen and Hjørland (2007) argue that Bradford's distribution is not as objective a tool as may appear, since a first necessity is to specify a subject for analysis, and the way in which the subject is defined will lead to very different results. They suggest that 'the fact that it is difficult to find any examples of its actual use in practice may be an indication that such problems have intuitively been foreseen'.

Certainly, great reliance on informetrics for collection development has been limited. Most practitioners seem to take the view well summarized by Norton (2010, 142):

> Core and scatter has important implications but should be tempered, as should most bibliographic methods, with additional information, more than one measurement system, and common sense based upon the underlying requirements of the collection, facility or research.

This is confirmed by a thorough comparison of reported methods for constructing core journal lists (Corby, 2003), in which a blend of informetric methods (particularly Bradford and citation rankings) with other approaches was found to be most appropriate.

Another practical example is the study of *obsolescence*, the rate at which literature loses its value over time, with implications for the maintenance of collections by 'weeding'; this is typically assessed by the rate of citation, on the basis that when material ceases to be cited, it is no longer of current interest. In this way, the 'half-life' for a source, typically an academic journal, may be calculated as the period at which it has had half the use it will receive. However, as Nicholas et al. (2010, 2481) say in their detailed review of the topic, 'Outwardly, the concept of obsolescence appears to be a relatively straightforward one, but on closer inspection much of its straightforwardness disappears'. Rates of obsolescence are very varied, between subjects and in different contexts, and may be affected by many factors. This is one area where an uncritical use of informetric data in practice may be particularly unwise.

Structure of literature and of scholarship

A second very important application has been in the *understanding of the structure of literatures, of disciplines and of collaborating groups*. Bibliographic coupling and co-citation linking are two techniques which aid such analyses.

Bibliographic coupling involves counting the number of references that a given pair of documents have in common. The relationship between documents is believed to be stronger if they have more cited documents in common. This relationship is static over time and retrospective. Co-citation analysis involves counting the number of times that a given pair of documents (or authors or journals) are co-cited by third parties. The more papers co-cite the pair, the stronger the relationship. This relationship is dynamic (new papers may be published which cite the pair) and forward-looking. Webometrics uses many of the same techniques, with hyperlinks replacing the reference or citation as the function linking documents (Thelwall, 2006).

Citation and co-citation analysis has been much used to produce 'maps' of subjects and disciplines, and combined with other methods to identify the underlying social and intellectual relationships. This method was used to produce the maps of information science mentioned in Chapter 1, and some of the images in the visually stunning *Atlas of Science* mentioned above (Börner, 2010). Other examples, to show the scope of this technique, are a study of a small group of information researchers at University College London, comparing citation linkages with social networks (Johnson and Oppenheim, 2007), a mapping of the structure of the Arts and Humanities Citation Index database (Leydesdorff, Hammarfelt and Salah, 2011), and an analysis of the relations between library and information departments and institutions, based on citation networks, nationality, geographic distance and academic collaboration (Yan and Sugimoto, 2011). The use of these techniques for identifying and mapping small research specialities is reviewed by Morris and Martens (2008).

Understanding resources

Informetric studies may also be used to increase *understanding of particular resources*; a journal for example, of a small group of journals in a niche subject area. Examples are detailed comparisons of the bibliometrics of small numbers of academic journals of information science (Tsay, 2011; Nebelong-Bonnevie and Frandsen, 2006).

Informetrics may also be used to *follow changing resources and communication patterns*. An example is a study of the increase over time in citations to web resources in a number of toxicology journals (Robinson, 2007).

Evaluating impact

Already mentioned as an important application is the use of informetrics data for the *assessment of impact and influence*: of journals, authors, departments, institutions and countries.

One aspect of this in which informetric analyses have found particularly controversial application is in the evaluation of research outcomes. Bibliometric measures of research productivity, impact and quality have been given an increasing role in supporting and developing science policy. Seeking the highest return for the resources invested, policy-makers have been attracted by availability of low-cost 'objective' bibliometric indicators (such as counts of published works, articles in refereed journals, citation impact, and so on). A good example is the use of bibliometric indicators to assess and map the impact of British biomedical research during the 1990s (Webster, 2005).

This is an area where there has been heated debate as to how well informetric measures truly capture 'quality', and how much reliance can be placed on them. There was considerable controversy, for example, in both Australia and the United Kingdom during 2010–11 as to whether, and how, bibliometric data should be used in upcoming national research evaluation programmes.

Journal impact factors measure the frequency with which an 'average article' in a journal has been cited in a particular year or period, thus offering a quantitative tool for ranking, evaluating, categorizing and comparing journals. Impact factors have found a variety of practical applications: from guiding editorial and advertising policy to evaluating the scientific quality of individuals and research groups. Although researchers have drawn attention to limitations associated with impact factors (as an example, see Reedijk and Moed, 2008), the fact remains that they offer a simple, easily understood and practical measure of the relative standing and influence of a given journal title. Although the impact factor is best known, there are alternative metrics for a journal's influence; for example, the 'diffusion factor', which measures the breadth of influence across the literature according to how many other sources cite it (Frandsen, Rousseau and Rowlands, 2006). Other summary metrics for journals include 'immediacy' and 'half-life', measuring respectively the rapidity with which the journal's material makes an impact, and how long it remains useful. Attempts have been made to produce analogous web impact factors.

A relatively new development is the use of the 'h-index', as a measure of the impact of journals, departments and – more controversially – of individuals. The h-index is a measure of 'overall impact': an author has an index of N, if at least N of their publications have been cited N times, but N+1 of their papers have not been cited N+1 times. It was devised as a way of avoiding the simplicity of 'citation counts', which can be greatly influenced by a single highly cited paper. It is now increasingly used as a single measure of academic 'quality'. For reviews, see Egghe (2009; 2010) and Norris and Openheim (2010), and for examples of its use in 'rating' library and information academics from the UK and USA see Meho and Spurgin (2005), Oppenheim (2006), Sanderson (2008) and Li et al. (2010), and for an international group of researchers in human-computer interaction see Meho and Rogers (2008).

Bibliometrics for retrieval

Finally, bibliometrics may be used as an *adjunct to retrieval*. A number of search engines have incorporated bibliometric concepts into their design. Google's PageRank, which calculates a quality ranking for each web page, an objective measure of its importance based largely on the number of inlinks, is best known.

It is also possible for someone searching bibliographic databases, e.g. those provided by ProQuest's Dialog, to use simple bibliometrics themselves, as a way of improving searches, or of summarizing search results. It is possible in some databases to search for, or display, the number of times an item has been cited. This makes it possible to identify items which have had a high impact – though this is not at all the same as saying they are 'the best' – and this can be a way of identifying the most significant items out of a list of articles retrieved by subject searching. It may also be a quick and convenient way of identifying important or influential authors, institutions, journals, etc. for a subject.

If the search system supports simple bibliometrics, a searcher can quickly summarize factors such as year of publication, language, country of publication, source journal or subject area, and thereby to provide a useful synopsis of the content of a large amount of material retrieved. Having retrieved the set of material by subject searching, this approach allows a quick and convenient analysis to answer questions such as what are the major languages in which the work was published, what are the most significant journals or other sources, at what time period was publication most active, etc.

Summary
Informetrics has developed from a straightforward counting of the attributes of printed resources to a subject in its own right with a high degree of mathematical and technical sophistication, applied to information environments very different from its origins. Nonetheless, its adoption in the practice of library and information work remains limited, and its use for research evaluation is highly controversial. It is a central topic for information science, now and in the future, and it is important that both researchers and practitioners are fully aware of its promise and limitations.

- The fundamental theories of informetrics – Bradford, Lotka, Zipf, small worlds – are well understood mathematically, but their origin remains a matter for debate.
- Application – for practice and for policy – has lagged behind theory.
- Informetrics is a fundamental part of the information sciences.

Key readings
N. De Bellis, *Bibliometrics and citation analysis: from the Science Citation Index to cybermetrics*, Lanham MD: Scarecrow Press, 2009.

[A good textbook covering many topics thoroughly.]

Ronald Rousseau, Informetric laws, *Encyclopedia of Library and Information Sciences* (3rd edn), London: Taylor & Francis, 1:1, 2010, 2747–75.

[A short and accessible summary of the laws.]

L. Egghe, *Power laws in the information production process: Lotkaian informetrics*, Amsterdam: Elsevier, 2005.

[A detailed and thorough treatment, but only for readers comfortable with mathematics.]

References

Baird, L. M. and Oppenheim, C. (1994) Do citations matter?, *Journal of Information Science*, 20(1), 2–25.

Banay, G. L. (1945) The use of research publication in mental disease, *Bulletin of the Medical Library Association*, 33(1), 50–9.

Bar-Ilan, J. (2008) Informetrics at the beginning of the 21st century – a review, *Journal of Informetrics*, 2(1), 1–52.

Bar-Ilan, J. (2010) Informetrics, *Encyclopedia of Library and Information Science* (3rd edn), London: Taylor & Francis, 1:1, 2755–64.

Bensman, S. J. (2007) Garfield and the impact factor, *Annual Review of Information Science and Technology*, 41, 93–155.

Bhavnani, S. K. and Peck, F. A. (2010) Scatter matters: Regularities and implications for the scatter of healthcare information on the Web, *Journal of the American Society for Information Science and Technology*, 61(4), 659–76.

Björneborn, L. (2006) 'Mini small worlds' of shortest link paths crossing domain boundaries in an academic Web space, *Scientometrics*, 68(3), 395–414.

Björneborn, L. and Ingwersen, P. (2004) Toward a basic framework for webometrics, *Journal of the American Society for Information Science and Technology*, 55(14), 1216–27.

Borgman, C. L. and Furner, J. (2002) Scholarly communication and bibliometrics, *Annual Review of Information Science and Technology*, 36(1), 2–72.

Börner, K. (2010) *Atlas of Science: Visualizing what we know*, Cambridge MA: MIT Press.

Börner, K., Chen, C. and Boyack, K. W. (2003) Visualizing knowledge domains, *Annual Review of Information Science and Technology*, 37, 179–255.

Börner, K., Sanyal, S. and Vespignani, A. (2007) Network science, *Annual Review of Information Science and Technology*, 41, 537–607.

Bradford, S. C. (1934) Sources of information on specific subjects, *Engineering: an illustrated weekly journal*, 137(no. 3550, 26 January 1934), 85–6. Reprinted in *Journal of Information Science*, 1985, 10(4), 176–80.

Buckland, M. K. and Hindle, A. (1969) Library Zipf, *Journal of Documentation*, 25(1), 52–7.

Cole, F. J. and Eales, N. B. (1917) The history of comparative anatomy: Part 1. A statistical analysis of the literature, *Science Progress*, 11(April 1917), 578–96.

Corby, K. (2003) Constructing core journal lists: mixing science and alchemy, *portal: Libraries and the academy*, 3(2), 207–17.

Cronin, B. (1998) Metatheorizing citation, *Scientometrics*, 43(6), 45–55.

Cronin, B. (2001) Bibliometrics and beyond: some thought on web-based citation analysis, *Journal of Information Science*, 27(1), 1–7.

Davis, C. H. and Shaw, D. (eds) (2011) *Introduction to information science and technology*, Medford NJ: Information Today.

De Bellis, N. (2009) *Bibliometrics and citation analysis: from the Science Citation Index to cybermetrics*, Lanham MD: Scarecrow Press.

Egghe, L. (1985) Consequences of Lotka's law for the law of Bradford, *Journal of Documentation*, 41(30), 173–89.

Egghe, L. (2005) *Power laws in the information production process: Lotkaian informetrics*, Amsterdam: Elsevier.

Egghe, L. (2009) Mathematical study of the h-index sequence, *Information Processing and Management*, 45(2), 288–97.

Egghe, L. (2010) The Hirsch index and related impact measures, *Annual Review of Information Science and Technology*, 44, 65–114.

Enger, K. (2009) Using citation analysis to develop core book collections in academic libraries, *Library and Information Science Research*, 31(2), 107–12.

Fairthorne, R. A. (1969) Empirical hyperbolic distributions (Bradford-Zipf-Mandelbrot) for informetric description and prediction, *Journal of Documentation*, 25(4), 319–45.

Frandsen, T. F., Rousseau, R. and Rowlands, I. (2006) Diffusion factors, *Journal of Documentation*, 62(1), 58–72.

Garfield, E. (1955) Citation indexes for science: a new dimension in documentation through association of ideas, *Science*, 122(no. 3159), 108–11.

Garfield, E. (1972) Citation analysis as a tool in journal evaluation, *Science*, 178(no. 4060), 471–78.

Gleick, J. (2011) *The information: a history, a theory, a flood*, London: Fourth Estate.

Gross, P. L. K. and Gross, E. M. (1927) College libraries and chemical education, *Science*, New Series, 66, no. 1713(October 28 1927), 385–9.

Hertzel, D. H. (1987) Bibliometric research: history, *Encyclopedia of Library and Information Science*, 1987, reprinted as an ELIS Classic in the 3rd edn, 2010, 1:1, 546–86.

Hilbert, M. and Lopez, P. (2011) The world's technological capacity to store, communicate and compute information, *Science*, 332, no. 6025, 60–5.

Hood, W. W. and Wilson, C. S. (2001) The literature of bibliometrics, scientometrics and informetrics, *Scientometrics*, 52(2), 291–314.

Jacso, P. (2010) Pragmatic issues in calculating and comparing the quantity and quality of research through rating and ranking of researchers based on peer reviews and bibliometric indicators from Web of Science, Scopus and Google Scholar, *Online Information Review*, 34(6), 972–82.

James, K. (2006) Six degrees of information seeking: Stanley Milgram and the small world of the library, *Journal of Academic Librarianship*, 32(5), 527–32.

Johnson, B. and Oppenheim, C. (2007) How socially connected are citers to those that they cite?, *Journal of Documentation*, 63(5), 609–37.

Keiser J. and Utzinger J. (2005) Trends in the core literature on tropical medicine: a bibliometric analysis from 1952–2002, *Scientometrics*, 62(3), 351–65.

Kurtz, M. J. and Bollen, J. (2010) Usage bibliometrics, *Annual Review of Information Science and Technology*, 44, 3–64.

Leimkuhler, F. F. (1967) The Bradford distribution, *Journal of Documentation*, 23(3), 197–207.

Leydesdorff, L., Hammarfelt, B. and Salah, A. (2011) The structure of the Arts & Humanities Citation Index: A mapping on the basis of aggregated citations among 1,157 journals., *Journal of the American Society for Information Science and Technology*, 62(12), 2414–26.

Li, J.A., Sanderson, M., Willett, P., Norris, M. and Oppenheim, C. (2010) Ranking of library and information science researchers: comparison of data sources for correlating citation data and expert judgement, *Journal of Informetrics*, 4(4), 554–63.

Line, M. B. (1994) Libraries and their management, in Vickery, B. C. (ed.), *Fifty years of information progress: a Journal of Documentation review*, London: Aslib, 189–223.

Lotka, A. J. (1926) The frequency distribution of scientific productivity, *Journal of the Washington Academy of Sciences*, 16(12), 317–23.

Meho, L. I. and Rogers, Y. (2008) Citation counting, citation ranking and h-index of human-computer interaction researchers: a comparison of Scopus and Web of Science, *Journal of the American Society for Information Science and Technology*, 59(11), 1711–26.

Meho, L. I. and Spurgin, K. M. (2005) Ranking the research productivity of library and information science faculty and schools: an evaluation of data sources and research methods, *Journal of the American Society for Information Science and Technology*, 56(12), 1314–31.

Molyneux, R. E. and Williams, R. V. (1999) Measuring the Internet, *Annual Review of Information Science and Technology*, 34, 287–339.

Morris, S. A. and Martens, B. V. (2008) Mapping research specialities, *Annual Review of Information Science and Technology*, 42, 213–95.

Nebelong-Bonnevie, E. and Frandsen, T. F. (2006) Journal citation identity and journal citation image, *Journal of Documentation*, 62(1), 30–57.

Neuhaus, C. and Daniel, H.-D. (2008) Data sources for performing citation analysis: an overview, *Journal of Documentation*, 64(2), 193–210.

Newman, M. E. J. (2005) Power laws, Pareto distributions and Zipf's Law, *Contemporary Physics*, 46(5), 323–51.

Nicholas, D., Rowlands, I., Huntington, P. and Jamali, H. (2010) Information obsolescence, *Encyclopedia of Library and Information Sciences* (3rd edn), London: Taylor & Francis, 1:1, 2475–82.

Nicolaisen, J. (2007) Citation analysis, *Annual Review of Information Science and Technology*, 41, 609–41.

Nicolaisen, J. and Hjørland, B. (2007) Practical potentials of Bradford's Law: a critical examination of the received view, *Journal of Documentation*, 63(3), 359–77.

Nisonger, T. E. (1998) *Management of serials in libraries*, Englewood CO: Libraries Unlimited.

Norris, M. and Oppenheim, C. (2010) The h-index: a broad review of a new bibliometric indicator, *Journal of Documentation*, 66(5), 681–705.

Norton, M. J. (2010) *Introductory concepts in information science* (2nd edn), Medford NJ: Information Today.

Oppenheim, C. (2006) Using the h-index to rank influential British researchers in information science and librarianship, *Journal of the American Society for Information Science and Technology*, 58(2), 297–301.

Otte, E. and Rousseau, R. (2002) Social network analysis: a powerful strategy, also for the information sciences, *Journal of Information Science*, 28(6), 441–53.

Pastro-Satorras, R. and Vespignani, A. (2004) *Evolution and structure of the Internet: a statistical physics approach*, Cambridge: Cambridge University Press.

Pritchard, A. (1969) Statistical bibliography or bibliometrics?, *Journal of Documentation*, 25(4), 348–49.

Reedijk, J. and Moed, H. F. (2008) Is the impact of journal impact factors declining?, *Journal of Documentation*, 64(2), 183–192.

Robinson, L. (2007) Impact of digital information resources in the toxicology literature, *Aslib Proceedings*, 59(4/5), 342–51.

Rousseau, R. (2005) Robert Fairthorne and the empirical power laws, *Journal of Documentation*, 61(2), 194–202.

Rousseau, R. (2010) Informetric laws, *Encyclopedia of Library and Information Sciences* (3rd edn), London: Taylor & Francis, 1:1, 2747–54.

Sanderson, M. (2008) Revisiting h: measured on UK LIS and IR academics, *Journal of the American Society for Information Science and Technology*, 59(7), 1184–90.

Schlögl, C. (2005) Information and knowledge management: dimensions and approaches, *Information Research*, 10(4), paper 235 [online] available at http://InformationR.net/ir/10-4/paper235.html.

Schlögl, C. and Gorraiz, J. (2011) Global usage versus global citation metrics: the case of pharmacology journals, *Journal of the American Society for Information Science and Technology*, 62(1), 161–70.

SIMS (2003) *How much information? 2003 Executive summary*, School of Information Management and Systems, University of California Berkeley, available at http://www2.sims.berkeley.edu/research/projects/how-much-info-2003/execsum.htm.

Small, H. (1973) Co-citation in the scientific literature: a measure of the relationship between two documents, *Journal of the American Society for Information Science*, 24(4), 265–9.

Tabah, A. N. (1999) Literature dynamics: studies on growth, diffusion and epidemics,

Annual Review of Information Science and Technology, 34, 249–86.

Tague-Sutcliffe, J. (1992) An introduction to informetrics, *Information Processing and Management*, 28(1), 103.

Tague-Sutcliffe, J. (1994) Quantitative methods in documentation, in Vickery, B. C. (ed.), *Fifty years of information progress: a Journal of Documentation review*, London: Aslib, 147–88.

Thelwall, M. (2006) Interpreting social science link analysis research: a theoretical framework, *Journal of the American Society of Information Science and Technology*, 57(1), 60–8.

Thelwall, M. (2008) Bibliometrics to webometrics, *Journal of Information Science*, 34(4), 605–22.

Thelwall, M. (2010) Webometrics: emergent or doomed?, *Information Research*, 15(4), paper colis713 [online], available at http://informationr.net/ir/15-4/colis713.html.

Thelwall, M., Vaughan, L. and Björneborn, L. (2005) Webometrics, *Annual Review of Information Science and Technology*, 39, 81–135.

Tsay, M. Y. (2011) A bibliometric analysis and comparison on three information science journals: JASIST, IPM, JOD, 1998–2008, *Scientometrics*, 89(2), 591–606.

Webster, B. M. (2005) International presence and impact of UK biomedical research, 1989–2000, *Aslib Proceedings*, 57(1), 22–47.

White, H. D. and McCain, K. W. (1989) Bibliometrics, *Annual Review of Information Science and Technology*, 24, 119–86.

Wilson, C. S. (1999) Informetrics, *Annual Review of Information Science and Technology*, 34, 107–247.

Wyndham Hulme, E. (1923) *Statistical bibliography in relation to the growth of modern civilisation*, London: Butler and Tanner Grafton.

Yan, E. and Sugimoto, C. R. (2011) Institutional interactions: Exploring social, cognitive, and geographic relationships between institutions as demonstrated through citation networks, *Journal of the American Society for Information Science and Technology*, 62(8), 1498–1514.

Zipf, P. K. (1935) *The psycho-biology of language*, Cambridge MA: MIT Press.

Zipf, P. K. (1949) *Human behavior and the principle of least effort*, Reading MA: Addison-Wesley.

CHAPTER 9

Information behaviour

One thing we know now . . . is that underlying human propensities with regard to information emerge again and again, as each new technology becomes familiar and its use second nature.

Marcia Bates (2010, 2385)

All people are individuals and will seek and use information in different ways . . . [information gathering] is an integral part of our personalities, and we all do it differently. There is no such thing as a homogenous body of information users.

Maurice Line (1998, 223)

Introduction

Information behaviour, the ways in which it is studied, and the significance for practice of the results of such studies, are central topics within information science. Without reliable knowledge of the way in which people find and use information, provision of effective services can be based only on guesswork and prejudice.

This has been a very popular area of information research, and one of the richest for the creation of models and frameworks to explain the complex data produced.

As Case (2006, 295) writes, the information behaviour literature presents a 'bewildering array of topics, populations, samples, sites, theories and methods. Readers wishing to investigate this topic in depth are well served by numerous thorough and detailed overviews, including books (Case, 2007; 2012), review articles (Wilson, 2000; Pettigrew, Fidel and Bruce, 2001; Case, 2006; Savolainen, 2007; Fisher and Julien, 2009; Julien, Pecoskie and Reed, 2011) and encyclopaedia articles (Bates, 2010). Urquhart (2011) even provides a review of recent reviews, while Case (2006) identifies sources reviewing older material. Faced with this plethora of material, this chapter will try only to draw out the main issues and findings, and provide some examples.

We will first consider the question of what information behaviour is, and how it relates to similar ideas, and then briefly outline the historical development of the subject, emphasizing the different ways it has been regarded and studied. A section of theories and models takes a very select look at the wide variety which have been proposed, followed by a summary of research methods used. We then look at some examples of studies of the information behaviour of different groups, and at the idea of individual styles of information behaviour. The summary section looks at what general lessons have been learned about information behaviour.

What is information behaviour?

'Information behaviour' has two connotations, nicely summarized by Bates (2010, 2381) as:

> the many ways in which human beings interact with information, in particular the ways in which people seek and utilize information . . . [and also] . . . a subdiscipline [of library and information science] that engages in a wide range of types of research conducted in order to understand the human relationship to information.

It is usually defined in a rather broad way. Wilson (2000, 49), for example, defined it as:

> the totality of human behavior in relation to sources and channels of information, including both active and passive information seeking and information use. Thus, it includes face-to-face communication with others, as well as the passive reception of information as in, for example, watching TV advertisements, without any intention to act on the information given.

Some commentators, such as Case (2006) have warned against too wide a broadening of scope; ultimately there may be nothing in the information sciences which could not be called 'information behaviour'. They suggest that system evaluations, searching strategies, etc., should be left outside the definition, and this is the approach taken in this chapter. Wilson (1999) gave a useful pictorial model of the components of information behaviour, shown in an expanded form in Figure 9.1 below.

This shows 'information behaviour' as a wide concept, set within the whole of an individual's life world. Within it is 'information seeking': the purposeful activities of looking for information to meet a need, solve a problem, or increase understanding. Within that, in turn, is 'information retrieval': the seeking for some definite information within some kind of information system.

The idea of information behaviour, and its more specific components, is closely tied up with two other concepts: information use and information need. Information use was discussed in Chapter 4, where we saw that it was far from a simple concept; see Savolainen (2009) and Fleming-May (2011). The idea of

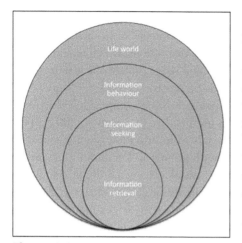

Figure 9.1
The nested model of information behaviour

an 'information need' poses similar problems. Information needs (or 'wants' or 'demands') are a part of overall information behaviour, and can only be understood in the wider context of the use of information in work, in study and in life generally. They may be expressed explicitly – 'what I want to know is . . .' – or implicitly – 'I am a doctor (so obviously I need to know about) . . .'. Over 30 years ago, Wilson (1981, 5) commented that 'within the field of user studies the investigation of "information needs" has presented seemingly intractable problems . . . progress towards some theoretical understanding of the concept of "information need" has been slow'. The situation has not improved much since then, Case (2007, 69) writing that 'not only has a definition of "information need" been difficult to establish, describing exactly how it influences human behavior has also been controversial.'

There is no accepted definition of an information need, though there have been numerous suggestions (Case, 2012, Chapter 4). Most revolve around the idea of a need being some kind of 'recognized gap' between what one knows and what one wants to know: associated with a desire to seek answers, reduce uncertainty, or make sense.

The whole idea of an 'information need' is a contested concept, some writers arguing that there is no such thing. Some scholars argue either that information needs are 'really' other kinds of need – so that a need for information on the location of the nearest pizza restaurant is 'really' an expression of a need for food – or that information needs are 'only' an expression of a psychological state of mind.

In any event, it is clear that an information need is an abstract concept. Not directly observable, such needs exist only 'inside someone's head'. Observation can give only indirect information about such needs. They can only be found directly by asking someone to describe their own need, which they may find difficult to do, as the needs may be implicit, too obvious to be mentioned, not recognized, etc.

Returning to the idea of information behaviour, there have been two objections to the term itself (Savolainen, 2007). One is grammatical; information cannot behave, so the correct term should be 'information-related behaviour'. While recognizing the validity of this point, we accept that the grammatically incorrect term is ubiquitous, so we use it here. The second is more substantial: 'behaviour' has connotations of the discredited psychological concept of behaviourism, and could be taken to be limited to observable, objective actions, which would greatly limit the scope of the idea. However, in general usage, behaviour is here taken to include cognitive behaviour: needs, opinions, motives, knowledge, and so on.

The alternative concept of 'information practice' has become widely discussed since 2000, although the phrase had been used earlier (Savolainen, 2007). This approach brings a more sociological approach to information seeking and use, treating them and phenomena associated with groups and communities, rather than with individuals; it therefore has some similarities with domain analysis, discussed in Chapter 5. Although many previous studies, as we shall see, focused on groups of individual information users defined by their occupation or role, information practice considers information activities to be embedded in the wider social practices of the group, and particularly on the cultural factors affecting information sharing. Savolainen (2007) gives a review of the concept, and a distinction from information behaviour; an early study of 'everyday life information seeking' based on the idea provides a good example (McKenzie, 2003). The term 'information work' (not to be confused with the use of that phrase to mean the work of an information specialist) has also been used to imply something rather similar to information practice; see Savolainen (2007) for a discussion, and Palmer and Neumann (2002) for an example, in a study of humanities scholars.

Notwithstanding these developments, we will use information behaviour as the umbrella term for the remainder of this chapter.

As was just noted, we will not in this chapter look at studies of the way in which people use particular information systems. This is the area of human-computer interaction (HCI), usability, system evaluation, and search strategies and tactics. These have, of course, an overlap with more general information behaviour; they are presented in an integrated way, for example, in Chowdhury and Chowdhury's 2011 book on 'users and usability'. These are considered in the chapter dealing with information technologies.

Origins and development of information behaviour studies

A specific concern for users of information has been evident from the earliest days of the information professions. Bates (2010) reminds us that Samuel Green, one of the founders of the library profession in the USA, who began his 1891 Presidential Address to the American Library Association with 'The function of the library is to serve its users', was writing as early as 1876 that librarians should 'mingle freely' with their users, and 'help them in every way' (Green, 1876, 78). However, although Green pointed out that one benefit of such mingling was that 'you find out what books the actual users of the library need . . . what subjects the constituency of the institution are interested in, and what is the degree of simplicity they require in the presentation of knowledge', systematic research into the needs and behaviours of users came only later.

The early developments are outlined by Wilson (1994; 2000; 2008), who identifies studies of library use and users dating back to 1916, reviewed by McDiarmid in 1940. However, like much else in the information sciences, research into information behaviour was stimulated by a concern for improved methods for handling scientific and technical information, catalysed by the 1948 London conference of the Royal Society, at which use of documents and libraries was discussed. By the time of the follow-up 1958 Washington conference on scientific information, a significant part of the programme was devoted to information needs and sources.

As a consequence, the first major programme of research on the topic was carried out during the 1950s and 1960s on the information needs and behaviours of academics and practitioners in STEM (science, technology, engineering and medicine) subjects, mainly using quantitative surveys. These early studies are reviewed by Menzel (1966) and Meadows (1974). From this first phase of information behaviour research activity emerged many ideas of wider significance, such as the 'information gatekeeper' (a person who acts as an information resource for colleagues) and the 'invisible college' (a network for communicating academic and professional information outside the formal publication process).

During the 1960s and 1970s, there was an expansion of interest in information behaviour relevant to the social sciences, including business and management; initially that of academic and professional groups in the area, and then spreading to an interest in 'ordinary people', and to information from outside formal published sources. Project INISS, a major study of information needs and behaviour in UK social services, is a good example, and was highly influential in the development of concerns and methods (Streatfield and Wilson, 1982). These developments were fuelled by an enthusiasm, particularly in the USA, for 'evaluation' studies of government programmes to address poverty, inequality, poor education, discrimination, and so on: this provided both new areas for information behaviour studies, and new tools – both quantitative and qualitative – to address them (Bawden, 1990).

The term 'information behaviour' began to be used widely during the 1970s; previously such research had been classed as 'user studies', 'information needs and use', 'communication behaviour', and so on. Coincident with this was a new interest in social science methodology, qualitative studies, and creation of conceptual models of information behaviour (Ellis, 2011).

Only during the 1990s did attention turn to the information behaviours of academics and practitioners in the arts and humanities. This progress of interest in information behaviours – beginning with the STEM subjects, progressing to the social sciences, and culminating with the humanities – both is a response to the external factors noted and also reflects the general advancement of information services in different domains. The introduction of online information services, for example, and other technological developments followed exactly the same pattern. Given that much of the focus of behaviour studies has been in seeing how people adapt to new information technologies, the way they have developed is understandable. From the 1980s, much attention was paid to the use of digital tools: online and CD-ROM databases, online catalogues and, later, internet resources.

From 1990 onwards there was a very great increase in academic interest in the area. This manifested itself not just in a larger number of studies, but also an increase in the range of research methods used, and of theories, models and frameworks adopted; both methods and models will be discussed below. The concept of 'information seeking' as an area of study emerged, broader than user studies or information retrieval and allowing for greater consideration of the context in which the information was sought and used.

Theories and models

Information behaviour is the area within the information sciences which has led to the greatest proliferation of theories and models; the 2005 book edited by Karen Fisher, Sandra Erdelez and Lynne McKechnie lists no fewer than 73. We will make no attempt to list, still less discuss and compare them all. Rather, we will give a categorization, and briefly describe some important examples; readers with an interest in the topic will find further information on these examples, and others, in Case (2006; 2012), Wilson (1999; 2010), Fisher and Julien (2009), Fisher, Erdelez and McKechnie (2005), Pettigrew, Fidel and Bruce (2001) and Robson and Robinson (2012). We also show some of the models in diagram form, as this helps make their nature immediately obvious; note, however, that most have extensive text description to go with the pictures. While most of these models have been derived by information science researchers, there is some overlap with models originating in communication science (Robson and Robinson, 2012; McQuail and Windahl, 1993).

It is difficult to distinguish clearly between a 'theory' and a 'model' in this subject and so we will consider them together. 'Theories' here are usually qualitative descriptions and explanations, rather than the mathematical and predictive theories used in the sciences. 'Models' are generally rather simple 'conceptual models', taking the form of flow charts or diagrams; very different from the mathematical models used in science and economics, and the physical or computer models used by architects to picture new buildings and by chemists to display the structure of chemical substances. Their aim is to show the factors involved in information behaviour, and how they relate to one another, to depict the stages and processes of information seeking and use, and sometimes to illustrate a person's thought processes and changing cognitive state as they deal with information (Wilson, 2010; Järvelin and Wilson, 2003).

The idea of conceptual models for information behaviour has been advocated most strongly by Tom Wilson over many years. Wilson, a British information science professor who has spent most of his career at Sheffield University, was one of the leaders in the investigation of information use in the social sciences, and in the application of qualitative methods for studying information behaviour. He was instrumental in establishing the series of 'Information Seeking in Context' (ISIC) international conferences, which have been very influential in promoting the study of the wider contexts of information use. His 1981 paper 'On user studies and information needs' was the first to try to establish a set of definitions and models for the area, and was highly influential (Bawden, 2006). He has derived a number of information behaviour models, whose development he reviews in Wilson (1981; 1999; 2005; 2010).

We can divide the numerous models of this area into four rough categories, depending on their purpose and scope.

Descriptive models

The first class of models we may call *descriptive*. These simply list the factors and activities involved in the aspects of information behaviour being considered; they may be presented graphically or just as a list.

The earliest of these was a diagrammatic representation of a very general information communication model, showing relations between users and information resources, mediated by technology and tools, published by Tom Wilson (1981), and shown, in a simplified form, in Figure 9.2 on the next page.

A later model in this category, and one which attracted much interest, was the behavioural model, derived by David Ellis, another British information science professor originally from the Sheffield school, and now at the University of Aberystwyth. The model, developed in two stages (Ellis, 1989; Ellis, Cox and Hall, 1993), identified eight features of behaviour within information seeking:

- starting – activities at the start of information seeking
- chaining – following references, citations, etc.
- browsing – scanning areas of interest
- differentiating – filtering material by source and quality
- monitoring – keeping up to date by checking sources regularly
- extracting – systematically working through a source
- verifying – checking accuracy of information
- ending – concluding steps.

The model does not define the interrelations between the features, nor the order in which they are carried out; that is determined for each situation. This has

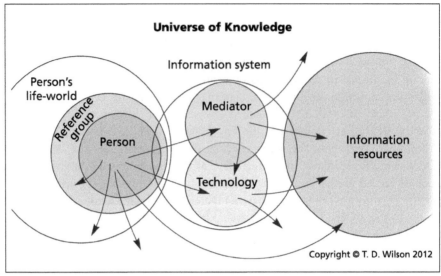

Figure 9.2 *Wilson's descriptive model (reproduced courtesy of Tom Wilson)*

been one of the most tested of all information behaviour models, having been used with studies of groups including scientists and engineers, lawyers, web users and social science researchers.

Process models

Models of this first kind have the limitation that they simply enumerate or display the stages or activities of information seeking, and the entities which affect them. The second class of models for information behaviour comprises *process* models, showing what happens in what order for the information behaviour being illustrated; typically, these are represented as flow-charts or process diagrams.

Wilson (1981) was again the innovator here, deriving the model shown (in a slightly revised form) in Figure 9.3, which is often termed Wilson's first model; he acknowledged its limitations, suggesting that it was little more than a map of the area to be explored, with little explanatory power.

A similar simple model was produced by Krikelas (1983). Later models of this kind were based on studies of occupational groups, and included specific mention of tasks and work roles. Examples are the models of Byström and Järvelin (1995) and of Leckie, Pettigrew and Sylvain (1996); the latter is shown in Figure 9.4.

This model has been used with groups including engineers, lawyers, doctors, nurses and dentists.

Cognitive models

The previous class of models has the limitation that they can, for the most part,

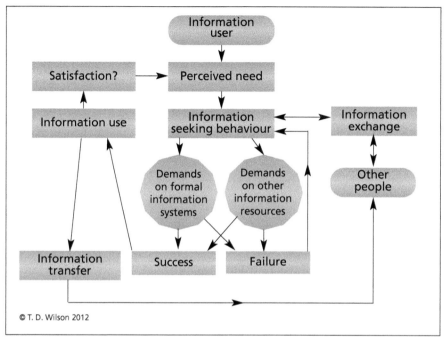

Figure 9.3 *Wilson's first model of information behaviour (reproduced courtesy of Tom Wilson)*

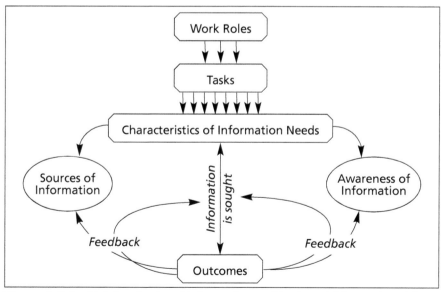

Figure 9.4 *Leckie's 'professional information seeking' model (reproduced from Leckie, Pettigrew and Sylvain, 1996, by permission of University of Chicago Press)*

show only observable behaviours and activities. A third category of models, which may be called *cognitive process*, add the thoughts and motivations of people to the actions and entities shown in the second category.

Arguably the best known of these is what is usually referred to as Wilson's 'expanded model'. The final development of a series of models developed by Tom Wilson (Wilson and Walsh, 1996), it added contextual and cognitive elements. It is shown in Figure 9.5, though this diagram does not do full justice to the ideas, since it subsumes some of Wilson's earlier models without displaying all their detail.

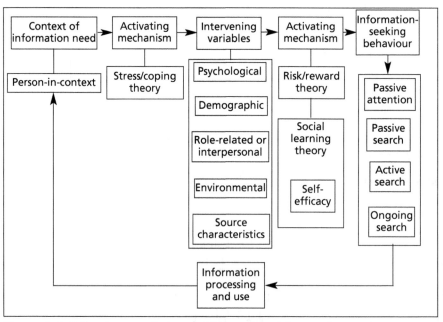

Figure 9.5 *Wilson's expanded model (Reproduced from Wilson and Walsh, 1996. © the British Library Board)*

Other models involving cognitive aspects were presented by Ingwersen (1996), focusing specifically on the information retrieval aspects of information seeking, and by Choo (2006), taking a wider scope of all information needs, seeking and use.

Finally in this category, we should mention the 'information search process' model, derived by Carol Kuhlthau, a library science professor with a long career at Rutgers University. This model, developed between 1980 and 2000, considers six stages of a search process: initiation, selection, exploration, formulation, collection and presentation. For each of these stages, three aspects are described: thoughts, feelings, and actions. This is a rather different kind of model from the others: it is focused on the user's subjective experience as the search progresses, has to be understood holistically, and is not usually displayed as a diagram (Kuhlthau, 2003; 2005). It has been particularly used in studies of school and college students, and also with occupational groups.

Complex models

The models considered so far all tend to explain information behaviour as a linear, ordered set of stages, and to focus on specifically information-related action and cognition. In the fourth and last category are a group of more elaborate models, which we might call *complex*. These introduce a greater degree of context and an increased number of perspectives, and are typically non-linear or multidirectional, rather than having a single sequence of steps.

The non-linear nature of information seeking in the real world has been most clearly captured in the model devised by Alan Foster, another British academic originally from the Sheffield school and now at Aberystwyth. This model defines three 'contexts of interaction' for the information seeker: external (e.g. the social or organizational setting); internal (e.g. feeling and thoughts), and their cognitive approach (e.g. openness). They influence three 'core processes': opening (e.g. browsing); orientation (e.g. problem definition); and consolidation (e.g. verifying). Behaviour patterns described in this way are likened to an artist's palette, able to be combined in any way, to reflect the dynamic and holistic nature of information seeking (Foster, 2004).

Another in this category, described as a 'comprehensive model of information seeking', and aiming to include factors not included in previous information behaviour models, was devised to explain the information behaviour of cancer patients, although it has also been used with engineers (Johnson, 1997; Johnson, Andrews and Allard, 2001). Using some of the ideas of Dervin's Sense-Making (see below), it focuses on the factors relating to people and sources, and on the reasons for particular forms of information seeking, rather than the details of information seeking, and is shown in Figure 9.6 on the next page.

Other models in this category include two 'general models of information behaviour'. Niedzwiedzka (2003) develops Wilson's expanded model, by extending it to broader areas of information behaviour and emphasizing the character of the activities. Godbold (2006) combines Wilson's model with that of Ellis and with Dervin's Sense-Making to the same ends. Another model of this kind develops Ingwersen's original cognitive model in similar ways (Ingwersen and Järvelin, 2005).

While these more sophisticated models undoubtedly capture more of the complexity of information behaviour in the real world, this very fact means that it is less easy to employ them in the straightforward way that the simpler models can be used.

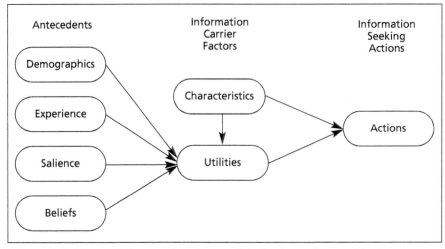

Figure 9.6 *Johnson's 'comprehensive model of information seeking'
(reproduced from Johnson, Andrews and Allard, 2001, by
permission of Elsevier)*

Individual perception theories

Another approach to explaining information behaviour has been to put forward
theories or frameworks based on a constructivist approach, focusing on the
subjective perceptions of individuals as they go about dealing with information.
Usually a very wide scope is taken in what counts as information behaviour; there
is certainly no limitation to formal sources and retrieval processes.

Of these theories, the most influential has certainly been Brenda Dervin's
'Sense-Making' methodology (always with a capital 'S' and 'M', to indicate the
specific use of the phrase). Dervin, a US academic whose work straddles the
information and communication sciences, has developed the idea over several
decades, to provide a very general methodology, rather than a specific model or
theory, for understanding how people derive meaning from information, and
thereby understand their information behaviour in the widest sense (Dervin,
2005; Dervin, Foreman-Wernet and Lauterbach, 2003; Savolainen, 2006). The
ideas, as noted above, have influenced several more specific models of
information behaviour.

There are other examples of this kind of theory, of which we will mention
four well known ones. Reijo Savolainen's 'everyday life information seeking'
(ELIS) gives a holistic framework for understanding the social and psychological
factors underlying the way people use information in everyday settings
(Savolainen, 1995; 2005). Elfreda Chatman's 'life in the round' or 'small world'
theories similarly seek to explain the everyday information behaviour of people
in their social context (Chatman, 1999; Fulton, 2005). The 'information grounds'

theory, developed by Karen Pettigrew and Karen Fisher, concentrates on the detail of the social contexts in which people find and share information (Fisher, 2005). These are many and varied; as well as libraries and information centres, they include clinics, playgrounds, shops, restaurants, and transport settings. Finally, Sandra Erdelez's concept of 'information encountering' focuses on the ways in which people make unexpected discoveries of interesting information, and the extent to which they actively seek to make this happen (Erdelez, 2004).

Evolution and ecology

Finally, in our rapid survey of models and theories of information behaviour, we should mention two general approaches which have arisen from analogies with the biological world. *Information ecology* examines the contexts of information behaviour by analogy with ecological habitats and niches, identifying behaviours in biological terms such as 'foraging' (see, for example, Nardi and O'Day, 1999; Pirolli, 2007; and Huvila, 2009), while Amanda Spink (2010) has put forward an evolutionary perspective for information behaviour.

Methods for studying information behaviour

We will consider information research methods in Chapter 14, but we should note here that a wide variety of research methods has been used to investigate information behaviour. The texts and reviews mentioned above give more details and examples; the books by Donald Case (2007; 2012) are particularly helpful. In summary, we can say that interviews of one kind or another have been the most common method, but many others have applied to some extent, including: questionnaires; telephone and web surveys; focus groups; observation; diaries, logs, audio journals, and photo diaries; think aloud; ethnography, critical success factors, critical incidents, and vignettes; web log analysis; content and discourse analysis; document analysis; and meta-synthesis of the literature.

In general terms, there has been a move from largely quantitative survey methods, almost universal in the first decades of 'user studies', to greater use of in-depth qualitative techniques, as interest has moved towards investigating information behaviour in wider contexts. The focus has similarly changed. Initial studies were generally carried out from a systems perspective, investigating which systems and services were used, by whom, and to what extent, with limited consideration of the purpose or success of their use. Later studies considered the information behaviour of individuals, from a cognitive viewpoint, while a primarily social viewpoint, including detailed consideration of information in the wider context of the life and work of social groups, followed.

As a simple illustration of the range of methods currently employed, the following list shows a selection of papers published between 2008 and 2011, with a note of the methods used.

Information behaviour research examples

Krampen, G., Fell, C. and Schui, G. (2011) Psychologists' research activities and professional information-seeking behaviour, *Journal of Information Science*, 47(4), 439–50. [Online survey.]

Vilar, P. and Žumer, M. (2011) Information searching behaviour of young Slovenian researchers, *Program*, 45(3), 279–93. [Computer session recordings, questionnaires.]

Lu, L. and Yuan, Y. C. (2011) Shall I Google it or ask the competent villain down the hall? The moderating role of information need in information source selection, *Journal of the American Society for Information Science and Technology*, 62(1), 133–45. [Interviews, questionnaires.]

Bartlett, J. C., Ishimura, Y. and Kloda, L. A. (2011) Why choose this one? Factors in scientists' selection of bioinformatics tools, *Information Research*, 2011, 16(1), paper 463, available from http://InformationR.net/ir/16-1/paper463.html. [Diaries, interviews.]

Pilerot, O. and Limberg, L. (2011) Information sharing as a means to reach collective understanding: a study of design scholars' information practices, *Journal of Documentation*, 67(2), 312–33. [In-depth interviews, discourse analysis.]

Mason, H. and Robinson, L. (2011) The information-related behaviour of emerging artists and designers: inspiration and guidance for new practitioners, *Journal of Documentation*, 67(1), 159–80. [Online questionnaires.]

Brine, A. and Feather, J. (2010) The information needs of UK historic houses: mapping the ground, *Journal of Documentation*, 66(1), 28–45. [Postal questionnaires and interviews.]

Robinson, M. A. (2010) An empirical analysis of engineers' information behaviours, *Journal of the American Society for Information Science and Technology*, 61(4), 640–58. [Self-reporting using PDAs.]

Niu, X. et al. (2010) National study of information seeking behavior of academic researchers in the United States, *Journal of the American Society for Information Science and Technology*, 61(5), 869–90. [Web-based in-depth questionnaire.]

Medaille, A. (2010) Creativity and craft: the information seeking behavior of theatre artists, *Journal of Documentation*, 66(3), 327–47. [Online questionnaires and interviews.]

Nicholas, D. et al. (2010) Diversity in the e-journal use and information-seeking behaviour of UK researchers, *Journal of Documentation*, 66(3), 409–33. [Web log analysis.]

Martinez-Silveira, M. S. and Oddone, N. (2009) Information-seeking behavior of medical residents in clinical practice in Bahia, Brazil, *Journal of the*

Medical Library Association, 96(4), 381–84. [Questionnaire, critical incidents.]

Tenopir, C., King, D. W., Edwards, S. and Wu, L. (2009) Electronic journals and changes in scholarly article seeking and reading patterns, *Aslib Proceedings*, 61(1), 5–32. [Questionnaires, critical incidents, comparison over time.]

Hider, P. N., Griffin, G., Walker, M. and Coughlan, E. (2009) The information seeking behaviour of clinical staff in a large health care organization, *Journal of the Medical Library Association*, 97(1), 47–50. [Postal questionnaires.]

Hemmig, W. S. (2008) The information seeking behaviour of visual artists: a literature review, *Journal of Documentation*, 64(3), 343–62. [Literature analysis.]

Trotter, M. I. and Morgan, D. W. (2008) Patients' use of the Internet for health related matters: a study of Internet usage in 2000 and 2006, *Health Informatics Journal*, 14(3), 175–81. [Questionnaires, comparison over time.]

Reddy, M. C. and Spence, P. R. (2008) Collaborative information seeking: a field study of a multidisciplinary patient care team, *Information Processing and Management*, 44(1), 242–55. [Ethnography.]

Inskip, C., Butterworth, R. and MacFarlane, A. (2008) A study of the information needs of the users of a folk music library and the implications for the design of a digital library system, *Information Processing and Management*, 44(2), 647–62. [Context analysis, conceptual framework derived, individual interviews.]

Miranda, S. V. and Tarapanoff, K. M. A. (2008) Information needs and information competencies: a case study of the off-site supervision of financial institutions in Brazil, *Information Research*, 13(2), paper 344, available from http://informationr.net/ir/13-2/paper344.html. [Content analysis, interviews, focus groups, observation, document analysis.]

Information behaviour of groups

Information research has focused on a wide variety of groups of user, becoming wider as time has passed, from an initial focus on academic and professional groups; again, the texts and reviews give full details. We give some examples of the kind of groups studied below, following Case (2006; 2007; 2012) in categorizing the groups studied as defined by occupation or discipline, by role or by demographic status. Occupational groups have been most studied, and almost all research has been carried out in the developed world. For examples of the limited number of studies in the developing world, see Mooko (2005) and Musoke (2007). Some examples of groups studied are:

By occupation or discipline
Scientists, engineers, doctors, nurses, pharmacists, social scientists, humanities scholars, psychologists, industrial managers, journalists, lawyers, farmers, artists, police officers, arts administrators, theologians, architects, teachers, janitors.

By role
Patients, carers, students, researchers, professors, citizens, job-seekers, genealogists, hobbyists (e.g. cooks, coin buyers, knitters), library users, shoppers, readers, internet users.

By demographic
Children, teenagers, women, mothers, older people, immigrants, poor people, homeless people, retired persons. Inhabitants of particular countries or areas, ethnic minorities.

Copious individual examples are given in the books and general review articles noted above. For readers interested in an overview of the kind of studies involved, and the understanding gained, there are overviews for all categories. As examples of reviews of the literature on studies by occupation or discipline, see Case (2007) (scientists and engineers, lawyers, journalists), Robinson (2010) (healthcare workers), Hemmig (2008) (visual artists) and Kloda and Bartlett (2009) (rehabilitation therapists). As examples of reviews by role, see Case (2007) (citizens, consumers, patients, students) and Savolainen (2008) (unemployed people, environmental activists); and as examples of reviews by demography, see Urquhart and Yeoman (2010) (women), Caidi, Allard and Quirke (2010) (immigrants), Spink and Heinström (2011) (young children) and Dutta (2009) (inhabitants of developing countries).

Individual information behaviour styles
As we have seen, several of the models and frameworks mentioned above focus on the individual information user; their actions, thoughts and motivations. An interesting extension of this is to try to determine, and label or categorize, an individual's typical pattern of information behaviour, which we might call their 'information style'.

This area has been reviewed in detail (Bawden and Robinson, 2011), so here we will only mention some main points and examples. Much of the work in this area has analysed the relation between personality factors and interaction with computer systems, typically web searching; as with search strategies and tactics, this is a 'micro' level of information behaviour which was discussed in Chapter 7.

One way in which this kind of 'information style' emerges is as an almost accidental by-product of a wider study. An early example is that of Palmer's study of scientists working at an agricultural research organization, based on semi-structured interviews and questionnaires (Palmer, 1991a; 1991b). Cluster analysis of the results showed the participants falling into five groups, which were denoted as:

- 'non-seekers', for whom information access was not a priority
- 'lone, wide rangers', preferring to work alone, reading and scanning widely, and relying on serendipitous information discovery
- 'unsettled, self-conscious seekers', concerned about missing important information
- 'confident collectors', amassing their own information collections, rather than routinely searching for information
- 'hunters', with regular information-gathering routines, and a focus on currently relevant information.

Palmer then went on to derive an alternative and, by her description, subjective six-fold typology, based on her appreciation of participants' information habits, and including such factors as appearance, body language and intonation in response to questions:

- 'information overlord', operating an extensive and controlled information environment
- 'information entrepreneur', creating an information-rich environment, using many sources and strategies
- 'information hunter', organized and predictable information gatherer, in narrowly focused areas
- 'information pragmatist', occasional gatherer of information, only when need arises
- 'information plodder', rarely seeking information, relying on own knowledge or personal contacts
- 'information derelict', seeming to neither need nor use information.

Classifications of this kind are great fun and may spark insights, and there are a number in the literature; however, they are never consistent with one another, and their objective validity has to be doubted.

Another, and more systematic, approach is to try to determine information behaviour by some kind of survey, and then to compare the results with personality as assessed by some psychometric test. An example is the work of Jannica Heinström (2003, 2005), who assessed information behaviour of students by survey, identifying three behavioural patterns: fast surfing, broad scanning and deep diving. These behaviour patterns could then be related to personality and learning style, identified from another survey. For example, the fast surfing behaviour – associated with a rapid search for a few highly relevant documents, ideally supporting already formed viewpoints – was related to neuroticism, to cautiousness (low openness to experience) and to carelessness (low conscientiousness), as well as to a typically superficial and non-strategic approach to study. These ideas have been elaborated in a book, which identifies five 'information attitudes', linked to personality traits, and resulting in typical patterns of information behaviour: invitational; exploring; purposeful; passive; and avoiding (Heinström, 2010).

These studies, and others reviewed by Bawden and Robinson (2011), open the intriguing potential for a categorization of individual information behaviour. Knowledge of individual 'information styles' could be valuable for information service provision in several ways, such as customization of interfaces, or provision of training and support in the most appropriate way; it has long been recognized that information users, even with the same subject interests and same education level, cannot be treated as a homogenous mass (see, for example, Line, 1998). However, we still have no agreed method for determining such styles reliably.

Summary: so what do we know?

There have been, as the account above makes clear, very many studies of information behaviour. These have produced much information about the detailed behaviours of many different kinds of people: from the academic and professional groups who were the main focus of early studies to the much more diverse groups and individuals studied since. While there is therefore a large body of good evidence to support the practice of information provision to a variety of user groups, it is not so clear that many general findings have emerged. What, after over 50 years of effort, do we know about information behaviour in general?

As the quote from Marcia Bates which opened this chapter reminds us, one thing we know is that technology does not change our basic ways of dealing with information, although the details of sources and systems, search tactics and access methods, will obviously change markedly.

One general finding is that, the more carefully it is investigated, the more subtle and differentiated information behaviour is found to be. Behaviours are often not what would be expected; sometimes they are counter-intuitive, and sometimes difficult to interpret.

The law which governs information behaviour has been found, over and over again, to be Zipf's law of least effort. Familiarity of sources, and ease of access and use, is usually (though not invariably) more important than perceived quality. This principle is sometimes expressed as the 'good enough', sometimes as 'satisficing'; it can be found in virtually all information environments.

Perhaps, to the chagrin of an early generation of information researchers, who believed that their findings would be used mainly to improve traditional library and information services, personal and informal sources have always held a very high place, in academic and professional contexts as well as with the general public. The ubiquity of social media now raises this effect to a new level. Similarly, unstructured and serendipitous information seeking is often found to be more important than the use of formal sources in a structured way.

Domains are important. To a large extent information behaviour is correlated with membership of a domain: occupation, academic discipline, role, etc. But, as the opening quote from Maurice Line reminds us, that is not the whole story: individual personality is important, even if we do not yet have a reliable way of assessing individual information styles.

Information behaviour cannot be considered in isolation; we need to explicitly understand the wider context. Information skills and behaviour are usually pragmatic and problem-based: most of the time, people are trying to solve problems, to make sense of the world, and to do things, not to find information for its own sake. Experience has shown that the more context can be brought into the understanding of information behaviour, the more realistic and helpful are the results.

There are now many alternative models for information behaviour: a good indication that none is wholly adequate. The recent trend is to try to combine and improve them, rather than to create new ones. Similarly, the initial trend for quantitative surveys, and the subsequent enthusiasm for qualitative methods, have been replaced by the recognition that both are needed; the subject is too complex for any single solution.

> - Information behaviour has been studied for over 50 years, using a wide variety of research methods.
> - There are numerous conceptual models and qualitative theories accounting for different aspects of information behaviour.
> - Information behaviour is determined primarily by domain (occupation, academic subject, etc.) but is also affected by personality differences.
> - A great deal is known about information behaviour within particular domains, but there are few general principles.

Key readings

K. E. Fisher, S. Erdelez, and L. E. F. McKechnie (eds), *Theories of information behavior*, Medford NJ: Information Today, 2005.
   [A very accessible set of short descriptions of many theories and models.]

Donald Case, *Looking for information: a survey of research on information seeking, needs and behavior* (3rd edn), Bingley: Emerald, 2012.
[A thorough and detailed coverage of all aspects, equally valuable for reference as for tutorial reading; the two earlier editions of the book are also valuable for older material.]

References

Bates, M. J. (2010) Information behavior, *Encyclopedia of Library and Information Sciences* (3rd edn), London: Taylor & Francis, 1:1, 2381–91.

Bawden, D. (1990) *User-oriented evaluation of information systems and services*, Aldershot: Gower.

Bawden, D. (2006) Users, user studies and human information behaviour: a three-decade perspective on Tom Wilson's 'On user studies and information needs'. *Journal of Documentation*, 62(6), 671–79.

Bawden, D. and Robinson, L. (2011) Individual differences in information-related behaviour; what do we know about information styles?, in Spink, A. and Heinström, J. (eds), *New directions in information behaviour*, Bingley: Emerald, pp 127–58.

Byström, K. and Järvelin, K. (1995) Task complexity affects information seeking and use, *Information Processing and Management*, 31(2), 193–213.

Caidi, N., Allard D. and Quirke, L. (2010) Information practices of immigrants, *Annual Review of Information Science and Technology*, 44, 493–531.

Case, D. O. (2006) Information behavior, *Annual Review of Information Science and Technology*, 40, 293–327.

Case, D. O. (2007) *Looking for information: a survey of research on information seeking, needs and behavior* (2nd edn), New York: Academic Press.

Case, D. O. (2012) *Looking for information: a survey of research on information seeking, needs and behavior* (3rd edn), Bingley: Emerald.

Chatman, E. (1999) A theory of life in the round, *Journal of the American Society for Information Science*, 50(3), 207–17.

Choo, C. W. (2006) *The knowing organization* (2nd edn), Oxford: Oxford University Press.

Chowdhury, G. G. and Chowdhury, S. (2011) *Information users and usability in the digital age*, London: Facet Publishing.

Devin, B. (2005) What methodology does to theory: Sense-Making methodology as exemplar, in Fisher, K. E., Erdelez, S. and McKechnie, L. E. F. (eds), *Theories of information behavior*, Medford NJ: Information Today, 25–30.

Dervin, B., Foreman-Wernet, L. and Lauterbach, E. (2003) *Sense-Making methodology reader: selected writings of Brenda Devin*, Cresskill NJ: Hampton Press.

Dutta, R. (2009) Information needs and information-seeking behavior in developing countries, *International Information and Library Review*, 41(1), 44–51.

Ellis, D. (1989) A behavioural approach to information retrieval system design. *Journal of Documentation*, 45(3), 171–212.

Ellis, D. (2011) The emergence of conceptual modelling in information behaviour research, in Spink, A. and Heinström, J. (eds), *New directions in information behaviour*, Bingley: Emerald, 17–35.

Ellis D., Cox D. and Hall K. (1993) A comparison of the information seeking patterns of researchers in the physical and social sciences, *Journal of Documentation*, 49(4), 356–69.

Erdelez, S. (2004) Investigation of information encountering in the controlled research environment, *Information Processing and Management*, 40(6), 1013–25.

Fisher, K. E. (2005) Information grounds, in Fisher, K. E., Erdelez, S. and McKechnie, L. E. F. (eds), *Theories of information behavior*, Medford NJ: Information Today, 185–90.

Fisher, K. E., Erdelez, S. and McKechnie, L. E. F. (eds) (2005) *Theories of information behavior*, Medford NJ: Information Today.

Fisher, K. E. and Julien, H. (2009) Information behavior, *Annual Review of Information Science and Technology*, 43, 317–58.

Foster A. (2004) A non-linear model of information seeking behavior, *Journal of the American Society for Information Science and Technology*, 55(3), 228–37.

Fleming-May, R. A. (2011) What is library use? Facets of concept and a typology of its application in the literature of library and information science, *Library Quarterly*, 81(3), 297–320.

Fulton, C. (2005) Chatman's life in the round, in Fisher, K. E., Erdelez, S. and McKechnie, L. E. F. (eds), *Theories of information behavior*, Medford NJ: Information Today, 79–82.

Godbold N. (2006) Beyond information seeking: towards a general model of information behaviour, *Information Research*, 11(4) paper 269, available at http://InformationR.net/ir/11-4/paper269.html.

Green, S. S. (1876) Personal relations between librarians and readers, *American Library Journal*, 1(2/3), 74–81.

Heinström, J. (2003) Five personality dimensions and their influence on information behaviour, *Information Research*, 9(1) paper 195, available at http://informationR.net/ir/9-1/paper165.html.

Heinström, J. (2005) Fast surfing, broad scanning and deep diving: the influence of personality and study approach on students' information-seeking behaviour, *Journal of Documentation*, 61(2), 228–47.

Heinström, J. (2010) *From fear to flow: personality and information interaction*, Oxford: Chandos.

Hemmig, W. (2008) The information-seeking behaviour of visual artists: a literature review, *Journal of Documentation*, 64(3), 343–62.

Huvila, I. (2009) Ecological framework of information interactions and information infrastructures, *Journal of Information Science*, 35(6), 695–708.

Ingwesen, P. (1996) Cognitive perspectives of information retrieval interaction, *Journal of Documentation*, 52(1), 3–50.

Ingwersen. P. and Järvelin, K. (2005) *The turn: integration of information seeking and retrieval in context*, Dordrecht: Springer.

Järvelin, K. and Wilson, T. D. (2003) On conceptual models for information seeking and retrieval research. *Information Research*, 9(1), paper 163, available at http://informationr.net/ir/9-1/paper163.html.

Johnson J. D. (1997) *Cancer-related Information Seeking*, Creskill, NJ: Hampton Press.

Johnson J. D., Andrews, J. E. and Allard S. (2001) A model for understanding and affecting cancer genetics information seeking, *Library & Information Science Research*, 23(4), 335–49.

Julien, H., Pecoskie, J. L. and Reed, K. (2011) Trends in information behavior research, 1999–2008: a content analysis, *Library and Information Science Research*, 33(1), 19–24.

Kloda, L. A. and Bartlett, J. C. (2009) Clinical information behavior of rehabilitation therapists: a review of the research on occupational therapists, physical therapists, and speech-language pathologists, *Journal of the Medical Library Association*, 97(3), 194–202.

Krikelas, J. (1983) Information-seeking behaviour: patterns and concepts, *Drexel Library Quarterly*, 19(1), 5–20.

Kuhlthau, C. C. (2003) *Seeking meaning: a process approach to library and information services* (2nd edn), Santa Barbara CA: Libraries Unlimited.

Kuhlthau, C. C. (2005) Kuhlthau's information search process, in Fisher, K. E., Erdelez, S. and McKechnie, L. E. F. (eds), *Theories of information behavior*, Medford NJ: Information Today, 230–34.

Leckie, G. J., Pettigrew, K. E. and Sylvain, C. (1996) Modeling the information seeking of professionals: a general model derived from research on engineers, health care professionals, and lawyers, *Library Quarterly*, 66(2), 161–93.

Line, M. B. (1998) Designing libraries round human beings, *Aslib Proceedings*, 50(8), 221–29.

McDiarmid, E. W. (1940) *The library survey: problems and methods*, Chicago: American Library Association.

McKenzie, P. J. (2003) A model of information practices in accounts of everyday life information seeking, *Journal of Documentation*, 59(1), 19–40.

McQuail, D. and Windahl, S. (1993) *Communication models for the study of mass communication* (2nd edn), New York NY: Longman.

Meadows, A. J. (1974) *Communication in science*, London: Butterworth.

Menzel, H. (1966) Information needs and uses in science and technology, *Annual Review of Information Science and Technology*, 1, 41–69.

Mooko, N. P. (2005) The information behaviours of rural women in Botswana, *Library and Information Science Research*, 27(1), 115–27.

Musoke, M. G. N. (2007) Information behaviour of primary care providers in rural Uganda, *Journal of Documentation*, 63(3), 299–322.

Nardi, B. A. and O'Day, V. L. (1999) *Information ecologies: using technology with heart*, Cambridge MA: MIT Press.

Niedzwiedzka, B. (2003) A proposed general model of information behaviour. *Information Research*, 9(1), paper 164, available at http://informationr.net/ir/9-1/paper164.html.

Palmer, J. (1991a) Scientists and information. 1. Using cluster analysis to identify information style, *Journal of Documentation*, 47(2), 105–29.

Palmer, J. (1991b) Scientists and information. 2. Personal factors in information behaviour, *Journal of Documentation*, 47(3), 254–75.

Palmer, C. L. and Neumann, L. J. (2002) The information work of interdisciplinary humanities scholars: exploration and translation, *Library Quarterly*, 72(1), 85–117.

Pettigrew, K. E., Fidel, R. and Bruce, H. (2001) Conceptual frameworks in information behavior, *Annual Review of Information Science and Technology*, 35, 43–78.

Pirolli, P. (2007) *Information foraging theory: adaptive interaction with information*, Oxford: Oxford University Press.

Robinson, L. (2010) *Understanding healthcare information*, London: Facet Publishing.

Robson, A. and Robinson, L. (2012) Building on models of information behaviour: linking information seeking and communication, *Journal of Documentation*, in press.

Savolainen, R. (1995) Everyday life information seeking: approaching information seeking in the context of 'way of life', *Library and Information Science Research*, 17(3), 259–94.

Savolainen, R. (2005) Everyday life information seeking, in Fisher, K. E., Erdelez, S. and McKechnie, L. E. F. (eds), *Theories of information behavior*, Medford NJ: Information Today, 143–48.

Savolainen, R. (2006) Information use as gap-bridging: the viewpoint of Sense-Making methodology, *Journal of the American Society for Information Science and Technology*, 57(8), 1116–25.

Savolainen, R. (2007) Information behavior and information practice: reviewing the 'umbrella concepts' of information-seeking studies, *Library Quarterly*, 77(2), 109–32.

Savolainen, R. (2008) *Everyday information practices: a social phenomenological perspective*, Lanham MD: Scarecrow Press.

Savolainen, R. (2009) Information use and information processing: comparison of conceptualizations, *Journal of Documentation*, 65(2), 187–207.

Spink, A. (2010) *Information behaviour: an evolutionary instinct*, Heidelberg: Springer.

Spink, A. and Heinström, J. (2011) Information behaviour development in early childhood, in Spink, A. and Heinström, J. (eds), *New directions in information behaviour*, Bingley: Emerald, 17–35.

Streatfield, D. R. and Wilson, T. D. (1982) Information innovations in social services departments: a third report on Project INISS, *Journal of Documentation*, 38(4), 273–81.

Urquhart, C. (2011) Meta-synthesis of research on information seeking behaviour, *Information Research*, 16(1), paper 455, [online] available at http://InformationR.net/ir/16-1/paper455.html.

Urquhart, C. and Yeoman, A. (2010) Information behaviour of women: theoretical perspectives on gender, *Journal of Documentation*, 66(1), 113–39.

Wilson, T. (1994) Information needs and uses: fifty years of progress' in Vickery, B. C. (ed.), *Fifty years of information progress: a Journal of Documentation review*, London: Aslib, 15–51.

Wilson, T. (2008) The information user: past, present and future, *Journal of Information Science*, 34(4), 457–64.

Wilson, T. D. (1981) On user studies and information needs, *Journal of Documentation*, 37(1), 3–15.

Wilson, T. D. (1999) Models in information behaviour research, *Journal of Documentation*, 55(3), 249–70.

Wilson, T. D. (2000) Human information behaviour, *Informing Science*, 3(2), 49–55.

Wilson, T. D. (2005) Evolution in information behavior modelling: Wilson's model, in Fisher, K. E., Erdelez, S. and McKechnie, L. E. F. (eds), *Theories of information behavior*, Medford NJ: Information Today, 31–6.

Wilson, T. D. (2010) Information behavior models, *Encyclopedia of Information Science and Technology* (3rd edn), London: Taylor & Francis, 1:1, 2392–2400.

Wilson, T. and Walsh C. (1996) *Information behaviour: an interdisciplinary perspective. British Library Research and Innovation Report 10*. London: British Library, available at: http://informationr.net/tdw/publ/infbehav.

CHAPTER 10

Communicating information: changing contexts

We are all patrons of the Library of Babel now, and we are the librarians too.

James Gleick (2011, 426)

If you want to truly understand something, try to change it.

Kurt Lewin, German-American psychologist

It is not necessary to change. Survival is not mandatory.

W. Edwards Deming, American statistician

Introduction

In this chapter, we will look at some of the changes which have occurred, and are still occurring, to the way in which recorded information is communicated. These changes are largely a result of new technologies, specifically the 'digital transition' to a world in which most information is in digital form most of the time, but also reflect economic and social factors.

The significance of these changes for the information sciences is two-fold. The environment in which information practitioners work is very different indeed to what it was 30 years ago, and we may expect it to change equally dramatically in the coming decades. A full understanding of these changes, and an appreciation of what is to come, is essential for effective information provision. Perhaps more positively, the information sciences can make very significant contributions to steering these changes, so as to take best advantage of new capabilities without losing the best of past practices.

We will mainly consider the present situation in this chapter, having looked at historical developments in Chapter 2, and leaving consideration of future trends to the final chapter. We will first look at some general frameworks to help understand the issues, before examining the digital transition from the print-based information environment, changing economic factors and new forms of recorded communication. We will then look at some new forms of research and scholarly activity which both take advantage of, and contribute to, new communication formats, and conclude with a reflection on changing information spaces and places.

Much of the material in this chapter deals with publishing and scholarly communication. Relevant though these areas are for the information environment, and hence for the information sciences, we will only be able to cover them in outline, referring readers to other sources for more detail.

Communication frameworks

As we saw in Chapter 2, the information environment which persisted to the end of the 20th century was established in outline with the introduction of printing in Europe in the 15th century, and formed in detail with the communications revolution of the 19th century. Significant changes began to appear with the advent of the digital computer in about 1960, and proceeded with an increasing pace and complexity ever since. The arrival of new formats, new forms of information resources and new ways of providing the older formats give a complicated, and sometimes bewildering, picture for anyone trying to understand the whole picture of the communication of recorded information.

Two kinds of conceptual models can help to make sense of this, and to remain unchanged in outline despite great changes in detail. These are the communication chain for recorded information and frameworks for categorizing information resources.

Information chains and lifecycles

As we noted in Chapter 1, the idea of a communication chain, or information chain, or information lifecycle, of recorded information is a fundamental one for the information sciences, and it is also commonly invoked in explanations of information and digital literacies. This chain describes the processes from creation, through dissemination, organization, indexing, storage and use to disposal.

There have been many variants of this chain and lifecycle used over the years to explain the nature of information dissemination in particular, and the changes brought about to it by technological and other factors (Duff, 1997; Robinson, 2009; Paulus, 2011). A typical example is shown in Figure 10.1; recent adaptations of the chain for books and for archival records are shown in Figures 10.2 and 10.3. However, the general processes within the chain remain invariant; information resources must be created by someone, disseminated in some way, etc. The communication chain conceptual model is therefore a simple but effective way of categorizing and understanding changes in the information landscape.

Resource frameworks

To understand information resources in a changing environment, we need a framework to categorize them, and to include new forms of resource, and new formats of existing resource types. Four typologies of materials have commonly been used, either alone or in combination, in resource guides:

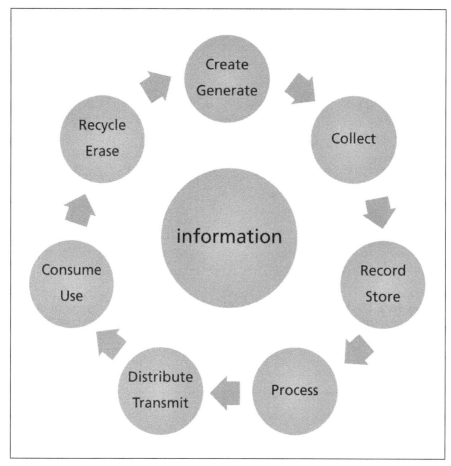

Figure 10.1 *The information lifecycle (reproduced from L. Floridi, Information: a very short introduction, by permission of Oxford University Press)*

- by subject, e.g. civil engineering
- by format, e.g. podcast
- by location, e.g. North America
- by type of material, e.g. peer-reviewed journal article.

While all are useful in some respects, the last, organizing by type of material, is generally regarded as the most helpful in most circumstances. A typology of very long standing divides resources into categories by level: primary, secondary, tertiary, etc.

There are various forms of this kind of framework; some include categories independent of the levels, such as 'incidental information' or 'popularizations';

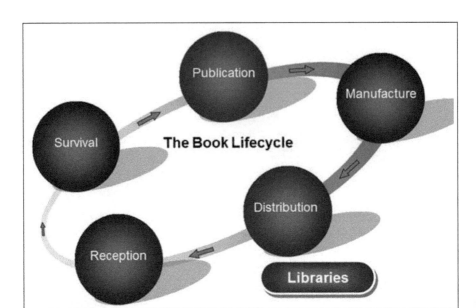

Figure 10.2 *The book lifecycle (reproduced from Paulus, 2011, by permission of the Johns Hopkins University Press)*

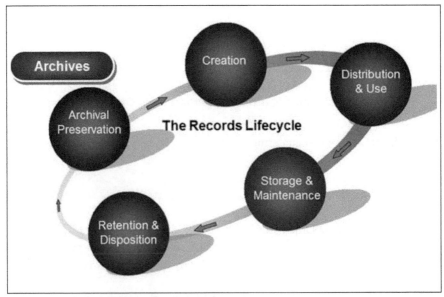

Figure 10.3 *The archival record lifecycle (reproduced from Paulus, 2011, by permission of the Johns Hopkins University Press)*

see, for example, Søndergaard, Andresen and Hjørland (2003) and Davis and Shaw (2011, section 11.1). The most comprehensively focused on resource levels, and hence most stable amid changes in forms and formats, is a variant originally proposed by Robinson (2000) and used in a simplified form for detailed analyses of healthcare and pharmaceutical resources (Robinson, 2010; Bawden and Robinson, 2010), which denotes resources as:

- zeroth: raw information before it enters the communication chain, for example the output from laboratory instruments
- primary: the 'original information', e.g. journal articles
- secondary: value-added information, from some organization of primary material, e.g. textbooks, reviews, abstracts
- tertiary: materials pointing to, and aiding the use of, primary and secondary materials, e.g bibliographies, directories
- quaternary: giving access to resource listings at a higher level, essentially 'lists of lists'
- quintenary: lists of lists of lists.

The two highest levels have proliferated in the web environment, whereas in days of print a few quaternary 'bibliographies of bibliographies' were all that could be found.

Categorizations of this sort are necessarily subjective according to how the resource is used. A bibliography of medical articles, for example, would normally be taken as a tertiary resource, but to a future historian of healthcare information it would be a primary document. Nonetheless, they are very helpful in understanding resources in times of change.

Changing information landscapes

With these two simple models for understanding the information environment in mind, we will now look at the effects of the main factors changing the information landscape. The most significant of these is the digitization of the print-on-paper environment, with consequent changes to the mechanisms and economics of publishing and dissemination generally. We will look only at some main trends and issues; for fuller accounts of their development and significance, see the books by Woodard and Estelle (2010), Hughes (2012), Deegan and Sutherland (2009), Cope and Phillips (2006; 2009), Feather (2006) and Thompson (2005). See also Gleick (2011) for an overview of changes in the wider information landscape in which the developments on which we will focus are embedded. Meadows (1998) gives a detailed account of scholarly communication at the end of the 20th century, just as structural transformation began.

Digitizing the world of print

The digital computer began to be applied on a routine basis in the publishing sector during the 1970s, following the first experiments in computer typesetting in the 1960s. Although this made the production of printed materials more efficient, it had no impact on the form of these materials, or the ways in which they were used (Twyman, 1998).

The first transformational change came with the conversion of printed abstracting and indexing services to computerized form. This began with STEM (science, technology, engineering and medicine) services in the 1970s; see Bourne and Hahn (2003) for an account of the early developments. The proceedings of the first of the well known yearly London International Online Information Meetings in 1977 includes papers restricted to applications in STEM subjects, with some online library systems, and the first generation of numeric databanks, again almost entirely in STEM areas (Learned Information, 1977). Application in other subject areas came in the next decade. Computerized indexes, allowing Boolean searching, were much simpler and quicker to use, and those who – like the authors of this book – had to spend lengthy periods looking up and cross-referencing entries in printed index volumes do not miss the old ways. Even here, however, some lamented that a degree of serendipity had been lost; there are many anecdotes of the interesting things found only because they happened to be next to what had been looked up on the printed page of an abstracting journal.

Academic and professional journals were the next to be digitized. Again, this has largely been received positively; users mainly look at articles across many journals, and this is much more easily done digitally than by leafing through printed volumes. This convenience comes, again, with some cost. When articles are retrieved directly through some form of search engine, rather then by looking through indexes and issues of a printed journal, the identity of the journal itself is, to some extent, lost. In the future, journals may be seen as a kind of brand identifying a collection of articles of a certain kind, rather than a publication with volumes and issues.

Abstracting and indexing services, some journals, and a very few books, moved to digital form before the advent of the world wide web. But it was the web which caused the major change to the printed information environment. The convenience of the web environment led to the mass migration of journals to electronic form, and to all other forms of printed products gaining a digital dimension.

E-books have long been heralded, but slow to arrive. Reference works, with their requirement for rapid and frequent updating, were a natural candidate, and these moved rapidly to the web, and to mobile devices for ease of access; Buckland (2008), Singer (2010) and Detmering and Sproles (2012) all analyse the consequences of this. Other book formats have been slower to move; reading a book, particularly for pleasure, on a computer has proved to be unappealing, and portable e-book readers were slower to gain acceptance than many had predicted. The 'tipping point', at which e-books compete with print for most purposes, was believed by many to have been reached with the introduction of Amazon's Kindle and Apple's iPad in 2007 and 2010 respectively, but this remains to be seen.

One effect of introduction of digital printing processes for books in the 1980s has been that the unit cost becomes independent of print run; the cost of printing each book is the same, whether ten books are produced at a time, or ten thousand. This has led to the wide availability of *print on demand*, to produce small numbers, or even single copies, of specialist or old titles. As Breede (2006) points out, this returns us to the situation before the introduction of printing, when hand-written manuscript books were typically produced to order.

While arguments about the viability of digital formats for newly published books raged, mass digitization of older materials was proceeding more quietly, though with some controversies over copyright and access in the programmes run by companies such as Google and Microsoft. The prospect of all published information being digitally available has often been proclaimed, but remains as yet a good way off. The processes of, and issues in, digitization and the creation of digital collections is clearly described by Zhang and Gourley (2008).

Newspapers and magazines, like popular books, have had a slow progress to digital format, with many concerns about user acceptability and about economic viability. The tablet computer format, particularly the iPad and its successors, is generally seen as the most likely way forward, with print versions slowly declining.

One whole format of material, the printed brochure which publicizes organizations, products and services, has largely moved from print to web. An important part of the job of the information specialist in many environments used to be to keep an updated collection of printed brochures and catalogues; this is now largely a matter of the past, except for those cases where an attractive printed brochure has value as a marketing tool, alongside a web presence. A similar situation can be seen with data compilations of all kinds, which no longer exist as printed volumes. Much of what is sometimes referred to as 'grey literature' – reports, and similar documents, disseminated by the organizations which produce them, rather than through formal publishing channels – has migrated wholesale from print to the web environment.

We can see, therefore, a mixed picture. Some forms of information resources – abstracting and indexing services, academic journals, reference works, brochures and catalogues – have largely moved to the web, and their complete demise in print form would not be unexpected. For others – most books, newspapers, magazines – the picture is less clear; print, for the moment at least, lives happily alongside digital.

The new information environment; homogenized simplicity

One final change can be noted. Most people, most of the time, now access all their information through a single search engine interface, perhaps augmented by social media such as Facebook and Twitter, and by news media. Contrast this with the situation in the early 1990s. At that time, to get a full coverage one would have had to use a variety of online host systems, catalogues and directories, plus the emerging internet services of Gopher, WAIS, FTP, and web, as well as the full array of printed sources and services, at that time largely unaffected by the digital transition. The new environment is undoubtedly much simpler, but at the cost of homogenization: all information looks the same in a web browser, and it takes a great effort to consciously analyse what it is that the search engine is offering. A greater degree of digital literacy, as discussed in Chapter 13 is needed to have full understanding of the context of the information which can be so readily found; see Godwin and Parker (2012) for discussions of the literacies needed in this new environment.

These changes have had obvious effects on collection-centred institutions, most obviously libraries and information centres. Some have moved to an all-digital format; all have moved to a hybrid, partly digital, condition, with consequences for their physical structure and use of space, as well as for the nature of the services which they provide, as we will see later. Archives and records centres have also been affected, as they have had to deal with complexities of preserving digital materials, as noted in the chapter on information technologies. The decision by the Library of Congress in 2010 to archive all Twitter messages since that service's inception in 2006 is the most ambitious attempt to deal with this; at the time of the decision, this amounted to fifty million messages per day. Perhaps most difficult are the fundamental questions of what – in the new environment – counts as a 'record', and what should be preserved; for a clear account of the issues, see Millar (2010, Chapter 9).

Moving to mobile

Another general development is the move to mobile, context-aware and pervasive information provision, now mainly through smartphones and tablet computers. Initially this has taken the form of mobile versions of familiar resources; a good example are medical reference works and pharmacopoeias, which were among the first resources to be placed on early 'personal digital assistant' (PDA) devices, and are now migrating to newer devices (Robinson, 2010). Many information providers are now seeking to provide convenient mobile interfaces for resources ranging from books and journals to library catalogues and social media. New forms of resource for this type of device are now emerging, as we will see later.

Alongside, and often stemming from, technological advances, have come changes to the economic and contractual aspects of information service provision, which we will now consider.

Changing economic models

When resources are in digital form, the economic model changes for an institution, or indeed an individual, from ownership of physical information items to access to digital material. Rather than purchasing a book or a series of issues of a journal, the user buys a licence to access the digital equivalent. In the early days of digital materials, when both users and providers were finding their way to the most appropriate form of contracts for purchasing these new forms, there were numerous widely reported 'horror stories'. Libraries who cancelled journal subscriptions found that they lost access to the older material, whereas with printed issues they would have owned them in perpetuity. Individuals who had purchased e-books found that the books disappeared from their e-readers, and the price refunded, when the supplier encountered a copyright problem. Libraries with e-books found themselves restricted to a certain number of uses per year, whereas a physical library book can be used as often as needed. These, and other, problems are being resolved as experience is gained as to what is acceptable in digital licences. However the new environment, even with all these problems ironed out, is still an unfamiliar one.

The most dramatic change has been in the way journal subscriptions are dealt with. In the days of print, a library would choose its journals individually, and purchase them through a subscription agent. In the digital environment, it is more usual to choose a 'journal bundle', including a large number of titles, from a supplier or publisher such as ScienceDirect, Ebsco or Emeraldinsight. This bulk purchasing, the so-called 'Big Deal' arrangement, has advantages of convenience, especially as a search interface is usually provided. However it does, to an extent, dilute one of the traditional roles of the information practitioner – the careful selection of individual sources – and there has been pressure for different models with more control by the purchaser.

A combination of concern over rising journal prices, and the opportunities offered by the digital environment, has led to a number of initiatives to change the economic model in favour of the library and the reader. One of these is the consortium deal, aimed at providing favourable terms for e-journal access to library consortia, particularly in the developing world. Examples are the programmes of the INASP/PERii, EIFL and WHO's HINARI; for the origins of these, and other similar programmes, see Rowland (2005). A more fundamental change is brought in by the move to open access and to repositories, to which we now turn.

Open access and repositories

The open access (OA) movement stemmed from a belief that the traditional system for dissemination of research, with research articles published in commercial journals purchased by, mainly, academic libraries, was inherently unfair. Academic institutions, whose researchers provided most of the articles and also acted as journal editors and peer reviewers, had to 'buy back' their own work from the publishers for their libraries. The move to a largely digital format for academic journals allowed an alternative; open access, in various forms, essentially meaning access to academic and research literature free of any charge. The focus has been on journal articles, but academic monographs are also now being included. There has also been an analogous concern for open access to the scientific data in publications, to allow its free re-use; for the detailed rationale for this Open Data (OD) position, see Murray-Rust (2008; 2011).

We will look at some features of open access publishing below: for an overview of its origins and continuing issues see Jacobs (2006), Drott (2006), Oppenheim (2008) and Cope and Phillips (2009), and for recent developments and examples see Ayris (2011) and Ferwerda (2010).

There have been lengthy debates about the best method of providing open access, and currently three models are available:

1 *Green* open access: an article is published by a conventional subscription journal, and a copy is archived in a freely accessible source, usually an institutional repository.
2 *Gold* open access: an article is published in a conventional journal, but is available freely; either the journal makes all articles open access, or just allows access to some without subscription (this, of course, is only possible in a digital environment). Authors of articles are charged for publication.
3 *Platinum* open access: articles are published in fully open access journals, with no charge to the author.

The platinum route is in principle the best, and is made possible by easy-to-use free software for e-journal publication; the best-known example is the Open Journals Systems (OJS) software. However, it relies on volunteer effort to undertake all the publishing tasks which are still necessary, as well as an institution to provide the computing resources. In effect, therefore, journals of this kind are effectively subsidized by academic institutions and professional societies; their numbers as yet are very few. For a case study of such a journal of library science, see Haschak (2007). Other examples in our disciplines are *Information Research, Library and Information Research* and *Evidence-based Library and Information Practice*.

Gold open access requires authors to have a source of funding to pay for publication. One widely touted suggestion is that libraries and information centres could take on this role, as effectively the publishing arm of their institution, using the monies saved by the cancellation of journal subscriptions.

Green open access is the simplest, and the most widely established. It can be achieved by authors 'self-archiving' a copy of a paper without the publisher's mark-up on their personal web pages. Or it may involve using an archive for material in a particular subject area, such as the pioneering physics open access archive arXiv, established in 1991. It is now usually achieved by an *institutional repository*, which have now been established for many universities and research institutes, which are increasingly mandating, i.e. requiring, their staff to deposit all their publications in such a repository.

These repositories are databases of publications, and sometimes other materials, such as student dissertations and theses, book chapters and unpublished research reports. They typically use self-archiving software, such as DSpace or EPrints, and conform to the Open Access Initiative Protocol for Metadata Harvesting (OAIPMH) to provide a consistent form of metadata for ease of access. Because the materials in this kind of repository are freely available to anyone, they are sometimes called 'open access archives'. A 'quality assured' listing of active academic open access repositories throughout the world is given by the splendidly acronymed OpenDOAR (Directory of Open Access Repositories) directory, to be found on the web (as of December 2011) at http://www.opendoar.org. This is useful for finding and comparing repositories which are located in particular countries or regions of the world, or which serve a particular purpose.

The technical and economic changes described above, while they have certainly affected the details of the communication chain, and the roles of different actors within it, have done little to change the nature of the information resources being created and disseminated. We are still dealing with books and their constituent chapters, with journals and their constituent articles, with reports, legislation, and so on. The resources themselves would have been familiar to information practitioners a hundred years ago, though the format of their delivery has changed. But the digital transition has also created entirely new forms of resource, which we will now consider.

New forms of communication

One of the factors which make the job of the information provider ever more complicated is the way in which new types of information resource appear, usually adding to, rather than replacing, what is already there. Perhaps ironically, some of the more recent types of resource have disappeared first; who now remembers the Gopher, WAIS and FTP searching facilities, which were the staple of 'Internet for information professionals' courses in the 1990s?

We have already mentioned web pages for institutional and product information. Other examples are:

- blogs; although many are personal and ephemeral, a substantial proportion carry significant information
- 'microblogging' services, such as Twitter, which – despite the brevity of their entries and their wide use for triviality – can in some cases be valuable resources, and pointers to other resources
- wikis, allowing collaborative resource construction; both well known and general sources such as Wikipedia, and numerous specialized sources
- social media, such as Facebook, LinkedIn, and numerous professional forums
- aggregators, which integrate a variety of other sources, particularly for updating purposes and for news
- apps for mobile devices – smartphones and tablets – which either provide convenient 'anywhere anytime' access to information resources, particularly quick reference sources, or give context-aware information on collections, particularly in museums, galleries and heritage libraries, or – particularly for tablets – offer multimedia versions of reference works.

These forms of communication also have the potential to change the nature of more traditional forms of information dissemination. Textbooks and monographs sometimes now come with an associated website or blog, to allow for the authors' corrections and updates to, and readers' comments on, the original text. Journals are beginning to allow online comments on articles, replacing the tradition 'letter to the editor'. This may lead to still more disruptive changes; it is proposed that journal articles might be published without the traditional 'peer review' approval, and be judged instead by readers' comments on the journal's website or blog. For an account and critique of traditional peer review see Weller (2001) and Bornmann (2011), and for newer alternatives see Ware (2011) and Poschl (2010). However, evidence suggests that changes are coming relatively slowly, and that new forms of resource are only slowly penetrating the traditional scholarly communication system; see, for example, Robinson (2007), who shows the rather limited extent of referencing of newer types of resources in the scientific literature, and Feng and Widén-Wulff (2011).

Several of the trends noted above – open access, open data, new forms of peer review, and the wiki style of encyclopedia – are all manifestations of the new 'open information' and 'crowdsourcing' concepts, made possible by web facilities. We might also add other manifestations: the folksonomies and social tagging discussed in Chapter 6, which supplant or replace professional classification and indexing, 'wikimap' initiatives, such as OpenStreetMap, which claims to provide digital maps with the same quality as, and greater timeliness than, conventional mapmaking, and the products of so-called 'citizen journalism', by which traditional news sources are similarly supplanted or replaced by blogs and Twitter. Despite their undoubted successes and popularity, this kind of development has led to concerns about declining quality, shallowness of understanding, and the 'death of expertise'. For detailed analyses of one of the most prominent examples, Wikipedia, see Reagle (2010), Huvila (2010) and O'Sullivan (2009).

Not only are the changes stemming from the digital transition affecting resources in the communication chain, but they are leading to prospects of new forms of academic work. The information sciences play a part in the development of these new initiatives, and in turn they influence the work and roles of the information practitioner.

New forms of research and scholarship

The widespread availability of digital information resources and networked computing facilities, coupled with systems for communication, sharing and collaboration in their use, has led to the development of a new style of research and scholarship, generally described as *e-science* or *e-research*. In essence, this is collaborative work among researchers in different institutions, and typically widely spread geographically, of a sort that is made possible by the ability to manipulate large amounts of data and information in a collaborative manner. Standards for metadata description, data storage, text mark-up and so on are essential to enable data sharing and combination, as is open access to such data. For this reason, this type of research is sometimes described as *data-intensive* or *information-intensive*. Borgman (2007) and Dutton and Jeffreys (2010) give wide-ranging overviews of examples, comparisons of e-research in different subject areas, and analysis of issues. Systems which support these forms of working are sometimes referred to as 'collaboratories' or 'virtual research environments' (VREs). Kowalczyk and Shankar (2011) outline aspects of infrastructure which make the necessary information sharing possible. A tension can be seen between an emphasis on the provision of the maximum amount of open data in whatever form is available, and a focus on carefully curated datasets, with good metadata and quality control; the instinct of most information specialists will be to support the latter, but this is not necessarily the way in which things will develop.

Examples in the sciences include *bioinformatics*, with the collection, storage and analysis of large quantities of genetic and biochemical data, and *chem(o)informatics*, dealing with information on chemical substances and reactions (Lesk, 2008; Leach and Gillett, 2007; Murray-Rust, 2011). In the 'opposite corner' of the academic world, *digital humanities* allows research on digitized texts of many kinds, of archaeological materials, and other unconventional forms of document (Warwick, Terras and Nyhan, 2012; Dalbello, 2011). In the social sciences, large amounts of 'social records' of diverse kinds – housing, shopping, transport, employment, education, and many more – are becoming amenable to collaborative processing and analysis (Jankowski, 2009).

As noted above, the information sciences can contribute to these developments in various ways. Michael Buckland (2011), for example, advocates a role in the management of the large numeric datasets necessary for e-research, commenting that this is just a modern instantiation of our traditional concern for bibliography, Kretzschmar and Potter (2010) discuss involvement with digital humanities, while Gore (2011) reviews a variety of examples in e-science. There has also been interest in setting up collaboratories to support research and practice within the information sciences themselves; see, for example, Sonnenwald et al. (2009).

The move to a largely digital information environment, and its various implications and effects, have led to a reconsideration of libraries and information centres as 'information spaces', as we will now see.

Information places and spaces

We must now think of information spaces (and often also information products) as comprising both physical and virtual parts, within which individual information users operate and with which they interact. We can think of these two parts as equivalent to Karl Popper's Worlds 1 and 3 respectively. A useful way of visualizing this is given by the American library scholar Walt Crawford, who speaks of a 'complex' library. By analogy with a 'complex number' in mathematics, which comprises both a real and an imaginary part, so a complex library – or any other complex information space – comprises both a real (physical) and a virtual (digital) part. Pomerantz and Marchionini (2007) give a clear analysis of the changing nature of information spaces.

One particularly notable example has been a move to 'virtual reference', with the traditional face-to-face or telephone interaction, situated in a part of a library with a printed reference collection, supplanted by e-mail, instant messaging, web chat, text messaging, or even virtual reality; see, for example, Olszewski and Rumbaugh (2010) and Devine, Paladino and Davis (2011).

As information resources become increasingly digital, so the function of libraries and information centres moves away from that of essentially a storage space for physical information products. If they retain a physical space at all, what is its purpose? A store or archive for the residuum of physical materials? A quiet place for study and reflection? A stimulating environment for creative innovation? A social space, or community meeting place? There are many possible answers, and the best solutions still have to be worked out. Many public and academic libraries appear to be going down the 'social hub' route, providing a space for meetings and collaborative work, and for cultural activities, to complement information provision; as examples for academic libraries, see Bryant, Matthews and Walton (2009) and Waxman et al. (2007), and for a public library example, see May and Black (2010). Commercial, research and STEM information centres seem rather to be moving towards a transformation to the 'thinking place' or the 'knowedge exchange'; as an example, see Kao and Chen (2011) on a medical library whose design encourages its users 'slow down and take a mind break'. These new concepts have strong implications for the design of new 'information spaces' (McDonald, 2010; Beard and Dale, 2010; Latimer, 2011; Black, 2011; Niegaard, 2011).

Summary

We see in many ways a mixed, and somewhat confusing, picture of the information environment, resulting from technical and other changes. The move to a largely digital information world is unstoppable, and in some sectors and subjects virtually complete, but printed sources and physical information places retain their importance. A few types of resource have all but disappeared, but much more common is the situation of new resource types and formats existing alongside older forms. New forms of research and scholarship, and new forms of information spaces, have been introduced, but the old have by no means disappeared, so that it may be commented that 'the revolution has yet to materialise' (Hahn, Burright and Duggan, 2011, 24). It seems that the information sciences are destined to live in changing times for the foreseeable future.

- Technological and economic factors are changing the information environment in many complex ways.
- Changes relate not merely to specific formats and forms or resources, but also new ways of working and using information.
- Simple conceptual models of the communication chain, of types of information resources, and of the 'complex library', can help understand changes in the information environment.

Key readings

B. Cope and A. Phillips (eds), *The future of the book in the digital age*, Oxford: Chandos, 2006.

B. Cope and A. Phillips (eds), *The future of the academic journal*, Oxford: Chandos, 2009.

[Two edited books which, while dated in detail, give a good overview of many of the trends and issues in changing information resources.]

W. H. Dutton and P. W. Jeffreys (eds), *World wide research: reshaping the sciences and humanities*, Cambridge MA: MIT Press, 2010.
[Good overview of new forms of digital scholarship.]
J. Pomerantz and G. Marchionini, The digital library as place, *Journal of Documentation*, 2007, 63(4), 505–33.
[A thoughtful essay on the nature of information places and spaces.]

References

Ayris, P. (2011) University and research libraries in Europe working towards open access, *Liber Quarterly*, 20(3–4), 332–46.

Bawden, D. and Robinson, L. (2010) Pharmaceutical information; a 30-year perspective on the literature, *Annual Review of Information Science and Technology*, 45, 63–119.

Beard, J. and Dale, P. (2010) Library design, learning spaces and academic literacy, *New Library World*, 111(11/12), 480–92.

Black, A. (2011) 'We don't do public libraries like we used to': attitudes to public library buildings in the UK at the start of the 21st century, *Journal of Librarianship and Information Science*, 43(1), 30–45.

Borgman, C. L. (2007) *Scholarship in the digital age: information, infrastructure and the Internet*, Cambridge MA: MIT Press.

Bornmann, L. (2011) Scientific peer review, *Annual Review of Information Science and Technology*, 45, 199–245.

Bourne, C. P. and Hahn, T. B. (2003) *A history of online information services 1963–1976*, Cambridge MA: MIT Press.

Breede, M. H. (2006) Plus ça change . . . print on demand reverts book publishing to its pre-industrial beginnings, in Cope, B. and Phillips, A. (eds), *The future of the book in the digital age*, Oxford: Chandos, pp 27–46.

Bryant, J., Matthews, G. and Walton, G. (2009) Academic libraries and social and learning space: a case study of Loughborough University Library, *Journal of Librarianship and Information Science*, 41(1), 29–38.

Buckland, M. K. (2008) Reference library service in the digital environment, *Library and Information Science Research*, 30(2), 81–5.

Buckland, M. K. (2011) Data management as bibliography, *Bulletin of the American Society for Information Science and Technology*, 37(6), 3–37.

Cope, B. and Phillips, A. (eds) (2006) *The future of the book in the digital age*, Oxford: Chandos.

Cope, B. and Phillips, A. (eds) (2009) *The future of the academic journal*, Oxford: Chandos.

Dalbello, M. (2011) A genealogy of digital humanities, *Journal of Documentation*, 67(3), 480–506.

Davis, C. H. and Shaw, D. (eds) (2011) *Introduction to Information Science and Technology*, Medford NJ: Information Today.

Deegan, M. and Sutherland, K. (2009) *Transferred illusions: digital technology and the forms of print*, Farnham: Ashgate.

Detmering, R. and Sproles, K. (2012) Reference in transition: a case study in reference collection development, *Collection Building*, 31(1), 19–22.

Devine, C., Paladino, E. B. and Davis, J. A. (2011) Chat reference training after one decade: the results of a national survey of academic libraries, *Journal of Academic Librarianship*, 37(3), 197–206.

Drott, M. C. (2006) Open access, *Annual Review of Information Science and Technology*, 40, 79–109.

Duff, A. S. (1997) Some post-war models of the information chain, *Journal of Librarianship and Information Science*, 29(4), 179–87.

Dutton, W. H. and Jeffreys, P. W. (eds) (2010) *World wide research: reshaping the sciences and humanities*, Cambridge MA: MIT Press.

Feather, J. (2006) *A history of British publishing* (2nd edn), Abingdon: Routledge.

Feng, G. and Widén-Wulff, G. (2011) Scholarly communication and possible changes in the context of social media: a Finnish case study, *Electronic Library*, 29(6), 762–76.

Ferwerda, E. (2010) Open access monographic publishing in the humanities, *Information Services and Use*, 30(3–4), 135–41.

Gleick, J. (2011) *The information: a history, a theory, a flood*, London: Fourth Estate.

Godwin, P. and Parker, J. (eds) (2012) *Information literacy beyond Library 2.0*, London: Facet Publishing.

Gore, S. (2011) e-Science and data management resources on the Web, *Medical Reference Services Quarterly*, 30(2), 167–77.

Hahn, T. B., Burright, M. and Duggan, H. N. (2011) Has the revolution in scholarly communication lived up to its promise?, *Bulletin of the American Society for Information Science and Technology*, 37(5), 24–8.

Haschak, P. G. (2007) The 'platinum route' to open access: a case study of E-JASL: the Electronic Journal of Academic and Special Librarianship, *Information Research*, 12(4), paper 321 [online], available at http://InformationR.net/ir/12-4/paper321.html.

Hughes, L. M. (ed.) (2012) *Evaluating and measuring the value, use and impact of digital collections*, London: Facet Publishing.

Huvila, I. (2010) Where does the information come from? Information source use patterns in Wikipedia, *Information Research*, 15(3), paper 433 [online] available at http://informationr.net/ir/15-3/paper433.html.

Jacobs, N. (ed.) (2006) *Open access: key strategic, technical and economic aspects*, Oxford: Chandos.

Jankowski, N. W. (ed.) (2009) *e-Research*, London: Routledge.

Kao, P. and Chen, K. (2011) A park in the library: The 'New Reading Paradise' in the National Taiwan University Medical Library, *New Library World*, 112(1/2), 76–85.

Kowalczyk, S. and Shankar, K. (2011) Data sharing in the sciences, *Annual Review of*

Information Science and Technology, 45, 247–94.

Kretzschmar, W. A. and Potter, W. G. (2010) Library involvement with large digital humanities projects, *Literary and Linguistic Computing*, 25(4), 439–45.

Latimer, K. (2011) Collections to connections: changing spaces and new challenges in academic library buildings, *Library Trends*, 60(1), 112–33.

Leach, A. R. and Gillett, V. J. (2007) *An introduction to chemoinformatics: revised edition*, Dordrecht: Springer.

Learned Information (1977) *Proceedings of the 1st International On-Line Information Meeting, London, 13–15 December 1977*, Oxford: Learned Information.

Lesk, A. (2008) *Introduction to bioinformatics* (3rd edn), Oxford: Oxford University Press.

May, F. and Black, F. (2010) The life of the space: evidence from Nova Scotia public libraries, *Evidence Based Library and Information Practice*, 5(2), 5–34, [online] available at http://ejournals.library.ualberta.ca/index.php/EBLIP/article/view/6497.

McDonald, A. (2010) Libraries as places: challenges for the future, in S. McKnight (ed.), *Envisioning future academic library services: initiatives, ideas and challenges*, London: Facet Publishing, 31–54.

Meadows, A. J. (1998) *Communicating research*, London: Academic Press.

Millar, L. A. (2010) *Archives: principles and practice*, London: Facet Publishing.

Murray-Rust, P. (2008) Open Data in science, *Serials Review*, 34(1), 52–64.

Murray-Rust, P. (2011) Semantic science and its communication – a personal view, *Journal of Cheminformatics*, 3:48 [online] available at http://www.jcheminf.com/content/3/1/48.

Niegaard, H. (2011) Library space and digital challenges, *Library Trends*, 60(1), 174–89.

Olszewski, L. and Rumbaugh, P. (2010) An international comparison of virtual reference services, *Reference and User Services Quarterly*, 49(4), 360–68.

Oppenheim, C. (2008) Electronic scholarly publishing and open access, *Journal of Information Science*, 34(4), 577–90.

O'Sullivan, D. (2009) *Wikipedia: a new community of practice?*, Farnham: Ashgate.

Paulus, M. J. (2011) Reconceptualizing academic libraries and archives in the digital age, *portal: Libraries and the Academy*, 11(4), 939–53.

Pomerantz, J. and Marchionini, G. (2007) The digital library as place, *Journal of Documentation*, 63(4), 505–33.

Poschl, U. (2010) Interactive open access publishing and public peer review: the effectiveness of transparency and self-regulation in scientific quality assurance, *IFLA Journal*, 36(1), 40–6.

Reagle, J. M. (2010) *Good faith collaboration: the culture of Wikipedia*, Cambridge MA: MIT Press.

Robinson, L. (2000) A strategic approach to research using Internet tools and resources, *Aslib Proceedings*, 52(1), 11–19.

Robinson, L. (2007) Impact of digital information resources in the toxicology literature, *Aslib Proceedings*, 59(4/5), 342–51.

Robinson, L. (2009) Information Science: communication chain and domain analysis, *Journal of Documentation*, 65(4), 578–91.

Robinson, L. (2010) *Understanding healthcare information*, London: Facet Publishing.

Rowland, F. (2005) Journal access programmes for developing countries, *Serials*, 18(2), 104–6.

Singer, C. A. (2010) Ready reference collections: a history, *Reference and User Services Quarterly*, 49(3), 253–64.

Sonnenwald, D.H., Lassi, M., Olson, N., Ponti, M. and Axelsson, A-S. (2009) Exploring new ways of working using virtual research environments in library and information science, *Library Hi-Tech*, 27(2), 191–204.

Søndergaard, T. F., Andresen, J. and Hjørland, B. (2003) Documents and the communication of scientific and scholarly information: revising and updating the UNISIST model, *Journal of Documentation*, 59(3), 278–320 .

Thompson, J. B. (2005) *Books in the digital age*, Cambridge: Polity Press.

Twyman, M. (1998) *British Library guide to printing history*, London: British Library.

Warwick, C., Terras, M. and Nyhan, J. (eds) (2012) *Digital humanities in practice*, London: Facet Publishing.

Ware, M. (2011) Peer review: recent experience and future directions, *New Review of Information Networking*, 16(1), 25–53.

Waxman, L. et al. (2007) The library as place: providing students with opportunities for socialising, relaxation and refreshment, *New Library World*, 108(9/10), 424–34.

Weller, A. C. (2001) *Editorial peer review: its strengths and weaknesses*, Medford NJ: Information Today.

Woodward, H. and Estelle, L. (2010) *Digital information: order or anarchy?*, London: Facet Publishing.

Zhang, A. B. and Gourley, D. (2008) *Creating digital collections: a practical guide*, Oxford: Chandos.

CHAPTER 11

Information society

We can see now that information is what our world runs on: the blood and the fuel, the vital principle.

James Gleick (2011, 8)

Dort, wo man Bücher verbrennt, verbrennt man auch am Ende Menschen.
(Wherever they burn books, they will in the end burn human beings.)

Heinrich Heine

Common sense is a deposit of prejudices laid down in the mind before you reach 18.

Albert Einstein

Introduction

Since the later years of the 20th century, it has become commonplace for commentators to declare that we are living in an 'information society'. If this is true, and it must be pointed out that some expert commentators find the whole idea unhelpful, then this must surely have major implications for the information sciences. It is beyond doubt that social issues impinge on the work of information scholars and practitioners alike.

In this chapter, we will first consider the nature of, and criteria for, an information society. We will then look at some of the frameworks – policies, laws, and ethics – which structure the ways in which information is used in society, and the organizations and infrastructures which support its use. We conclude with the role of information in the development of society, and some of the problems and issues which it brings with it.

What is the information society?

We will begin by considering the nature of an information society; how we know one when we see one. We will do so in outline only, referring interested readers to excellent and detailed texts (Feather, 2008; Webster, 2003; 2006; Cornelius, 2010).

There are a number of criteria by which present day Western society may be judged an 'information society'. None of them is entirely convincing. For one thing, as we have seen in Chapter 2, every society for some thousands of years has had some form of recorded information, and has often regarded these records as important and valuable; yet we do not regard these as information societies. Nor is it sufficient to point to the evident fact that information is abundant and prominent in our society. Everyone on the planet has to eat food: in Western societies everyone eats several meals a day; a large and important industry produces and distributes foodstuffs; whole bookshops and television channels are devoted to cookery, and chefs achieve celebrity status. And yet we do not speak of a 'food society'.

The economic information society

Perhaps the most objective conception of the information society is based on economics. When most of the economic activity and wealth of a society is based on intangible, information-based goods, then it seems reasonable to describe this as an information society. Luciano Floridi (2010a), who takes this view, points out that the countries of the G7 group must be counted as information societies, since more than 70% of the Gross Domestic Product is accounted for by intangible goods. This viewpoint builds on the studies of scholars such as Fritz Machlup, Peter Drucker and particularly Marc Porat, who pioneered the idea of the 'information economy' in the 1970s. It has been developed into a model of a *triple helix* knowledge economy, with synergistic activity of government, academia and commerce and industry (Leydesdorf, 2010).

The occupational information society

A related argument is based on occupations. When most people are employed as 'information workers', rather than as manual workers, then the society should be called an information society. This viewpoint was pioneered in the 1960s by the American sociologist Daniel Bell, with his idea of the 'post-industrial society'. These views were developed in the 1990s in the 'knowledge society' idea of the German sociologist Nico Stehr, who examined the extent to which non-information occupations were increasingly knowledge-based.

While these economic and occupational arguments seem generally convincing, they have been criticized on a number of grounds; most particularly because supporters of these viewpoints tend to adopt an imprecise, and perhaps unreasonably broad, idea of what may be counted as 'information work' or 'information-based goods'.

The technological information society

An alternative, and perhaps the most popular, explanation is based on technology.

When a society has sufficiently powerful and widespread information and communication technologies (ICTs), then it should be counted as an information society. The problem here is to determine what counts as an 'information technology', and how much of it there must be to create an information society. Similar problems beset attempts to define an information society on the basis of increases in the production and consumption of media (for example Skogerbø and Syvertsen, 2004).

The political information society

There is an approach which seeks to understand the issue in political terms. An information society is one in which information, and ICT, issues become the subject of political debate and action at local, national and international levels. Here there is the problem of how much debate is necessary. Governments, and powerful individuals, have been trying to censor and 'spin' information since the earliest times; does this imply that these were information societies?

The socio-cultural information society

Then there are social and cultural accounts; most notably the ideas of the 'network society', put forward by the Spanish sociologist Manuel Castells in the 1990s. These point to the power of information, and specifically information networks, to change our perceptions of time and distance, and to change the way we behave and interact in all aspects of our social dealings. Early comments in this vein were made by Karl Popper who, in 1945, foresaw an *abstract society*, in which 'men practically never meet face-to-face; in which all business is conducted by individuals in isolation, who communicate by typed letters or by telegrams'. The rise of social media since such ideas were first advanced has only served to further promote this idea. It seems undeniable that society, in those parts of the world affected by these trends, has changed greatly; but again it is problematic to say exactly when, and why, it became an information society.

The theoretical information society

Finally, the British sociologist (and our colleague at City University London) Frank Webster has argued along rather different lines; that an information society should be understood as one in which abstract theoretical knowledge achieves an importance as the main guide to practical action.

Open society

We can mention one other concept which, though in no way a theory of the information society, has some resonance with it. This is Karl Popper's idea of an 'open society', which he initially proposed in the 1940s, as an alternative to the closed societies of fascism and communism. Popper's open society is a society based on the rule of law, in which everyone knows the law and is equal before it, in which those who are responsible for making the laws can be changed without the use of force, and in which society is advanced by rational argument and open criticism of the *status quo*. It is therefore a form of society dependent on the free flow of information, and Popper's principles can be used as a guide for information providers (Robinson and Bawden, 2001). Popper's protégé, the financier and philanthropist George Soros, used these idea as the basis for his Open Society Institute, which works to advance the idea in practice, and which has always supported library and information programmes as an important strand of its work; for one example, support for the professional development of information specialists in countries in transition, see Robinson and Glosiene (2007).

With these ideas of the nature of an information society in mind, we will move on to look at some of the frameworks which govern information within societies.

Frameworks for information society

We will consider three overlapping categories of frameworks: policies, laws, and ethics and values.

Information policies

We will examine information policies in more detail in the next chapter, as they are an important aspect of information management at all levels. Here, we will simply note that national, and to an extent international, policies have a major effect in determining the form of information society in their part of the world. This is not to underestimate the part played by non-governmental agencies, and philanthropic foundations, such as the Open Society Institute and the Bill and Melinda Gates Foundation in promoting the development of information societies. But it is governments, and international bodies, which have the power to enact the laws and regulations, discussed below, which provide the framework for such societies. These control the nature of intellectual property and copyright, data protection and privacy, freedom of information and censorship in any region. Governments and international bodies may also choose to fund the development of the physical and digital information infrastructure, promote education and training for information literacy, advocate e-procurement and e-commerce, and so on. And they are able to lead by example, since governments are among the largest producers, collectors, preservers and users of information, and can promote e-government, giving citizens digital access to government information and services.

The nature of information policies varies greatly between countries and regions. The UK and the USA are examples of countries with rather partial and reactive policy provisions (Jaeger, 2007; Orna, 2008; Rubin, 2010); France and

example of a more co-ordinated approach (Cacaly and Le Coadic, 2007). The European Union is an example of an international body with a proactive approach, while the United Nations has actively promoted information literacy programmes, as we will see in Chapter 13. For further discussion of these issues, see Cornelius (2010), Yusof, Basri and Zin (2010) and Feather (2008).

The legal framework for information

We will not attempt to describe 'information law' in any detail. The legal framework is complex, and, crucially, differs from country to country. We will give an outline of the issues, and refer the reader to any of the authoritative books on the topic; for example Pedley (2011) and Stead (2008) for a UK perspective on the specific topics below, and Rubin (2010) for a US perspective.

At the risk of oversimplification, we can say that there are four main areas of law affecting information within society.

The first is the legal protection given to 'intellectual property'; abstract products of the human mind, recorded in some form of document. The most obvious aspect of this is copyright law, which gives protection to original intellectual works, usually instantiated in some form of document, preventing copying and other unreasonable use without the copyright holder's permission. See Cornish (2009) and Padfield (2010) for a UK perspective, and Rubin (2010) and Crews (2012) for a US perspective. As with so many other aspects of the information environment, the move to digital information has caused problems, as it is much less clear what a digital 'copy' is; see Pedley (2007) for an introduction to digital copyright issues. There are particular difficulties with copyright issues in programmes of mass digitization of older books; both the necessity of dealing with many individual copyright holders, and also the problem of 'orphan works', for whom the copyright holder cannot be identified or contacted.

Other forms of intellectual property are *patents*, monopolies granted to an inventor in exchange for their revealing details of their invention in a patent specification, *designs* of products, and *trademarks*, associated with a commercial brand, which may be registered by their owner.

In the case of patents, the inventor provides a written account, made publicly available, of the invention – which must be new and useful – and how it works. The state then gives a limited-time monopoly for the inventor to exploit it. In addition to their legal importance, patents form a valuable information resource in their own right, both giving substantive information about their subject – and forming a particularly valuable resource for science and technology – and also a source of business and competitor intelligence. Patents information has for many years been an important speciality for information practitioners; see Adams (2011) for both legal and informational aspects of patents.

Trademarks are usually words or images, but may also be colours, sounds or smells. They serve only to distinguish a brand, and need not be in any way descriptive; they therefore do not form an information resource in the same way that patents do. Registered designs, which protect the appearance of mass-produced items, similarly have a legal rather than an informational function.

Intellectual property rights are governed by the laws of each country, overseen by the United Nations' World Intellectual Property Organization (WIPO). Copyright in the UK is governed by UK law, increasingly interrelated with European Union Directives. See the texts mentioned above for details of this complex topic.

The second is the general area of intellectual freedom, subsuming issues such as freedom of information, data protection, privacy, breach of confidence and censorship. These are essentially questions of to what extent, and how, information may be freely used and accessed. They often reflect opposing 'rights': what one person sees as a straightforward right to privacy may be seen by another as censorship of free expression. See Jones (2009) and Office for Intellectual Freedom (2010) for a US perspective on these issues, and Wacks (2010) on the privacy concept.

The third is a set of issues affecting the legal status of certain collections of documents. Examples are *legal deposit*, by which certain institutions, typically national libraries, are entitled to a copy of everything published in their region; regulations specifying a time period after which official archives may make materials publicly available, for example the UK '30-year rule'; and issues around the proper re-use of public sector information, particularly by commercial organizations.

Finally, there are a number of 'information crimes', which have become possible only in a digital networked environment: so-called cybercrimes. Examples are 'hacking', 'phishing' and 'cyberstalking'.

Above and beyond formally enacted, and precisely stated, laws, there is the more nebulous area of values and ethical standards relevant to information matters.

Information ethics and values

Although having less substantive force than laws, ethics and values are arguably more pervasive and influential in directing the ways in which information is, and is not, used in society.

Dictionaries typically define ethics as a system of morals or rules of behaviour. A definition constructed for an ethics course for library and information students is 'ethics is the art and science that seeks to bring sensitivity and method to the discernment of moral values and action' (Carbo, 2008, 11).

In academic and professional contexts, the idea is often conflated with the requirements of the law as 'legal and ethical issues'. Ethics itself is associated with right behaviour when there is no law to say what to do; or in the extreme in deciding when it is right to ignore the law. Ethical principles are also usually held to be derived from, or at least strongly associated with, 'professional values'.

For the information sciences, ethical issues may arise in both research and practice. They have much in common with similar issues for other disciplines and professions, although they will centre around a specific set of 'information ethics'. This is an area of much current interest, and Himma (2007) goes so far as to say that information ethics is as 'hot' as medical ethics. We can only cover the issues briefly here, leaving the interested reader to follow up the references.

The ethics of information research will be discussed in Chapter 14. We will just note here that the issues are essentially the same as for other social science and computing disciplines: treating research participants correctly and observing good practice in data collection and use.

For the practice of the information disciplines, a number of important ethical issues have been identified. These are typically grouped together under the heading 'information ethics'. This concept has grown from an initial focus on the activities of librarians and information specialists to a wide concern for information in society as a whole; for which, obviously, information specialists feel a particular responsibility.

It abuts the related ideas of computer ethics, network ethics and cyberethics. The move to a largely digital information environment, while it may not affect ethical principles *per se*, brings about new practical issues. For example, use of computerized issuing systems, availability of many resources in digital form, and use of RFID identifiers in printed materials, make it much easier to create a record of which users accessed which items and how they used them; this has implications for privacy of information use, and anonymity in information research.

Some of the main areas of concern within information ethics include: censorship and intellectual freedom; privacy, confidentiality and data protection; ownership of information, and commercial use of public information; universal access, information poverty and the digital divide; respect for intellectual property combined with fair use; and issues of balance and bias in information provision, collection development and metadata creation. The area is reviewed from various perspectives by Sturges (2009), Frohmann (2008), Carbo and Smith (2008) and Fallis (2007). Himma (2007) and Carbo (2008), with older literature reviewed by Smith (1998) and a specifically historical perspective given by Bynum (2010).

Some of these aspects are affected by laws – copyright and censorship, for example – while others are covered by professional codes of conduct. There are a variety of these, some of which are reviewed and compared by Sturges (2009) and by Rubin (2010, Chapter 10). The most relevant for the information sciences are arguably the Professional Guidelines of the American Society for Information Science and Technology, and the Ethical Principles for Library and Information Professionals of UK's CILIP; both are to be found on the website of the organization. These both emphasize that information specialists have an ethical duty to their employers, clients and patrons, to the wider society, and to their profession. Several other national and international bodies for librarians, archivists and other information specialists have similar codes. They may be criticized on the grounds that they provide some general principles, but little guidance on how they are to be applied in specific cases.

Ethical dilemmas in the information disciplines typically focus around how a particular person is to be treated, or how particular documents should be handled, or how services should be provided. Some examples, mainly taken from Rubin (2010), Jones (2009) and Fallis (2007), are shown in the box here.

Ethical dilemmas in information; some examples

Should librarians put internet filters on all computers in a public library?

Should librarians ever tell the police what a patron has been reading?

Should books donated by organizations with racist or religious fundamentalist views be included in library collections?

Should homeless people with challenging behaviour and poor personal hygiene be allowed to use a public library?

Should charges be made for specialist services in public libraries?

Should an information officer in a pharmaceutical company agree to provide marketing executives with literature comparing their products favourably with competitors, but not the other way round?

Should a school librarian make multiple copies of a copyrighted article for a class, when the school cannot afford to purchase multiple copies of the book itself?

Should warning notices be put on encyclopedias containing clearly inaccurate medical information?

Should reference librarians give information to patrons asking about ways of making car-bombs? or ways to commit suicide? or how to take illegal drugs?

Should a college librarian tell a professor which students had looked at their required reading material?

Should a commercial information service ever charge for supplying material which is provided freely by public bodies?

Should a college librarian agree to a request to shelve material on creationism and intelligent design in a 'science' section, even if the cataloguing-in-publication classification is 'religion'?

While dilemmas of this kind will occur in a particular context, and may have to be dealt with pragmatically as they occur, many commentators have suggested that the information professions would benefit from a more structured and systematic way of deciding such questions. Unfortunately, there is no universally agreed set of ethical principles which would help. For an example of a thoughtful discussion of such dilemmas, see the discussion by Thornley et al. (2011) on the ethical implications of adoption of RFID devices.

One approach is to rely on professional *values* as a guide. Michael Gorman, for example, as we saw in Chapter 3, lists eight 'enduring values' of librarianship: stewardship, service, intellectual freedom, rationalism, literacy and learning, equity of access to recorded knowledge and information, privacy and democracy (Gorman, 2000). Richard Rubin lists seven values of library and information science: service, reading and the book are important, respect for truth and the search for truth, tolerance, the public good, justice and aesthetics (Rubin, 2010). While such value lists may be valuable as a basis for discussion, they are – like the rather similar codes and guidelines mentioned above – of limited value in specific situations; however, see McMenemy (2010) for an analysis of a specific issue using Gorman's value of 'rationalism'.

We should also mention the well known set of 'Five Laws of Librarianship', put forward by the Indian librarian and scholar S. R. Ranganathan in 1931:

- Books are for use
- Every reader his book
- Every book its reader
- Save the time of the reader
- The library is a growing organism.

Although not put forward as professional values, they have been regarded as such, and have been highly influential and spawned several extensions and modifications (McMenemy, 2007).

Ethical principles

We may look for guidance in general principles of ethics, often propounded by famous philosophers of the past, though these have not been widely applied to questions of information ethics. Fallis (2007) argues that there are four general types of ethical theory which may be useful, giving examples of their application in information contexts:

1 *Consequence-based theories* – these hold that the right action is that which brings about the best outcome for the greatest number. The best-known example is the philosophy of *utilitarianism*, as originally advocated by John

Stuart Mill. This approach may be used in information ethics to argue, for example, that we should not censor potentially offensive materials, even though we know that not doing so will cause distress to some people.

2 *Duty-based theories* – these argue that there are certain ethical duties which must always be obeyed, regardless of their consequences. These are justified by our moral intuition; the best-known example is Kant's idea of the *categorical imperative*. In an information context, we could, for example, argue that we always have a duty to provide full and correct information, which overrides any other consideration.

3 *Rights-based theories* – these suggest that the right thing to do in any situation is determined by the rights we assign to others. This approach was first propounded by John Locke, and recently developed by John Rawls for the rights of members of a society. This approach may be particularly useful for 'code-based' information ethics, since these are often expressed as the rights which people have: to have access to information, to be treated respectfully and equally by information providers, to privacy in their information dealings, and so on. Budd (2006) has argued for a rights-based approach to information ethics, giving practical guidance to librarians in particular.

4 *Virtue-based theories* – these suggest that the right thing to do in any situation is what a virtuous person would do. Traced back to Aristotle, these theories ascribe to the virtuous person traits such as courage, calmness and friendliness; these are indeed valuable attributes for the information provider.

While all of these approaches have some value for the information context, none is a panacea and none is without problems in application to specific cases. Perhaps the main value of such ethical theories is that they force us to be clear about how we approach specific ethical dilemmas, and to be explicit about how we try to solve them. The same is true of a variety of conceptual frameworks derived to help clarify and explain the issues: Carbo (2008) analyses several of those used in the teaching of ethics to library and information students.

Some have argued that we need an entirely new form of ethics to deal with information issues, based on the centrality of information as a universal entity. This has been put forward most fully by Luciano Floridi, as a part of his Philosophy of Information (Floridi, 2010a, Chapter 8; 2010b), but was preceded by earlier writers such as Norbert Wiener (1954). 'Information ethics' focuses on information itself, rather than on any particular technologies, and on the idea that a person may use information as a *resource*, to generate other information as a *product*, which in turn may transform the informational environment as a *target*. Floridi argues that all things which exist should be regarded as 'informational entities': this certainly includes people, but also animals, plants, paintings, books, stars and stones. Information ethics is that set of principles which enable all information entities to flourish; specifically by minimizing *entropy*. Floridi here uses entropy not in the sense of physical, thermodynamic entropy, nor in the sense in which the word is used in Shannon's theory, but rather to mean any destruction or corruption of an informational entity. He does not mean that all information should be protected, nor that e-mails or encyclopedia entries should be assigned a moral worth; rather that ethical dealing with all that exists in the universe should rest upon an appreciation of their informational nature. Floridi derives four main principles of information ethics, for the 'infosphere' – the universe understood in informational terms:

- entropy ought not to be caused
- entropy ought to be prevented
- entropy ought to be removed
- the flourishing of informational entities as well as of the whole infosphere ought to be promoted by preserving, cultivating and enriching their properties.

This is an ambitious attempt to set up a whole system of ethics with information as its basic concept; not, as Floridi reminds us, to replace other ethical systems and principles, but to augment them. It remains to be seen whether it will lead to a more coherent and practically useful way of dealing with the ethical problems of the information disciplines and professions than earlier frameworks.

These legal and ethical frameworks are, in many respects, the main supporting infrastructure of the information society, albeit an intangible framework. We may also regard Jesse Shera's social epistemology, discussed in Chapter 3, as another piece of an intangible infrastructure. We will now look at more tangible infrastructures: both physical and digital.

Information society infrastructures

We can consider the tangible infrastructures which underpin an information society in two main categories: technological and organizational, the latter predating concepts on information society by many years.

The technological infrastructure is, for the most part, the expansion throughout society of the hardware and software systems discussed in Chapter 7. National policies aimed at such things as promoting high-speed networks, ensuring that rural and underdeveloped regions have access to network connectivity, and providing access to computers and networks in schools, public libraries, etc., may be seen as directly supporting the development of information society.

More specific support is provided by developments in the kind of systems termed *social informatics*, most simply understood as 'the systematic study of social aspects of computerization' (Kling, Rosenbaum and Sawyer, 2005, 3). The term refers both to research into the way in which ICTs affect, and are affected by, societies and social relations, and also the proactive development of ICTs for social development. It uses an eclectic mix of methods, from the analytical and technical to the ethnographic, and also includes a strong element of action research (Davenport, 2008; Kling, Rosenbaum and Sawyer, 2005). Focusing on tasks, practices, communities and tacit knowledge, and the ways in which these are affected by ICTs, and in turn affect the way they are used, it has a strong overlap with ideas of knowledge management, to be discussed in the next chapter.

We may also mention two specific ICT applications regarded as central to the development of an information society. One is *e-government*, the use of ICTs to provide access to government information and services, and to support interactions between government and citizens. The second is *e-commerce*, whereby ICTs are used both for retail – the success of Amazon being the most obvious example – and for business-to-business transactions. One specific example of the latter is e-procurement by governments; not only does this give support to ICT use, but it has proved a useful tool for ensuring transparency and minimizing corruption in some countries, and thereby contributed to the development of civil society. For an example of these initiatives in a developing country, see Tigre (2003), and for an example from the USA see Thomas and Streib (2005).

A main organizational support of information society is the public library service, established in most of the developed world in the 19th century; for overviews see McMenemy (2009) for the UK, and Koontz and Gubin (2010) for international perspectives. This is sometimes perceived as in decline, at least in the USA and UK, threatened by economic problems, and with its long-standing core mission of provision of recreational reading and reference information challenged by a variety of factors, from Google and Wikipedia to Amazon and e-books. However, in many countries the public library service is a major force for developing the information society beyond wealthy and urban elites, adding to its remit the provision of ICT equipment and networking for those without, promotion of information and digital literacy, and linking with government departments and agencies for provision of public information and services. While in some countries there are alternative sources of public information – for example, the respected and long-standing Citizens' Advice Bureau in the UK – the public library service is generally the leader in this respect. Examples of these public library roles come from Denmark (Nielsen and Borlund, 2011), Singapore (Luyt, 2010) and the USA (Jaeger and Bertot, 2011; Mandel et al., 2010; Kinney, 2010).

To conclude this chapter, we will look at some perceived problematic issues within the information society, and particularly the kinds of 'divides' which have been identified.

Problems and divides within the information society

Whatever definition may be taken for an information society, it necessarily implies availability of a great deal of information, in a great variety of forms. While we may agree that this is, in general, a Good Thing, it has given rise to a variety of problems and difficulties. This stems from two main factors. The wealth of information available leads to laments of TMI (Too Much Information). And this, and the diversity of formats and channels available, leads us to confront the 'paradox of choice': we become paralysed by the sheer volume of choices available, and resort to crude heuristics (do what you did last time; do what that person is doing; and so on) as a way of coping. These issues, and the resulting problems, are reviewed by Bawden and Robinson (2009).

Overload and anxiety

The most publicized of these issues is *information overload*; the situation which arises when there is so much relevant and potentially useful information available that it becomes a hindrance rather then a help. This problem first came to prominence in the 1990s, with a series of reports showing the waste of time, decrease in efficiency, and even ill-health, allegedly caused by information overload. In truth, this is not a new problem, although, as James Gleick (2011) points out, it has always felt new. Complaints about there being too much to read have been made for some hundreds of years, even since the introduction of printing: for examples, see Gleick's book and the paper by Bawden and Robinson (2009). For more recent examples and discussion, see Davis (2011), MacDonald, Bath and Booth (2011) and Koltay (2011).

A related issue is 'perfect remembering', brought by the preservation of our thoughts and actions in digital media. Mayer-Schönberger (2009) extols the virtues of forgetting, and advocates an explicit place for it in a digital world.

Other named pathologies of an information society include information anxiety, information fatigue, infoglut, information obesity, and data smog; Bawden and Robinson (2009) and Johnson (2012) explain and exemplify these. There is also concern that the availability of information and communication sources leads to an inability to focus or concentrate: a state termed *continuous partial attention*. This has led a number of commentators to bemoan the increasingly superficial way in which information and knowledge is handled; Carr (2010) is one well publicized example. It is alleged that deep engagement with information and knowledge – reading a book from start to finish, for example – has been largely supplanted by a scanning of snippets: articles are supplanted by blog postings are supplanted by tweets.

Quite how valid these concerns are – and if valid, how new, and how serious – is very much a matter of debate. Bawden and Robinson (2009) summarize the solutions proposed: most often these involve either good organizational or personal information management, considered in the next chapter, or the promotion of digital literacy, considered in Chapter 13.

Information poverty and digital divide

As we noted above, equality of access to information is often cited as a fundamental value of the information sciences and disciplines. Many commentators have held that this is violated by discernable divides into information 'haves and have nots', whether this divide is economic (rich versus poor), national (developed world versus developing world), regional (city versus rural area), and so on.

This divide is often expressed as that between the information rich and the information poor. 'Information poverty' has been, and is, understood in various ways: as lacking money to pay for information; as living in a region where access to information sources is limited; as living under a government which deliberately restricts access to information; or as lacking the basic education or the information literacy necessary to use a range of information resources. See Feather (2008) and Haider and Bawden (2007) for analyses of the concepts of information rich and poor. Note that the term is sometimes used for those who, though not fitting any of the categories above, have problems in finding necessary information for some tasks, as in a study of UK healthcare information managers by MacDonald, Bath and Booth (2011).

This is sometimes expressed more specifically as a 'digital divide'; between those who have access to digital resources, the money to pay for them and the ability to use them effectively, and those who lack one or more of the requisites. The advent of ICTs is often held to have worsened the divide between those who have ready access to information and those who do not. On the other hand, it may be argued that a range of new ICTs, from open access e-journals to smartphones, will enable developing countries to catch up with the developed world in information terms, in a way that would be impossible without such technologies. As examples of the debate around this issue, see Vicente and Lopez (2011) for an analysis of the digital divide across the countries of the European Union, Kinney (2010) for the perspective of the US public library sector and Stevenson (2009) for a critique of the whole concept.

Information generations

Another form of divide which has caused concern is the divide between generations. It is argued that people of different ages form distinct 'generations' with different attitudes and behaviours (Edmunds and Turner, 2005). This includes information behaviour, due to their growing up in very different information environments; a reflection of the quote from Einstein which opens this chapter. The 'babyboomer' generation, brought up with the 'novelties' of television, vinyl records and paperback books, will be very different from the 'Millennials' brought up with the web, the mobile phone and the computer game, and so on.

This is seen as a problem in various ways: different generations may need different forms of information provision; older generations, unfamiliar with new ICTs, may form a group of 'information poor' in their own right; and that the younger generations, while very confident with new ICTs, may be unable to engage with information resources in a deep and sustained way. The latter is a specifically generational variant of the concerns about superficial information behaviour noted above.

Against these viewpoints, it has to be said that many concerns are based on anecdote and opinion, rather than sustained research. The few rigorous studies which have been done do not show very sharp and consistent generational differences, although information services, particularly those serving reasonably homogenous age groups, do need to be aware of typical generational attitudes and preferences; see, for example, Holman (2011) and Rowlands et al. (2008).

Summary

It is generally agreed that we live in an information society, but there is no general agreement about exactly what this means, other than that information is somehow central to the way in which the society works. Alternative theories invoke technology, politics, economics, occupations and roles, networks and communication, knowledge and abstract theory, and other factors, as the basis for the idea. In truth, it is probably best understood in terms of a combination of these.

The framework which holds this kind of society together is composed of both tangible and intangible components. Tangible networks and computers are balanced by intangible policies, laws and regulations, and even vaguer values and attitudes.

Despite the wealth of information available, unimagined by previous generations, the paradox of choice, the pressure of 'too much information', and the inequitable nature of access have led to concerns about information overload, information anxiety, the digital divide and the rest. Whether these will fade away into insignificance, as societies adapt to their new nature, or whether they will continue to require active treatment, through information management and digital literacy, remains to be seen.

- Information society is a concept with no single agreed definition; it may be understood in a number of ways, expressed as theories or frameworks.
- The idea of information society is closely related to other concepts: network society, knowledge society, information economy and post-industrial society.
- Although ICTs are crucial, the form of the information society is determined equally by national and international policies, laws, and regulations.
- Perceived problems of information societies include information overload, information poverty, and the digital divide.

Key readings

John Feather, *The information society: a study of continuity and change* (5th edn), London: Facet Publishing, 2008.

Frank Webster, *Theories of the information society* (3rd edn), London: Routledge, 2006.

Ian Cornelius, *Information policies and strategies*, London: Facet Publishing, 2010.

[Three textbooks which cover the issues raised in this chapter from rather different perspectives.]

References

Adams, S. (2011) *Information sources in patents* (3rd edn), Berlin: de Gruyter.

Bawden, D. and Robinson, L. (2009) The dark side of information: overload, anxiety and other paradoxes and pathologies, *Journal of Information Science*, 35(2), 180–91.

Budd, J. M. (2006) Toward a practical and normative ethics for librarianship, *Library Quarterly*, 76(3), 251–69.

Bynum, T. W. (2010) The historical roots of information and computer ethics, in Floridi, L. (ed.), *The Cambridge Handbook of Information and Computer Ethics*, Cambridge: Cambridge University Press, 20–38.

Cacaly, S. and Le Coadic, Y. (2007) Fifty years of scientific and technical information policy in France (1955–2005), *Journal of Information Science*, 33(3), 377–84.

Carbo, T. (2008) Ethics education for information professionals, *Journal of Library Administration*, 47(3/4), 5–25.

Carbo. T. and Smith, M. M. (2008) Global information ethics: intercultural perspectives on past and future research, *Journal of the American Society for Information Science and Technology*, 59(7), 1111–23.

Carr, N. (2010) *The Shallows: how the Internet is changing the way we think*, London: Atlantic Books.

Cornelius, I. (2010) *Information policies and strategies*, London: Facet Publishing.

Cornish, G. P. (2009) *Copyright: interpreting the law for libraries, archives and information services* (5th edn), London: Facet Publishing.

Crews, K. D. (2012) *Copyright law for librarians and educators: creative strategies and practical solutions* (3rd edn), Chicago: American Library Association.

Davenport, E. (2008) Social informatics and socio-technical research: a view from the UK, *Journal of Information Science*, 34(4), 519–30.

Davis, N. (2011) Information overload, reloaded, *Bulletin of the American Society for Information Science and Technology*, 37(5), 45–9.

Edmunds, J. and Turner, B. S. (2005) Global generations: social change in the twentieth century, *British Journal of Sociology*, 56(4), 559–77.

Fallis, D. (2007) Information ethics for twenty-first century library professionals, *Library Hi Tech*, 25(1), 23–36.

Feather, J. (2008) *The information society: a study of continuity and change* (5th edn), London: Facet Publishing.

Floridi, L. (2010a) *Information – a very short introduction*, Oxford: Oxford University Press.

Floridi. L. (2010b) Information ethics, in Floridi, L. (ed.), *The Cambridge Handbook of Information and Computer Ethics*, Cambridge: Cambridge University Press, 77–9.

Frohmann, B. (2008) Subjectivity and information ethics, *Journal of the American Society for Information Science and Technology*, 59(2), 267–77.

Gleick, J. (2011) *The information: a history, a theory, a flood*, London: Fourth Estate.

Gorman, M. (2000) Our enduring values: librarianship in the 21st century, Chicago: American Library Association.

Haider, J. and Bawden, D. (2007) Conceptions of 'information poverty' in library and information science: a discourse analysis, *Journal of Documentation*, 63(4), 534–57.

Himma, K. E. (2007) Foundational issues in information ethics, *Library Hi Tech*, 25(1), 79–94.

Holman, L. (2011) Millennial students' mental models of search: implications for academic librarians and database developers, *Journal of Academic Librarianship*, 37(1), 19–27.

Jaeger, P. T. (2007) Information policy, information access, and democratic participation: the national and international implications of the Bush administration's information policies, *Government Information Quarterly*, 24(4), 840–59.

Jaeger, P. T. and Bertot, J. C. (2011) Responsibility rolls down: Public libraries and the social and policy obligations of ensuring access to E-government and government information, *Public Library Quarterly*, 30(2), 91–116.

Johnson, C. A. (2012) *The information diet: a case for conscious consumption*, Sebastopol CA: O'Reilly.

Jones, B. M. (2009) *Protecting intellectual freedom in your academic library: scenarios from the front lines*, Chicago: American Library Association.

Kinney, B. (2010) The internet, public libraries, and the digital divide, *Public Library Quarterly*, 29(2), 104–61.

Kling, R., Rosenbaum, H. and Sawyer, S. (2005) *Understanding and communicating social informatics: a framework for studying and teaching the human contexts of information and communication technologies*, Medford NJ: Information Today.

Koltay, T. (2011) Information overload, information architecture and digital literacy, *Bulletin of the American Society for Information Science and Technology*, 38(1), 33–5.

Koontz, C. and Gubin, B. (eds) (2010) *IFLA public library service guidelines* (2nd edn), IFLA Publications No. 147, Berlin: de Gruyter.

Leydesdorff, L. (2010) The knowledge-based economy and the triple helix model, *Annual Review of Information Science and Technology*, 44, 367–417.

Luyt, B. (2010) Imagining the internet: learning and access to information in Singapore's public libraries, *Journal of Documentation*, 66(4), 475–90.

MacDonald, J., Bath, P. and Booth, A. (2011) Information overload and poverty: challenges for healthcare services managers?, *Journal of Documentation*, 67(2), 238–63.

Mandel, L. H., Bishop, B. W., McClure, C. R., Bertot, J. C. and Jaeger, P. T. (2010) Broadband for public libraries: Importance, issues, and research needs, *Government Information Quarterly*, 27(3), 280–91.

Mayer-Schönberger, V. (2009) *Delete: The virtue of forgetting in the digital age*, Princeton NJ: Princeton University Press.

McMenemy, D. (2007) Ranganathan's relevance in the 21st century, *Library Review*, 56(2), 97–101.

McMenemy, D. (2009) *The public library*, London: Facet Publishing.

McMenemy, D. (2010) Whither rational thought: the responsibilities of the information and library profession in ensuring balance, *Library Review*, 59(1), 5–8.

Nielsen, B. G. and Borlund, P. (2011) Information literacy, learning, and the public library: A study of Danish high school students, *Journal of Librarianship and Information Science*, 43(2), 106–19.

Office for Intellectual Freedom (2010) *Intellectual Freedom Manual* (8th edn), Chicago: American Library Association.

Orna, E. (2008) Information policies: yesterday, today, tomorrow, *Journal of Information Science*, 34(4), 547–65.

Padfield, Y. (2010) *Copyright for archivists and records managers* (4th edn), London: Facet Publishing.

Pedley, P. (2007) *Digital copyright* (2nd edn), London: Facet Publishing.

Pedley, P. (2011) *Essential law for information professionals* (3rd edn), London: Facet Publishing.

Robinson, L. and Bawden, D. (2001) Libraries and open society: Popper, Soros and digital information, *Aslib Proceedings*, 53(5), 167–78.

Robinson, L. and Glosiene, A. (2007) Continuing professional development for library and information science: case study of a network of training centres, *Aslib Proceedings*, 59(4/5), 462–74.

Rowlands, I., Nicholas, D., Williams, P., Huntington, P., Fieldhouse, M., Gunter, B., Withey, R., Jamali, H. R., Dobrowolski, T. and Tenopir, C. (2008) The Google generation: the information behaviour of the researcher of the future, *Aslib Proceedings*, 60(4), 290–310.

Rubin, R. E. (2010) *Foundations of Library and Information Science* (3rd edn), New York NY: Neal-Schuman.

Skogerbø, E. and Syvertsen, T. (2004) Towards an information society? The value of media production and consumption, *Javnost – The Public*, 11(1), 45–60.

Smith, M. M. (1998) Information ethics, *Annual Review of Information Science and Technology*, 32, 339–66.

Stead, A. (2008) *Information rights in practice: the non-legal professional's guide*, London: Facet Publishing.

Stevenson, S. (2009) Digital divide: a discursive move away from the real inequalities, *Information Society*, 25(1), 1–22.

Sturges, P. (2009) Information ethics in the twenty-first century, *Australian Academic and Research Libraries*, 40(4), 241–51.

Thornley, C., Ferguson, S., Weckert, J. and Gibb, F. (2011) Do RFIDs (radio frequency identifier devices) provide new ethical dilemmas for librarians and information professionals?, *International Journal of Information Management*, 31(6), 546–55.

Thomas, J. C. and Streib, G. (2005) E-democracy, e-commerce and e-research, *Administration and Society*, 37(3), 259–80.

Tigre, P. B. (2003) Brazil in the age of electronic commerce, *Information Society*, 19(1), 33–43.

Vicente, M. R. and Lopez, A. J. (2011) Assessing the regional digital divide across the European Union 27, *Telecommunication Policy*, 35(3), 220–37.

Wacks, R. (2010) *Privacy: a very short introduction*, Oxford: Oxford University Press.

Webster, F. (ed.) (2003) *The information society reader*, London: Routledge.

Webster, F. (2006) *Theories of the information society* (3rd edn), London: Routledge.

Wiener, N. (1954) *The human use of human beings: cybernetics and society* (revised edition), Boston MA: Houghton Mifflin.

Yusof, Z. M., Basri, M. and Zin, N. A. M. (2010) Classification of issues underlying the development of information policy, *Information Development*, 26(3), 204–13.

CHAPTER 12

Information management and policy

The information that your institution creates and uses can either represent an asset or a liability. Into which of these camps it falls is largely dependent on how it is managed.

UK Joint Information Systems Committee, JISC (2007, 4)

Knowledge and wisdom, far from being one
Have oft-times no connection. Knowledge dwells
In heads replete with thoughts of other men;
Wisdom in minds attentive to their own.
Knowledge is proud that he has learned so much,
Wisdom is humble that he knows no more.

William Cowper (*The winter walk at noon*, Book 6 of *The Task*, 1785)

If you try to improve the performance of a system of people, machines and procedures by setting numerical goals for the improvement of individual parts of the system, the system will defeat your efforts, and you will pay a price where you least expect it. [Tribus' Perversity Principle.]

Myron Tribus (*Quality First*, Washington DC:
National Society of Professional Engineers, 1992)

Introduction

Information management is a complicated subject, and can be understood in different ways. Sometimes it is understood as a wide and all-embracing concept, including records management, knowledge management, library management and so on, and sometimes with a much narrower focus. It may, or may not, be taken to include the processes of 'ordinary' management – budgeting, managing people, and so on – which are as necessary in an information-providing institution or department as in any other. And it may be considered from a variety of perspectives, emphasizing information resources, technologies, organizational structures, and others; see Detlor (2010), Schlögl (2005), Bouthillier and Shearer (2002) and Rowley (1998) for examples.

In this chapter, we will take information management to include all the concepts, techniques and processes which underlie and enable information service provision. We take a wide view, including all the environments in which information, in all its guises, is managed. We focus on the ideas that recorded information, instantiated in documents, can be understood as a resource, though perhaps an unusual one in some respects; that information has a value, though this may be difficult to determine; and that information management processes can be related to the communication chains and information lifecycles mentioned in previous chapters. This covers a wide area and in this chapter, perhaps even more than others in this book, we will have to give only a brief account of the issues, leaving readers to follow up topics of interest via the recommended resources. Even so, it is a relatively long chapter, emphasizing the wide range of the topic.

We cannot deal with general management topics, for lack of space; for coverage of these issues oriented to the perspective of information service provision see Bryson (2011) and Edwards, Layzell Ward and Rugaas (2000), though we will mention marketing and promotion of services as a particularly important issue. And important though the legal and ethical framework is, within which information management operates, we will make only brief mention of it, as these topics have been covered in the previous chapter. For insights into the historical development of information management, see Black and Brunt (1999) and Black, Muddiman and Plant (2007).

We will first look at some of the very basic ideas of information management, and then give an overview of some of the contexts in which it occurs; records management, library management, knowledge management, etc. Four important general issues – information governance and information risk, information policies and strategies, information auditing and mapping, and valuing information: assessing the effectiveness and impact of information provision – are then covered. Finally, we will briefly consider information provided in support of creativity and innovation.

Information management basics

Fundamental to information management is the idea that information, and the documents in which it is carried, has a chain or lifecycle of clearly defined stages. There is a variety of these, as introduced in previous chapters, and they will vary in detail according to their context, and will change in detail with a changing information environment (Robinson, 2009; Paulus, 2011). But without this general concept it will not be possible to plan to manage information resources in any logical way. The management process focuses on understanding the operation of the chain as a whole, and on ensuring effective working of each of its parts.

Information management also assumes that information may be regarded, to some extent, as a resource. The term 'information resource management' (IRM) had a period of popularity for a specific approach; we do not use it here, since all forms of information management rely on the idea, to some extent. This assumes that information resources may be identified, counted, and their cost, use (actual and potential) and value assessed; this underlies the idea of the information audit, to be discussed later. Information, considered as a resource, has some unusual, and indeed paradoxical, qualities. Information has multiple and unpredictable lifecycles, so that its use and value does not change with time in a regular manner; it is 'diffusive', tending to leak from any straightjacket of control, and the more it leaks the more there is; it is sharable, not exchangeable, it can be given away and retained at the same time; and its value is subjective, depending upon its context and intended use by particular persons on particular occasions. Information cannot be managed as any other resource, including valuation in the same manner, without doing violence to those attributes of information which make it an inarguable resource, in the sense of being a dynamic force for innovation and progress. For more discussion of these issues, see Eaton and Bawden (1991), Yates-Mercer and Bawden (2002), Holtham (2001), Meyer (2005) and Budd (2011).

Although, as we shall see in detail later, the value of information may be difficult to determine, any approach to information management must make some attempt to do so, or there will be little rationality behind management decisions. It is also assumed that it is possible to add value to information by appropriate processes. An influential model for understanding value-added processes in information lifecycles was introduced in the 1980s by Robert Taylor (1982; 1986), and has since then 'been woven into the broad fabric of LIS' (Pimental, 2010, 58). It provides a framework within which value-adding processes – such as classifying and relating, evaluating and interpreting, presenting options, and making choices – are carried out within information systems of all kinds. Information management is, to a large degree, a matter of enabling these processes to occur in an efficient manner.

Ironically, as Rubin (2010, 289–90) notes, the more efficient an information service is at adding value in these ways, the less its work may be obvious to its users; an example emphasizing the importance of marketing and promotion. This is one of the aspects of 'general management' which is generally agreed to be of particular importance within information management. Information services have all too often been rather poor at this, with the result that their contributions are all too often overlooked or underrated. Best practices are outlined in the general management references, and in Gould (2009); key messages from the older literature are reviewed by Koontz, Gupta and Webber (2006). Information marketing has to have clear objectives, with ways of monitoring success, based on careful analysis of the context, with a general strategy for promoting the service generally and with tactics for addressing distinct user groups, rather than the casual approach sometimes adopted; see Vasileiou and Rowley (2011) for an example of the marketing of e-book services. To the traditional methods of brochures, flyers, presentations, web page and e-mail notices are now added Web 2.0 tools, and mobile, viral, ambush and guerrilla marketing (Ratzek, 2011; Savard and Gupta, 2011).

Effective promotion of services requires a good understanding of the users of a service, and their information needs; indeed, this is an essential prerequisite for effective information management. As we saw in Chapters 4 and 9, information use is a not a simple concept, but nonetheless much progress has been made in understanding user behaviour. In Chapter 14 we will look at the methods which can be used to assess user needs; Case (2007; 2012) gives good coverage of the nature of information needs and their investigation. Several models for investigating and understanding user needs have been proposed; as examples, see Agosta and Hughes-Hassell (2006) and Hepworth (2004).

Users need to be understood as individuals as well as *en masse*. We are concerned here with information management as an organizational activity, but we should note that there is a well established idea of *personal information management* or *personal knowledge management*, concerned with how individuals deal with their own information. This overlaps with what is known of individual information behaviour and with the need for digital literacy; for more details, see Bedford (2012), Pauleen and Gorman (2011), Whittaker (2011), Fourie (2011), Jones (2007a; 2007b), and Jones and Teevan (2007). It is, of course, of relevance here because an effective organizational information programme will rely on a knowledge of the personal information practices of the individual people it serves; this also enables personalized support and assistance towards good information practices.

Having introduced some of the universal aspects of information management, we will now look, in outline, at its practice in particular contexts.

Contexts of information management

There are inevitable overlaps between any set of sub-categories of information management (IM), as these are neither precisely defined nor exactly named and have – in any case – much in common: McDonald (2010), for example, argues that data management and records management are essentially the same thing. Accepting these limitations, and choosing those IM aspects commonly distinguished, we will consider, in no significant order: data management; document and content management; records management and archiving; library and repository management; management of documentation in museums and galleries; collection management; knowledge management; and business intelligence.

Data management

By data management we mean the management of structured sets of facts and figures, rather than bodies of text. It is usually taken to encompass database systems, data modelling, metadata, data quality and security issues and the maintenance of data warehouses, archives and repositories; see, for example, Gordon (2007).

We saw in the last chapter that the management of large data sets is coming within the ambit of the information sciences as part of the new style of e-research, and bringing data management firmly within the remit of library and information specialists (Buckland, 2011). Before this development, however, data management was seen as lying on the boundaries between library and information science and computer science and information systems, and perhaps more naturally belonging to the latter. This led to a split, with documents and data typically being managed through different processes, and with different systems. In some sectors, however, particularly those involving chemical or biomedical research, library and information services have a long involvement with data management, the pharmaceutical industry being an evident example (Bawden and Robinson, 2010).

The split between data management and other forms of information management may be expected to narrow and disappear in the near future, particularly as e-research develops, and as newer technologies close the rather artificial gap between the handling of data and of information.

Document and content management

Document management and content management are terms which are often used synonymously, with content management sometimes implying a wider scope; increasingly these concepts are described as enterprise content management (ECM) (Cameron, 2011). They refer to processes of creating, revising, tracking, disseminating and storing electronic documents, which may sometimes be images of paper documents. This is usually in the context of publishing, in a very broad sense. It may be 'traditional' publishing, creating e-books, e-journals, and so on; or it may be the generation of internal documentation, such as procedures or handbooks; or of documents for specific external dissemination, such as regulatory documents in the pharmaceutical industry.

There is interaction with the forms of information management more familiar to information practitioners, in that content management systems both draw material from databases and store their products in repositories and archives. Practitioners are often involved in one form of internal document management, the maintenance of an institutional intranet (White, 2011).

Records and archives management

These two aspects of information management are often treated as synonymous, or as on a continuum – and are often integrated in practice in smaller organizations – although there are distinct differences between the two. For detailed accounts of records management see Shepherd and Yeo (2003) and McLeod and Hare (2005), for archive management see Millar (2010), Hill (2011) and Shepherd (2009), and for a practical guide see the 'infokit' on managing the information lifecycle from the UK Joint Information Systems Committee (JISC, 2007).

Documents are regarded as *records* when they are created or acquired by an organization, as part of a business process, so that their existence provides evidence of the fact that the process took place. Most records are created internally, but incoming messages and other documents, if they are used as part of a business process, are also records. They are distinguished from *reference material*, other documents which are used by the business but which do not qualify as records according to the above understanding. These are not kept with the records collection. Note that 'business' is not restricted to the commercial world; records are as important for education, government, charities, etc.

A record therefore has two main purposes. While it is 'active' it supports the business process for which it was created or acquired; later it serves as a memory of the past, with respect to that process. In some cases, this 'memory' function is so important that the record is kept indefinitely; this is the function of archives.

Records management is usually understood to be the systematic and consistent control of records throughout their lifetime. More than most other kinds of document, records have a distinct and predictable lifecycle, encompassing the stages from creation or acquisition, circulation, use, storage, and final destruction or preservation. A good example is shown in Figure 12.1, based on a model proposed by the UK's Joint Information Systems Committee (JISC, 2007).

It is usual to categorize records in three stages over their lifetime:

1 *Active records* are those which are in use, needed for the purposes of the organization.
2 *Semi-active records* are those which are no longer in use, but which must be retained and kept accessible for a defined period of time. This may be for a variety of reasons: they may be needed, perhaps unpredictably, for business purposes in the future. Or there may be a requirement to keep them for some time for legal or regulatory reasons.
3 *Inactive records* are those which are no longer required, and need not be kept. When a record becomes inactive, the decision is made to destroy it or to preserve it.

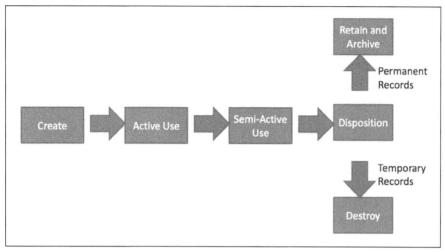

Figure 12.1 *The records management lifecycle*

Although records normally move logically through these stages, there may be occasions when matters go 'in reverse'. Non-current records for example, may become current again, if there is renewed and unexpected interest in their content.

Those records which are preserved permanently – for historic, cultural or reference purposes – become *archival records*, and are dealt with by the methods of *archive management*.

The basic processes of records management are therefore:

- categorization organization and indexing of records
- storage of records appropriately, so that they are secure, and can be retrieved when needed
- providing access to records, and ensuring that potential users are aware of the collection, and how it may be accessed
- retaining records so long as they are needed, and then destroying them or sending them for archival preservation.

The processes of archive management are similar, except that the last of the four points becomes:

- retaining archival records indefinitely, or until archive policy, with respect to particular records, changes.

Records rarely if ever occur singly, and the basic unit to be managed is the *record series*, a collection of records of similar nature, e.g. an organization's annual report, or staff monthly expense accounts. This may in turn be divided into *files*, usually the unit which is stored and retrieved, and within files are individual documents. Records which are vital to the continuance of the business are known, reasonably enough, as *vital records*. An issue of particular importance in records and archives management is that of *provenance*; by whom was the record created or acquired, and in what context. This will determine how it is treated.

Both physical and digital records are generally arranged according to a *file plan* or *file classification*, based on the functions and processes within the organization which the records support and reflect. Accompanying the file plan is the *retention schedule*, which specifies the lifecycle of each record series: in particular, how long it is to be kept at each stage, where (in the case of physical records) it is to be kept, and how it is finally to be disposed of, i.e. destroyed or archived. This is usually accompanied by a *records retention authority*, a formal policy document which specifies the retention schedule and the reasons for it.

Managers of both physical and digital records have to give considerable attention to secure preservation of records, perhaps more than other information managers, since the loss of some records can cause the failure of the business on which they rely. The move to digital records and archives, as with other forms of document collection, has brought advantages and problems. Issues of physical storage, and of the problems of records which may fit into two or more places in a file plan, become less pressing. There is no longer the issue of keeping current records separate, and more immediately accessible, than non-current, or making particular provision for vital records. Nor is there any need to make duplicate copies, for whatever purpose.

On the other hand, issues of records held on obsolescent storage media can cause great problems; particularly if it is held that transferring the records to newer media means that they are no longer 'the original'. This problem of 'format obsolescence' is also one of the main issues for archive managers.

National archives are often a good source of information not merely about their own activities but about approaches to records and archives management. Good examples are the information provided by the national archives of the UK, the USA, and Australia (as of December 2011) to be found on their web pages at http://www.nationalarchives.gov.uk, http://www.archives.gov and http://www.naa. gov.au respectively.

Library and repository management

The term 'library management' is often used to refer to the 'general management' issues involved in running a library, perhaps with some sector-specific issues included. For example, the journal *Library Management* lists as its coverage (as of December 2011): strategic management; human resources; cultural diversity; information use; managing change; quality management; leadership; teamwork; marketing; outsourcing; automation; library finance; charging; performance measurement; and data protection and copyright. An American Library Association book offering tips for library management (Smallwood, 2011) focuses on issues of people management, time management, using IT, acquisitions, meetings, partnerships, and public relations, while Hayes' (2001) classic text on library management and planning focuses on quantitative models for optimizing workloads and staffing levels, and for assisting management decisions generally. The phrase has also been widely used in the context of the *library management systems* (LMS), discussed in the chapter on information technologies.

More in keeping with our idea of information management as based around an information chain or lifecycle is the 'collection-centred' idea of library services; see, for example, Gorman (2000) and Chowdhury, Burton, McMenemy and Poulter (2008). These can be summarized as:

1 Select and acquire.
2 Organize, classify, index.
3 Provide access and circulation.
4 Preserve and conserve.
5 Assist and advise users.
6 Weed and dispose.

Traditionally, these kinds of library management activities would have been referred to as library 'services' rather than library management (Gorman specifically adds to them 'manage and administer the library'), and divided into technical services (1, 2, 4, and 6) and public services (3 and 5). These distinctions are increasing irrelevant, in view of the changes to lifecycles and chains noted in Chapter 10, which affect libraries as much as any other information institution.

The management of largely or fully digital libraries follows this same pattern, though with the details of each process amended to the digital environment, as discussed in earlier chapters. *Repository management*, dealing with institutional and discipline repositories, is largely the same, and indeed is usually dealt with by an institution's library. The process of selection at the start is replaced by a task of encouraging the deposit of relevant materials, and – as a repository is a *de facto* archive – weeding and disposal are not usually necessary.

Museum and gallery information management

As we have seen in earlier chapters, the items in collections of museums, galleries and other heritage institutions may be regarded as documents in their own right.

This brings the necessity for their description, categorization and indexing, in a way analogous to other forms of documents, in libraries, archives, etc. Three decades ago Roberts and Light (1980, 42 and 44) were stating that 'museums throughout the world have an overwhelming documentation problem . . . every museum needs a documentation system for collections management purposes'.

Indeed, the kind of materials found in the collections of museums, archives and heritage libraries, and galleries to a lesser extent, may overlap considerably. The IM processes involved have usually been described as *museum documentation*, as exemplified by the work of the UK Museum Documentation Association, founded as early as 1977. A particular issue is the need for specialized vocabularies for describing this kind of material. Otherwise, the processes are much the same as in other contexts, especially archives, with the obvious proviso that weeding and disposal is much less relevant to collections which usually have a high proportion of valuable and rare objects. A survey by Marty (2007) found that over three-quarters of US museum professionals were active in information management, including the application of systems for collection management and content management. A good account of the principles of museum information management, though dated in detail, is given by Orna and Pettitt (1998); for a more recent survey, see the collection of case studies edited by White (2012).

Collection management

In some ways, it may not be appropriate to distinguish this as a separate context for information management; rather it is the kind of IM which is fundamental in all 'memory institutions' – libraries, record centres, archives, museums and galleries – which have just been discussed. Manzuch (2009) argues that the definitive features of archives, libraries and museums are collections and information management processes, and these are clearly central to the convergence (or re-convergence) of these institutions (Given and McTavish, 2010).

However, as the term is in common use, we will consider what are the common features of, and issues for, collection management in all situations. We have already seen, in Chapter 4, something of the nature of collections, and how the concept itself is being changed by the digital transition.

Four fundamental questions underlie all collection management (see, for example, Kovacs, 2009):

1 What purpose/s does the collection serve ?
2 For whom is the collection being maintained ?
3 What type of resources or items will be collected ?
4 How best can the collection be organized ?

Collection management is usually understood as comprising all the processes which are involved in the creation and maintenance of a collection, in the light of the answers to the above questions. These processes will differ in nature and emphasis according to the context, as seen in the examples above, but usually include:

- selection
- acquisition
- processing of material so that it is integrated into the collection
- preservation
- provision of access
- assessment of the quality and adequacy of the collection
- evaluation of use
- weeding and disposal.

A detailed account of these processes, written for the library context but more widely applicable, is given by Fieldhouse and Marshall (2012); for special collections , see Cullingford (2011); for specific issues of digital collections, see Zhang and Gourley (2008) and Hughes (2012); and for an example of a newer style of the management of museums' collections and associated information, see Forbes (2012).

Knowledge management

The idea of knowledge management (KM) originated in the 1980s and came into prominence in the 1990s as a widely promoted business concept; Koenig and Neveroski (2010) give an interesting account of its origins. It was soon hailed an important new field within the information sciences, although it was dismissed by some as a fad or a gimmick, and one eminent commentator went so far as to call it a 'nonsense' (Wilson, 2002). The initial hype has long died down, and the phrase 'knowledge management' is no longer so much in vogue; terms such as *business intelligence* are to a degree replacing it. Nonetheless, the basic idea remains important.

This is, in essence, the management of 'tacit knowledge'; the subjective knowledge in people's heads, which it is difficult, or perhaps impossible, to convey to others. This is sometimes categorized as personal, rather than propositional, knowledge: 'knowing how' rather than 'knowing that'. It is the kind of knowledge gained by experience, and by following example, rather than by reading and formal education, and is usually associated with some practical skill or competence. It is what Popper would claim belongs to his 'World 2', although KM theorists usually prefer to refer back to Michael Polanyi's (1962) theory of knowledge, encapsulated in his dictum 'we may know more than we can tell'; see Day (2005), Tsoukas (2005) and Baumard (2010) for the significance of Polanyi's views for KM. We noted in the last chapter that there are overlaps with the ideas of social informatics.

There are usually three elements to a knowledge management programme, though one often predominates, according to circumstances:

1 Content, the type of knowledge to be shared, and the way in which it is represented.
2 Technology, the means by which it is shared.
3 Culture, promoting the sharing of knowledge.

This means that there can be no 'one size fits all' best solution.

Two main approaches have been adopted. One, seeing KM as an extension of conventional information management, focuses on creating 'know-how databases', to which members of an organization are encouraged to contribute their practical knowledge. The second, considering that personal and tacit knowledge, by its nature, cannot be captured in this explicit way, focuses on putting people in touch with one another, through tools such as 'indexes of expertise' or 'corporate yellow pages'. An increasingly popular method is the 'community of practice': a group of practitioners who come together to share knowledge and experience, largely informally.

KM has generated a large literature of its own: for helpful overviews, see Desouza and Paquette (2011), Srikantaiah and Koenig (2008) and Martin (2008).

This is, of course, largely focused on Western concepts of knowledge. As we noted in Chapter 4, the indigenous knowledge of the developing world may take very different forms. Nonetheless there has been concern for using ideas of knowledge management to capture and preserve such knowledge, and ensure that it is made, and remains, accessible; as examples, see Stevens (2008), Lwoga (2011), Greyling and Zulu (2010), Dweba and Mearns (2011) and Maina (2012).

Environment scanning

Rather than a form of information management, this is a business activity which is often associated with the IM function. It is somewhat broader than the *competitor/competitive intelligence* (CI) activity, from which it has grown, and it is sometimes regarded, with KM, as a part of business intelligence. It involves a systematic analysis, from sources both formal and informal, and both internal and external, of changes in the environment in which a business operates; certainly including the activities of competitors, but also including legal and regulatory issues, economic, demographic, social and political issues, etc. Usually associated with the commercial world, it is increasingly practised by educational and other non-profit organizations. An information service may be asked to undertake this work, or its results may be integrated with an IM or KM service.

Choo (2001; 2009) reviews environmental scanning, which he explains as 'the acquisition and use of information about events, trends and relationships in an organization's external environment, the knowledge of which would assist management in planning the organization's future course of action', distinguishing it from competitor and competitive intelligence, and from business intelligence. He relates this to information-seeking behaviour, and presents a model of different forms of scanning: undirected viewing, a passive, casual and opportunistic information gathering; conditioned viewing, a more focused, but still passive, information gathering; enacting, taking action and seeing what happens; and searching, actively seeking required information. This links environment scanning closely with knowledge management and other information functions.

Aspinall (2011) gives a detailed account of competitive intelligence in the biopharmaceutical industry, taking a very broad approach to include information on customers and distributors, and on changes in the wider environment, and emphasizing its links with knowledge management. She identifies a specific CI cycle: identification of key intelligence topics and questions; collection; analysis; interpretation and dissemination.

Having examined various contexts for information management, and found a good deal of commonality and convergence, we will now look at some IM issues which have relevance to all contexts, beginning with information governance and information risk.

Information governance and information risk

These are ideas which have come to prominence under these names relatively recently in many information management contexts, although they build on earlier concerns. Information governance is an umbrella concept, referring to the sets of policies, processes and standards which are applied within an organization to ensure that all stages of the information lifecycle are managed correctly, so that the organization observes all relevant laws and regulations, avoids risk and uses its information in a way which is both effective and ethically correct (Kooper, Maes and Lindgreen, 2011).

The concept of information governance is interpreted differently according to the organization's context. Usually there is a focus on the legal framework for IM; legislation on matters like data protection, freedom of information, privacy, copyright, intellectual property and so on, discussed in the last chapter, together with any sector-specific regulations or issues affecting the way information is managed. In the British health services, for example, information governance is particularly concerned with safeguarding information about patients, and ensuring that it is used to best effect in planning treatment.

Correct dealing with information often involves a formal assessment of the quality of procedures; the information governance concept largely subsumes concerns which were previously expressed as quality control and application of standards in information management. Lomas (2010) shows how international standards for records management and for information security contribute to information governance.

Information risk is another relatively new concept, stemming from the realization that information problems can become serious business problems, and can – in extreme cases – threaten the survival of a commercial organization, or the credibility and ability to function of a government department. These typically arise from the release of information which should remain confidential, or from the loss of vital information. Those with morbid tastes may like to consider an account of 'great information disasters' throughout (Horton and Lewis, 1990). Examples of more recent problems are shown in the box. Information governance is intended to remove the possibility for such errors.

Information governance, as well as all of information management, rests on clearly stated policies and strategies, expressed in plans and procedures, and we now consider these.

Information policies and strategies

Policies and strategies, plans and objectives, mission and visions: these form the framework, albeit one with a very inconsistent use of terminology, for information management. We will look at the components of this framework, illustrating them by examples to give a flavour of how they are applied. Orna (2008) gives an excellent short coverage of the field and Cornelius (2010) a longer one, focusing on national information policies. Orna (1999; 2004) gives a wide variety of detailed examples of organizational policies and strategies.

Information policies, and equivalents, may be applied at widely different levels: from a small department or function within an organization to a large organization, a grouping of organizations within the public or private sector (e.g. 'UK higher education'), a region, a nation, a grouping of nations, or even the whole world. National information policies have already been mentioned in the last chapter as one of the frameworks for an information society.

Organizations began formally to state information policies in the 1980s, coinciding with the widespread adoption of what were then termed 'new ICTs' (information and communication technologies). Governments had begun to state national information policies in the previous decade, though elements of what would later be termed information policy can be traced back to at least the start of the 20th century. All countries have *de facto* some information policy provision, but only a minority have a clear and fully explicit statement of such; the UK does not. National policies tend to focus first on technological infrastructures, second on skills (often in a rather limited 'computer literacy'

Some recent 'information disasters'

HM Revenue and Customs (the British tax authorities) lost a CD, which had been sent by unsecure post, with personal details of 25 million taxpayers; this led to a new Code of Practice for UK government data.

A minister in the British government, working on official correspondence in St James Park, London, in his lunch break, discarded papers in a park litter bin.

Facebook arbitrarily changed the default privacy settings for its users to 'disclose everything', and was criticized by various national authorities.

A London healthcare trust 'misplaced' personal and health records for 160,000 children.

A large insurance company lost the personal data on 46,000 policy holders during transfer to a processing centre; the company was heavily fined by the authorities.

A laptop computer, stolen from the car of a British government defence official, contained the personal details of 600,000 applicants to join the armed forces.

Details of 9000 school children on unencrypted memory sticks were stolen in a burglary of the home of London education officer.

Google's StreetView camera cars collected passwords and email addresses from unsecured Wi-Fi systems; although the company stated that this was inadvertent, and no use would be made of the data collected, they were heavily criticized, and in response created a Privacy Director role.

The organ donation preferences of over 400,000 people were recorded wrongly on a UK organ donation register, due to a software error.

A British internet provider sent an e-mail to thousands of its subscribers with over 3000 customer records appended, and a British bank similarly appended details of 500 confidential customer transactions in a widely circulated e-mail.

A London borough authority admitted the complete loss of the details of over 100 people, owing to the disappearance of paper files and theft of laptop computers.

context) and third on the legal framework, covering copyright, access rights, etc., with content and other 'library and information issues' taking a smaller place. Brown (1997) gives a clear account, though dated in details, of the basic issues underlying information policies, particularly at the national level.

In the beginning there may be an explicit *mission statement*, or perhaps a *purpose*. This is a statement of what the information service is and does. From this, everything else can be derived. Some mission statements are very brief, others are quite verbose:

Advancing the world's knowledge.   British Library, 2010

The Library's mission is to make its resources available and useful to the Congress and the American people and to sustain and preserve a universal collection of knowledge and creativity for future generations.

Library of Congress, 2008

Our mission is to become the best public library in the world by being so tuned in to the people we serve and so supportive of each other's efforts that we are able to provide highly responsive service. We strive to inform, enrich and empower every person in our community by creating and promoting easy access to a vast array of ideas and information, and by supporting an informed citizenry, lifelong learning and love of reading; ensure access to information sources throughout the nation and around the world; serve our public with expert and caring assistance; and reach out to all members of our community.

Seattle Public Library, 2008

This is often accompanied by a statement of *vision*: where the service would like to be, and what it aspires to.

In 2020 the British Library will be a leading hub in the global information network, advancing knowledge through our collections, expertise and partnerships, for the benefit of the economy and society and the enrichment of cultural life.

'Our vision', British Library '2020 Vision', 2010

The Library leads the nation in ensuring access to knowledge and information and in promoting its creative use for the Congress and its constituents.

Vision statement, Library of Congress, 2008

In the knowledge and information society, libraries are perceived as places where knowledge and culture flow freely, in contrast to the selective offerings of the media, and of the educational system.

Vision for the Finnish public library system for 2010

The next level down, which will be the entry level if there is no explicit purpose or vision, is the *policy*, in this case an information policy. This usually specifies how and why information is used in the environment covered by the policy, which kinds of information and knowledge are relevant and important, and which are vital in achieving the organization's purpose, the principles that will be applied in managing it, how various technologies will be applied, and how various groups of people will be affected. An information policy is usually a tool for developing information strategies. It is a statement of principle rather than detail, typically fairly short, and is 'meant to last'; a policy will not normally be changed frequently.

> Safeguard the privacy and confidentiality of personal health information.
> Ensure that health information systems are efficient and effective.
> Promote the optimal use of health information.
> Ensure the high quality of health information.
>
>   Principles within the Irish national health information strategy, 2004

Policies may also be devised to cover particular aspects of the overall activities of library and information services; collection management policies, for example, are quite popular.

Below the level of policy, typically come a number of *strategies*. These state in some detail how the policy will be achieved, and provide a detailed framework within which information management is carried out.

A strategy is usually accompanied by specific *objectives*; verifiable and achievable aims, the successful achievement of which shows the success of the strategy. Information management (potentially including both knowledge management and records management) is often described as the implementation of an information strategy. A strategy will often be written to cover a defined period of time, typically 3–5 years, and may be reviewed and modified frequently as circumstances change.

> We aim to provide resources and services needed to achieve national health priorities such as the National Service Frameworks and local priorities such as impact on patient care, CNST requirements and the provision of new services within the Trust.
>
> We aim to provide a truly multidisciplinary library service with equity of access and with resources, services and facilities tailored to meet the needs of all types of healthcare staff.
>
>   Examples of objectives from the Library Services of the
>   George Eliot Hospital NHS Trust, Nuneaton, England, 2007

Five 'key themes which set out strategic priorities' from the British Library's 2011–2015 strategy are:

1   Guarantee access for future generations.
2   Enable access to everyone who wants to do research.
3   Support research communities in key areas for social and economic benefit.
4   Enrich the cultural life of the nation.
5   Lead and collaborate in growing the world's knowledge base.

These lead to objectives and actions, for example:

> Priority
> 2   Enable access to everyone who wants to do research
> Objective
> Champion the importance of datasets in scholarly communication across all disciplines
> Action
> Create a network of national and international organisations who assign persistent identifiers to datasets, so that they can be located and re-used and their impact as a research asset measured.

A similar approach is seen in the Wellcome Trust Library Strategy:

> Objective: Developing audiences – identifying and analysing the research and learning needs of current and potential audiences – in order to increase use of resources
> Strengthen links with history of medicine centres of excellence and groups in related fields
> Planned programme of visits with key contacts agreed
> Analyse usage, surveys, trends and benchmarking data to drive service change and to demonstrate impact
> Library Advisory Committee to review six months test data from National Specialist Libraries Benchmarking project
>
> Examples of an objective and associated
> targets and indicators of progress from the
> Wellcome Trust Library Strategy (2006–2009)

The term *plan* is used with particular inconsistency. Sometimes, typically in the form of a *strategic plan*, it will be a high-level concept, similar to what is more often called policy, though with more concrete objectives. In the form of a *business plan*, it will focus on financial and budgetary predictions and objectives, though may include higher-level issues, such as overall purpose and vision. Harriman (2008) gives a practical guide to the implementation of business plans for library and information services, with examples form several countries. On other occasions, a plan may be a lower-level and detailed prescription for how a particular objective is to be achieved.

Good examples of fully developed policies of a rather different nature are the strategies and policies of the British Library, the strategic plan of the Library of Congress and the digitization strategy of the Wellcome Trust, to be found respectively (as at mid 2012) at http://www.bl.uk/aboutus/stratpolprog/strategy1115, http://www.loc.gov/about/mission.html and http://library. wellcome.ac.uk/node351.html.

Implementation of an information policy or strategy, particularly within an organization, requires a good knowledge of the available information resources, and the ways of investigating these is our next topic.

Information auditing and mapping

One of the criteria of a 'resource' is that it may be audited within an organization; the financial audit is most familiar, but other forms are common. Information resources, too, can be audited, and the *information audit* is a staple tool of information management. At its simplest, an information audit may be a listing, as complete as possible, of the information resources available, with a note of who is responsible for maintaining them. Their cost will also usually be included. More ambitious audits will attempt to establish the use and value of the resources and the effectiveness with which information is brought into the organization and communicated within it.

Details and examples of information audits are given by Orna (1999; 2004) and by Buchanan and Gibb (2007; 2008). A variety of methods may be used, including examination of documents and systems, observations, interviews and focus groups, and questionnaires; these will be discussed later in the chapter on research methods. These are, of course, standard library and information research methods, and largely qualitative; it has been argued that it is desirable for information audits to use more of the methods associated with financial audit, to give a more 'hard-nosed' quantitative account of the value of information resources; see, for example, Griffiths (2010).

Information mapping is sometimes distinguished as that form of information audit, or a part of a wider audit, which focuses on how information flows within an organization, or a part of it. Graphical means are typically used to visualize the results.

The idea of auditing implies that what is being audited – information and the documents and systems which convey it – has a definable value. This is a vexed question, to which we now turn.

Valuing information

It has been understood for many years that a particular difficulty for information management lies in the difficulty of assigning a value – particularly a specific monetary value – to information. This applies to specific pieces of information, such as facts provided in answer to reference query or documents retrieved from a database, to collections of information and to the totality of an information service. See Braman (2006) for an extensive review of past literature on economic aspects of information.

This is due to what Koenig and Manzari (2010, 4305) term the 'elastic and amorphous nature of information and information services and the difficulty of quantifying them and in turn measuring their impact'. Although the *cost* of providing a particular item or collection of information can be known accurately, its *value* will depend upon the circumstances of its use, and their consequences, which cannot usually be known in advance. Furthermore, it is notoriously difficult, even after the event, to determine exactly what results may be said to be due to some particular information being available.

This has led to many experts abandoning the attempt to provide a quantitative value for information, and rely on asserting a broad qualitative educational or moral value. Raban (2007) compares several such social and user-centred approaches to valuing information. Alternatively, some surrogate for 'true' value is used, such as estimated time saved, which may be related to cost, and expressed user satisfaction. These approaches, however, are generally unconvincing to funders and managers, and ways of assessing numerical and cost values are constantly being sought. Aabø (2009) reviews ways in which library and information services have attempted to show return on investment in financial terms.

Away from the library sector, there is a slow move to treat information more generally as a quantifiable asset in monetary terms: see Oppenheim, Stenson and Wilson (2003) for an account of the conceptual basis, and Wilson and Stenson (2008) and Cummins and Bawden (2010) for descriptions of how valuations of information assets are beginning to appear on the balance sheets of companies.

A popular approach at the present time is the idea of *contingent valuation*, which starts from the view that the value of information is simply what someone is willing to pay for it. This idea of 'willingness to pay' for information has been studied in many experimental tests, with inconclusive results; see, for example, Raban and Sheizaf (2006) and Sakalaki and Smaragda (2007).

Contingent valuation applies this idea to 'real world' information services, and derives methods for assessing the perceptions of users of free information services of how much they would be willing to pay to have the services maintained, and what would be the economic costs of their withdrawal. These methods have been tested over many years with other forms of goods and services which are free at the point of use. They have the advantage that they are approved by governments and commercial organizations as a valid approach to cost-benefit analysis.

The approach has been applied to various kinds of information services, particularly public and national libraries, in a number of studies; see Hider (2008a), Chung (2008) and Lee, Chung, and Jung (2010) for examples, reviews and critiques. Specific examples include:

1 An estimation of the value of the borrowing of books from British public

libraries, by asking library patrons to estimate the value of the benefit which they had obtained from books borrowed, and how much they would have been willing to pay for this. The typical value was 8% of the purchase price of the books (Morris, Sumsion and Hawkins, 2002).

2 A study by the British Library (BL) to assess the value of its national library services; both the direct benefits to users and the indirect benefits to the nation. This involved a variety of user surveys, including questions on what users would have done if BL services were not available, and what the consequent costs would have been, and what amount of money users would think was adequate compensation for the loss of all BL services, if the BL did not exist. The study results suggested that the BL generated a value to the nation of about four times its costs (British Library, 2004).

3 A study of the perceived value of the Norwegian public library service, presenting library users with a scenario in which the municipality was considering closing a library, and asking either what they would be willing to pay to keep the library open, or alternatively what they would be willing to accept as compensation for its closure. By combining the results, it could be shown that the amount users would be willing to pay is roughly equivalent to current library costs per head of population (Aabø, 2005).

4 A study of the perceived value of technical services – collection management, cataloguing, etc. – in a public library service; this showed the perceived value of these functions to be considerably higher than that of the library service *per* se (Hider, 2008b).

Despite some acknowledged shortcomings and oversimplifications, contingent valuation methods seem the most acceptable means at present of evaluating cost-benefit of information services. It is likely that they will be further developed and used in the future.

Effectiveness and impact

Contingent valuation is one approach to the evaluation of effectiveness of information provision; an intrinsic part of information management. There is a long history of efforts to find the best ways to achieve this; see Lancaster (1993) for an influential summary of practice in earlier days, Rapp (2008) for an account of early evaluations at the US National Library of Medicine, which has been a leader in this area, and Matthews (2007) and Kyrillidou and Cook (2008), Tenopir (2012) and Hughes (2012) for surveys of recent practice.

All evaluations must 'measure' something, by either quantitative or qualitative assessment, or by a hybrid approach. A useful six-way typology of what may be measured, originally suggested by the American library science professor Wilfred Lancaster, is as follows:

1 *Cost:* measures what a service costs to provide, a collection to purchase, etc. This can usually be known with accuracy, and replacement costs can be assessed by standard financial techniques. It will be included in an information audit.

2 *Effectiveness:* shows how well the system is working, compared to what it is expected to do. It may often be measured quantitatively, using, for example, performance metrics, or expressed user satisfaction.

3 *Benefit:* implies a knowledge of the 'true' value of a system or service, and is notoriously difficult to measure. It is usually approached by qualitative or semi-qualitative measures.

4 *Cost-effectiveness:* attempts to relate the measured effectiveness of a system or service with its known costs. Usually this approach is used on an isolated component of a total information service, and usually in a comparison between two alternatives, e.g. whether to subscribe to information from provider A or B, or whether to outsource some function.

5 *Cost-benefit:* attempts to relate the cost of providing a service to its 'real' benefits, but there are few convincing examples. Impact studies and the application of techniques such as contingent valuation are among them.

6 *Cost-performance-benefit:* aims at the investigation of the whole set of relationships between the costs, performance, and benefits of an information service. No convincing study of this type has ever been carried out.

Most effectiveness measures rely either on user satisfaction surveys or on some form of performance metrics. The former evaluate information provision by focusing on the behaviour and opinions of its users, applying a variety of survey methods, both quantitative and qualitative, as we will discuss in the chapter on research methods. Inevitably they only give a partial picture, since they cannot include those who could use the service, but do not.

Performance metrics give quantitative measures of effectiveness, which allow comparison between information services if standard sets of performance indicators are used; they are particularly popular with large library services, although Funk (2008) gives examples of such metrics being used to compare the performance of smaller healthcare library and information services. For detailed overviews of information performance metrics, see Heaney (2009) and Dugan, Hernon, and Nitecki (2009). An ISO standard – ISO 11620 'Information and documentation: library performance indicators (2008)' – lists 45 indicators meant for all types of library, and a set of 30 indicators especially suitable for national libraries has been devised, as an adjunct to this standard (Poll, 2008). An IFLA handbook (Poll and te Boekhorst, 2007) lists 40 indicators, with example results. Many national sets of indicators have also been derived, though they are increasingly being replaced by the international standards.

These indicators are quantitative measures of service effectiveness, such as: number of loans; occupancy of seats in reading rooms; number of accesses to e-resources; availability of required items; speed of retrieval from closed stacks; cost per loan; and rate of satisfactorily answered reference requests. Advantages of such indicators are that they should be available from a library's management information with a minimum of extra work required, and they are readily comparable with similar libraries, and year-on-year within one library. Drawbacks are they are rather oriented towards traditional paper-based library and information services, and that they give little qualitative insight into the reasons for adequacy, or otherwise, of the service. The data also needs to be interpreted with sensitivity to user needs: the relative importance of the speed of an inter-library loan and of its cost, for example, be very different for a medical library serving a critical care department and for an academic departmental library serving mainly humanities research students.

In some cases, performance metrics for information services have been incorporated into an adaptation of the 'balanced scorecard' quality management approach, which identifies critical success factors for a service's objectives, and tests these with performance metrics; see, for example, Lloyd (2006).

User satisfaction ratings, in a rather limited fashion, may be included in such metrics. In some sectors, a standard format for assessing this factor is used, for comparability. This is particularly common within academic libraries in particular countries. In the UK, for example, the Society of College, National and University Libraries (SCONUL) recommends and promotes such surveys through its 'Performance Portal' (as of December 2011 to be found at http://vamp.diglib. shrivenham.cranfield.ac.uk), while the SERVQUAL protocol, a standard 'service industry' instrument, has been widely used in some countries; see Yu et al. (2008) for a critique based on Chinese experience. A similar protocol, specifically devised for assessing user satisfaction in library and information services, LibQUAL, has also had wide use: see Greenwood, Watson and Dennis (2011) and Russell (2010) for accounts of its use in the USA and Ireland respectively.

Impact studies are particularly desirable for service evaluation, since they aim to show the actual impacts made on the users of information services by the information provided, and on the business of the organization of which the services are a part. In an academic library, for example, we might want to show that use of the library and information services results in students getting better grades in assessments, fewer students dropping out, researchers obtaining more grants, lecturers writing more papers, and so on. In a healthcare setting, we would like to show that information services result in fewer patient deaths, faster recovery, less hospital-acquired infection, etc. In a commercial context, we might look for more innovations, and products getting to market more quickly. Oakleaf

(2010) gives an overview of methods of assessing value in academic libraries, although many of the points are more generally applicable.

Often, however, hard data to support such conclusions is lacking, and evaluators must rely on expert opinion. A good example is the study of the value of academic libraries to researchers, carried out by the UK Research Information Network (RIN, 2011). Quantitative studies of statistical and bibliometric data give limited results, so that the study relied on qualitative evidence from interviews and focus groups, but was able to conclude that 'the evidence on the value of libraries . . . is robust and unequivocal' (RIN, 2011, 4). Botha, Erasmus and Van Deventer (2009) give an example of this kind of impact assessment of information services in a scientific research institution.

As with anything attempting to show the 'real value' of information, impact studies are difficult to carry out and relatively few really convincing individual examples have been described. However, as Koenig and Manzari (2010, 4305) say 'when pulled together, the literature is impressively consistent in showing that library and similar information services have a substantial positive impact'.

This style of evaluation has been studied more in the health information sector than elsewhere, perhaps because this sector is 'evidence-based' in general, perhaps because the results are clearly measurable, and important both in humanitarian and economic terms; for reviews, see Weightman et al. (2009) and Marshall (2007). However, it has proved difficult to show a conclusive relation between library and information provision and the desirable outcomes. Nonetheless, these studies suggest that while this direct impact is difficult to establish without doubt, there is an increasing body of evidence that information provided by a library service can influence patient care outcomes and that assessment of impact at a local level is possible by careful choice of evaluation methods. See Robinson and Bawden (2007) for a more detailed account of such a study.

The methods described above give some insight into the usefulness, value and impact of library and information services. Other, complementary, approaches aim to give an understanding of the detail of how and why the services provide value.

One classic example is the 'Value Project' (Urquhart and Hepworth, 1995), a study that explored an approach to assessing the effectiveness of UK healthcare libraries as information providers and their effect on clinical decision-making and patient care. The study resulted in the development of a toolkit aimed at health sector information professionals to enable them to demonstrate the contribution their services were making. There are some similarities with the 'impact' studies noted above, but the Value Toolkit aimed at identifying more long-term and intangible benefits. Although devised for the medical library environment, this toolkit has been adapted for use in other kinds of information service, for example assessing the value of the use of material in public libraries (Bawden et al., 2010).

Studies of this sort may give valuable detailed information of exactly how and why information services are effective in helping particular user groups. And in general we can expect much more attention to be paid to developing methods for showing the 'real' value and impact of information provision.

We now conclude the chapter by considering the idea of managing information specifically in support of creativity and innovation.

Information for creativity and innovation

One important function for information management in some contexts is to provide systems and services which support and promote innovation and creativity. But here we encounter the paradox put forward by the poet Lord Byron:

> To be perfectly original one should think much and read little and this is impossible, for one must have read before one has learnt to think.

On the other hand, as Karl Popper reminds us (Popper and Eccles, 1984, 208):

> Einstein once said 'My pencil is clever than I'. What he meant could perhaps be put thus: armed with a pencil, we can be more than twice as clever as we are without. Armed with a computer (a typical World 3 object), we can perhaps be more than a hundred times as clever as we are without.

Innovation and creativity can certainly be aided by information tools, since they depend on the 'prepared mind', which will generally rely on the input from more conventional information systems. But there may be some specific features of information, rather unconventional, which may support creativity, for example:

- inclusion of peripheral and speculative (even incorrect) material
- provision of interdisciplinary information
- representations of information to bring out analogies, patterns, exceptions, etc.
- emphasis on browsing facilities
- encouragement of informal channels
- information geared to individual preferences and requirements.

Some techniques for promoting creativity rely on group interactions; but as Theodore Von Kármán, the Hungarian-American engineer, wrote 'The finest creative thoughts come, not out of organized teams, but out of the quiet of one's own world'. Information management in support of creativity and innovation must support both groups and individuals.

There are also some examples of information systems specifically geared to *literature discovery*, by identifying patterns and relationships in information collections; for example, common title words, index terms or citations (Kostoff et al., 2009). The idea of knowledge discovery from literature databases was pioneered by Don Swanson and his colleagues (see, for example, Swanson and Smalheiser, 1999). It can be seen as a specific example of the more general idea of *data mining* or *data analytics*; extracting information implicit in large data collections, through statistical and pattern recognition techniques (Chen and Liu, 2004; Han, Kamber and Pei, 2011).

A browsing approach to information has often been associated with creativity. As we saw in Chapter 7, while it seems clear what browsing is in practice, precise definitions are few, and not generally agreed, perhaps because the term can cover a variety of activities and purposes: it has been described as 'seeking and selecting information by skimming, scanning and other similar activities', and as 'the art of not knowing what you want until you find it'. The finding may be in itself a Eureka moment, again emphasizing the link between browsing and innovation and creativity. The whole area of information and creativity is an intriguing one; for more detail and examples, see two reviews spanning a wide time period (Bawden, 1986; 2011).

Summary
The quotation from Myron Tribus, the American engineer, which began this chapter reminds us that all complicated systems, including information management systems, need to be managed in a holistic manner. We have tried, in this chapter, to illustrate the general principles, models and frameworks which underlie the diverse forms of information management discussed. We have deliberately taken a wide scope, including records and archive management, knowledge management, data management, business intelligence and so on, which others consider separate subjects. We believe that it is sensible to consider all these under the information management heading, because of the increasing extent of convergence between them: silo building is a foolish activity under these circumstances. Practitioners of the information sciences are likely to have

- Information management is a complicated field, encompassing different forms of information and types of documents in diverse environments.
- A variety of models and frameworks can be used to understand information management, based around ideas of the communication chain and information lifecycle, and to value-added processes.
- Demonstrating the value and impact of information and information provision is a major challenge for information management.

to deal with any or all of these functions in the future. The important task will not be to distinguish between these aspects of information management, but rather to treat them holistically, and to attend to issues of information governance and of establishing the value and impact of information provision, which will become even more important in the future.

Key readings

Elizabeth Orna, Information policies: yesterday, today, tomorrow, *Journal of Information Science*, 2008, 34(4), 547–66.

B. Detlor, Information management, *International Journal of Information Management*, 2010, 30(2), 103–108.

[Two articles which give clear short overviews of the topics.]

Elizabeth Orna, *Information strategy in practice*, Aldershot, Gower, 2004.

Ian Cornelius, *Information policies and strategies*, London: Facet Publishing, 2010.

[Two books which give a range of examples as well as explaining the principles.]

References

Aabø, S. (2005) Are public libraries worth their price ?, *New Library World*, 106(11/12), 487–95.

Aabø, S. (2009) Libraries and return on investment (ROI): a meta-analysis, *New Library World*, 110(7/8), 311–24.

Agosta, D. E. and Hughes-Hassell, S. (2006) Toward a model of the everyday life information needs of urban teenagers, part 1: theoretical model, *Journal of the American Society for Information Science and Technology*, 57(10), 1394–1403.

Aspinall, Y. (2011) Competitive intelligence in the biopharmaceutical industry: the key elements, *Business Information Review*, 28(2), 101–4.

Baumard, P. (2010) Knowledge: tacit and explicit, *Encyclopedia of Library and Information Sciences* (3rd edn), London: Taylor & Francis, 1:1, 3184–94.

Bawden, D. (1986) Information systems and the stimulation of creativity, *Journal of Information Science*, 12(5), 203–16 [reprinted in R. L. Ruggles, (ed.), *Knowledge Management Tools*, Boston: Butterworth-Heinnemann, Boston, 79–101].

Bawden, D. (2011) Encountering on the road to Serendip? Browsing in new information environments, in A. Foster and P. Rafferty (eds), *Innovations in IR: Perspectives for theory and practice*, London: Facet Publishing, 1–22.

Bawden, D., Calvert, A., Robinson, L., Urquhart, C., Bray, C. and Amosford, J. (2010) Understanding our value: assessing the nature of the impact of library services, *Library and Information Research*, 33(105), 62–89 [online] available at http://www.lirg.org.uk/lir/ojs/index.php/lir.

Bawden, D. and Robinson, L. (2010) Pharmaceutical information; a 30-year perspective on the literature, *Annual Review of Information Science and Technology*, 45, 63–119.

Bedford, D. A. D. (2012) Enabling personal knowledge management with collaborative and semantic technologies, *Bulletin of the American Society for Information Science and Technology*, 38(2), 32–9.

Black, A. and Brunt, R. (1999) Information management in business, libraries and British military intelligence: towards a history of information management, *Journal of Documentation*, 55(4), 361–74.

Black, A., Muddiman, D. and Plant, H. (2007) *The early information society: information management in Britain before the computer*, Aldershot: Ashgate.

Botha, E., Erasmus, R. and Van Deventer, M. (2009) Evaluating the impact of a special library and information service, *Journal of Librarianship and Information Science*, 41(2), 108–23.

Bouthillier, F. and Shearer, K. (2002) Understanding knowledge management and information management: the need for an empirical perspective, *Information Research*, 8(1), paper 141 [online] available at http://InformationR.net/ir/8-1/paper141.html.

Braman, S. (2006) The micro- and macro-economics of information, *Annual Review of Information Science and Technology*, 40, 3–52.

British Library (2004) *Measuring our value*, [online] available from http://www.bl.uk/pdf/measuringourvalue.pdf.

Brown, M. (1997) The field of information policy. 1. Fundamental concepts, *Journal of Information Science*, 23(4), 261–75.

Bryson, J. (2011) *Managing information services: a sustainable approach* (3rd edn), Farnham: Ashgate.

Buchanan, S. and Gibb, F. (2007) The information audit: role and scope, *International Journal of Information Management*, 27(3), 159–72.

Buchanan, S. and Gibb, F. (2008) The information audit: methodology selection, *International Journal of Information Management*, 28(1), 3–11.

Buckland, M. K. (2011) Data management as bibliography, *Bulletin of the American Society for Information Science and Technology*, 37(6), 34–7.

Budd, J. M. (2011) Meaning, truth and information: prolegomena to a theory, *Journal of Documentation*, 67(1), 56–74.

Cameron, S. A. (2011) *Enterprise content management: a business and technical guide*, Swindon: British Computer Society.

Case, D. O. (2007) *Looking for information: a survey of research on information seeking, needs, and behaviour* (2nd edn), New York: Academic Press.

Case, D. O. (2012) *Looking for information: a survey of research on information seeking, needs and behavior* (3rd edn), Bingley: Emerald.

Chen, S. Y. and Liu, X. (2004) The contribution of data mining to information science, *Journal of Information Science*, 30(6), 550–8.

Choo, C. W. (2001) Environmental scanning as information seeking and organizational learning, *Information Research*, 7(1), paper 112 [online] available at http://informationr.net/ir/7-1/paper112.html.

Choo, C. W. (2009) The art of scanning the environment, *Bulletin of the American Society for Information Science*, 25(3), available from http://www.asis.org/Bulletin/Feb-99/choo.html.

Chowdhury, G. G., Burton, P. F., McMenemy, D. and Poulter, A. (2008) *Librarianship: an introduction*, London: Facet Publishing.

Chung, H. K. (2008) The contingent valuation method in public libraries, *Journal of Librarianship and Information Science*, 40(2), 71–80.

Cornelius, I. (2010) *Information policies and strategies*, London: Facet Publishing.

Cullingford, A. (2011) *The special collection handbook*, London: Facet Publishing.

Cummins, J. and Bawden, D. (2010) Accounting for information: information and knowledge in the annual reports of FTSE 100 companies, *Journal of Information Science*, 36(3), 283–305.

Day, R. E. (2005) Clearing up 'implicit knowledge': implications for knowledge management, information science, psychology, and social epistemology, *Journal of the American Society for Information Science and Technology*, 56(6), 630–35.

Detlor, B. (2010) Information management, *International Journal of Information Management*, 30(2), 103–8.

Desouza, K. C. and Paquette, S. (2011) *Knowledge management: an introduction*, London: Facet Publishing.

Dugan, R. E., Hernon, P. and Nitecki, D. A. (2009) *Viewing library metrics from different perspectives: inputs, outputs and outcomes*, Westport CT: Libraries Unlimited.

Dweba, T. P. and Mearns, M. A. (2011) Conserving indigenous knowledge as the key to the current and future use of traditional vegetables, *International Journal of Information Management*, 31(6), 564–71.

Eaton, J. J. and Bawden, D. (1991) What kind of resource is information?, *International Journal of Information Management*, 11(2), 156–65 .

Edwards, G. E., Layzell Ward, P. and Rugaas, B. (2000) *Management basics for information professionals*, New York: Neal Schumann.

Fieldhouse, M. and Marshall, A. (eds) (2012) Collection development in the digital age, London: Facet Publishing.

Forbes, M. (2012) CollectionSpace: a story of open-source software development and user-centered design, *Bulletin of the American Society for Information Science and Technology*, 38(3), 22–6.

Fourie, I. (2011) Personal information management (PIM), reference management and mind maps: the way to creative librarians?, *Library Hi Tech*, 29(4), 764–71.

Funk, C. J. (2008) Using standards to make your case: examples from the medical library community, *New Library World*, 109(5-6), 251–57.

Given, L. M. and McTavish, L. (2010) What's old is new again: the reconvergence of libraries, archives and museums in the digital age, *Library Quarterly*, 80(1), 7–32.

Gordon. K. (2007) *Principles of data management: facilitating information sharing*, Swindon: British Computer Society.

Gorman, M. (2000) *Our enduring values: librarianship in the 21st century*, Chicago: American Library Association.

Gould, M. R. (2009) *The library PR handbook: high-impact communications*, Chicago: American Library Association.

Greenwood, J. T., Watson, A. P. and Dennis, M. (2011) Ten years of LibQUAL: A study of qualitative and quantitative survey results at the University of Mississippi 2001–2010, *Journal of Academic Librarianship*, 37(4), 312–18.

Greyling, E. and Zulu, S. (2010) Content development in an indigenous digital library: A case study in community participation, *IFLA Journal*, 36(1), 30–9.

Griffiths, P. (2010) Where next for information audit?, *Business Information Review*, 27(4), 216–24.

Han, J., Kamber, M. and Pei, J. (2011) *Data mining: concepts and techniques*, San Francisco: Morgan Kaufman.

Harriman, J .H. P. (2008) *Creating your library's business plan: a how to do it manual*, London: Facet Publishing.

Hayes, R. M. (2001) *Models for library management, decision-making and planning*, Amsterdam: Academic Press.

Heaney, M. (ed.) (2009) Library statistics for the twenty-first century world, IFLA Publications no. 138, Munich: K. G. Saur.

Hepworth, M. (2004) A framework for understanding user requirements for an information service: defining the needs of informal carers, *Journal of the American Society for Information Science and Technology*, 55(8), 695–708.

Hider, P. (2008a) Using the contingent valuation method for dollar valuations of library services, *Library Quarterly*, 78(4), 437–58.

Hider, P. (2008b) How much are technical services worth? Using the contingent valuation method to estimate the added value of collection management and access, *Library Resources and Technical Services*, 52(4), 254–62.

Hill, J. (ed.) (2011) *The future of archives and recordkeeping: a reader*, London: Facet Publishing.

Holtham, C. (2001) Valuation has its price, *Library Association Record*, 103(4), 232–33.

Horton, F. W. and Lewis, D. (eds) (1990) *Great information disasters*, London: Aslib.

Hughes, L. M. (ed.) (2012) *Evaluating and measuring the value, use and impact of digital collections*, London: Facet Publishing.

JISC (2007) Managing the information lifecycle, [online] available at http://www.jiscinfonet.ac.uk/infokits/information-lifecycle/Information-Lifecycle.pdf.

Jones, W. (2007a) *Keeping found things found: the study and practice of personal information management*, San Francisco: Morgan Kaufmann.

Jones, W. (2007b) Personal information management, *Annual Review of Information Science and Technology*, 41, 453–504.

Jones, W. and Teevan, J. (2007) *Personal information management*, Seattle: University of Washington Press.

Koenig, M. and Manzari, L. (2010) Productivity impacts of libraries and information services, *Encyclopedia of Library and Information Sciences* (3rd edn), London: Taylor Francis, 1:1, 4305–4314.

Koenig, M. and Neveroski, K. (2010) Knowledge management: early development, *Encyclopedia of Library and Information Sciences* (3rd edn), London: Taylor & Francis, 1:1, 3155–63.

Koontz, C. M., Gupta, D. and Webber, S. (2006) Key publications in library marketing: a review, *IFLA Journal*, 32(2), 224–31.

Kooper, M. N., Maes, R. and Lindgreen, E. E. O. R. (2011) On the governance of information: introducing a new concept of governance to support the management of information, *International Journal of Information Management*, 31(3), 195–200.

Kostoff, R. N., Block, J. A., Solka, J. L., Briggs, M. B., Rushenberg, R. L., Stump, J. A., Johnson, D., Lyons, T. J. and Wyatt, J. R. (2009) Literature-based discovery, *Annual Review of Information Science and Technology*, 43, 241–85.

Kovacs, D. E. (2009) *The Kovacs guide to electronic library collection development* (2nd edn), New York NY: Neal Schuman.

Kyrillidou, M. and Cook, C. (2008) The evolution of measurement and evaluation of libraries: a perspective from the Association of Research Libraries, *Library Trends*, 56(4), 888–909.

Lancaster, F. W. (1993) *If you want to evaluate your library* (2nd edn), London: Library Association Publishing.

Lee, S., Chung, H. and Jung, E. (2010) Assessing the warm glow effect in contingent valuations for public libraries, *Journal of Librarianship and Information Science*, 42(4), 236–44 .

Lloyd, S. (2006) Building library success using the balanced scorecard, *Library Quarterly*, 76(3), 352–61.

Lomas, E. (2010) Information governance: information security and access within a UK context, *Records Management Journal*, 20(2), 182–98.

Lwoga, E. (2011) Knowledge management approaches in managing agricultural indigenous and exogenous knowledge in Tanzania, *Journal of Documentation*, 67(3), 407–30.

Maina, C. K. (2012) Traditional knowledge management and preservation: intersections with library and information science, *International Information and Library Review*, 44(1), 13–27.

Manzuch, Z. (2009) Archives, libraries and museums as communicators of memory in the European Union projects, *Information Research*, 14(2), paper 400 [online] available at http://informationr.net/ir/14-2/paper400.html.

Marshall, J. G., (2007) Measuring the value and impact of health library and information services: past reflections, future possibilities, *Health Information and*

Libraries Journal, 24(1), 4–17.

Martin, B. (2008) Knowledge management, *Annual Review of Information Science and Technology*, 42, 371–424.

Marty, P. F. (2007) Museum professionals and the relevance of LIS expertise, *Library and Information Science Research*, 29(2), 252–276.

Matthews, J. R. (2007) *The evaluation and measurement of library services*, Westport CT: Libraries Unlimited.

McDonald, J. (2010) Records management and data management: closing the gap, *Records Management Journal*, 20(1), 53–60.

McLeod, J. and Hare, C. (eds) (2005) *Managing electronic records*, London: Facet Publishing.

Meyer, H. W. J. (2005) The nature of information and the effective use of information in rural development, *Information Research*, 10(2), paper 214 [online] available at http://InformationR.net/ir/10-2/paper214.html.

Millar, L. A. (2010) *Archives: principles and practice*, London: Facet Publishing.

Morris, A., Sumsion, J. and Hawkins, M. (2002) Economic value of public libraries in the UK, *Libri*, 52(2), 78–87.

Oakleaf, M. (2010) *Value of academic libraries: a comprehensive research review and report*, Chicago, American Library Association [online] available at http://www.ala.org/ala/mgrps/divs/acrl/issues/value/val_report.pdf.

Oppenheim, C., Stenson, J. and Wilson, R. M. S. (2003) Studies on information as an asset 1: definitions, *Journal of Information Science*, 29(3), 159–66.

Orna, E. (1999) *Practical information policies* (2nd edn), Aldershot, Gower.

Orna, E. (2004) *Information strategy in practice*, Aldershot, Gower.

Orna, E. (2008) Information policies: yesterday, today, tomorrow, *Journal of Information Science*, 34(4), 547–66.

Orna, E. and Pettitt, C. (1998) *Information management in museums* (2nd edn), Aldershot: Gower.

Paulus, M. J. (2011) Reconceptualizing academic libraries and archives in the digital age, *portal: Libraries and the Academy*, 11(4), 939–53.

Pauleen, D. J. and Gorman, G. E. (eds) (2011) *Personal knowledge management: individual, organizational and social perspectives*: Farnham: Gower.

Pimental, D. M. (2010) Examining the KO roots of Taylor's value-added model, *Knowledge Organization*, 37(1), 58–64.

Polanyi, M. (1962) *Personal Knowledge*, Chicago Il: University of Chicago Press.

Poll, R. (2008) Quality indicators for national libraries: the new standard, paper presented at the 74th IFLA Congress, Quebec, August 2008, available from http://www.ifla.org/IV/ifla74/papers/160-Poll-en.pdf.

Poll, R. and te Boekhorst, P. (2007) *Measuring quality: performance measurement in libraries* (2nd edn), IFLA Publications no, 127, Munich: K. G. Saur.

Popper, K. R. and Eccles, J. C. (1984) *The self and its brain*, London: Routledge.

Raban, D. R. (2007) User-centred evaluation of information: a research challenge, *Internet Research*, 17(3), 306–22.

Raban, D. R. and Sheizaf, R. (2006) The effect of source nature and status on the subjective value of information, *Journal of the American Society for Information Science and Technology*, 57(3), 321–29.

Rapp, B. A. (2008) Excellence in evaluation: early landmarks at the National Library of Medicine, *Library Trends*, 56(4), 859–87 [examples of some 'classic' early service evaluations.]

Ratzek, W. (2011) The mutations of marketing and libraries, *IFLA Journal*, 37(2), 139–51.

RIN (2011) *The value of libraries for research and researchers*, London: Research Information Network, available from http://www.rin.ac.uk/our-work/using-and-accessing-information-resources/value-libraries-research-and-researchers.

Roberts, D. A. and Light, R. E. (1980) Museum documentation, *Journal of Documentation*, 36(1), 42–84.

Robinson, L. (2009) Information Science: communication chain and domain analysis, *Journal of Documentation*, 65(4), 578–91.

Robinson, L. and Bawden, D. (2007) Evaluation of outreach services for primary care and mental health: assessing the impact, *Health Information and Libraries Journal*, 24(s1), 57–66.

Rowley, J. (1998) Towards a framework for information management, *International Journal of Information Management*, 18(5), 359–69.

Rubin, R. E. (2010) *Foundations of Library and Information Science* (3rd edn), New York NY: Neal-Schuman.

Russell, P. (2010) Measuring up: The experience of LibQUAL at ITT Dublin library. *SCONUL Focus*, (49), 47–51.

Sakalaki, M. and Smaragda, K. (2007) How much is information worth? Willingness to pay for expert and non-expert informational goods compared to material goods in lay economic thinking, *Journal of Information Science*, 33(3), 315–25.

Savard, R. and Gupta, D. K. (eds) (2011) *Marketing libraries in a Web 2.0 world*, Munich: de Gruyter.

Schlögl, C. (2005) Information and knowledge management: dimensions and approaches, *Information Research*, 10(4), paper 235 [online] available from http://www.informationr.net/ir/10-4/paper235.html.

Shepherd, E. (2009) *Archives and archivists in 20th century England*, Farnham: Ashgate.

Shepherd, E. and Yeo, G. (2003) *Managing records: a handbook of principles and practice*, London: Facet Publishing.

Smallwood, C. (2011) *Library management tips that work*, Chicago: American Library Association.

Srikantaiah, T. K. and Koenig M. E. D. (eds) (2008) *Knowledge management in practice: connections and context*, Medford NJ: Information Today.

Stevens, A. (2008) A different way of knowing: tools and strategies for managing indigenous knowledge, *Libri*, 58(1), 25–33.

Swanson, D. R. and Smalheiser, N. R. (1999) Implicit text linkages between Medline records: using Arrowsmith as an aid to scientific discovery, *Library Trends*, 48(1), 48–59.

Taylor, R. (1982) Value-added processes in the information life cycle, *Journal of the American Society for Information Science*, 33(5), 341–46.

Taylor, R. S. (1986) *Value-added processes in information systems*, Norwood NJ: Ablex.

Tenopir, C. (2012) Beyond usage: measuring library outcomes and value, *Library Management*, 33(1/2), 5–13.

Tsoukas, T. (2005) *Complex knowledge: studies in organizational epistemology*, Oxford: Oxford University Press.

Urquhart C. and Hepworth J. (1995) The value of information supplied to clinicians by health libraries: devising an outcomes-based assessment of the contribution of libraries to clinical decision making, *Health Libraries Review*, 12(3), 201–13.

Vasileiou, M. and Rowley, J. (2011) Marketing and promotion of e-books in academic libraries, *Journal of Documentation*, 67(4), 624–43.

Weightman, A., Urquhart, C., Spink, S. and Thomas, R. (2009) The value and impact of information provided through library services for patient care: developing guidance for best practice, *Health Libraries and Information Journal*, 26(1), 63–71.

White, L. (2012) Introduction to Museum Informatics: something new, something more, *Bulletin of the American Society for Information Science and Technology*, 38(3), 15–21.

White, M. (2011) *The intranet management handbook*, London: Facet Publishing.

Whittaker, S. (2011) Personal information management: from information consumption to curation, *Annual Review of Information Science and Technology*, 45, 3–62.

Wilson, R. M. and Stenson, J. A. (2008) Valuation of information assets on the balance sheet: the recognition and approaches to the valuation of intangible assets, *Business Information Review*, 25(3), 167–82.

Wilson, T. D. (2002) The nonsense of knowledge management, *Information Research*, 8(1), paper 144 [online] available from http://www.informationr.net/ir/8-1/paper144.html.

Yates-Mercer, P. A. and Bawden, D. (2002) Managing the paradox: the valuation of knowledge and knowledge management, *Journal of Information Science*, 28(1), 19–29.

Yu, L. et al. (2008) An epistemological critique of gap theory based library assessment: The case of SERVQUAL, *Journal of Documentation*, 64(4), 511–51.

Zhang, A. B. and Gourley, B. (2008) *Creating digital collections: a practical guide*, Oxford: Chandos.

CHAPTER 13

Digital literacy

> Any attempt to constitute an umbrella definition or overarching frame of digital literacy will necessarily involve reconciling the claims of myriad concepts of digital literacy, a veritable legion of digital literacies.
>
> Colin Lankshear and Michele Knobel (Lankshear and Knobel, 2008, 4)

Introduction

As the quotation above illustrates, understanding digital literacy, and similar ideas, can be complicated; we will give a simplified account, picking out the most important aspects, without attempting to cover every definition or perspective.

Digital literacy refers to the ability to use information effectively, in all formats, in a largely digital information environment This is a vital 'life skill' for anyone in today's world. All those aiming to work as an information specialist must have a high level of digital literacy themselves, and will be expected to help others achieve the same.

'Digital literacy' is a relatively new term, describing a set of knowledge, skills and attitudes needed to handle information effectively in a digital age. The term was first popularized by Paul Gilster, in a book of the same name, published in 1997. There have been – as we shall see below – several terms used to refer to these skills and competences, but we believe digital literacy to be the most appropriate.

Although, as we shall see, the library and information community has made substantial contributions in this area, so have other disciplines, particularly computer science and education. Gilster himself epitomizes this eclectic mix: originally a specialist in medieval literature, he has been a flight instructor, a full-time writer on internet topics, and most recently a blogger on developments towards interstellar exploration (Gilster, 2011).

There are various detailed definitions and explanations of digital literacy, but in general we can say that:

> Digital literacy is the set of attitudes, understanding and skills needed
> to find, communicate and use information effectively, in a variety of
> media and formats.

While it relies on an underpinning of basic literacy and of ICT skills, it is more concerned with understanding information resources, and their expression in various formats, and with the ability to evaluate, synthesize, organize and communicate information effectively. Although much information is in digital form, an important aspect of digital literacy is knowing when to use a non-digital source: printed sources, people, etc.

The idea of digital literacy is a broad one, and it builds on the older and simpler concepts of 'information literacy' and 'computer literacy'. Unfortunately, these 'literacy' terms, and others such as media literacy, are not used consistently (Bawden, 2001; 2008), and there is often difficulty in finding an appropriate equivalent term in languages other then English (Chevillotte, 2010). Not only must the idea of digital literacy find its place among information literacy, computer literacy, ICT literacy, e-literacy, network literacy, and media literacy, but it must also be matched against terms which avoid mentioning 'literacy', such as informacy and information fluency. In some circumstances, even 'information' is not mentioned, as in 'basic skills', 'Internet savvy' or 'smart working' (Robinson et.al., 2005). Often, unfortunately, these approaches have been pursued in isolation, with limited collaboration, and much reinventing of wheels.

We will first look at the original ideas: information and computer literacy.

Information and computer literacies

Computer literacy (sometimes called 'IT literacy' or 'ICT literacy') is a term dating back to the early 1980s, and promoted by the IT community. It refers to the skills and knowledge needed to use IT systems effectively – usually a set of specific competences with computer hardware and standard software packages. A typical example is the set of knowledge and skills promoted by the ECDL (European Computer Driving Licence) training. Computer, or ICT, literacy is rather limited, since it does not imply any understanding of the information being handled, nor any 'softer' skills of information evaluation, organization, etc.

Information literacy is usually understood as a broader approach to information handling, incorporating softer non-technical skills, and mainly promoted by the library community, especially in universities and colleges, and increasingly in schools. The phrase was first used in 1974, in a report by the then president of the American Information Industry Association, Paul Zurkowski, but has been used with various meanings since (Bawden, 2001): indeed, writes Sylvie Chevillote (2010, 2422) 'there seems to be almost as many ways of defining [information literacy] as there are authors writing about it'.

A typical explanation, originally put forward by the American Library Association in 1989, and which has considerable influence, particularly in library and information contexts, is:

> Information Literacy is defined as the ability to know when there is a need for information, to be able to identify, locate, evaluate, and effectively use that information for the issue or problem at hand.

Most views of information literacy have been based on this, giving typically a six-stage process:

1 Recognizing a need for information.
2 Identifying what information is needed.
3 Finding the information.
4 Evaluating the information.
5 Organizing the information.
6 Using the information effectively .

Of course, the final stage – using the information – usually leads to new information needs, so that the whole process forms a circle; or perhaps a spiral, since we are going upwards all the time, gaining new information. There are numerous variants on this 'knowledge spiral', which usually result in extra steps being added. Sometimes, 'finding the information' is broken down into several discrete steps, e.g.

- identifying the best source
- searching and retrieving information
- accessing and viewing information.

Others add alternatives to 'using information', such as:

- communicating information
- sharing information
- storing or archiving information
- destroying or discarding information.

An example of a broader approach is the 'seven pillars' model, developed by SCONUL (Society of College, National and University Libraries) in the UK in

1999 (Lock, 2003), which distinguished seven aspects, themselves relying on basic library literacy and computer literacy capability:

- recognize information need
- distinguish ways of addressing gap
- construct strategies for locating
- locate and access
- compare and evaluate
- organize, apply and communicate
- synthesize and create.

This model is shown diagrammatically in Figure 13.1.

This goes beyond the skills-based computer literacy model, by including softer skills such as evaluation of information and recognition of information need, but is still a rather prescriptive and formal approach, based on the assumption of an explicit information need. It is a model widely used for planning training courses in information literacy, particularly in academic libraries, and also forms the basis for interactive tutorials.

The information-literate person

During the 1990s, an alternative viewpoint emerged, though it never challenged the popularity of the 'six stages' or 'seven pillars' style of model. Information literacy was seen less as a series of competences to be mastered, and more as a set of general knowledge and attitudes to be possessed by an information-literate person. A well known example is the set of seven key characteristics presented by Christine Bruce, a professor in Queensland, Australia, such that the information-literate person is one who (Bruce, 1994; 1997):

- engages in independent self-directed learning
- uses information processes
- uses a variety of information technologies and systems
- has internalized values that promote information use
- has a sound knowledge of the world of information
- approaches information critically
- has a personal information style.

Some of these are very different from the specific skills espoused in other models. Such a person should have developed an appreciation of the value of appropriate information so that they will automatically seek it out (Bruce's 'internalised values'), and will be aware of the ways in which they prefer to find and use information (Bruce's 'personal style'). This latter might be, for example,

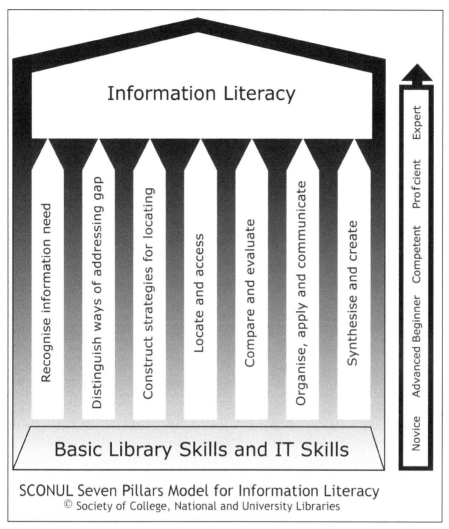

Figure 13.1 *SCONUL's 'seven pillars' model of information literacy (reproduced by permission of SCONUL)*

a preference for collecting and organizing interesting information for when it is needed rather than searching at the moment of need, or a preference for browsing widely rather than searching narrowly and specifically; or *vice versa* in either case.

In 2011, SCONUL revised their 'seven pillars' model 'to reflect more clearly the range of different terminologies and concepts which we now understand as information literacy' (SCONUL, 2011). The generic version of this model

displays the attributes of an information-literate person, in a manner rather
similar to Bruce's formulation, as shown in Figure 13.2.

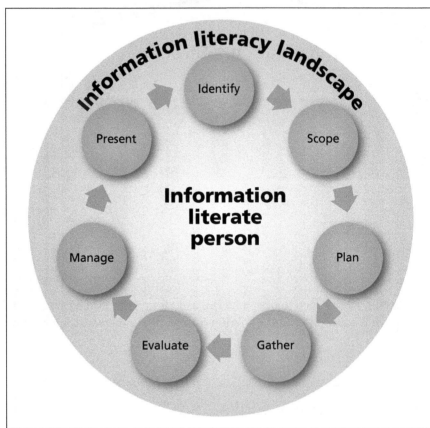

Figure 13.2 *SCONUL's revised model of information literacy (reproduced by
permission of SCONUL)*

Each 'pillar' is explained in rather general terms; for example, 'scope' involves
assessing current knowledge and identifying gaps. These can then be linked to
the necessary knowledge and skills. 'Scope' requires an understanding of what
types of information are available, characteristics of different types and formats
and what services are available to access them, and the skills of 'knowing what
you don't know', identifying appropriate types and formats of information and
available tools and resources, and keeping aware of new tools and resources.
These, still rather general, attributes can be explained in specific detail, with
exemplification of relevant databases, search engines, etc., for particular
contexts; e.g. undergraduate history students, or medical researchers.

An even broader approach is that of US educational specialists Jeremy Shapiro and Shelley Hughes (1996), who envisaged a concept of, and curriculum for, a kind of computer literacy comprising seven components:

- Tool literacy – competence in using hardware and software tools.
- Resource literacy – understanding forms of, and access to, information resources.
- Social-structural literacy – understanding the production and social significance of information.
- Research literacy – using IT tools for research and scholarship.
- Publishing literacy – ability to communicate and publish information.
- Emerging technologies literacy – understanding of new developments in IT.
- Critical literacy – ability to evaluate the benefits of new technologies (note this is not the same as 'critical thinking', which is often regarded as a component of information literacy).

Somewhat similar broad concepts, combining general knowledge and attitudes with specific skills have also been described under the headings of 'network literacy' (McClure, 1994), 'informacy' (Neelameghan, 1995), and 'mediacy' (Inoue, Naito and Koshizuka, 1997); for comparisons of these, see Bawden (2001; 2008), Bawden and Robinson (2002) and Pinto, Cordon and Diaz (2010). These general capabilities also underpin a capacity for personal information management, discussed in the last chapter.

The concept of digital literacy

Paul Gilster (1997), introducing the concept of digital literacy as the term is now generally used, did not provide lists of skills, competences or attitudes defining what it is to be digitally literate. He explained it as an ability to understand and to use information from a variety of digital sources, and regarded it simply as literacy in the digital age: an updated version of the traditional idea of literacy, the ability to read, write and otherwise deal with information using the technologies and formats of one's own time, and an essential life skill. This rather general expression of the idea, although it has irritated some commentators, is one of the strengths of Gilster's concept. It can be applied without the restrictive 'competence lists' which have afflicted some other descriptions of the literacies of information.

In his book, Gilster repeatedly emphasizes that digital literacy is about mastering ideas and concepts, not keystrokes, thus distinguishing his conception from the more limited 'technical skills' view of digital literacy. It is, he says (1997, 2),

. . . cognition of what you see on the computer screen when you use a networked medium. It places demands upon you that were always present, though less visible, in the analog media of newspapers and TV. At the same time, it conjures up a new set of challenges that require you to approach networked computers without preconceptions. Not only must you acquire the skill of finding things, you must also acquire the ability to use these things in your life.

Gilster gives, as perhaps the single clearest explanation in the book, the idea that digital literacy is 'the ability to understand and use information in multiple formats from a wide variety of sources when it is presented via computers' (1997, 1) – he does not forget that there are non-digital formats as well. He specifically notes that digital literacy involves an understanding of how to complement digital resources with such things as reference works in libraries, printed newspapers and magazines, radio and television, and printed works of literature. He even says how much he enjoys reading traditional printed books.

The book does not give a particularly structured or detailed account of digital literacy itself, or of the skills and attitudes which underlie it; it is an impressionistic and wide-ranging account, which some reviewers have suggested may make it difficult to set the ideas in a framework, or decide which are most important. Although there is nowhere in the book any specified list of skills, competences, etc. associated with the general idea of digital literacy, a list may be derived from the text (Bawden, 2001; 2008). In brief, this includes:

- 'knowledge assembly', building a 'reliable information hoard' from diverse sources
- retrieval skills, plus 'critical thinking' to making informed judgements about retrieved information, with wariness about the validity and completeness of internet sources
- reading and understanding non-sequential and dynamic material, of the kind found on the web: liable to change continually and browsable by hyperlinks, by contrast with the static linear text of formally published materials
- awareness of the value of traditional tools in conjunction with networked media
- awareness of 'people networks' as sources of advice and help
- using filters and agents to manage incoming information; an example is software for categorizing and prioritizing emails as they are received
- being comfortable with publishing and communicating information, as well as accessing it.

Variants on digital literacy
To add to the confusion, other terms have been used for what appears to be very

much Gilster's idea of digital literacy. The phrase 'e-literacy', still sometimes used as a synonym for skills-based computer literacy, is being widely adopted as synonymous with digital literacy; as is 'media literacy', expanded from its original meaning of a familiarity with the mass media.

Allan Martin, an IT education specialist, for example, presents e-literacy as a central concept, drawing on a range of other literacies – information, media, computer and ICT and even 'moral literacy' – and involving awareness, understanding and reflective evaluation as well as skills (Martin, 2003). This seems very similar to Gilster's idea, and indeed, Martin (2006) suggests that digital literacy and e-literacy are synonymous.

The digital literacy concept has also been central to the European Union's DigEuLit project; it is perhaps ironic that, although the term was originated by an American, many subsequent descriptions of, and developments in, digital literacy have been in Europe. DigEuLit, a collaborative project of the EU's e-learning programme between 11 universities and colleges in Western and Central Europe in 2005–6, took a 'Gilster-like' broad approach in defining digital literacy as:

> . . . the awareness, attitude and ability of individuals to appropriately use digital tools and facilities to identify, access, manage, integrate, evaluate, analyse and synthesize digital resources, construct new knowledge, create media expressions, and communicate with others, in the context of specific life situations, in order to enable constructive social action; and to reflect upon this process.
>
> Martin (2006, 156)

This is extended into a description of 13 specific processes – evaluation, synthesis, reflection, etc. – drawn from this definition, rather in the manner of the linear information literacy models described earlier. Martin (2006) argues that it is broader than information literacy, ICT literacy, etc., and subsumes a number of these individual literacies. He notes that it is also a quality that will vary according to each individual's life circumstances, and will change and develop over time, since it involves attitudes and personal qualities as well as knowledge and skills. Like Gilster, he sees it as a life skill, not particularly associated with formal education. For other recent thoughtful analyses of similar issues, see Buschman (2009) and Mackey and Jacobson (2011).

Finally, we should notice that what is commonly taken as the central theme of digital literacy – an ability to synthesize and integrate information from varied sources – is gaining increased attention in its own right. An interesting example is the concept of the 'synthesising mind', devised by US psychologist Howard Gardner (2006), which was identified as a 'breakthrough idea' by the *Harvard Business Review*.

A model for digital literacy

As we have seen, the ideas of information literacy and of digital literacy have been debated and amended ever since they were introduced. A complication has been the inconsistent way in which the terms have been used.

To try to get an overall understanding, we can set out the generally agreed components of digital literacy, as they emerge from the authors quoted above, in this way:

Underpinnings

* Literacy *per se*
* Computer and ICT literacy.

Background knowledge

* The world of information
* Nature of information resources.

Central competencies

* Reading and understanding digital and non-digital formats
* Creating and communicating digital information
* Evaluation of information
* Knowledge assembly
* Information literacy
* Media literacy.

Attitudes and perspectives

* Independent learning
* Moral and social literacy.

The 'underpinnings' give the basic skill sets without which little can be achieved. The 'background knowledge' complements them, by giving the necessary understanding of the way in which digital and non-digital information are created and communicated, and of the various forms of resources which result. The competencies are essentially those proposed by Gilster, phrased in the terms of later authors. 'Information literacy' implies competences in actively finding and using information in 'pull' mode, while 'media literacy' implies an ability to deal with information formats 'pushed' at the user. (The distinction is between 'pull' where the user actively seeks and acquires information from, for example, a search engine, a directory or an e-journal and 'push', where the user passively receives information via, for example, e-mail circulation, Twitter, or text messaging.) Finally, the attitudes and perspectives reflect the idea that the ultimate purpose of digital literacy is to help each person learn what is necessary for their particular situation. 'Moral and social literacy' reflects the need for an understanding of sensible and correct behaviour in the digital environment, and may include issues of privacy and security, reflecting some of the issues discussed in Chapter 11.

At the heart of this conception are ideas of understanding, meaning, and context (Bawden, 2001; Bawden, 2008; Pilerot, 2006), following Gilster's 'ideas, not keystrokes'. It seems reasonable to regard this kind of literacy, expressed appropriately according to the context, as an essential requirement for life in a digital age, as well as for minimizing specific problems such as information overload (Koltay, 2011). Supporting and promoting it must be one of the most important tasks for information scientists, and other information specialists.

Importance of digital literacy

As we have noted, digital literacy was first recognized as important within university, college and – to a lesser extent – school libraries, meeting the need to help students deal effectively with the greater range and diversity of information resources available. Only later did it grow into a concern for workplaces, though often not using the 'literacy' designation, with training and awareness programmes being created for staff (Bawden and Robinson, 2002; Robinson et al., 2005; Secker, Boden and Price, 2007; Coysh, 2011). Even later, and more slowly, it became recognized as required for everyone in society. Lloyd (2010; 2011) gives wide-ranging analyses of the idea across several sectors. Activity was largely focused initially in the English-speaking world; for perspectives on later developments worldwide, see Virkus (2003), Lau (2008) and Chevillotte (2010).

In an international context, strong claims have been made for the importance of societal information literacy, and for it to be regarded as one of the basic human rights. It has been the subject of two UNESCO conferences, each of which has generated a significant final document.

The Prague Declaration of 2003 (at the time of writing to be found at http://portal.unesco.org) stated that

> [Information literacy] is a prerequisite for participating effectively in the Information Society . . . [and] plays a leading role in reducing the inequities within and between countries and peoples, and in promoting tolerance and mutual understanding.

The Alexandria Proclamation of 2005 (at the time of writing to be found at http://archive.ifla.org/III/wsis/BeaconInfSoc.html) stated that:

> Information Literacy lies at the core of lifelong learning. It empowers people in all walks of life to seek, evaluate, use and create information effectively to achieve their personal, social, occupational and educational goals. It is a basic human right in a digital world and promotes social inclusion of all nations

and that

> Information literacy and lifelong learning are the beacons of the Information Society, illuminating the courses to development, prosperity and freedom.

The idea of information and digital literacy as a human right is analysed in detail by Sturges and Gastinger (2010). A caveat, criticizing a 'one size fits all' international imposition of a single idea of information literacy is given by Pilerot and Lindberg (2011).

Within Europe, digital literacy and media literacy are being promoted by the European Commission as essential for the development of, and promotion of, active citizenship within the European knowledge society (European Commission, 2011).

There seems no doubt that the promotion of digital literacy will be a major concern for information specialists for many years to come.

Promoting digital literacy

A wide variety of methods has been used for training, teaching and promoting digital literacy, or information literacy. To a large extent they follow on from 'user education' or 'bibliographic instruction' in library settings. They give a good example of the techniques which information specialists need to understand, and be able to use, when they are asked to train and instruct users in any aspect of information use. Sadly, although comparative studies have been done, there is no evidence that any training method is 'best'; it depends very much on the context – the subject, audience and situation.

One issue specific to digital literacy training is whether there can be such a thing as generic 'digital literacy' or 'information skills' training, applicable to everyone, or whether it has to be set in a particular context: 'digital literacy for medical students', 'information skills for tourist guides', etc. The general opinion seems to be that there is a core of general principles, relevant to any context, which can be used as the basis for all digital literacy training, but that they must be customized to a particular context. This might involve using appropriate examples of information needs and information resources, treating things at different levels of sophistication, and emphasizing particular aspects or components of digital literacy – the evaluation of information, for example, might be very important in one context, and irrelevant in another. Subject specific information literacy promotion has a good deal in common with aspects of domain analysis, as discussed in Chapter 5.

A variety of teaching and training methods can be used in digital literacy training, including: lectures and presentations; demonstrations; case studies and 'story telling'; practical exercises and hands-on practice; and one-to-one advice and consultancy. These are usually delivered face to face, but may also be provided through e-media, such as podcasts, video and audio streaming, chat and interactive web applications. They may be backed up by resources (paper or virtual) such as: guides to sources, searching and evaluation; FAQ (frequently asked questions) files and 'best practice' notes; textbooks and articles; discussion lists and blogs; and interactive tutorials.

Given that there is no single 'best' method of training, the usual advice is to try to provide a variety of approaches, to suit different learning styles. Overviews and examples are given in Bawden and Robinson (2002), Robinson et al. (2005), Martin and Madigan (2006), and Secker, Boden, and Price (2007).

A variety of interactive web-based tutorials for various aspects of digital literacy is available. Most are aimed at promoting 'generic' digital literacy to students. A majority are also based on the 'linear' competence models of information literacy discussed above, although all vary slightly, and some address more general issues of understanding.

For example, the UK Open University's *Safari* tutorial (located at the time of writing at http://www.open.ac.uk/safari) has seven sections:

1 Understanding information
2 Unpacking information
3 Planning a search
4 Searching for information
5 Evaluating information
6 Organizing information
7 Where do I go from here?

The US University of Wyoming's *Tutorial for Information Power* (at the time of writing at http://tip.uwyo.edu) has five sections:

1 Investigating
2 Searching
3 Locating
4 Evaluating
5 Utilizing.

Although the detailed structure and degree of generality varies, this illustrates how tutorials of this kind mainly follow the ALA/SCONUL kind of model of information literacy. This makes the tutorials easier to create, but may mean that they are of value only to specific groups or for particular purposes; most are aimed at college and university students. Notess (2006) reviews their advantages and disadvantages.

Summary

We have seen how the idea of being literate, or fluent, with information has grown from being associated with specific skills in the use of computers, libraries, etc. to a much broader and all-encompassing concern for attitudes and values, as well as skills and understanding, in making good use of information. Beginning as largely a concern for formal education, information and digital literacy is now recognized as being of concern to all aspects of society. Promoting digital literacy has been primarily the job of the information specialists, although other disciplines, such as educators and publishers, also play a major part. It is likely that concerns about this kind of literacy will increase, rather than decrease in the future: few people now take the optimistic view that our young people are so at home with computers that this is no longer an issue. While the specific issues to be addressed, and the ways in which digital literacy is encouraged and promoted, will no doubt change in future years, this topic is likely to remain a central one for information science.

- There is inconsistency in the way in which several 'literacies of information' have been described over more than 20 years.
- Digital literacy is a set of attitudes, understanding and skills which allow information and knowledge to be communicated effectively, using a variety of media and formats.
- Digital literacy is important in education, in the workplace and in society generally.
- The promotion of digital literacy in all environments is an important task for information specialists.

Key readings

Paul Gilster, *Digital literacy*, New York, NY: Wiley, 1997.
  [Introduces the digital literacy concept.]
David Bawden, Origins and concepts of digital literacy, in Lankshear and Knobel (eds), *Digital literacies: concepts, policies and practices*, New York NY: Peter Lang, 2008, 15–32.
  [Analysis of the development of the idea.]

References

Bawden, D. (2001) Information and digital literacies: a review of concepts, *Journal of Documentation*, 57(2), 218–59.

Bawden, D. (2008) Origins and concepts of digital literacy, in Lankshear, C. and Knobel, M. (eds), *Digital literacies: concepts, policies and practices*, New York NY: Peter Lang, 15–32.

Bawden, D. and Robinson, L. (2002) Promoting literacy in a digital age: approaches to training for information literacy, *Learned Publishing*, 15(4), 297–301 .

Bruce, C. (1994) Portrait of an information literate person, *HERDSA News*, 16(3), 9–11.

Bruce, C. (1997) *The seven faces of information literacy*, Adelaide: Auslib Press.

Buschman, J. (2009) Information literacy, 'new' literacies and literacy, *Library Quarterly*, 79(1), 95–118.

Chevillotte, S. (2010) Information literacy, in *Encyclopedia of Library and Information Science* (3rd edn), Abingdon: Taylor & Francis, 1:1, 2421–28.

Coysh, L. (2011) Further developing the library curriculum: skills for life delivery, *Health Information and Libraries Journal*, 28(1), 82–6.

Gardner, H. (2006) *Five minds for the future*, Boston MA: Harvard Business School Press.

Gilster, P. (1997) *Digital literacy*, New York, NY: Wiley.

Gilster, P. (2011) *Centauri Dreams: news forum of the Tau Zero Foundation*, available at http://www.centauri-dreams.org.

European Commission (2011) Media Literacy, [online] http://ec.europa.eu/culture/media/literacy.

Inoue, H., Naito, E. and Koshizuka, M. (1997) Mediacy: what is it?, *International Information and Library Review*, 29(3/4), 403–13.

Koltay, T. (2011) Information overload, information architecture and digital literacy, *Bulletin of the American Society for Information Science and Technology*, 38(1), 33–5.

Lankshear, C. and Knobel, M. (2008) *Digital literacies: concepts, policies and practices*, New York NY: Peter Lang.

Lau, J. (ed.) (2008) *Information literacy: international perspectives*, IFLA Publications No. 131, Munich: K. G. Saur.

Lloyd, A. (2010) *Information literacy landscapes: information literacy in education, workplace and everyday contexts*, Oxford: Chandos.

Lloyd, A. (2011) Trapped between a rock and a hard place: what counts as information literacy in the workplace and how is it conceptualized?, *Library Trends*, 60(2), 277–96.

Lock, S. (2003) Information skills in higher education: a SCONUL position paper, [online] http://www.sconul.ac.uk/groups/information_literacy/papers/seven_pillars.html.

Mackey, T. P. and Jacobson, T. E. (2011) Reframing information literacy as a metaliteracy, *College and Research Libraries*, 72(1), 62–78.

Martin, A. (2003) Towards e-literacy, in Martin, A. and Rader, H. (eds), *Information and IT literacy: enabling learning in the 21st century*, London: Facet Publishing, 3–23.

Martin, A. (2006) A European framework for digital literacy, *Nordic Journal of Digital Literacy*, 2006(2), 151–160 , available at http://www.idunn.no/ts/dk/2006/02/a_european_framework_for_digital_literacy?languageId=2.

Martin, A. and Madigan, D. (eds) (2006) Digital literacies for learning, London: Facet Publishing.

McClure, C. R. (1994) Network literacy: a role for libraries, *Information Technology and Libraries*, 13(2), 115–25.

Neelameghan, A. (1995) Literacy, numeracy . . . informacy, *Information Studies*, 1(4), 239–49.

Notess, G. R. (2006) *Teaching web search skills*, Medford NJ: Information Today.

Pilerot, O. (2006) Information literacy – an overview, in Martin, A. and Madigan, D. (eds), *Digital literacies for learning*, London: Facet Publishing, 80–8.

Pilerot, O. and Lindberg, J. (2011) The concept of information literacy in policy making texts: an imperialistic project?, *Library Trends*, 60(2), 338–60.

Pinto, M., Cordon, J. A. and Diaz, R. G. (2010) Thirty years of information literacy (1977–2007): A terminological, conceptual and statistical analysis, *Journal of Librarianship and Information Science*, 42(1), 3–19.

Robinson, L., Hilger-Ellis, J., Osborne, L., Rowlands, J., Smith, J. M., Weist, A., Whetherly, J. and Phillips, R. (2005) Healthcare librarians and learner support: competences and methods, *Health Information and Libraries Journal*, 22 (supplement 2), 42–50.

Secker, J., Boden, D. and Price, G. (eds) (2007) *The information literacy cookbook: ingredients, recipes and tips for success*, Oxford: Chandos.

SCONUL (2011) The seven pillars of information literacy, [online] available at http://www.sconul.ac.uk/groups/information_literacy/seven_pillars.html.

Shapiro, J. J. and Hughes, S. K. (1996) Information technology as a liberal art, *Educom Review*, 31(2), March/April 1996, [online], available at http://net.educause.edu/apps/er/review/reviewarticles/31231.html.

Sturges, P. and Gastinger, A. (2010) Information literacy as a human right, *Libri*, 60(3), 195–202.

Virkus, S. (2003) Information literacy in Europe: a literature review, *Information Research*, 8(4), paper 159, available from: http://informationr.net/ir/8-4/paper159.html.

CHAPTER 14

Information science research: what and how?

Research is to see what everybody else has seen, and to think what nobody else has thought.

Albert Szent-Györgi, Hungarian biochemist

There is nothing like looking, if you want to find something. You certainly usually find something, if you look, but it is not always quite the something you were after.

J. R. R. Tolkien (*The Hobbit*)

This is not a field that produces Wunderkinder, bright young things who make their mark at a precocious age. In fact, some of our sample members have kept their best wine until last. Creativity in academic information science is clearly not the preserve of callow youth . . .

Blaise Cronin and Lokman Meho (2007, 1954)

Avoiding useless results requires openness and transparency about how the data were gathered and a reasonable judgement that does not exaggerate what these data could possibly mean.

Elke Greifeneder and Michael Seadle (2010, 7)

Introduction
In this chapter we will consider the nature and purpose of information research, and the methods used to carry it out. We will give an overview with examples, without trying to go into the detail of any particular aspects.

There are a number of good textbooks covering information research methods. These all cover many of the topics in this chapter in much more detail than we give here. We will mention them now, and refer to them again only when they offer some particularly useful material. They should, however, be considered as valuable references for all of this chapter, offering a fuller treatment to material which we treat briefly here.

Two good texts giving a detailed coverage of the area are Alison Pickard's *Research methods in information* (2007), and Briony Oates' *Researching information systems and computing* (2006). Lawal (2009) gives a guide aimed specifically at library and information practitioners and students considering carrying out research, while Moore (2006) focuses on planning and managing information research. Texts on research methods generally may also be valuable, for example Denscombe's (2010) guide to social research methods. So also may be some texts on particular aspects of the information sciences; Donald Case's books (2007; 2012) on information and use, for example, give a very good overview of the research processes and methods used in this area.

Research is most simply regarded as the creation of new knowledge, though there are many different understandings as to what constitutes 'research'. For our purposes, it is helpful to restrict its meaning to the creation of knowledge which is new to everyone, not just to the researcher, in a form which can be communicated through objective information, and which builds on existing knowledge.

For disciplines with associated professional activities, such as the information sciences, research has two purposes: academic, to improve the discipline's knowledge base; and professional, to improve practice. This is the traditional difference between 'pure' and 'applied' research, but the divide is, in practice, rarely entirely clear.

Information research may be carried out by university professors and researchers, doctoral students, students doing dissertations as part of a taught course, research institutes and consultancies, government agencies, system and service designers and suppliers, and practitioners. An interaction between academics and practitioners is beneficial for both, as we will discuss later. As the opening quote from Cronin and Meho indicates, it can be carried out at any stage of a career, and is certainly not only for young people.

Research has been a part of the information sciences since they emerged as distinguishable disciplines and professions. The chapters on information behaviour, informetrics, information organization and information technology give examples of early research in these topics, and the ways in which the focus and methods of information research have developed.

Styles of information research

All styles of research are based in a philosophical viewpoint or paradigm, of the kind discussed in Chapter 3, though this is not always explicitly recognized by researchers. A 'broad brush' distinction can be made between studies conducted from a positivist viewpoint, where it is assumed that an objective reality exists, which the researcher may identify and study, and those conducted from a constructivist viewpoint which assumes that reality is subjective, and must be constructed or interpreted by the researcher. For information research, the former assumes, for example, that concepts such as the meaning or relevance of a piece of information to a user, or the proper role of an information service, are objective facts which may be determined correctly, while the latter assumes that they are subjective, and created and modified by those involved. While information researchers need not be philosophers, it is important to recognize what assumptions are implicit in the methods used, and what assumptions or viewpoints they themselves hold which may affect their approach; see, for example, Burke (2007) for examples in the context of information management research.

A common distinction is between *quantitative* and *qualitative* research. These describe a difference in general style and ethos: in essence whether the focus is on measuring, counting and testing formally stated hypotheses or on an interpretation of the meaning of events, issues and opinions, in an attempt to gain understanding. In practice there is overlap. Few studies are solely one or the other. Each has its own ways of analysing the data generated in the research process. This may be statistical in nature for quantitative studies, where the research questions may be phrased as hypotheses to be proved or disproved at a certain level of statistical significance. Many information research studies, however, can find answers to their research questions by simpler quantitative methods, using mainly descriptive statistics. It is, of course, essential to plan the research starting with the questions, and working through the kind of results needed to answer them, and then to the data collection and analysis methods which will give those results. Collecting data first, and then wondering how to analyse it, is a recipe for failure, or at best wasted time.

It is sometimes believed that qualitative studies are somehow 'easier' than quantitative, but this is not so. Gorman and Clayton (2005) give a good overview of qualitative methods for information research, emphasizing that they are in no way less rigorous than quantitative methods.

General aspects of research methods

There is a very wide range of research methods and techniques used in our discipline. We consider them later in this chapter in three rough categories – surveys; experimenting, evaluating and observing; and desk research. This reflects the general crude categorization that, to find out about something we can: ask someone who has some insight; observe what happens; or examine relevant documents. In practice, in any real research or evaluation, there is some overlap, and 'mixed method' studies are increasingly common. The term 'triangulation' is used to describe studies which mainly rely on one method, but then use a second method to check the validity of the results; for example, questionnaire surveys which include some interviews. For more discussion and examples of triangulation and mixed methods, see Huntington and Gunter (2006) and Fidel (2008).

Evaluation is such an important part of research in many subjects, including the information sciences, that it is often treated separately. Evaluation may be carried out on a micro level, evaluating, for example, the content of a small set of literature, or a macro level, evaluating systems and services. Powell (2006) gives an overview of evaluation research in information topics. Research embedded in a practice context, where the aim of the research is the improvement of practice rather than an objective study of the situation, may be termed *action research.*

All research of whatever kind will involve an element of *desk research*, in the form of a literature review for context setting, and to establish if similar studies have already been done. For desk research proper, this will form an introduction; for example, a literature review of subject X will begin with a description and analysis of any previous reviews of that subject. 'Literature' here is defined very broadly, as it may include information in sources other than academic and professional literature. We will discuss these points, under the headings of desk research and of finding and evaluating earlier research.

All research which has any element of data collection will need to consider the question of sampling: how to know that an adequate number and range of cases have been included for the results to be valid, and how to know how generalizable to other situations the results will be. The sampling issue can be avoided only when all relevant cases are considered; for example, if one is studying some aspect of national libraries in the British Isles, it is feasible to study all of them. The extreme example of this is the case study, where a single example is studied in great detail. We will discuss sampling in more detail later.

Advances in information and communication technologies, allowing greatly increased options for communication between researchers, and for collection, integration and analysis of large amounts of data, are leading to the new style of research, termed 'e-research' or 'e-science', as discussed in Chapter 10. This may affect information research directly, and information specialists may have a role in promoting and facilitating it.

All research, even small-scale and relatively informal studies, require careful planning; in particular, to ensure that all the resources needed, including access to people and systems to be studied, are in place, and that everything happens in the right order. All research also requires attention to: the analysis of the data collected, which must be planned before the collection stage; ethical issues; and presentation of results.

Research and the practitioner

It has always been considered desirable that information practitioners should carry out research and use research results, and academics in the information sciences should be aware of practice issues in planning and carrying out research. There has in the past, as with many disciplines, been a divide between academics and researchers, and practitioners. The latter have been held to be uninterested in research results, still less in carrying out research themselves; the counter-prejudice has been that information researchers undertake 'useless' research, ignoring the needs of practice. Thirty years ago, Alan Blick, a well known information manager in the British pharmaceutical industry, was presenting this as a kind of contest or conflict between practitioners and researchers in information science (Blick, 1983). The debate rumbles on; see, for example, Haddow and Klobas (2004), Greifeneder and Seadle (2010), Powell, Baker and Mika (2002) and Hall (2010).

There is now a greater pressure for practitioners to be more involved in research, and in using its results, and for academics and other researchers to pay greater attention to dissemination of results in a way useful for practice: funders of research are increasingly requiring attention to be given to practical impact. Communication between the two groups is of obvious importance: some publishers are asking for statements of implications for practice to be made in the abstracts of information research articles. However, a study of the extent to which reports of research into information-seeking behaviour addressed the implications for practice found that while a majority did so, they did not do it well; most recommendations for practice were stated only vaguely (McKechnie et al., 2008). Wilson (2008) also comments on an increasing disconnection between the interests of researchers and practitioners in studies of users and user behaviour. There is still a long way to go, in this respect.

From the other side, it is of course necessary that practitioners are reminded of the value of using research in a routine way. A good example of the kind of promotion that would help here is IFLA's guidance on using research to promote literacy and reading (Farmer and Stricevic, 2011). Application of the ideas of *knowledge translation* may help in this respect (Garnett, 2011).

Much practitioner research is an integral part of reflective practice, and usually aimed at service evaluation and improvement. This has led some commentators to argue for library and information service provision to be fully 'evidence-based', i.e. with practice based explicitly on research results; we are very far from that situation. The idea of 'evidence-based practice' itself has been criticized as too narrow and mechanical an approach, by those who argue for practitioners to have a fuller understanding of research and theory; see Booth and Brice (2004) and Hjørland (2011) for viewpoints.

Research methods for information science

As we have noted, there are many different methods which can be used for information research, ranging from the experimental to the conceptual (Cronin and Meho, 2007). These may be categorized in various ways; each of the textbooks has its own categorization. Hider and Pymm (2008) describe various detailed classifications of information research methods, and propose nine strategies: historical research; ethnography; surveys; evaluation; case study; action research; experiment; other strategy; mixed strategies. They also define 15 forms of data collection, which to an extent overlap with methods: questionnaire or interview; focus groups; journal entries; observation; inspection; content analysis; protocol analysis; bibliometric analysis; transaction log analysis; task analysis; historical source analysis; dataset construction; use of data collected earlier; other technique; more than one technique. They conclude, from an analysis of the literature and comparison with similar studies in the past, that all of this wide range of methods is important for information research, but that surveys and experiments are the predominant methods.

We will use the simpler three-way classification, justified above, to consider the main forms of information research, and the methods used for each: surveys; experimenting, evaluating and observing; and desk research. We will do so only in outline, as full details of each are given in relevant chapters of the textbooks referred to earlier. We will give some examples of each from the literature; we emphasize that these are not intended as the 'best' examples, simply as typical of what is in the literature.

Research methods – surveys

This is, and has always been, the most common method for carrying out research in library and information science. It is the, crudely expressed, 'asking someone' style of research, and usually involves asking for the opinions and experiences of information users (actual and potential) and information providers. It is a method very much in the social science research tradition.

This approach is very commonly used in mixed-methods research, typically combining a survey with some form of observation. A small number of interviews will often be incorporated into research mainly relying on desk research or on some form of observation. Conversely, survey research will usually incorporate some element of desk research, if only for the initial literature survey.

Most library and information surveys are small-scale, rarely involving more than 100 participants, and are usually aimed at a closely defined group of people. They do not therefore usually adopt the rigorous methods of sampling and analysis used for purposes such as public opinion polling or large-scale market research. The main methods used for library and information surveys are questionnaires and interviews.

Questionnaires are usually regarded as being in the positivist/objective style of research, since they assume that the researcher and those surveyed share a common perspective of the situation. A series of short, structured questions, with prescribed answers (yes/no, Lickert scale, multiple-choice) is generally used, with limited opportunity for expressing extra information, giving reasons, or raising other topics. This approach is appropriate for getting large numbers of responses quickly and simply, and for giving results which can be analysed quantitatively. However, the value of the results relies on the researcher having understood all the relevant factors, and expressed them in a way which the participants can understand.

Questionnaires are increasingly likely to be administered electronically, using software such as SurveyMonkey, rather than in printed form. This is convenient, and gives greater 'reach', but may mean that the population sampled, the response rate, and any bias in response, is unknown. If such a survey is placed on a website, for example, all that can be known is those who replied to it; the number who saw it, and did not respond, cannot usually be established, nor can whether there is anything different about those who responded and those who did not.

Interviews are regarded as appropriate for getting a greater, and richer, amount of information from a smaller number of participants. There are several forms of interview. *Structured interviews* resemble questionnaires, in that a pre-defined set of questions is asked, often requiring a choice of answer from a list. At the opposite extreme *unstructured interviews* have no predefined structure, and resemble a free-flowing conversation; they are most appropriately used in an exploratory way, in situations where the interviewer does not have a good understanding of the issues or context. An intermediate form, and often regarded as most appropriate for most library and information research is the *semi-structured interview*, where a number of predefined questions are always asked, but subsequent questioning will depend on the responses given. Interviews are sometimes referred to as *research conversations*, if the intention is to reach a consensus with the interviewee, or even to affect their views, rather than simply to gain information from them.

There are a number of issues around the conduct of interviews, which must be decided for each study, and often will be determined by practicality rather than theoretical considerations. They include:

- Whether it is carried out face to face, or by telephone, internet chat, e-mail, or other means. In general, all other things being equal, those methods which allow tone of voice, facial expression, etc., to be noted will give richer information than others.
- The location of face-to-face interviews; interviewees are usually more relaxed and forthcoming in their own space.
- Whether interviews are recorded, videoed, or taken down verbatim, or whether the interviewer takes notes; unless it is essential to have the exact words used, or to have a permanent record of the interview to ensure research quality or to allow checking by someone else, simple note-taking is often best, since it avoids worrying about technical issues, and allows

immediate feedback to be given to the interviewee on what the interviewer understands them to have said.

Interviews are usually carried out one-to-one, but may involve an interviewer with a group of interviewees. This may be useful on grounds of practicality and time saving, and also in allowing interviewees to discuss issues, reach consensus and spark ideas off each other; but equally they run the risk of being dominated by a small number of senior, or noisy, participants, so that other views are not heard. The terms *group interview* and *focus group* are used for this method; the latter more commonly when the motive is obtaining a 'group viewpoint' rather than just interviewing several people at once for convenience.

A tool specifically designed for reaching consensus within a group is a *Delphi study*. This brings a virtual group of participants together, typically by e-mail. They are asked individually to state their views on some topic. The researcher writes a summary of their responses, and sends it out to them for further comment; this process is repeated as many times as necessary. Usually two or three 'rounds' are enough to reach consensus, or to establish that there are two or more incompatible viewpoints.

An approach which may be used with any of the above methods is the *critical incident* technique. This asks participants to specify one particular occurrence of what is under investigation; for example, one occasion when use of a particular information source made a difference to their work. This approach avoids very general and bland responses, and is particularly useful in assessing impact of information systems and services.

When a survey is begun, the researchers may not be sure that the survey instrument (interview schedule, questionnaire, etc.) is quite right. A *pilot study* may therefore be carried out, with a small number of participants, to check the validity of the survey, and allow for changes to be made for the main survey. In a large-scale study, particularly if it is analysed quantitatively, the results of the pilot study would not be included, though in smaller surveys they are sometimes included.

The following list gives a selection of information research articles based on various forms of survey method.

Examples of surveys in information research
Please note that these are not recommended as 'best practice', simply as recent relevant examples.

Questionnaires
Attfield, S. J., Adams, A. and Blandford, A. (2006) Patient information needs: pre- and post-consultation, *Health Informatics Journal*, 12(2), 165–77.

Bennett, R. (2007) Sources and use of marketing information by marketing managers, *Journal of Documentation*, 63(5), 702–26.

Pálsdóttir, Á. (2010) The connection between purposive information seeking and information encountering: a study of Icelanders' health and lifestyle information seeking, *Journal of Documentation*, 66(2), 224–44.

Interviews

Savolainen, R. (2010) Source preference criteria in the context of everyday projects: relevance judgements made by prospective home buyers, *Journal of Documentation*, 66(1), 70–92.

Marcella, R. et. al. (2007) The information needs and information-seeking behaviour of the users of the European Parliamentary Documentation Centre: a customer knowledge survey, *Journal of Documentation*, 63(6), 920–34.

Mansourian, Y. and Ford, N. (2007) Web searchers' attributions of success and failure: an empirical study, *Journal of Documentation*, 63(5), 659–79.

Focus groups

White, M. D., Matteson, M. and Abels, E. G. (2008) Beyond dictionaries: understanding information behaviour of professional translators, *Journal of Documentation*, 64(4), 576–601.

Zuccala, A. (2010) Open access and civic scientific information literacy, *Information Research*, 15(1), paper 426, available from http://InformationR.net/ir/15-1/paper426.html.

Burhanna, K. J. et al. (2009) No natives here: a focus group study of student perceptions of Web 2.0 and the academic library, *Journal of Academic Librarianship*, 35(6), 523–32.

Delphi studies

Zhang, Y. and Salaba, A. (2009), What is next for Functional Requirements for Bibliographic Records? A Delphi study, *Library Quarterly*, 79(2), 233–55.

Saunders, L. (2009) The future of information literacy in academic libraries: a Delphi study, *Portal: Libraries and the Academy*, 9(1), 99–114.

Zins, C. (2007) Conceptions of information science, *Journal of the American Society for Information Science and Technology*, 58(3), 335–50.

Critical incidents

Tenopir, C. et al. (2009) Electronic journals and changes in scholarly article seeking and reading patterns, *Aslib Proceedings*, 61(1), 5–32.

Kraaijenbrink, J. (2007) Engineers and the web: an analysis of real life gaps in information usage, *Information Processing and Management*, 43(5), 1368–82.

Weightman, A., Urquhart, C., Spink, S. and Thomas, R. (2009) The value and impact of information provided through library services for patient care: developing guidance for best practice, *Health Information and Libraries Journal*, 26(1), 63–71.

Mixed methods

Nicholas, D., Rowlands, I. and Jamali, H. R. (2010) e-textbook use, information seeking behaviour and its impact: case study – business and management, *Aslib Proceedings*, 36(2), 263–80 [questionnaires, focus groups, web log analysis, analysis of sales and library circulation data].

Craven, J., Johnson, F. and Butters, G. (2010) The usability and functionality of an online catalogue, *Aslib Proceedings*, 62(1), 70–84 [interviews, focus group, observation with 'think aloud'].

Wilson, K. and Corrall, S. (2008) Developing public library managers as leaders: evaluation of a national leadership development programme, *Library Management*, 29(6–7), 473–88
[Interviews, focus groups, questionnaires, observation].

Research methods – experimenting, evaluating and observing

This category of research covers a variety of methods. At one end of the spectrum are those described as *experimental*, based in a positivist, scientific world-view. At the other are methods of *observation* and interpretation, based in the traditions of ethnography and similar disciplines. They often have a common set of purposes, however, in being used to understand information behaviour, to evaluate the use and performance of information systems and services, and to give a basis for the improvement of such systems and services, and the design of new ones.

The experimental style of research in library and information science derives from the methods of the experimental sciences. The topic to be studied is isolated, so far as possible, from the complexities of the 'real world', so that all the variable factors in the situation can be held constant, apart from the ones being studied. Its opposite is *operation evaluation*, analysing the totality of an information service, and including all the 'messiness' of the real-world context. Experiment is an approach used particularly often in research into information retrieval and human-computer interaction, typically comparing algorithms and interfaces. Where users are involved, data on their success at using the system may be augmented by data gathered from special equipment, such as eye-tracking devices to see where they look on the screen, and by user opinions given by conventional interview, or by 'talk/think aloud' or 'talk/think after' features of the experiment.

At the other extreme, observation is usually regarded as a technique for understanding a real-world situation, without affecting or controlling it at all (Baker, 2006); hence a phrase commonly used in the past, *unobtrusive observation*. The use of the so-called *mystery shopper* or *mystery visitor* is a modern variant.

The current trend is for observation, often used in conjunction with other data gathering methods, to be used in a way which draws from subjects and approaches such as anthropology, ethnography, and phenomenology or phenomenography, which emphasize a detailed interpretation of the situation from the viewpoint of those observed, and understanding as much of the context of their situation as possible. For overviews, in addition to chapters in the research methods textbooks, see Goodman (2011) and Bruce (1999).

The more unstructured ways of gathering qualitative data, typically based around observation, are sometimes referred to as *grounded theory*; often incorrectly, since this involves precisely specified and rigorous forms of analysis; see relevant chapters in the research method textbooks, and the article by Tan (2010) for details. Grounded theory can be a valid and valuable method, as shown by the information research examples given below; however, it should only be used with an understanding of its nature.

A new form of observation has become possible with the move to a largely digital information environment; the ability to analyse the logs of websites and search engines, to establish exactly what a very large number of users are doing, in a way not possible with printed information. However, such log analysis cannot give any explanation for why users are doing what they do, nor how satisfied they are; it is therefore often combined with other methods, typically interviews.

Research studies of the kinds noted above can be used for the very practical purpose of the *evaluation* of the performance of information systems and services. Here, research overlaps very much with practice, since the monitoring of performance should be a routine activity for information providers, using tools such as standard sets of performance indicators, user-satisfaction surveys and cost-benefit analyses. 'Research', in the context of the evaluation of operational systems, tends to mean particular exercises or projects, such as an *information audit*, whose purpose is to enumerate and evaluate all the available information resources (Buchanan and Gibb, 2008), or an *impact study*, aiming to show the 'real benefit' to the users. Impact studies were discussed in Chapter 12 in the context of attempts to measure the value of information.

Similarly, they may lead to the equally practical issues of the design and implementation of new systems and services, or new features within existing systems. Again, there is an overlap with practice, as these are also normal tasks for the practitioner; they are typically regarded as 'research' when there is some novelty in the new system or feature, or when an established feature is introduced into a new context. Research into information needs and behaviour is also needed in order to develop or extend systems to go beyond incremental improvement of what is already available.

The next list gives a selection of information research articles based on various forms of experiment, evaluation and observation methods.

Examples of experiment, evaluation and observation in information research
Please note that these are not recommended as 'best practice', simply as recent relevant examples.

Experiment
Vilar, P. and Žumer, M. (2011) Information searching behaviour of young Slovenian researchers, *Program*, 45(3), 279–93.

Makri, S., Blandford, A. and Cox, A. L. (2010) This is what I'm doing and why: methodological reflections on a naturalistic think-aloud study of interactive information behaviour, *Information Processing and Management*, 47(3), 336–48.

Boryung, J. (2007) Does domain knowledge matter: mapping users' expertise to their information interactions, *Journal of the American Society for Information Science and Technology*, 58(13), 2007–20.

Observation
Reddy, M. C. and Spence, P. R. (2008) Collaborative information seeking: a field study of a multidisciplinary patient care team, *Information Processing and Management*, 44(1), 242–55.

Ulvik, S. (2010) 'Why should the library collect immigrants' memories?': a study of a multicultural memory group at a public library in Oslo, *New Library World*, 111(3–4), 154–60.

Allard, S., Levine, K. J. and Tenopir, C. (2009) Design engineers and technical professionals at work: observing information usage in the workplace, *Journal of the American Society for Information Science and Technology*, 60(3), 443–54.

Log analyses
Hider, P. M. (2007) Constructing an index of search goal redefinition through transaction log analysis, *Journal of Documentation*, 63(2), 175–87.

Borrego, A. and Urbano, C. (2007) Analysis of the behaviour of the users of a package of electronic journals in the field of chemistry, *Journal of*

Documentation, 63(2), 243–58.

Nicholas, D. et. al. (2009) Student digital information-seeking behaviour in context, *Journal of Documentation*, 65(1), 106–32.

Grounded theory

Camargo, M. R. (2008) A grounded theory study of the relationship between e-mail and burnout, *Information Research*, 13(4), paper 383, available from http://InformationR.net/ir/13-4/paper383.html.

Mutshewa, A. (2010) The use of information by environmental planners: a qualitative study using grounded theory, *Information Processing and Management*, 46(2), 212–32.

Makri, S. and Warwick, C. (2010) Information for inspiration: understanding architects' information seeking and use behaviors to inform design, *Journal of the American Society for Information Science and Technology*, 61(9), 1745–70.

Ethnographic and phenomenographic approaches

Prigoda, E. and McKenzie, P. J. (2007) Purls of wisdom: a collectivist study of human information behaviour in a public library knitting group, *Journal of Documentation*, 63(1), 90–114.

Boon, S., Johnson, B. and Webber, S. (2007) A phenomenographic study of English faculty's conceptions of information literacy, *Journal of Documentation*, 63(2), 204–28.

Gross, M. and Latham, D. (2011) Experiences with and perceptions of information: a phenomenographic study of first-year college students, *Library Quarterly*, 81(2), 161–86.

Service evaluation

Robinson L. and Bawden D. (2007) Evaluation of outreach services for primary care and mental health: assessing the impact, *Health Information and Libraries Journal*, 24(s1), 57–66.

Botha, E. et al. (2009) Evaluating the impact of a special library and information service, *Journal of Librarianship and Information Science*, 41(2), 108–23.

Bawden, D., Calvert, A., Robinson, L., Urquhart, C., Bray, C. and Amosford, J. (2010) Understanding our value: assessing the nature of the impact of library services, *Library and Information Research*, 33(105), 62–89, available from http://www.lirg.org.uk/lir/ojs/index.php/lir.

System and service design

Komlodi, A., Marchionini, G. and Soergel, D. (2007) Search history support for finding and using information: user interface design recommendations from a user study, *Information Processing and Management*, 43(1), 10–29.

Ahmed, S. M. Z., McKnight, C. and Oppenheim, C. (2006) A user-centred design and evaluation of IR interfaces, *Journal of Librarianship and Information Science*, 38(3), 157–72.

Westbrook, L. (2009) Unanswerable questions at the IPL: user expectations of e-mail reference, *Journal of Documentation*, 65(3), 367–95.

Research methods – desk research

The term 'desk research' covers the varied forms of research carried out by some kind of analysis of documents. This is a part of all research, in the form of a literature search to establish the context and to identify previous relevant work. It may provide the methods for studies in their own right, which are just as much valid research as any other, in as much as they have the potential to provide new knowledge and insights. Such studies will themselves be preceded by a literature review. See the section on 'Finding and evaluating research' below for more on the process.

Desk research is sometimes referred to as 'literature research' or, increasingly, 'internet research', although both these terms are too narrow to cover all forms of desk research. Several styles can be distinguished, although the distinctions are not sharp, and the terms are often loosely used; some studies cross the boundaries between styles.

Literature reviews are the most common form of desk research, and may form a study in their own right as well being a precursor to other research methods. They may be designated as *comprehensive* or *selective*, according to whether an attempt is made to cover all relevant material or only a subset which the reviewer finds significant. A *systematic review*, more common in subjects such as healthcare than library and information science, carefully defines and justifies the sources, search strategies and relevance criteria to be used, before material is identified. A review may be objective, in simply reporting what is in the literature, or subjective, in that the reviewer gives a judgement on the quality of the material and its content; the latter may be called a *critical* review. Reviews focused on an emergent or developing technology, and its prospects, may be termed *technology assessments*.

Meta-analysis and *meta-synthesis* are specific forms of literature review, in which a number of sources, typically individual research reports, are combined together, hopefully giving a more reliable and informative result than from any of the sources considered alone (Fink, 2010; Urquhart, 2010; Saxton, 2006). Meta-analysis deals with quantitative data by statistical analysis. It is difficult to perform this kind of analysis on the literature of the information sciences, because of the lack of comparable numeric data sets. Some library and information papers are unhelpfully termed meta-analyses, when they are in fact 'only' qualitative, or semi-quantitative, literature reviews. Meta-synthesis is an equivalent process, but aimed at combining the results of qualitative studies.

Conceptual or philosophical analysis, perhaps the most theoretical form of desk research, sets out to analyse and clarify terms, concepts and issues within the information sciences.

Historical analysis analyses the historical development of issues within the library and information disciplines and professions. The most common form of this has been the description of the development of libraries and information institutions. These have been joined by analyses of the development of systems, services, processes, and concepts, and by studies of information phenomena in society.

Content analysis is a diverse form of analysis, always involving some kind of quantitative assessment of the content of a set of documents, to assess the extent to which concepts and issues are mentioned, or not (White and Marsh, 2006). It may include a qualitative dimension, to record *how* concepts and issues are described.

Discourse analysis is a form of content analysis, focusing on 'discourse'; the way in which spoken or written language is used (Budd, 2006). It is used to analyse, often in detail, the way in which concepts and issues are mentioned, and what this shows about how they are understood.

Bibliometrics and *webliometrics* are quantitative methods for describing and analysing patterns of recorded communication. They are used to carry out research into such topics as: size and growth of information within disciplines; significant sources, authors, institutions and countries; linkages and influence between information producers; and changes in communication patterns. Results may be presented as simple counts or graphs, or complex maps. These methods have been discussed in more detail in the chapter dealing with informetrics.

The following list gives a selection of information research articles based on various forms of desk research.

Examples of desk research methods in information research
Please note that these are not recommended as 'best practice', simply as recent relevant examples.

Literature analysis
Davies, K. (2007) The information-seeking behaviour of doctors: a review of the evidence, *Health Information and Libraries Journal*, 24(2), 78–94.

Liew, C. L. (2009) Digital library research 1997–2007: organisational and people issues, *Journal of Documentation*, 65(2), 245–66.

Tanni, M. and Sormunen, E. (2008) A critical review of research on information behaviour in assigned learning tasks, *Journal of Documentation*, 64(6), 893–914.

Meta-analysis

Aabo, S. (2009) Libraries and return on investment (ROI): a meta-analysis, *New Library World*, 110(7–8), 311–24.

Julien, C., Leide, J. E. and Bouthillier, F. (2008) Controlled user evaluations of information visualization interfaces for text retrieval: literature review and meta-analysis, *Journal of the American Society for Information Science and Technology*, 59(6), 1012–24.

Webb, T. L. et al. (2010) Using the Internet to promote health behavior change: a systematic review and meta-analysis of the impact of theoretical basis, use of behaviour change techniques, and mode of delivery on efficacy, *Journal of Medical Internet Research*, 12(1), available from http://www.jmir.org/2010/1/e4/.

Content analysis

Cummins, J. and Bawden, D. (2010) Accounting for information: information and knowledge in the annual reports of FTSE 100 companies, *Journal of Information Science*, 36(3), 283–305.

Park, J., Lu, C. and Marion, L. (2009) Cataloging professionals in the digital environment: a content analysis of job descriptions, *Journal of the American Society for Information Science and Technology*, 60(4), 844–57.

Manzuch, Z. (2009) Archives, libraries and museums as communicators of memory in the European Union projects, *Information Research*, 14(2), paper 400, available from http://informationr.net/ir/14-2/paper400.html.

Discourse analysis

Kouper, I. (2010) Information about the synthesis of life-forms: a document-oriented approach, *Journal of Documentation*, 66(3), 348–69.

Haider, J. and Bawden, D. (2007) Conceptions of 'information poverty' in LIS: a discourse analysis, *Journal of Documentation*, 63(4), 534–57.

Foster, J. (2009) Understanding interaction in information seeking and use as a discourse: a dialogic approach, *Journal of Documentation*, 65(1), 83–105.

Philosophical/conceptual analysis

Robinson, L. and Maguire, M. (2010) The rhizome and the tree: changing metaphors for information organisation, *Journal of Documentation*, 66(4), 604–13.

Furner, J. (2009) Interrogating 'identity': a philosophical approach to an enduring issue in knowledge organization, *Knowledge Organization*, 36(1), 3–16.

Thornely, C. and Gibb, F. (2009) Meaning in philosophy and meaning in information retrieval (IR), *Journal of Documentation*, 65(1), 133–50.

Historical analysis

Weller, T. and Bawden, D. (2005) The social and technological origins of the information society: an analysis of the crisis of control in England, 1830–1890, *Journal of Documentation*, 61(6), 777–802.

Bowman, J. H. (2006) The development of description in cataloguing prior to ISBD, *Aslib Proceedings*, 58(1–2), 34–48.

Muddiman, D. (2005) A new history of ASLIB, 1924–1959, *Journal of Documentation*, 61(3), 402–28.

Bibliometrics

Frandsen, T. F. (2009) Attracted to open access journals: a bibliometric author analysis in the field of biology, *Journal of Documentation*, 65(1), 58–82.

Robinson, L. (2007) Impact of digital information resources in the toxicology literature, *Aslib Proceedings*, 59(4–5), 342–51.

Ying, D. (2010) Semantic web: who is who in the field – a bibliometric analysis, *Journal of Information Science*, 36(3), 335–56.

Having briefly examined the main methods of information research, we will look at some more general issues: sampling; research ethics; and identifying and evaluating research findings.

Sampling

'Sampling' is the procedure by which we choose a selection of entities (people, organizations, documents, etc.) to study, when there are too many possibilities for us to study them all. The aim of sampling is to choose them so that they are representative of the larger population from which they are drawn, so that the results obtained have a more general validity beyond the particular entities which were studied.

The issue of sampling very often arises in information research, regardless of the method used. It is often thought of in the context of surveys – how should we choose our participants? – but is equally applicable in, for example, the choice of documents for content or discourse analysis, or the choice of place and time for observations. It raises two questions: what kind of sample is to be used; and how to know when it is enough. These issues often cause angst to novice researchers. This is a very complex subject, and only some simple points are made here. The research methods textbooks cover it more thoroughly; Denscombe (2010) gives a particularly clear account.

Four general kinds of sample may be taken:

1   A *complete sample*, where we include all examples of the population. For instance, if we were studying archiving policies in local government in London, we might choose to interview the archivist in each of the London boroughs.

2   A *random sample* of our population. This has to be done formally, typically using tables of pseudo-random numbers. Many samples described as 'random' are no such thing, having simply been picked arbitrarily.

3   A *purposive sample*, chosen to include examples of different types within our population. For example, to get a sample of users of a website, we might choose to select by age, gender, nationality, education level, place of residence, occupation, etc. Having chosen these groups, we might then select individuals within them randomly. This is a complex process, and needs to be done carefully according to the nature of the research.

4   A *convenience sample*, where a set of appropriate participants is selected because they are available: family, friends, fellow students, regular users of an information service, etc. This may be an appropriate method for small-scale and exploratory studies, provided that (a) it is declared as such, and (b) no attempt is made to generalize the results, or to claim statistical validity; both of the latter would need a more formal sampling process.

The question 'how big a sample do I need' is very often asked, but is difficult to answer exactly. A numerical answer can only be given in rather specific cases; when we are comparing two circumstances, know the magnitude of the difference we are looking for and the level of statistical confidence we require for the answer, and where we are able to make assumptions about the underlying distributions of the variable. For example, if our study set out to decide whether students who use the library get better grades, if we were able to say that by 'better' we meant a difference of 5%, that we would take the question as settled if the difference we saw would occur by chance only once in a hundred times, and that we knew that the distributions of marks and of use of the library both observed certain statistical distributions: then we would be able to calculate that a sample of so many students would be enough. Denscombe (2010) gives a clear account of these issues.

In most information research, we know little about the underlying distributions, and have no particular reason to fix the other parameters. We have to judge whether the sample we have allows us to give a reasonably confident answer to our research questions. Usually this means two things: does my sample include all groups of the population I am studying; and do I have enough cases in each group? There is no formula to give the answer, and it must be decided by common sense in each case; usually, in small-scale studies, by doing as many cases as is feasible and – in the case of qualitative studies – stopping when no new information is being found. There are a number of 'rules of thumb' for this. Lawal (2009), for example, suggests that a sample of 100 items or people is enough; if groups are being compared, then 30 in each group. Another often quoted 'rule' is that adequate insight into a topic is gained from 5 in-depth interviews or 50 questionnaire responses. These 'rules' are based purely on 'custom and practice', and common sense, rather than any methodological validity.

Information research ethics

Information ethics in general were discussed in Chapter 11, and the basic principles hold good here. For information research, ethical issues and dilemmas will be much the same as for research in similar social and computing disciplines. Two standard texts of information research methods (Pickard, 2007 and Oates, 2006) mention as the main issues:

- gaining access – being open and honest about the purpose and nature of the research, who is funding it, how the results will be disseminated, etc.
- informed consent – making sure that everyone being studied in any way is aware of the research, and has the chance to refuse to take part, and to withdraw from the study
- ensuring anonymity and/or confidentiality of results, as necessary
- protecting participants' rights – particularly for 'vulnerable' people, such as children or sick people
- online and internet research – particularly with its possibilities for anonymous observation and interaction
- researcher integrity – for example, observing relevant codes of conduct, and collecting only those data which are really needed for the research.

Finding and evaluating research

Research does not consist of a collection of isolated studies and findings; it is a process of cumulative growth of knowledge, each study building on and extending earlier work. An essential first step is therefore to identify and evaluate previous studies.

This is the process generally referred to as *literature searching* or *desk research*; as we have seen above, it may form a research study in itself, as well as being the starting point for all research activity. 'Literature' has to be understood quite widely. As well as the journal articles, research reports and monographs which are the traditional ways in which research is reported, we must now consider web pages, blogs, datasets, and other newer media for the communication of research. Resources for identifying such materials include bibliographic databases, web search engines, web portals and specialized searching tools for particular subjects and formats. Search strategies and tactics may need to be adapted to the sources used, as described in the information technology chapter. A selection of useful sources for identifying information research is given in the list of additional resources. Detailed advice on finding, analysing and organizing literature material is given in the research methods textbooks, and in Fink (2010), Rumsey (2008) and Ridley (2008).

Once identified, the material must be evaluated, to assess whether it is relevant and useful, and organized, so that it may be used. Information evaluation, of particular relevance to the meta-analysis, meta-synthesis and systematic reviewing mentioned earlier as examples of desk research, is also necessary as a starting point for all research. The formal methods of the systematic review, and of *critical thinking*, which has some similarities, are not usually necessary here. Rather, a checklist of issues can be applied to decide the quality and usefulness of material. This will typically include criteria such as: authority; coverage; accuracy; reliability; bias; timeliness; accessibility; language; and uniqueness.

More specifically, if we are evaluating a typical research report or journal article, we will ask a series of questions such as those in the box here.

Information evaluation by information professionals has been pioneered in the healthcare sector: two useful resources from that sector are a paper by Booth (2007) and a short book by Greenhalgh (2010). Although both refer to the healthcare context specifically, the points they make are much more widely applicable to critical appraisal of any form of literature.

If the studies being evaluated involve quantitative data, then an assessment of the statistics used is necessary. This can be complex, and specialist advice may be necessary: basic guidance is given in the research methods textbooks, in Greenhalgh (2010), and in a variety of guides to statistics: good examples of the latter are Campbell (2009) and Hand (2008).

Summary

Research is fundamental to the information disciplines and professions. Without it, the academic knowledge base will stagnate, and enhancements and improvements in practice will be made more difficult. Academics and practitioners have a joint duty to carry out appropriate research, to be aware of – and make use of – existing research findings, and to communicate across the academic-practitioner divide on these issues. The UK's Library and Information Science Research Coalition, set up in 2009, is one approach to addressing these matters (Hall, 2010).

The range of methods available for, and used in, information research has expanded greatly since the origins of formal research in our discipline, and nove

Evaluating a research article or report

Who are the authors, and what are their qualifications? Who published the study?

Is the purpose of the research clearly stated? Are there clear research questions?

What are the background assumptions, presuppositions, and theoretical positions? Are they stated clearly?

Is the context of the research stated clearly?

Is there an appropriate literature review?

Is the review claimed to be comprehensive or systematic? If so, is it?

Do the references listed give a fair representation of the available evidence? Have the authors interpreted the evidence from the references correctly?

Are the research methods clearly described and justified?

Are the methods appropriate to answer the research questions?

If questionnaires, interviews or similar data collection methods are used, are they fully described, and have they been validated?

Are the results presented fully and clearly; are the original data given, or is it stated where they can be found?

If it is a quantitative study, are appropriate statistical techniques used? Are the data presented in appropriate tabular and graphical forms, with appropriate levels of precision?

If it is a qualitative study, are the methods for collecting and analysing data explained fully? Are they careful and rigorous enough? Are the data set out clearly?

Is there any evidence of bias, or undue subjectivity, on the part of the authors?

Do the authors draw appropriate conclusions from the findings? Do they answer the questions that the study was designed to answer?

Are the findings integrated with previous work?

Is any practical relevance of the findings made clear?

Are there any ethical issues; is it clear how the work has been funded, and does this matter?

Is the style and presentation appropriate for the intended audience?

methods still arise. Research is likely to be even more important in the future, to help deal with the dramatic changes in the information landscape that we are seeing, in response to a variety of factors, most particularly new technologies. In the next, and final, chapter, we will look at the future research agenda for information science.

- Research is essential for the future of the information disciplines and professions.
- Practitioners and academic researchers have a joint responsibility to carry out appropriate research and to make use of existing research.
- A wide variety of methods is available for information research, but these must be chosen and applied correctly in each study.

Key readings

A. J. Pickard, *Research methods in information*, London: Facet Publishing, 2007.

B. J. Oates, *Researching information systems and computing*, London: Sage, 2006.
[Two good textbooks, giving detailed coverage of the material in this chapter.]

P. Hider and B. Pymm, Empirical research methods reported in high-profile LIS journal literature, *Library and Information Science Research*, 2008, 30(2), 108–14.
[A careful analysis of information research methods and their relative importance.]

References

Baker, L. M. (2006) Observation: a complex research method, *Library Trends*, 55(1), 171–89.

Blick, A. R. (1983) Information science research versus the practitioner, *Nachrichten fur Dokumentation*, 34(6), 261–65.

Booth, A. (2007) Who will appraise the appraisers? The paper, the instrument and the user, *Health Information and Libraries Journal*, 24(1), 72–6.

Booth, A. and Brice, A. (2004) *Evidence-based practice for information professionals*, London: Facet Publishing.

Bruce, C. (1999) Phenomenography: opening a new territory for library and information science, *New Review of Information and Library Research*, 5, 31–47.

Buchanan, S. and Gibb, F. (2008) The information audit: methodology selection, *International Journal of Information Management*, 28(1), 3–11.

Budd, J. M. (2006) Discourse analysis and the study of communication in LIS, *Library Trends*, 55(1), 65–82.

Burke, M. E. (2007) Making choices: research paradigms and information management: practical applications of philosophy in IM research, *Library Review*, 56(6), 476–84.

Campbell, M. J. (2009) *Statistics at square one* (11th edn), Chichester: Wiley-Blackwell.

Case, D. O. (2007) *Looking for information: a survey of research on information seeking, needs and behavior*, New York NY: Academic Press.

Case, D. O. (2012) *Looking for information: a survey of research on information seeking, needs and behavior* (3rd edn), Bingley: Emerald.

Cronin, B. and Meho, L. I. (2007) Timelines of creativity: A study of intellectual innovators in information science, *Journal of the American Society for Information*

Science and Technology, 58(13), 1948–59.

Denscombe, M. (2010) *The good research guide, for small-scale social research projects* (4th edn), Maidenhead: Open University Press.

Farmer, L. and Stricevic, I. (2011) *Using research to promote literacy and reading in libraries: Guidelines for librarians*, IFLA Professional Reports No. 125, The Hague: International Federation of Library Associations, available from http://www.ifla.org/files/hq/publications/professional-report/125.pdf.

Fidel, R. (2008) Are we there yet? Mixed methods research in library and information science, *Library and Information Science Research*, 30(4), 265–72.

Fink, A. (2010) *Conducting research literature reviews* (3rd edn), Thousand Oaks CA: Sage.

Garnett, A. (2011) Information science as knowledge translation, *Bulletin of the American Society for Information Science and Technology*, 37(5), 50–3.

Goodman, V. D. (2011) Applying ethnographic research methods in library and information science, *Libri*, 61(1), 1–11.

Gorman, G. E. and Clayton, P. (2005) *Qualitative research for the information professional: a practical handbook* (2nd edn), London: Facet Publishing.

Greenhalgh, T. (2010) *How to read a paper: the basics of evidence-based medicine* (4th edn), Chichester: Wiley-Blackwell.

Greifeneder, E. and Seadle, M. S. (2010) Research for practice – avoiding useless results, *Library Hi-Tech*, 28(1), 5–7.

Haddow, G. and Klobas, J. E. (2004) Communication of research to practice in library and information science: closing the gap, *Library and Information Science Research*, 26(1), 29–43.

Hall, H. (2010) Promoting the priorities of practitioner research engagement, *Journal of Librarianship and Information Science*, 42(2), 83–8.

Hand, D. J. (2008) *Statistics: a very short introduction*, Oxford: Oxford University Press.

Hider, P. and Pymm, B. (2008) Empirical research methods reported in high-profile LIS journal literature, *Library and Information Science Research*, 30(2), 108–14.

Hjørland, B. (2011) Evidence-based practice: an analysis based on the philosophy of science, *Journal of the American Society for Information Science and Technology*, 62(7), 1301–10.

Huntington, P. and Gunter, B. (2006) Triangulating qualitative research and computer transaction logs in health information studies, *Aslib Proceedings*, 58(1/2), 129–39 .

Lawal, I. O. (2009) *Library and information science research in the 21st century: a guide for practising librarians and students*, Oxford: Chandos.

McKechnie, L., Julien, H., Genuis, S.K. and Oliphant, T. (2008) Communicating research findings to library and information science practitioners: a study of ISIC papers from 1996 to 2000, *Information Research*, 13(4), paper 375, available from http://InformationR.net/ir/13-4/paper375.html.

Moore, N. (2006) *How to do research: a practical guide to designing and managing research projects* (3rd edn), London: Facet Publishing.

Oates, B. J. (2006) *Researching information systems and computing*, London: Sage.

Pickard, A. J. (2007) *Research methods in information*, London: Facet Publishing.

Powell, R. R. (2006) Evaluation research: an overview, *Library Trends*, 55(1), 102–20.

Powell, R. R., Baker, L. M. and Mika, J. J. (2002) Library and information science practitioners and research, *Library and Information Science Research*, 24(1), 49–72.

Ridley, D. (2008) *The literature review: a step-by-step guide for students*, London: Sage.

Rumsey, S. (2008) *How to find information: a guide for researchers* (2nd edn), Maidenhead: Open University Press.

Saxton, M. L. (2006) Meta-analysis in library and information science: method, history, and recommendations for reporting research, *Library Trends*, 55(1), 158–70.

Tan, J. (2010) Grounded theory in practice: issues and discussion for new qualitative researchers, *Journal of Documentation*, 66(1), 93–112.

Urquhart, C. (2010) Systematic reviewing, meta-analysis and meta-synthesis for evidence-based library and information science, *Information Research*, 15(3), paper colis708, available from http://informationr.net/ir/15-3/colis7/colis708.html.

White, M. D. and Marsh, E. E. (2006) Content analysis: a flexible methodology, *Library Trends*, 55(1), 22–45.

Wilson, T. (2008) The information user: past, present and future, *Journal of Information Science*, 34(4), 457–64.

CHAPTER 15

The future of the information sciences

Prediction is very difficult, especially about the future.

> Robert Storm Petersen, Danish poet and philosopher –
> also attributed to the physicist Niels Bohr

If we have learned one thing from the history of invention and discovery, it is that, in the long run and often in the short one, the most daring prophecies seem laughably conservative.

> Sir Arthur C. Clarke

Librarianship has become preoccupied, perhaps to a point of obsession, with its own future. There seems to be a growing sense that change is now moving at such a rate that steering may have ceased to be an option.

> Ross Atkinson (2001, 3)

Neither a wise man nor a brave man lies down on the tracks of history to wait for the train of the future to run over him.

> Dwight D. Eisenhower

Introduction

In this final chapter, we give an overview of some ideas about the discipline and profession of information science. As the opening quotation from Ross Atkinson indicates, some of the information professions are very concerned about this, perhaps seeing signs of their own demise, overwhelmed by changing technical and social environments.

This is by no means a new concern. During the 1970s, Dennis Lewis, an information manager in the British chemical industry who later headed the professional association ASLIB, became well known for propounding the idea that 'There won't be an information profession by the year 2000' (Lewis, 1980). This became known as the 'Doomsday Scenario', and Lewis rather revelled in his nickname of Doomsday Den. This focused on the increasing computerization of printed indexes, particularly for the scientific and technical literature, and the increasing trend for academic and professional users who needed the information to find it for themselves, a phenomenon then termed 'end-user searching'. This, argued Lewis, would lead to the end of the 'intermediary' role, by which an information scientist carried out searches on behalf of those who needed the information, using their searching skills to deal with the 'difficult' online information resources of the time. With this role gone, there would be no place left for the information specialist, and the profession would disappear, leaving only a few librarians and archivists, carrying out custodial functions for heritage material. And Lewis, like all other experts of the time, had not envisaged anything like the web or Google (Bawden, 2007).

Lewis' predictions turned out to be wrong, and we suggest that most similarly apocalyptic claims about the end of information disciplines and professions are likely to be similarly wrong. It may be that some information skills and jobs will disappear entirely, just as the skills of hot-metal typesetting disappeared entirely from the publishing sector, but we do not think wholesale extinctions are likely.

But, as the quotation from Petersen and Bohr reminds us, predicting the future is very difficult, and most predictions of information futures have been very wrong. To see why this may be, we will first look at the nature of prediction and prophecy.

Predicting and prophesying

Arthur C. Clarke, writer of popular science books and science fiction novels, and originator of the concept of the communications satellite, identified two general problems in predicting the future. A 'failure of imagination' occurs when future developments are unforeseen because some necessary piece of knowledge was as yet unavailable; more common is the 'failure of nerve', in which all the relevant facts are known, yet not followed to their logical conclusion (Clarke, 1999).

Karl Popper distinguished between *prediction*, when using sufficient knowledge is available to make reasonable conclusions about future events, and *prophecy*, when statements are made about the future without the necessary knowledge being available for them to be rational or realistic. David Deutsch (2011) builds on this view to argue that the continuous development of knowledge of all kinds reduces all speculation about the future to prophesy, and almost inevitably in error.

An extreme example of this is the idea put forward by some commentators, notably the science fiction writer Vernor Vinge and the computer scientist Ray Kurzweil, who argue that rapid growth in technological capabilities will lead to a *technological singularity*, after which the world will be so unrecognizable that any kind of prediction becomes meaningless. This is usually associated with the emergence of artificial intelligences with capabilities so far beyond humans as to be incomprehensible.

These ideas make it clear that speculations about a future likely to be influenced by the growth of knowledge, and by the new technologies and capabilities arising from it, are likely to be just that: speculations, possibly interesting, but almost always wrong. The future of information handling is most certainly of this kind, and it is straightforward, if a little unkind, to reflect on the many poor predications of the value and use of information and communication technologies; see Bawden (1997) for some examples.

One way of dealing with these difficulties is to look at 'histories of the future'; looking back at past predictions and prophecies – few of which have come true in the way their originators envisaged – both for what they can teach us about the problems of prediction in this area, and perhaps also to remind us of some as yet unachieved possibilities. Well known examples of predictions which anticipated the internet and the world wide web are H.G. Wells' World Brain encyclopedia, Vanevar Bush's Memex and Ted Nelson's Xanadu 'docuverse'. None of these 'came true' as their originators envisaged: Berners-Lee's idea of the web proved more practicable than Xanadu, we do not use microforms to follow associative links as Bush imagined, and Wells' Brain has never been implemented, either as a printed encyclopedia or as an artificial intelligence. Nonetheless, the ideas were very influential in their time, and helped determine much of current information landscape; see Houston and Harmon (2007) for a detailed analysis of the influence of Bush and Memex. A similarly influential view of the future was Licklider's (1965) idea of the future computerized research library, which foresaw many of the attributes – though not the operational details – of today's digital libraries. Wilfred Lancaster's idea of paperless information systems, and hence a paperless society, first expounded in the 1970s and envisaging a totally paperless environment by 2000, has also been influential. His original predictions now seem very modest technically, but over-optimistic socially; though digital technologies have advanced very much beyond anything he imagined, he underestimated the resilience of print, and people's desire for paper documents (Young, 2008). Overviews of other ideas in the 'history of the future of information' are given by Sapp (2002), Liestman (2002) and Pennavaria (2002). Interesting specific examples are a reproduction of a popular article from 1894, explaining how the printing of books was about to be replaced by the new technology of the wax cylinder, and how libraries would become 'phonographoteks' (Uzanne, 1894), and a conference paper by one of the leading American librarians of his day, looking forward 100 years, and foreseeing developments such as library automation and inter-library loan (Cutter, 1883).

Even science fiction writings have proved an interesting source of ideas for he future of information. It is arguable that the American cyber-punk author William Gibson, in novels such as *Neuromancer*, has presented a better understanding of the significance of the internet and of pervasive computing than have more factual writers. (Gibson is also credited with first using the term 'cyberspace'.) A number of eminent computer scientists have commented on the influence of HAL, the fictional computer from the movie *2001: A Space Odyssey* (Stork, 1997). Perhaps authors of fictional materials find it easier to overcome the failure of imagination. Examples of earlier fictional views of future library and information provision are given by Griffen (1987), Gunn (1995) and Pennavaria (2002); they provide a kind of fictional 'history of the future'.

Having acknowledged the difficulties of speculating on information futures in detail, we will now look at some of the forces, visible today, which are influencing future developments.

Drivers for change

It is often assumed that technology is the only significant force changing the information landscape; certainly many commentators focus on this, almost to the exclusion of everything else. And indeed technology does seem to advance so rapidly as to overshadow other factors. Since the arrival of the first 'microcomputers' in the early 1980s, it has been sensible to assume that whatever can be envisaged for information provision will be possible technically, if it depends on processing speeds, storage capacities and transmission speeds. This is an interesting reversal of the situation with Babbage's mechanical computers of the 19th century; the abstract ideas were sound, but the technology of the time could not instantiate them.

Recent trends include: cloud computing, with information stored remotely, so that the idea of local collection disappears; mobile devices, such as smartphones and tablet computers, potentially removing any idea of an 'information place'; mass digitization projects, raising the prospect that all information is either digital, or temporarily not-yet-digital; and so-called ubiquitous or pervasive computing, with information processing embodied in everyday objects, such as books, whiteboards, household appliances, and even clothing, potentially removing the distinction between an information resource and any other sort of object.

Despite the evident significance of technology, other general factors affect the information landscape. These are most commonly categorized as economic, social, demographic and political factors. Changes in the information landscape are not isolated from more general issues, as witness the concern for the relation between information technology and systems and environmental issues and climate change; see, for example, Chowdhury (2010) and Jenkin, Webster and McShane (2011). Similarly, there has been great interest in the 'informational differences' between generations, as discussed in Chapter 11.

Although the drivers for changes may be categorized in ways such as that shown above, in reality change is often due to a complex mix of factors. We have, for example, seen the rise of 'platinum open access' journals, discussed in Chapter 10, whose articles are available freely without subscription, but also without any charges to authors. To what do we ascribe their success? To technical factors, providing the web tools, software, storage capacity and networks, which make them possible? To economic factors; specifically the pressure on library budgets, due to journal price increases? To social factors, such as the blurring of boundaries between professions; in this case, scholars, librarians and publishers. In truth, it is a complex mix of all these, and perhaps others; for a detailed case study, of the *Electronic Journal of Academic and Special Librarianship*, see Haschak (2007). Similarly, the changes seen in a variety of information environments – including public and academic libraries, healthcare information services, and corporate information centres – are again attributable to a mix of technical, economic, demographic and social causes.

We will now look at some general scenarios for the future of the information landscape, based on these kinds of changes. We are looking ahead no more than 20 years; beyond that, prediction, even of this very rough kind, becomes impossible.

What lies ahead for information professions and disciplines

Three general views of the information future have been typically presented by commentators and seers; we categorize these as 'business as usual', 'changing landscapes' and 'into the clouds'.

'Business as usual'

This first viewpoint implies a continuation of the current situation, with information services continuing, and perhaps growing in importance, in something very similar to their current form. It relies on ideas of inertia and resistance to change, on the good 'brand image' of libraries and other information services, on the continuing interest in physical books and 'information places', and even on a perceived renewed enthusiasm for the 'real' as opposed to the virtual. This was seen clearly in the resistance to public library closures in Britain in 2010–11. However, even its proponents accept that this will not apply in all sectors of information work.

'Changing landscapes'

This second viewpoint involves incremental changes to the current situation, with some forms of information provision and service diminishing, or even disappearing, others expanding, and all changing their nature considerably. It is easy to identify current examples of this: academic libraries in Europe and North America moving from a role purely as a rather passive information provider, to a more active involvement in teaching, and to provision of study spaces extending into a 'social space' dimension; UK public libraries morphing into 'Ideas Stores' and 'Discovery Centres'; public libraries throughout Europe and the USA integrating more closely in the wider social and cultural environment; commercial information services increasingly emphasizing knowledge management, though perhaps not using that term; healthcare information services rebranding themselves as 'evidence services'; and so on. The constant factor here is an emphasis on reformulating the nature of information services, and in particular the balance between physical and digital resources and spaces, while retaining the 'trusted brand' advantages.

'Into the clouds'

This third viewpoint foresees the disappearance of most current forms of information service, and their replacement – if they are replaced at all – by something very different to what has been seen before. 'Clouds', implies here both the entirely decentralized 'cloud computing' environment, seen in embryonic form in services such as Apple's iCloud and Google+ discussed in Chapter 7, and perhaps also the lack of clarity of such radical predictions. Digital information would be ubiquitous and largely openly and freely accessed: the antithesis of the traditionally locally owned collection. Printed materials would retain a place only as heritage objects, and the idea of the collection, personal or institutional, would cease to have meaning. Information services, other than archives and heritage libraries, would cease to exist as institutions, and might take the form simply of advisory services, assisting patrons with selection and use of digital materials. Lacking a physical location, and a managed collection, information services would, if they were to survive at all, have to become more deeply embedded in the life and work of their patrons.

A cautious prognosis

Given what we have written above about the dangers of prediction, we will not try to say what we believe the future will be, in any detail; we would certainly be wrong if we did so. However, we do not believe that the 'business as usual' scenario is feasible, outside a few niche areas, given already evident technical and social developments. Nor, based on the evidence of the inaccuracy of all the 'doomsday' predictions so far, are we able to confidently support the more radical prescriptions. We therefore tentatively suggest that most information provision in most sectors and environments will follow the incremental 'changing landscapes' model. But it is very likely that this will be influenced in ways that cannot be predicted, by developments that have not yet been imagined.

We therefore need to be cautious about paying over-much attention to anyone who claims to know many details of the future of the information disciplines and professions more than a very few years ahead. General thoughts and alternative scenarios are likely to be more valuable. An interesting example is a series of imaginative scenarios for the future of libraries, although some, especially in the earlier volume, are already very outdated and part of the history of the future (Shuman, 1989; 1997). Thoughtful reflections on various current issues and future developments over the longer term are given by Atkinson (2001), Pomerantz and Marchionini (2007) and Carpenter et al. (2011).

In order to try to anticipate this changing future, and to control developments, rather than letting them control us, we need to consider what information research is needed.

Information research agendas

It is easy to find articles and conference presentations suggesting which kind of research is needed in many aspects of the information sciences, and proposing 'research agendas'. Most of these, however, are short-term, quite detailed and rather parochial. Ideas for research designed to advance the knowledge base of the information sciences over the longer term, more than just the next few years, is much less common. However, four examples of suggestions for sets of research questions with a sufficiently broad scope and long-term outlook as to be useful for more than a very few years can be given. The first three come from an issue of the *Library Trends* journal (volume 51, issue 4, 2003) devoted to 'research questions for the twenty-first century', which includes other examples.

Michael Buckland, who has appeared several times in this book, proposes 'five grand challenges' for what he terms 'library research', although we think they have wider applicability in the information sciences (Buckland, 2003). They are less research questions than suggestions for whole areas of research:

- library service: could library services be made more meaningful?
- library theory: who knew what when?
- library design: have digital libraries been designed backwards?
- library values: how neutral can libraries be?
- library communities: how do communities differ?

Christine Borgman, another well known American library science academic, suggests four general foci for research, focusing on the role of traditional information providers in a new information landscape (Borgman, 2003):

- invisible infrastructure
- content and collections
- preservation and access
- institutional boundaries.

Deanna Marcum, a prominent US librarian, offers three general questions for the future of digital library environments (Marcum, 2003):

- how are digital resource users best served?
- what elements are needed for a coherent strategy for preserving both digital and physical materials?
- what education will be needed by those providing these services?

Finally, Claudio Gnoli (2008), the Italian librarian and scholar, poses ten 'long-term research questions in knowledge organization' (KO):

- can KO principles be extended to a broader scope, including hypertexts, multimedia, museum objects and monuments?
- can the basic approaches to KO, ontological and epistemological, be reconciled?
- can an ontological foundation for KO be identified?
- should disciplines continue to be the structural base of KO?
- how can viewpoint warrant be respected?
- how can KO be adapted to local collection needs?
- how can KO deal with changes in knowledge?
- how can KO systems represent all the relevant dimensions?
- how can software and formats be improved to better serve identified needs?
- who should 'do KO'? Information professionals, authors or readers?

We propose the following set of seven, rather general, research questions to influence the future of the information sciences. As might be expected from what has gone before in this book, they take a broad viewpoint, and advocate the value of theory, as well as of practice, and of history. They are:

1 What is the best theoretical basis for the information sciences (if indeed there is a single such basis)?
2 How is the concept of information in the information sciences related to the ideas of information in other domains?
3 How can principles of information science be applied to all sectors where documents and information resources (widely understood) are used?
4 How can lessons from the past be applied to current and future information environments?
5 How can we best operate in a world where an information glut, previously unimaginable, will be the norm?
6 How can we best show the impact and value of knowledge and information resources and services in changing environments?

7 How can information research and information practice best be linked, so
   that each informs the other?

Consideration of research questions, added to our thoughts on the future of the
information professions, leads us to a final question: what is the future of
information science as an academic discipline and as a profession?

The future of information science

It is probably fair to say that many, perhaps most, of the assessments of the
condition of information science made by commentators since 2000 have tended
towards the gloomy. Observing the closing and merger of academic departments
in this subject in several countries, the cut-backs in information and library
services in several sectors, and the increasing reliance on web search engines and
social media for finding information, they have concluded that the best days of
the information discipline and professions are behind them.

We do not share that gloom. Most fundamentally, if we believe, as we have
stated in previous chapters, that information science is concerned with the study
of the communication chain of recorded information, then so long as information
is communicated the discipline cannot become redundant. It may change its
nature, and its specific focus of interest – indeed, we think it is inevitable that
this will happen – but it will not disappear. There are, we believe, some
fundamentals of human information-related behaviour and of the organization
of information, which do not change. It is the business of the information
scientist to investigate them, and to show their relevance in whatever information
environment they may be instantiated.

Lewis' 'Doomsday' did not happen, although he was correct in his analysis of
the decline of the 'information intermediary' role; in fact, more correct than he
could have imagined, given the rise of web search engines. But this did not mean
the end of the information disciplines as a whole, nor will it, whatever new
technologies arrive.

Another frequently expressed concern is that information science will be
subsumed into the larger academic disciplines that are increasingly interested in
information communication: particularly computer science, information systems
and business management. While it is certainly desirable to retain the
information science perspective, which is not shared by other disciplines, there
is – we think – no need for gloom about an increasing overlap of boundaries. If
the insights of the information sciences are being shared more widely, and gaining
greater influence, then this is to be welcomed, as has been pointed out from
various perspectives by several commentators, including Meadows (2009),
Buckland (2009) and Wilson (2006). As this book was being written, we were
in a department with the 'Information Science' name; but elsewhere in our

university people were working on digital libraries in an HCI centre, on information society issues in the department of sociology, on retrieval algorithms in a computer science unit, and on information management in the business school. We cannot, and should not try to, claim all information sciences issues as belonging to that discipline; rather we should seek to ensure that their importance is recognized in the wider world.

Finally, concern is sometimes expressed about the fragmented nature of information science; its nature as a multifaceted field of study, and the multiplicity of perspectives and theoretical positions within it. We do not agree that this is a weakness; information, as has been emphasized throughout this book, is a pervasive concept, which requires a variety of approaches to deal with it. We agree with Nolin and Åström (2010) that the multifaceted nature of information science is a strength, rather than a weakness.

We therefore believe that information science has a bright future; although, for the reasons given above, it will be different from what anyone can at present imagine.

Summary

No one knows in detail what the future will be like. This applies particularly to a discipline such as information science, which will be greatly changed by new knowledge, in ways which it is not possible to imagine.

Thinking about the future in terms of current trends and issues is unhelpful beyond the next few years. We would do better to draw inspiration from histories of the future, from speculative writings, and even from science fiction.

Information science has a bright future, though its details cannot be known. Rather than attempting to defend their present disciplinary niche, academics and practitioners alike should concentrate on ensuring that the insights of information science are recognized and applied in wider contexts.

> - The detailed future of information science is inherently unpredictable, since it will depend on the growth of new knowledge.
> - Only rather general predictions of the future information landscape can be made; there are several possible scenarios.
> - Research agendas have been proposed to provide a knowledge base for future information science.
> - Information science has a bright future; but it will change in ways we cannot now imagine.

Key readings

David Bawden, The nature of prediction and the information future: Arthur C. Clarke's Odyssey vision, *Aslib Proceedings*, 1997, 49(3), 57–60.

[An overview, with examples, of the problems of prediction in this area.]
J. Nolin and F. Åström, Turning weakness into strength: strategies for future LIS, *Journal of Documentation*, 2010, 66(1), 7–27.
[A positive viewpoint on the future of the information sciences.]

References

Atkinson, R. (2001) Contingency and contradiction: the place(s) of the library at the dawn of the new millennium, *Journal of the American Society for Information Science and Technology*, 52(1), 3–11.

Bawden, D. (1997) The nature of prediction and the information future: Arthur C. Clarke's Odyssey vision, *Aslib Proceedings*, 49(3), 57–60.

Bawden, D. (2007) The doomsday of documentation, *Journal of Documentation*, 63(2), 173–74.

Borgman, C. L. (2003) The invisible library: paradox of the global information infrastructure, *Library Trends*, 51(4), 652–74.

Buckland, M. K. (2003) Five grand challenges for library research, *Library Trends*, 51(4), 675–86.

Buckland, M. K. (2009) Book review of 'Information Science in Transition', *Journal of the American Society for Information Science and Technology*, 61(7), 1505.

Carpenter, M., Graybill, J., Offord, J. and Piorun, M. (2011) Envisioning the library's role in scholarly communication in the year 2025, *portal: Libraries and the academy*, 11(2), 659–82.

Chowdhury, G. (2010) Carbon footprint of the knowledge sector: What's the future?, *Journal of Documentation*, 66(6), 934–46.

Clarke, A. C. (1999) *Profiles of the future* (Millennium edition), London: Gollancz.

Cutter, C. A. (1883) The Buffalo Public Library in 1983, *Library Journal*, 8 (September/October 1883), 211–17, available from http://en.wikisource.org/wiki/The_Buffalo_Public_Library_in_1983.

Deutsch, D. (2011) *The beginning of infinity*, London: Allen Lane.

Gnoli, C. (2008) Ten long-term research questions in knowledge organization. *Knowledge Organization*, 35(2–3), 137–49.

Griffen, A. M. (1987) Images of libraries in science fiction, *Library Journal*, 112(14), 137–42.

Gunn, J. (1995) Dreams written out: libraries in science fiction, *Wilson Library Bulletin*, 69(6), 26–9.

Haschak, P. G. (2007) The 'platinum route' to open access: a case study of *E-JASL: the Electronic Journal of Academic and Special Librarianship*, *Information Research*, 12(4), paper 321 [online], available at http://InformationR.net/ir/12-4/paper321.html.

Houston, R. D. and Harmon, G. (2007) Vannevar Bush and memex, *Annual Review of Information Science and Technology*, 41, 55–92.

Jenkin, T. A., Webster, J. and McShane, L. (2011) An agenda for 'green' information technology and systems research, *Information and Organization*, 21(1), 17–40.

Lewis, D. A. (1980) Today's challenge – tomorrow's choice: change or be changed, or the Doomsday Scenario Mk 2, *Journal of Information Science*, 2(2), 59–74.

Licklider, J. C. R. (1965) *Libraries of the future*, Cambridge MA: MIT Press.

Liestman, D. (2002) Looking back to the future: turn of the century librarians look ahead to the twentieth century, *Reference Librarian*, No. 78, 25–46.

Marcum, D. B. (2003) Research questions for the digital era library, *Library Trends*, 51(4), 636–51.

Meadows, J. (2009) Fifty years of UK research in information science, in Gilchrist, A. (ed.), *Information science in transition*, London: Facet Publishing, 1–21.

Nolin, J. and Åström. F. (2010) Turning weakness into strength: strategies for future LIS, *Journal of Documentation*, 66(1), 7–27.

Pennavaria, K. (2002) Representations of books and libraries in depictions of the future, *Libraries and Culture*, 37(3), 229–48.

Pomerantz, J. and Marchionini, G. (2007) The digital library as place, *Journal of Documentation*, 63(4), 505–33.

Sapp, G. (2002) *A brief history of the future of libraries*, Lanham MD: Scarecrow Press.

Shuman, B. A. (1989) *The Library of the Future: alternative scenarios for the information profession*, Englewood CO: Libraries Unlimited.

Shuman, B. A. (1997) *Beyond the Library of the Future: more alternative futures for the public library*, Englewood CO: Libraries Unlimited.

Stork, D. G. (ed.) (1997) *HAL's legacy: 2001's computer as dream and reality*, Cambridge MA: MIT Press.

Uzanne, O. (1894) The end of books, *Scribner's Illustrated Monthly*, 16 (August 1894), 221–31, available at http://www.uiowa.edu/~obermann/endofbooks/end_of_books01.html and at http://ebooks.adelaide.edu.au/u/uzanne/octave/end.

Wilson, T. D. (2006) Revisiting user studies and information needs, *Journal of Documentation*, 62(6), 680–84.

Young, A. P. (2008) Aftermath of a prediction: F. W. Lancaster and the paperless society, *Library Trends*, 56(4), 843–58.

Additional Resources

Although this book is intended to be self-contained, with the provision of extensive literature references for readers interested in any particular aspects, we should mention some important resources for the study of information science.

Other textbooks
Two texts are useful complements to this one. Rubin's book covers the topics from a library science and US perspective. The volume edited by Davis and Shaw – in an interesting wiki-based approach to which we both contributed – emphasizes IT aspects, and again a US perspective.

Richard E. Rubin, *Foundations of Library and Information Science* (3rd edn), New York NY: Neal-Schuman, 2010.
Charles H. Davis and Debora Shaw (eds), *Introduction to Information Science and Technology*, Langam MD: information Today, 2011.

The books by Norton and by Debons are well written introductions to the subject, which could be used a precursor to our more in-depth treatment of any topic.

Melanie J. Norton, *Introductory Concepts in Information Science* (2nd edn), Langham MD: Information Today, 2010.
Anthony Debons, *Information Science 101*, Lanham MD: Scarecrow Press, 2008.

Vickery and Vickery, while once the unquestioned major text on the subject is now mainly of historic interest, although it gives clear coverage of some basics.

Brian C. Vickery and Alina Vickery, *Information Science in Theory and Practice* (3rd edn), Munich: K. G. Saur, 2004.

Finally, the book edited by Gilchrist contains a variety of perceptive summaries and perspectives of many aspects of information science.

Alan Gilchrist (ed.), *Information Science in Transition*, London: Facet
   Publishing, 2009.

Journals
The information science literature is a good example of the 'scatter' discussed
in Chapter 8. Relevant papers will be found in journals on a wide variety of
subjects, from computer science to cultural studies, from librarianship to
business management, and from information systems to archiving. A selective
list of major journals follows.

Journal of Information Science
Journal of Librarianship and Information Science
Journal of the American Society of Information Science and Technology
Journal of Documentation
Information Processing and Management
Information Research
Library and Information Science Research
Library and Information Research
Aslib Journal of Information Management (formerly Aslib Proceedings)
International Journal of Information Management.

Abstracting and indexing services
Again, information science literature may be covered by a wide variety of
secondary sources, especially if it relates to information in a particular subject
area; *Medline*, for instance, covers healthcare information. However, the main
resources are:

LISA (Library and Information Science Abstracts)
LISTA (Library and Information Science Abstracts)
SSCI (Social Science Citation Index) part of the *Web of Knowledge* service.

Reference sources
The third edition of Taylor & Francis' *Encyclopedia of Library and Information
Sciences* is a valuable resource, with short accessible articles of generally good
quality covering a wide area.

   Annual Reviews of Information Science and Technology (ARIST) has very useful
critical reviews of many topics in the information sciences. Sadly, it ceased
publication in 2011.

   The *Epistemological Lifeboat* [http://www.iva.dk/jni/lifeboat], a web resource
edited by Birger Hjørland and Jeppe Nicolaisen, has a useful compilation of short
authoritative articles on concepts and theories in information science.

Index